Teaching Notes

for Trinity Guildhall
Piano examinations
2012-2014

Complete syllabus

Written by
Pamela Lidiard
& Michael Round

Published by
Trinity College London
Registered office:
89 Albert Embankment
London SE1 7TP UK

T +44 (0)20 7820 6100
F +44 (0)20 7820 6161
E music@trinityguildhall.co.uk
www.trinityguildhall.co.uk

Authors

Pamela Lidiard is Deputy Head of Keyboard Studies at the Guildhall School of Music & Drama. As well as teaching and coaching pianists and singers, she also co-ordinates the postgraduate course for accompanists.

Michael Round is a soloist, accompanist, arranger, editor and orchestral pianist. He is also a freelance writer for *Music Teacher* and *International Piano*, and teaches piano at Kingston University. He studied at Trinity College of Music and later taught there for many years.

Contents

Introduction

These notes have been prepared for the benefit of teachers and students preparing for piano exams using the 2012–2014 syllabus. There is of course no 'one' way to play any piece of music, and this holds good for exams just as much as for concert performances. Examiners will always be ready to accept many different ways of playing the pieces, so long as they are well prepared, carefully thought out and appropriate for the style of the music being performed.

From Initial to Grade 3 there is one list of pieces only, from which three pieces are freely chosen. From Grade 4 up to Grade 8 pieces are in two groups; two pieces are chosen from one group and one from the other. This arrangement allows candidates to play as much as possible of the music that they themselves enjoy and which shows off their skills in the best and most balanced way. As with all exam programmes, candidates should aim to demonstrate a variety of styles and techniques within their programme.

Marks are awarded separately to each piece for each of three main areas:

- Notational accuracy & fluency: how well the notes are prepared and delivered. More conveniently thought of as: 'Me and the Music'.

- Technical facility: instrumental control and the ability to draw the most from the instrument; tone colour, articulation, pedalling etc: 'Me and the Instrument'.

- Communication and interpretation: how well candidates give their performance, engage the audience and convey a sense of the meaning of the music they are playing: 'Me and the Audience'.

Detailed criteria for assessing each performance are published, and candidates and teachers should look carefully at those that relate to the grade being taken to make sure that their preparation is correctly focused.

All pieces should be prepared in full unless otherwise stated; repeats should be omitted unless instructed otherwise. All *da capo* and *dal segno* instructions should be observed.

A final word of advice: enjoy practising and performing the pieces – your enjoyment will come across to the examiner and it will make the exam a happier event for everyone involved.

Teachers may photocopy pages from this book to use with students; it may be helpful to enlarge the copy.

Where publisher details are given as Trinity Guildhall this indicates that the piece is included in the piano book for the grade.

Entry Level

At Entry Level (Initial), candidates will typically be able to show that they have acquired a basic foundation on their instrument; they will demonstrate some interpretation through variation in dynamics and articulation, with a limited variety of pace. They will perform audibly, with a sense of enthusiasm and enjoyment, and with some awareness of audience. These features will be demonstrated through material that is short enough to allow candidates at this level to maintain concentration through to the end. Content will be simple and straightforward, often with attractive titles relating to familiar subjects and contexts. The musical language will be simple and accessible.

Initial

Alexander   Sour Lemons!   Trinity Guildhall

Just thinking about the title makes the mouth tingle, and that is surely the effect Alexander wants in the opening bars. A sharp, stinging *staccato* – keep the fingers firm and close to the keys to ensure that the chords with black and white notes synchronise well. The rhythm is also intentionally misleading, initially implying three beats in a bar but a small accent on the first note of bar 3 will restore us to common time. Notice how each four-bar phrase ends: the move to the dominant in bar 16 will make this strongest; then bars 4 and 12, with their upward-moving melody seeming to end with less certainty than the finality of the middle C in bar 8.

Chwatal   Little Playmates   Trinity Guildhall

This is staple fare for young pianists: five-finger melodies in C position playing above and below tonic and dominant chords. A clear differentiation between the dynamic levels and an appropriate balance between melody and chordal accompaniment are essential, but these need to be allied to a brisk tempo and an energy in the fingers to bring a performance to life. The *marcato* on the second and fourth lines applies to the left hand, where it takes the tune for two bars. The suggested tempo is ideal to accommodate both even *legato* quavers and crisp *staccato* crotchets. Try thinking of colours for the dynamics, ranging from a bright scarlet for the f to a pale pink for the p. Excellent practice material!

Josef Gruber   Sunshine (duet)   Trinity Guildhall

This should make most pianists feel like smiling as the hands play in octaves and remain in a C position throughout. Still, there are quite a few other details to get right. Firstly the dynamics: there are phrases marked p, mf and f, as well as some hairpins. Scales can be practised at these different levels, with the aim of characterising the sound differently. Perhaps mf is cheerful, p quite shy, and f boastful? Then articulation: there are a couple of *staccato* notes, quite a few slurs and some *portamento,* and it is good to understand the different physical movements for each of these at this early stage.

Candidates are welcome to bring a teacher, parent, guardian or friend in to the exam to play the duet part with them.

Uli Gruber Kindergarten Blues Trinity Guildhall

The children are stomping around the classroom at the start of this piece. Excellent music for developing a rich, firm-fingered sound in the left hand. The right hand chords are neither a real *staccato* nor held for a full crotchet, but something in between. Keep listening to the balance with the melody – the left hand must always sound like the main voice – and be careful about the sneaky right-hand minim in bar 3. Feel the fingers treading gradually lighter for the *diminuendo* in bar 8.

The 'Blues' in the title refers to the E/Eb argument; try playing the first five notes of C major, but play an Eb instead of D. This is the beginning of a blues scale and fun can be had improvising around these notes.

Hall The Secret Garden Trinity Guildhall

The bass line that descends from tonic to dominant using the melodic minor provides endless possibilities for improvisation. Here Hall adds a triad to each note and these chords should be practised in both hands, checking for a well-balanced hand shape, with a rounded fifth finger and supportive bridge. All dynamics are relative and, although the opening is marked $\boldsymbol{p}$, there needs to be room to get quite a bit softer later on, both as the line descends to bar 8, and also for the magical $\boldsymbol{pp}$ ending. Imagine that the piano represents a mood – perhaps the wonder as the door to this mysterious garden is opened. A small *crescendo* in bar 16 will make the fading away in the last bars easier to achieve.

Kabalevsky The Little Twins (from *Twenty-Four Easy Pieces* op. 39) Trinity Guildhall

Kabalevsky wrote several similar pieces that play with patterns, with the hands in contrary motion or, as here, playing copy-cat. *The Little Twins* is much more straightforward to play than it is to read, and you may consider using that same game of copy-cat to teach this piece. The opening bar is one cell, bar 7 is another and the ascending or descending fifth is the third. Cells can be practised beginning on different notes – not forgetting the F♯ in the key signature – noting where the accents fall, and finding a clean, crisp *staccato* touch. These twins are full of mischievous energy, so candidates should aim for the upper metronome speed in performance and make sure the right hand enjoys having the last word.

Keyworth Alaskan Adventure Trinity Guildhall

The lively character of this piece will be achieved easily if the playing is rhythmic and the articulation crisply observed. This will capture the sense of movement across wide open spaces as suggested in the title. It is only by looking at the black notes that we can tell which white notes are which, so many beginners' books use the two and three black note clusters to help pianists navigate around the piano. They are also really helpful for countering those drooping wrists (which wrist-rests for computers seem to encourage!), as the whole arm moves further into the keyboard to play. So having a piece that moves between white and black notes, using the same pattern for each, is both fun and pedagogically useful. Get the hands used to the positions by playing chords first, feeling the different length of the black keys (their total length, not just what we see). Improvising in these two positions, playing with the different dynamic levels and articulation, will be excellent preparation for the piece itself. There is an equality between the hands in the first two lines, but later make sure the chords don't get in the way of projecting the solo line.

Lockhart	April Shower	Trinity Guildhall

If only all April showers were as gentle and brief as this one! Try different fingers on the opening left-hand note, and help pianists understand the weight and spring in the key by depressing the note silently, and gradually making the finger lighter and lighter until the key pushes the finger back up. Having this sensitivity in the fingers will make control of dynamic levels more successful, particularly if the hands stay fairly close to the keys. Real rain obeys no rules of rhythm and pulse, but here pianists need to keep a steady minim beat until the final *rallentando*. Here, subdividing the minim beat into crotchets and perhaps then into quavers will help this shower to die away most gradually and believably.

Macardle	Driving Force	Trinity Guildhall

This is a big, bold piece, full of energy and strength, and it makes an ideal contrast to *April Shower*. No light *staccato* here; these repeated notes and chords are weighty, the fingers sticking to them as long as possible before they have to release to re-strike. This means that the left-hand crotchet will effectively come off with the second quaver in the right hand. The slur in bar 2 implies extra weight on the first note, as well as *legato*. Listen to the length of the right-hand crotchet in bars 4 and 12 – it is shorter than expected. The extra left-hand note in bar 9 plus a little more weight will produce the *ff*, but keep listening to the tone quality and avoid anything that sounds forced or ugly.

	Russian Dance	
Goedicke	(from *More Classics to Moderns* book 1)	*Yorktown Music Press*

Although the tempo marking is only *allegro moderato* the time signature indicates that there are only two beats in a bar, so the crotchet pace needs to be quite brisk to capture the energetic spirit of this dance. Articulation is important; only slur where marked, otherwise slightly separate the crotchets. The left-hand chords will last until the beginning of the next bar, so good co-ordination of the hands is needed here and practising the different movements of each hand away from the keyboard may help – on knees perhaps, or on the piano lid. Ideally the top two parts in the last bar should be played *legato*, while the bottom G is released and replayed. Difficult, but worth spending time on; this sort of co-ordination gives the brain a good workout!

Kember	On the Run	*Schott*

This is a useful five-finger exercise and will probably be best learnt by rote, so that the emphasis is on listening to the quavers and finding a good movement of the hand that helps to shape them well. On approaching the last note of each group the wrist will gently rise, lifting the fingers to release the final note without an accent. The accompanying dotted minims could lift at the same time, or play *legato*. Notice the different dynamic levels. Practising scales at different dynamics, or in different moods, is good preparation for this, feeling that extra energy in the fingers as the dynamic level increases. This needs to be played at a fast tempo – a speed of ♩ = 138 is good, always maintaining the clarity and evenness of the quavers.

Kendell   Thoughtful (from *Moods*)   *Bosworth*

This piece has a serious mood and the opening bars, with their Lydian colouring, should be played with gentle authority. The B♭ in the next phrase sows some doubt and the opening returns at a lower dynamic, less sure of itself, finally fading to a **pp**. A smooth, rich bass line will provide a continuity of sound under the two-, three- and four-note slurs in the melody. Allow only small gaps in the top line, as though beginning each new group of notes with a consonant, using the wrist to help the fingers gently release the last notes of the slurs. Subdivide the last two bars into quavers to be sure of having a gradual, organic slowing down.

Milne   Flâneur (duet)   *Faber*

The relaxed mood of this stroll is an ideal starting point for thinking about the suppleness of the wrist and elbow, which will help to achieve a good sound quality. The sensation of playing should be easy, pleasurable – just like a stroll around a city. Small hands will find it easier to play the flats if the hand position is slightly further in towards the black notes. Care should be taken with the co-ordination in bars 2–3; the right hand needs to lift, but the left hand should maintain its *legato*. Use this descending bass line as a starting point for some improvisation. With the right hand in a C position, the pianist can make up endless melodies to play on top.

Candidates are welcome to bring a teacher, parent, guardian or friend in to the exam to play the duet part with them.

Salutrinskaya   The Shepherd's Tune   *Yorktown Music Press*

The left-hand fifth brings to mind the melancholy drone of bagpipes and the modal melody would sound well on a wind instrument – a pipe or flute. This piece captures the traditional picture of the lonely, solitary shepherd. The melody needs depth of sound, keeping the fingers well supported from the bridge and ensuring the wrist is supple. Save the really soft sounds for the **pp** and **ppp** at the end. This last chord needs careful judging. Pianists should look at where the hands are going before they start moving and concentrate on feeling the weight of the notes with the fingertips, pressing down slowly, but just fast enough for the notes to sound. There is much expression in this melody and singing it through will help pianists understand its shape more keenly.

Foundation Level

At Foundation Level (Grades 1–3), candidates will typically be able to apply their knowledge, understanding and skills to produce a performance that demonstrates careful preparation, understanding and the beginning of thoughtful interpretation based on some creative engagement with the material. Candidates will perform clearly and accurately, with a fluent technical command appropriate to the level and a sense of spontaneity, sustaining these qualities through to the end. Through variations in pace, volume, rhythm and articulation they will be able to create and convey mood. These features will be demonstrated through material of sufficient length to allow candidates to show their ability to establish and sustain their performance and interpretation. Content will include easily recognisable styles (e.g. minuet, blues) as the foundation for the exploration of musical styles outside their immediate experience. The musical language will contain a variety of expression across the three pieces and will demand awareness of balance and phrase.

Grade 1

Telemann   Gigue in G   Trinity Guildhall

Georg Philipp Telemann became the leading German composer of his generation, despite being a contemporary of J S Bach. Bach clearly respected him as a man as well as a composer, asking him to become C P E Bach's godfather.

Telemann incorporated elements of French and Italian style into his works, and there is a certain flamboyance in this gigue that fits well with more Southern climates. It proceeds in leaps and broken chords, primary chord harmonies and direct modulations. It needs a light but energised touch, a buoyancy in the fingers and definitely some detail of articulation and dynamic to enliven the texture. The shape of the left-hand quavers often echoes that of the right hand, and this dialogue could be highlighted by changing the main voice to the left hand in those places, especially in bars 13 and 14, where it seems completely natural to make a *crescendo* through the left hand.

coll. by L Mozart   Menuett in F (from *Notebook for Nannerl*)   Trinity Guildhall

Nannerl was Wolfgang Amadeus's elder sister and their father, Leopold, put together a collection of 60 pieces to use to teach her the piano. Wolfgang probably learnt from the book as well and, although it was usually Leopold who wrote the pieces in the book, it is known that some of these minuets were written by Wolfgang when he was as young as five.

Experts agree that this minuet is probably not by Wolfgang himself, but it follows the usual minuet pattern, both harmonically and structurally. Different articulations could work in the left hand: all the crotchets could be detached, or some could be slurred to match the right hand, for instance in the first and penultimate bars of the first half. Keep a graceful one-in-a-bar feel, with the music shaped in two-bar phrases. It may help the dynamic contrast on the third line to think of two groups of dancers: the first group gesturing to invite the second to join them, the second group gracefully accepting, leading to the *tutti* on the last line.

Czerny   Allegro in G   Trinity Guildhall

Most pianists associate Carl Czerny with interminable finger exercises, his name synonymous with building technique so that we can play 'real' music, like Beethoven. But Czerny was himself a pupil of Beethoven and also taught Liszt, and the perfectly balanced structure and infectious mood of this *allegro* is proof that he should not be under-estimated.

Spend some time becoming conversant with these typical G major chords, perhaps through some improvisation. Play all three left-hand notes together, being sure to support the little finger well so that sustaining the bass notes will be easy. The right-hand *staccato* should be crisp to fit the bright mood (*allegro* means lively, not just fast) and the left-hand chords will match this articulation whilst the bass knits the texture together. Dynamics are editorial, but a spirited f seems right for the opening music, with a sense of *crescendo* to bars 6 and 7. The chords in bar 12 are slightly tricky; take care not to rush here and stay calm for the return to p in the next bar.

Wohlfahrt   Allegretto   Trinity Guildhall

Allegretto is not a very imaginative title, although it does give some idea of the mood of this piece – light-hearted and graceful. There is a sense of mazurka in the first section, with the *staccato* bass notes propelling the left hand on to the held crotchet chords on the second beat. The chords are simple: V^7–I in C and G majors. All pianists spend many hours playing these chords in myriad guises, so make sure they are well understood in different inversions. The changes of position in the right hand will also be easier if it is noticed that the first three phrases have the same pattern, but begin on different notes of the C major triad. Each four-bar phrase leads towards the dominant chord, then relaxes back on to the tonic. These become two-bar phrases at the start of the second section. Take care here to release the third note of these left-hand figures, giving a more supple and expressive character to this half.

Trad. *arr.* Eben   Our Old Stove is Bust Again   Trinity Guildhall

Czech composer Petr Eben died just a few years ago in 2007. He had been imprisoned in Buchenwald during World War II and later suffered under the Soviet regime but, as the political situation eased, he frequently visited the UK and became composer-in-residence at both Aldeburgh and Dartington. Like his compatriot Janáček he collected folksongs in Moravia and it is probably one of these that he has arranged here.

The first two bars of each line are great fun to play, even if they are expressing frustration at a broken stove. Use arm weight, keeping the fingers close to the keys, to ensure the chords play exactly together. Then comes the challenge of playing softly in the usually dominant right hand, letting the left-hand theme sing *marcato*. Practise very slowly, feeling a velvety softness in the right hand and steely finger tips in the left. A good exercise is to play the f bass note first and then the p chord, initially a second or two apart, and then closer and closer together until they are played at the same time.

Barratt   Saturday Stomp   Trinity Guildhall

This is immediately engaging, with an extraordinary $f\!f$ bar towards the end to lift it out of the predictable. The 'leisurely' indication implies a relaxed approach to the dotted rhythms, finding something more akin to triplets than a crisp military precision, although the regularity of the pulse should not waver at all through the piece. The slurs towards the end also suggest that the main theme should be played with buoyancy rather than too smoothly, and make sure the final semiquavers in bars 11-13 don't linger into the next beat. Bar 18 should be quite shocking; non-*legato* and with a real kick on the accented note (and remember the C sharps, all of which have been naturals up to now). Keep the strength in the last crotchet of that bar, then immediately return to a straight-faced $\boldsymbol{p}$, as though nothing unusual happened at all. There is exactly one beat's rest to prepare for the final $\boldsymbol{pp}$, keeping fingers close to the keys to control the sound.

Hall & Drayton   The Very Vicious Velociraptor   Trinity Guildhall

As well as appealing to the imagination, this piece is also pedagogically sound, with the quaver patterns and accented chords ensuring that pianists are practising both fingerwork and good use of the arms. Playing 1-2-3-4-5 or 5-4-3-2-1 perfectly evenly is one of the most tricky things to do well and an F♯ on finger 4 in the left hand adds to the challenge. Check for a balanced hand position and small adjusting movements in the arm. You may want to experiment with other fingerings: 3-2-1-3-2 in the left hand and 2-3-1-3-2 in the right hand avoid using the weaker fingers, although admittedly, developing the weaker fingers is one thing this piece aims to achieve! Listen for a neat join between the hands in bars 12-14 and, as the velociraptor slinks away on the last line, notice that the accents disappear. No *ritardando*, just let his footsteps quietly disappear into the distance – perhaps with a sigh of relief!

Milne   Cat's Whiskers   Trinity Guildhall

Did you know that a cat's whisker is a fine wire in a crystal radio receiver? Almost certainly not what is referred to here, but something called the 'cat's whiskers' is something very fine indeed. This is a delightful piece for both performers and audience, and has detailed directions for articulation and dynamics, as well as a chromatic scale, which will provide plenty of lesson material.

We're told to play the quavers as triplets, but the rhythm still needs to be precise, listening especially for the rests. No holding on to the final quavers in those slurred groups; gently raise the wrist and release the note without a bump. Notice that some of the *diminuendos* only lower the dynamic temporarily; in the next bar there is a return to $\boldsymbol{mf}$. This changes in bar 13 – very careful counting needed in the left hand here – where coming down to $\boldsymbol{mp}$ allows an exciting *crescendo* for the full orchestra to join in the last verse. The accent in bar 19 is easily overlooked, and watch out for the nonchalant, soft, sustained low note at the very end.

Norton   Walking Together   Trinity Guildhall

This is a gentle stroll rather than a purposeful walk and requires some subtlety in the shaping. The title probably comes from the quavers that move together in tenths, sounding warm and companionable. But there is also room for some more animated discussion on this walk, with agitated agreement – or perhaps disagreement – in the middle section.

A flexible wrist is an absolute necessity here to achieve the requisite rounded sound and shapely phrasing. Make sure that the right hand releases at the end of its first phrase, so that the last note doesn't linger into the next beat. Often a sense of movement into the keyboard can help the quickly repeated chords in bars 9 and 10, with a slight raising thrust of the arm to help with the accent. This line needs to feel more energised to contrast with the lulling of the repeated phrases elsewhere.

Anon.   La Gamba   *A & C Black*

This dance immediately brings to mind countless films and plays set in the 16th century, with court musicians playing viols, recorders and tambourines. It needs a brisk tempo, with a sense of one beat in a bar. Repeats should be played in the exam and, given that most music of the period was semi-improvised, it is very likely that an extra instrument or two would have joined in or dropped out on the repeat, so vary the dynamics to recreate that sense of immediacy. The emphasis is on the second bar of each two-bar phrase, and detaching the crotchets in the first bar and making a slight *crescendo* into the *legato* top line in the second will help achieve the character of this galliard. The left-hand fingering in bar 5 is good – avoiding thumbs and fifth fingers on black notes is unrealistic – but starting with 3 or 4 would be more conventional. Some variation in the articulation would be completely stylistic, particularly in the second half, where some crotchets could be played detached and some *legato*.

Carroll   Raindrops   *Forsyth*

This is the fourth piece in Carroll's wander through the landscape, the collection entitled *The Countryside*. It followed his popular *Scenes at a Farm* and his stated aim was to inspire children's imagination, writing in the preface that teachers should ask pianists to describe the scene the title suggests to them. When playing this, imagine hearing the very first raindrops falling in the opening two bars, and then making a quick dash under the trees with the *mf* quavers. Listen for a real equality between the hands, with chords and quavers matching precisely in length and dynamic. Keep the pulse absolutely steady (around ♩ = 120 feels right), perhaps slightly placing the last chord, mainly to give it a sense of finality, but also to help ensure that the all the notes synchronise perfectly.

Duncombe   Fanfare   *Faber*

This is an enjoyably boisterous piece with straightforward patterns that will be easy to assimilate. Separating all the left-hand crotchets is one suggestion, in bars 5–7 as well as in bar 8, although those in the middle *mp* section may be played a little longer to suit the mood. Notice that the lower voice crotchets in the right hand at bar 7 should match the length of the left-hand notes. Yes, there needs to be a contrast in dynamics in the middle section, but it is also important that the thirds are secure and synchronised. Make sure that the arm is involved here and only *mp* – no lower. Try different fingerings at the opening; the thumb is not always the best finger for such repeated notes and using 2–4 may give a brighter sound. Similarly the thirds may be more comfortable with 4 and 2, giving a more balanced hand, so playing the quavers 4-3-2-1 would enable this. A small holding back at the end and, for once, those last left-hand notes could be bold and definite, rather than fading away.

Grechaninov   The Little Traveller op. 98 no. 14   *Schott*

You may find this piece with other titles elsewhere; Russian colleagues say that the original title means 'pilgrims' and this seems to fit the mood well – weary, but positive.

The right-hand melody is in a wonderfully rich part of the instrument and is ideal for practising a seamless, foot-dragging *legato*. Listen to the sound of each note, balancing it with those either side; this matching of tone will do much to create a good *legato*. Elsewhere there are smaller slurs, but keep in mind the overall shape of two-bar phrases. Notice that none of these phrases really resolve. There is an increased hopefulness after the double bar, with a small *accelerando* as you glimpse your goal ahead. And the slowing up and pause in the following bar — are they relief that you are nearly there? Disappointment that it was a false alarm? You need a story behind these bars to make them work convincingly before the opening music returns and you finally reach a cadence in C.

Gurlitt Allegretto Grazioso *Schott*

The notes here are fairly straightforward and the 2-bar/2-bar/4-bar phrasing is typically classical. The insistent repetition and alien Ab in the middle section adds a touch of drama; build to $\boldsymbol{f}$ in bar 16, noting that there will need to be a very quick and well-judged *diminuendo* to return back to the safety of C major in the following bar. Listen for the rests in this second line, as they will help it sound more breathless and questioning. Played at a gentle tempo, ♩ = c. 112, there is time to think about the movements that will achieve this *grazioso*, classical style. Try a small rotary movement in bars 5-8 and lift the hand from a supple wrist at the end of the slurs. Play only the first repeat in the exam to balance the two halves and a very slight *ritardando* in the penultimate bar would be appropriate.

Last On the Trot *Forsyth*

This comes from Joan Last's collection *Razzamajazz* and she suggests that pianists may not be able to read these rhythms, but will very quickly pick them up once they hear them. She also proposes that these jazzy pieces could be given as 'bribes' for learning exam pieces — little did Last know then that such pieces would soon feature in most exam syllabuses!

There are a variety of different articulations here: quaver and crotchet *staccatos*, accents and small slurs. Some of the slurs finish with a *staccato*, some without, as in bars 2 and 13. The former will have more intent, more decisiveness than the latter, which will generally be part of a 'drop-float' movement. Having a story behind the notes may help the dynamic levels; something happens on the fourth line to make the music slightly tearful perhaps before you trot back to the major at the end. Notice the final right-hand note will outlast the left hand. ♩ = 144 is an excellent tempo, but a touch slower would also be acceptable.

Rowley Fugue IV *Chester*

This does feel like a piece solely written to introduce fugal playing to young pianists, but it is straightforward to play and promotes an equality between the hands that is always welcome. A small *diminuendo* at the end of the three-bar fugue subject would help the left hand to step into the spotlight in bar 4 and the move towards $\boldsymbol{p}$ in bar 7 (which should begin on the second quaver). Release the left-hand E in bar 11 to allow the right hand to re-strike it; this is awkward, but fairly typical in contrapuntal work. Note the unusually early release of the right hand in bar 15 and enjoy the final *crescendo* without forcing the sound. Alec Rowley is now remembered mostly for his many educational piano works. He taught at Trinity College of Music, so it is fitting to see one of his pieces in the syllabus.

Satie	At Play with a Hoop	*Yorktown Music Press*

Erik Satie was enormously influential in a Paris where artistic movements rapidly succeeded one another. Known now the world over as the composer of the *Gymnopédies*, at the time he was defiantly controversial, and often wrote simple, repetitive, sometimes bizarre works that were much admired by Poulenc and Les Six. This creativity and imagination make him a perfect composer of children's pieces and the directness of this one will appeal to many.

Finding a good 'drop-float' movement is needed at the opening and some may find matching the fingering in both hands helps this, using for instance 4-2 in right hand and 2-4 (or 2-3) in left hand. The dynamic is *f*, but add some shading to keep it alive. So bars 8-12 move towards the subdominant, whereas the answering bars 13-16 return to the tonic, with a concomitant relaxing of the dynamic level. Keep subdividing in quavers, then semiquavers, to get a convincing *ritardando* at the end, which could be accompanied by a *crescendo*, noting the accent on the last note. Choose a brisk tempo, around ♩ = 126-144.

Wedgwood	Minnie Mouse Hits Town!	*Faber*

Pam Wedgwood is an expert in writing immediately engaging pieces that often also have sound educational value. Here I imagine Minnie Mouse dressed in an outrageously bright and extravagant outfit, strutting down Hollywood Boulevard, attracting the attention of all around her, then gradually walking off into the distance.

With the exception of two bars, this promenade takes place over a descending ground bass and is a perfect opportunity to do some improvisation work over these four notes. This works very well with the right hand beginning in a G minor position, gradually adding the odd F♯ or E♭. Encourage a good *legato* and fairly weighty sound for the left-hand minims with precise rhythms in the right hand (Minnie's probably in high heels!). There's much repetition here and clearly distinguishable dynamic levels are needed to maintain interest.

Grade 2

Mattheson	Menuet (from *Suite quatrième pour le clavecin*)	Trinity Guildhall

Johann Mattheson was a composer and musical scholar, active in Hamburg in the first half of the 18th century. He befriended Handel when they were both working for the Hamburg Opera, although the famous story of their quarrel ends with Handel being saved from Mattheson's sword by a large button on his jacket! Mattheson became an ambassador and diplomat, fluent in English and even translating novels like Defoe's *Moll Flanders* into German.

This menuet came to us in the form of a performer's facsimile, devoid of any markings of tempo, dynamics or phrasing. Note that the key is clearly G minor, even though there is only one flat in the key signature – quite common for the period. The repeats (which should be played in the exam) give performers an opportunity to vary the dynamics. It is also quite likely that harpsichordists of the time would have improvised more ornaments in repeats; this was common practice on the opera stage, and Mattheson was also a singer. This is not expected in an exam, but I would suggest an extra mordent on the last right-hand note of the first section which could be added on the repeat. A dignified tempo, with clean articulation, neat ornaments and a sense of poise in the dance rhythms will bring out the best of this rather elegant menuet.

Anon.   Bourrée in D minor   Trinity Guildhall

Like Nannerl's *Minuet* in Grade 1, this was one of the dances probably collected by Leopold Mozart to use for teaching his children, and this Bourrée appears in the *Notebook for Wolfgang*. The Bourrée nearly always begins its phrases with a crotchet upbeat, and has poise and grace, although the English name for it, Borry, seems to suggest something more boisterous!

One of the main things that will help achieve that poise and sense of the dance is the articulation. It would be stylistic to detach some of the left-hand crotchets, particularly in the I–V–I found in bar 4 and elsewhere. This is such a common figure it is worth practising in all keys; it usually has a gentle *diminuendo*. This is also a good piece to think about the more subtle varieties of articulation: for instance the As in the right hand of bar 2 will not all be the same; the final one begins a new phrase and will have a different emphasis from the previous one, which ends a phrase. Using words can be helpful to capture this nuance: 'I must catch a train to Winchelsea, where I'll meet a friend who's waiting for me' fits this perfectly!

Haydn   Scherzo (from *Divertimento in F*, Hob. XVI/9)   Trinity Guildhall

As both divertimento and scherzo imply, this is a light-hearted piece and, despite the look of all those semiquavers, it is skilfully written so that all the passagework follows predictable patterns and falls under the fingers. The dynamics are editorial and you can consider other possibilities, especially in the contrasting middle section. It would seem logical however to begin and end with a bright *f*.

The play between *staccato* and *legato* will do much to capture both the elegance and wit of the piece. The hands are often in disagreement – note especially the *tenuto* left-hand lower F in bar 4 against the gently released right-hand third, as the suspension resolves. Make sure the right hand sings a dynamic level or two above the left-hand semiquavers after the double bar (a well-supported little finger is needed for these). Probably the trickiest moment is the right hand in bars 14–15; keep the wrist flexible to allow the changes in direction and leap of a sixth to flow easily, and find other ways of working on this passage. For example, practising something backwards really makes you think about all of the notes.

Steibelt   Andante   Trinity Guildhall

By a composer of whom most of us will not have heard, this is a strangely touching piece with its hesitant phrases and sighing suspensions. A successful performance will demand much subtlety of phrasing and a gentle, unforced sound.

Daniel Gottlieb Steibelt was born in Germany but travelled widely, working in London and Paris, challenging Beethoven to a contest in Vienna, and finally settling in St Petersburg. Like many of the pianists of the time, he wrote both piano works for his own recitals, but also pieces for teaching and clearly this is one of the latter. The shaping is typically classical: a two-bar phrase leads to the dominant answered by one cadencing in the tonic; a four-bar phrase then takes us back to the dominant. The whole section is repeated, but with the final phrase returning us to the tonic. Although nearly every phrase ends with a resolving suspension, it is important to understand the structure so that the moves to the dominant have a sense of increasing tension, whilst those to the tonic a sense of relaxation. Another way of thinking about this is through question and answer, statement and agreement and this idea of a conversation will help to link the small phrases into longer shapes.

| Tchaikovsky | Mazurka (from *Album for the Young* op. 39) | **Trinity Guildhall** |

The mazurka is a national Polish dance, the most well-known mazurkas being of course by Chopin. In contrast to the minuet or waltz, this three-beat dance tends to throw the emphasis on to the second beat and traditionally the men, in full dress uniform, would make their spurs ring at cadence points as they clicked their heels together.

Tchaikovsky has captured the nobility and pride of the mazurka in this piece. The rhythms need to be absolutely precise; from the very beginning ensure that the semiquavers are always neatly and quickly connected to the next downbeat – any hesitation here is fatal to the dance rhythm. There is also much detail of articulation to note. This dance is never hurried – there is a certain upright poise in the rhythm – but the pulse is strict and the left-hand chords will need to be carefully practised and understood to enable this. It may take longer to explain the chord progressions, as opposed to just learning the notes, but ultimately it gives much greater security and enhanced musicianship.

| Lutosławski | Gaik (Mayday Dance) (from *Melodie Ludowe*) | **Trinity Guildhall** |

Lutosławski is one of the great 20th-century composers, with a very unique voice. This piece is a good introduction to his style – its driving rhythmic energy is found in many of his other works. It comes from a selection of Polish folk tunes that the composer arranged. Sometimes translated as a Mayday Dance, the word *Gaik* also means a small forest.

The piece works best with an absolutely unchanging pulse, right up to the very last note, and a fast tempo – there's a primal energy here. Lutosławski has marked nearly every note with some direction of articulation and the dynamics too are very precise. The left-hand off-beat chords should be kept light and clean, allowing the right-hand melody to be easily heard. Perhaps in the opening bars there could be more equality between the two hands, or you could even bring the left hand to the fore. Make sure that the p is a real contrast to the f, but that it allows you room to be even quieter in the ensuing *più* p phrases. Take a deep breath before you start and feel the energy building up inside you that will take you right through the piece in one burst of adrenalin.

| Plé | **Petit Mystère** | **Trinity Guildhall** |

The title invites us to invent our own story to go with the evocative sounds and suspended chords of this piece. 'Very singing and expressive,' Plé tells us, and the dynamic levels range from p to pp, with 'mysterious' and 'very gentle' qualifying these low levels. Touch is everything; pianist and teacher Tobias Matthay used to speak of 'steel fingers in a velvet glove', but here you need velvet finger pads as well to conjure some of these sounds.

The use of pedals is optional. If they can't be easily reached keeping the heel on the ground, then leave them out. It is only in the final phrase that the notes actually mingle in one long sustaining pedal, producing that wash of sound so often described as 'impressionist'. Otherwise there is only one place where the *legato* is difficult without the pedal, bar 7, and examiners will understand if there is a small break in the sound here. Similarly, imagine the effect of the *una corda* and save a special tone quality for these two phrases. Maybe try a more oblique touch, slightly pulling the fingers towards you so that the keys descend more slowly. Above all, listen. Listen for exactly the right moment to begin again after the pauses (counted pauses seldom have the same effect); listen to match one note to another, hearing how the longer notes fade, so that the next note will need to start at a lower level; and listen for exact synchronisation of the chords. Plenty here to inspire an imaginative pianist towards a poetic performance.

DeHolt	Summer Swing	Trinity Guildhall

'Swing' style implies that the dotted rhythms are played as triplets, and this should extend to the quaver–crotchet–quaver rhythm in bar 9 and elsewhere. The fact that DeHolt writes this pattern differently in bar 5 means that the 'correct', classical rhythm in bar 9 would be acceptable in the exam, but it feels a little pedantic to play it that way in such an easy-going piece.

The articulation presents us with another conundrum: does the slur over the final notes imply that elsewhere the melody should be played non-*legato*? Your decision! There are many different types of articulation and it would be good to explore the differences between, for instance, a gentle left-hand bounce (ping pong ball) at the opening, and something heavier and slightly longer (football) towards the end. The dynamic range is quite wide here, but aim for a rich, trombone and tuba *ff* rather than something too hard-sounding at the climax; the overall mood is relaxed and celebratory. You could add in the drums on the last chord – lots of arm thrust to achieve the *sforzando*.

Chappell	Fanfare for the Common Cold	Trinity Guildhall

This is a wonderfully descriptive piece and should really spark the imagination of young pianists. The allusion is of course to Copland's *Fanfare for the Common Man* and once the performer has heard this work it will be easier to capture the brassy sound required in the opening. Experiment with different ways of dividing the hands for this; it works well if all the accented notes are kept in one hand.

Good use of the arm is vital for the whole piece: to get the necessary weight into the sound; to ensure synchronisation of the chords; to achieve the *portamento* marked later in the left hand; and to help with the *glissandi* and tone clusters at the end. Have you tried any of Kurtág's *Játékok* (*Games*)? The first book in this series is for beginners, and uses a lot of *glissandi* and tone clusters precisely to ensure that pianists understand arm weight. Here Chappell is mimicking those moments when the sneeze won't quite come out. The *glissandi* are marked to finish on the top note of most pianos, but don't worry if yours are shorter. The important thing is to begin straightaway; if you stop on the first note it is often more tricky to get the *glissando* going without hurting your fingers. There are various ways of playing the last chord: if your hands are long enough, you may be able to cover the octave just by turning them sideways, but smaller hands will need to play with the forearm and fist as Chappell suggests. This is a dramatic effect; there's no need to force the sound, and don't worry if you overlap on to one or two extra notes.

Anon.	Menuet BWV Anh. 118 (from *Notebook for Anna Magdalena*)	*Any reliable edition*

There is a polonaise from *Notebook for Anna Magdalena* in the main syllabus for Grade 3 (page 21), and the notes there give a little background to the book. Here again we have a two-part dance, a graceful minuet, and performers will need to add phrasing, articulation and dynamic detail. Most of the two-bar phrases lead towards the second bar and the couple of four-bar phrases move towards the third bar. You may like to slightly detach the second and third crotchets in some bars to capture the sense of dance, for instance in the right hand of bar 5, and both hands in the penultimate bar. The appoggiaturas work well as crotchets, with an emphasis on the dissonance. The trill in bar 9 should begin on the upper note and a mordent or trill on the penultimate right-hand note would sound stylistic. Repeats should not be played in the exam, but there is room for some dynamic contrast: the music moves firstly towards the dominant, F major, and then C major is suggested before it returns back to the tonic via the dominant. Let the dynamics subtly reflect these modulations and the general shape of the music.

Bartók   Tramp's Song   *Editio Musica Budapest*

When Bartók was teaching he found that many of the pieces written for children, with the exception of teaching pieces by the likes of Bach and Schumann, had little musical value, so he decided to write his own. These became the collection entitled *For Children*, first published in 1909. Bartók used Hungarian and Slovak folk tunes, often keeping the melody intact, but adding wonderfully evocative harmonies 'tinged with the nostalgic melancholy of the countryside', as Barbara Nissman writes.

In the first English editions this piece was titled *Sorrow* and, although *Tramp's Song* may be more accurate, 'sorrow' reflects well the wilting, sighing, short melodic phrases. Both hands shape away from the first notes in the slurs, helping to emphasise the major/minor uncertainty. After these small hairpins the music returns to its former dynamic level. An attempt to move to C major in bars 5-6 results in a longer phrase with a *crescendo* to its mid-point but the music slumps back into minor despair two bars later, with some two-part writing in the left hand. The lower A in bar 8 can be omitted. The dynamic levels are restrained: *mp*, *p* and *più p*. The differences are subtle, but must be audible.

Cornick   Just Cruisin'   *Universal*

The detail of dynamics and articulation make this piece excellent for developing fine co-ordination. The constant *mp*/*mf* contrasts could be added in later but the articulation needs to be there from the outset. Unslurred quavers should be detached; crotchets are sometimes held for full length and sometimes *staccato*; and notice that the second quaver in those two-note slurs will always release before the next downbeat. The right-hand upbeats are detached, whereas the left-hand upbeats are generally slurred – the pianistic equivalent of patting your head while rubbing circles on your tummy! The slurs under the chords in the middle section suggest they are phrased in pairs and some sneaky pedalling during the right-hand rests will help the implied *legato*. Cornick's tempo marking is quite fast given this level of detail, so ♩ = 112 or 116 would also be acceptable. The main thing is that all the detail needs to be well practised-in and assimilated so that ultimately the mood is relaxed – or 'cool' as the title implies – with no suggestion of effort.

D'Indy   Petite pièce   *Schott*

Vincent d'Indy's music is largely out of fashion now, but in Paris at the turn of the 20th century he was an important composer, teacher, conductor and staunch advocate of other composers' music. Amongst those he admired were many of the old masters – Monteverdi and Rameau, as well as Bach – and echoes of the baroque style can be heard in this piece, in its close part writing and in the chorale-inflected cadence.

Notice where the lower voice takes the lead: in bar 9 it begins a reply to the right hand's bar 7, and then in bar 11 it restates the opening motif. It also pre-echoes the right hand in bar 4 – worth bringing out. With both parts in the treble clef for most of the piece, it will be important to identify which is the main voice so that, for instance, the second left-hand note in bar 3 does not sound like part of the right-hand line. The phrasing indications are quite sophisticated, and imply stress and relaxation perhaps more than obvious separation between notes. 'Assez' is sometimes confused with 'assai'; the former means 'quite', the latter 'very'. A speed of around ♩ = 72 will prevent it from dragging, but give time for the chromaticism on the middle line to make its mark.

| Gurlitt | Allegro non troppo | *Alfred* |

So many pieces feature the main melody in the right hand ('rightist' as one of my left-handed students called it), so it's good to redress the balance and spend time developing a good *cantabile* tone in the left hand. Even in *p* this line should sing – think perhaps of a mellow brass sound, with the tuba playing the answering phrases with those low As. When you move towards the relative major there is a natural *crescendo* and, even though not marked, the sequence in bar 12 – which takes us back to the D minor – will inevitably sound less confident and firm than the preceding phrase in F. The right-hand chords look straightforward, but finding an ideal balance with the melody will need attentive listening. We want to hear the undercurrent of excitement or perhaps nervousness of these chords, without being over-conscious of hearing every single one. Keep the fingers on the keys, feeling exactly how much weight is needed for the chords to sound at the required dynamic. Finding the right tempo will also help this; too slow and the quavers will be intrusive, so judge the tempo by the left-hand melody, hearing its arc in one gesture (♩ = c. 126). Gurlitt has written in *mf*, then *mp* and finally *pp* towards the end; in effect this is a gradual *diminuendo*, enhanced by a *ritardando*, to bring the music gradually and gently to a full stop.

| Harris | Hopscotch | *Faber* |

This piece comes from Faber's *Fingerprints* collection, which informs us that Richard Harris was born in Kent and likes drinking ice cold milk! This is fairly easy-going – a brisk tempo, but with swung quavers and quite a bit of repetition, often with small changes. Whether or not this is chosen for an exam may depend on the ability to play two against three, as found in bar 5. There is a clear difference in learning styles here: some pick this up very quickly by ear; some need to understand the mathematical division of the beat, subdividing into triplet quavers; and some find a rhythmical phrase, like 'nice cuppa tea' useful. As the quavers in this piece are played as triplets anyway, the middle one of these would work well here. Avoid too clipped a semiquaver in bar 16, interpreting this more as a triplet. Elsewhere, take care to notice the length of final notes in phrases. Those in bars 7 and 11 are short, releasing before the next bar. Detach the accented notes, playing the rest of the left hand with a spring in its crotchet steps.

| Neefe | Canzonet | *Faber* |

Composers in the classical period were often given composition exercises, *partimenti*, in which they wrote, for instance, minuets on a certain prescribed pattern. This canzonet could easily be one of these exercises, fulfilling exactly the expectations of a simple piece in ternary form, with its 2+2+4 phrasing and sequences in the middle section. It is quite charming and requires good shaping, particularly to achieve the release of tension as appoggiaturas resolve in bars 2, 3 and elsewhere. As well as shaping on that level, we need to keep in mind the overall phrase: the first bars move towards the dominant, and the answering phrase returns us to the tonic. This needs to be reflected in the sound. Andantino is always a tricky tempo marking to interpret, but a speed of around ♩ = 76 is appropriate.

Nevada   Wenn Paris träumt (When Paris Dreams)   *Schott*

A sophisticated choice for someone who can empathise with the atmosphere of quintessentially romantic Paris by night. Also for someone who can comfortably reach the pedal, which is essential for capturing this seductive mood and evocative sound world. The precise release and retake of the pedal have been marked, although in reality this should be done so quickly that it feels like one movement rather than two. The foot must remain in contact with the pedal, and on good pianos the movement will be quite small. Listen carefully to ensure the sound of the melody is *cantabile* and warm enough to project above the hazy harmonies. The left hand will need to play below *mf* to take account of the richer noise of the pedalled notes in this register. With one in a bar, allow a natural *rubato* to accompany the phrasing, the left hand making small *diminuendo*s away from its bass notes. The right-hand D in bar 16 is tied over the rest, and the *rit.* and *accelerando* should not feel too obvious – just an initial lingering on the upward scale followed by a gentle flow forward to a reprise of the opening.

Spindler   Song Without Words   *Schott*

Fritz Spindler was a 19th-century German pianist and composer who wrote over 300 piano pieces. 'Songs without words' are often associated with Mendelssohn and they are indicative of the desire in this period to concentrate more on tone quality and making the piano sing. Understanding how the arm is involved, keeping the wrist supple so that the weight is easily transferred to the fingers, is essential. These are long opening phrases, and feeling the music move towards the dominant in bars 5 and 13, then relaxing back to the tonic, will help to shape them. The acciaccatura in bar 14 should still feel part of the lyrical line, not snatched.

The left-hand slurs are confusing and the suggestion is that they imply a shaping away from the downbeat rather than an actual gap in the sound between the bars. The harmonies are basically primary triads and should be practised as chords, perhaps using them as a basis for some improvisation. Using the pedal would be entirely appropriate here, but not necessary. It's a tribute to Spindler's talent that he has composed this touching piece from such simple material.

Grade 3

<table>
<tr><td>**Anon.**</td><td>**Polonaise BWV Anh. 128**
(from *Notebook for Anna Magdalena*)</td><td>**Trinity Guildhall**</td></tr>
</table>

J S Bach gave his second wife, Anna Magdalena, two 'little keyboard books' in 1722 and 1725, but several members of the family, including C P E Bach, continued to add to these collections well into the 1740s. Some of the works are definitely by J S himself, some have been attributed to other composers, but quite a few remain anonymous. It is tantalising to think that Anna Magdalena, who added several pieces in her own handwriting, may have been the composer.

Most of the smaller pieces are simple, two-part dances such as marches and minuets. There are a total of six polonaises, proving the popularity of this Polish dance, which is quite strict and ceremonial in character. It is unlikely that this one is by J S – the last line seems wholly uncharacteristic – but it is a useful exercise for ornamentation. All the ornaments begin on the beat and will require neat fingerwork. It often helps to realise how important the release of each note is to enable quick repetition. Stay close to the keys; movements are small but precise. Above all, the ornaments should not interrupt the flow of the dance, but simply decorate the line and help sustain the longer notes. Dynamics are editorial but we have left choices about articulation to each performer. It would be entirely stylistic to slightly separate some of the bass line notes, particularly where the intervals are wider.

<table>
<tr><td>**Handel**</td><td>**Sonatina HWV 585**</td><td>**Trinity Guildhall**</td></tr>
</table>

Handel settled in London in 1710 and by the time he wrote this sonatina he was working for the new and lavishly funded opera company, the Royal Academy. In 1719 he was sent abroad to recruit singers for this new venture, in particular the castrato Senesino, and Handel then composed and directed operas for nine seasons before the company went bankrupt. Opera was an expensive business then, as now, and no doubt Handel turned his hand to the occasional bit of teaching to supplement his income.

This unusual, through-composed piece is strictly in two parts until the final chord, and imagining a lively conversation between a violin and cello, or oboe and bassoon, may help to encourage an equal weighting between the two hands. There needs to be a buoyancy and directness in the playing, firm fingers but a supple wrist, and a sense of forward movement. Keep the tempo steady and avoid slowing up at the cadence points. As with most pieces from the baroque period, the original has no marks of dynamic or articulation but these should be added when playing on a modern instrument. Some have been suggested here and the *staccato* upbeats will help to create the lightness and energy that the piece demands. Make sure that wrists do not tighten for the trills; this will make them stand out and disturb the phrasing. Quite a challenging piece, as it moves over the keyboard quite rapidly, but one that uses many patterns that will be later encountered in baroque suite movements.

Mozart   **Menuett in F, K. 5**   **Trinity Guildhall**

There is another minuet from the *Notebook for Nannerl* in Grade 1, but this one is almost definitely by Wolfgang Amadeus himself, although the manuscript is yet to be found. Several pages from the original book were removed and have gradually been discovered in various libraries; perhaps K. 5 is still hidden somewhere.

Pianists are asked to observe both repeats in this piece. Played at a good tempo it is very short, and the repeats give performers an opportunity to vary the dynamics – those in the score are only editorial suggestions. Should the last bar of each section have the same right-hand rhythm or should the appoggiatura in bar 10 be played as a crotchet? The rules tell us that an appoggiatura before a dotted note will be two-thirds the length of that note, but either possibility is acceptable here as the differing notation is ambiguous. Decisions on articulation will need to be made: the right-hand slur in bar 2 implies that the second and third crotchets are detached. You may want to echo this in the left hand and use this phrasing elsewhere, for instance in bar 3 and the left hand of bar 9. The repeated bars that extend the opening to a 10-bar phrase and the central sequences occur in nearly all of Mozart's early minuets, so he must have been following a prescribed pattern. Make sure it is the second semiquaver in each group of three that is given more importance and not the thumb on the first. These breathless semiquavers and the continual off-beat entries of the right hand lend an energy and joy to this minuet that almost puts it into the category of a Beethovenian scherzo. Enjoy!

Burgmüller   **Pastorale op. 100 no. 3**   **Trinity Guildhall**

Pieces with the title 'pastorale' are usually in compound duple time and often use a drone. The aim is to give the impression of the outdoors, of fresh air and open spaces, and some of that mood is captured in this detailed pastorale by Burgmüller.

Although not exactly a drone, the G and D fifth acts as a pedal for the opening six bars, after a shapely, quasi-improvised introduction. Keep the chords well in the background; the overall dynamic is *p*, but you may need to play a little more firmly than that in the right hand for the melody to project. Keep the acciaccaturas and grace notes melodic, but before the beat. The accompaniment changes in the middle section and here it is the thumb that needs to play quietly; make sure it moves independently of the hand. The harmonies are tonic-dominant until bar 15, hence the accent and the *portamento* articulation adding a touch of drama before the return to the opening *dolce* theme. A slight easing of tempo in the last three quavers of bar 18 will help this link. Focus on the left-hand bass notes at the return so that the move to the dominant 7th is clearly heard, and take care over the length of the final note – only a crotchet.

Mendelssohn   **Romance**   **Trinity Guildhall**

Felix Mendelssohn had already composed an opera and several symphonies whilst still in his teens and he is particularly known by pianists for his *Songs Without Words*, which became enormously popular in Victorian England. Text and narrative played a far more important part for many composers in the romantic period than in the classical, and even in this rather modest romance there is an element of declamation in the *portamento* markings and in the shapes of the phrases.

Mendelssohn's original metronome mark is quite fast, and we have suggested something that brings it more within the range of this grade. Nevertheless, the music mustn't flag; there should be space enough not to hurry the phrase endings, but the only actual *ritardando* is in the final two bars. The left-hand chords need care in voicing. The chords need weight, particularly to ensure good synchronisation, but aim to focus the sound on the lowest note so that the harmonic progression can clearly be heard, particularly the interrupted cadence into the third bar. Here too the chord is sustained for longer, as though we sink more deeply into this warm Eb harmony. The *staccato* under the right-hand slur here implies that the weight is carried from note to note, as though each note has a small emphasis, or begins with a consonant. After the hesitant opening phrases and speech-like phrasing of the opening, the central section is marked *mf* *legato* and modulates to a more open Bb major. But not for long; we are soon back to the gentle uncertainty of G minor, but now at the lowest dynamic level. This romance would seem destined to remain unfulfilled.

Sandré	Requiem for a Little Bird	Trinity Guildhall

Born in the middle of the 19th century and dying during World War II, Gustave Sandré spent much of his life in Nancy, where he became a professor at the local conservatoire and taught Florent Schmitt. This expressive piece was probably written earlier on in his life, owing more to the romantic tradition than the later French impressionist or symbolist styles. It needs a subtle approach to tonal shading and rhythmic flow. Sandré's title allows us to imagine the emotional landscape behind this music, and this will help to find the right mood and sound.

The richly mournful alto territory of the opening phrases metamorphoses into something altogether more pleading and grief-stricken when in the soprano voice – clarinet to oboe perhaps. The accompanying thirds need a good *legato*; check that the fingers are resting on the keys then feel the arm helping to play the chords, the weight transferring to the fingers through a cushioning wrist. The chords in bars 17–20 will need strong intent to communicate. Find an emotional journey that takes you through the *diminuendo*, the stark return to *mf* and then the resigned *pp* dominant 7th. Finally, supported and echoed by the left hand, the melody makes one last impassioned outcry before sinking on to a prayerful plagal cadence.

	Bange Frage (Anxious Question)	
Reger	(no. 8 from *Aus der Jugendzeit* op. 17)	Trinity Guildhall

Max Reger was born in 1873 and died in 1916, yet in this relatively short life he composed an extensive list of works, including many for piano and organ. He is little heard today and has a reputation for being overly academic but, in the right hands, this can be a very effective piece, requiring musical sophistication.

Several traits of the organist are here, particularly in the part-writing and the need to change fingers or even to slide between black and white notes to achieve a good *legato*. This can be seen in bars 11–12, where the distance between the soprano and alto parts demands careful choreography. It is always allowable, as has been suggested elsewhere, to re-distribute the notes between the hands. Fingering is personal and, although suggestions have been made here, working out something that suits the performer's own hands is going to be particularly vital in this piece, where at times you have four lines simultaneously in play. Clearly there is a conversation taking place, with the opening two bars forming the often repeated question to which there is never really a satisfactory response. Some subtle *rubato* will help: 'bange' means anxious or fearful, and this nervousness can be reflected in a slight sense of forward movement as the question is asked, letting it hang in mid-air on the pause. Notice how this question is heard in various parts from bar 15 onwards: in the soprano, then the tenor, the bass, and then in *stretto* building to a very effective climax at bar 25. Excellent preparation for future fugal work.

| Nakada | Song of Twilight | Trinity Guildhall |

One of the most telling features of much Japanese art is the inclusion of space – space to contemplate the image. That sense of contemplation and suspension of time is in this haunting piece, and the steady pulse of the chords must be unhurried and almost hypnotic. It will probably come as no surprise to hear that Yoshinao Nakada felt very close to the music of Chopin and Fauré.

The sustaining pedal is essential here to achieve both the *legato* between the chords and the ambiguous, twilight atmosphere. This is straightforward *legato* pedalling: as the new chord is played the foot gently releases the pedal, clearing the previous chord, then re-pedals, sustaining this new chord so that the hand can prepare the next one. The foot should keep contact with the pedal all the time to avoid any extraneous noise; on most pianos the movement needed is quite small. At the same time the chords will need careful balancing – make good use of arm weight for this – and it would make sense for the dynamic to reflect the growing richness of the chords as they make their way into the bass clef.

The rather haunting, memorable melody needs to project easily above the accompaniment, with a supple wrist giving access to enough weight to enable this. Use a good finger *legato* even though the pedal will join the notes, letting the phrasing follow the shape of the notes. Take care to hold the bass C♯ in bar 12 and you may like to play *una corda* when you return to the beginning (repeat should be played in the exam).

| Rollin | Jazzy Joey | Trinity Guildhall |

Pieces with the main material in the left hand are always welcome and Rollin's jaunty *Jazzy Joey* is bound to be a popular choice. Loosely based on a blues scale on D, there is one side-stepping modulation to E and a cheeky coda, but the main feature of the piece is the tension between stronger and weaker beats. All the chords, and consequently the most weight, fall on the second and fourth beats of the bar, mimicking the off-beat emphasis of some popular styles like disco and reggae. Even so, the chords should not cover the left-hand motifs and, again running counter to the usual classical phrasing, there is a *diminuendo* toward the dominant chords.

Once you've caught the right balance between the hands and between the nonchalance and energy of this style, check that the dynamic levels are scrupulously observed, especially on the last line and keep the forward momentum right up to the final accent.

| Bortkiewicz | Through the Desert | Schott |

Sergei Bortkiewicz died in 1952 but it is only relatively recently that his piano works have begun to find their way back into the repertoire. He studied in St Petersburg and Leipzig, and spent much of his later life in Vienna. His main works for the piano owe much to Chopin and Liszt, and it is less common to come across pieces written for younger students such as this.

Written strictly in two parts, the title suggests a caravanserai; camels slowly tracking each other across the desert, their humps swaying from side-to-side as each phrase gets louder then softer. Try playing both parts together first to get this shape of the phrases well into the fingers and ears before playing in canon. These camels are unhurried, almost regal, with a weighted, lazy tread. The crotchet pulse feels right around 80, but feel two beats in a bar rather than four. The *una corda* should only be used at the *più lento* if it can easily be reached, keeping the heel on the floor. Play the mordents before the beat, keeping the finger movements small and light to maintain the **pp**. The swaying has now stopped, or perhaps the camels are so far in the distance that it can no longer be seen, and a gentle cadence in A minor (notice the tied Es) brings the piece to a halt.

Nurse's Tale op. 119 no. 8
Grechaninov   (from *Das Grossvaterbuch* (The Grandfather's Album))   *Schott*

The first song in Moussorgsky's *Nursery* song cycle begins with the young child asking his 'nursey' to tell him a story. It is this sort of 'nurse' we should imagine here – the comfortably rounded, indeterminately aged, big-hearted, beloved Baboushka of many a Russian novel.

The left hand rocks back and forth around the dominant and the repeated melodic phrases are soothing. Or are they? There is more than one possible story here and you may decide that the two note slurs suggest a more broken, agitated line. *Andante* is suitably ambiguous about the mood and the precise choice of tempo will reflect an imagined story. There will need to be a good balance between the layers of music, with the alto voice staying unobtrusively in the background and the left-hand little finger taking care that the bass notes are played more lightly than the chords. If you can comfortably reach the pedal you may like to use it, interpreting the slurs as indications of phrasing rather than real gaps in the sound, but this is only one option. The music seems more anguished as Grechaninov takes us to the subdominant on the third line, but then more resigned as a quasi-sequence cadences in the relative major. Then, unwillingly, we slow down before returning to the opening theme. Has this contrasting section made it darker? Sadder? Gentler? Again the choice is yours, and the possibilities inherent in the title and music are surely what make this such an intriguing piece. Repeats should be played in the exam.

No. 1 of Six Secret Songs
Maxwell Davies   (from *A Century of Piano Music* Grades 1–4)   *Bosworth*

Some of the phrasing in this seems counter-intuitive. You may automatically want to phrase the opening as it appears later, with upbeat crotchets to bars 2 and 3. But the title *Secret Songs* suggests that there may be words behind the melody that make sense of the phrase lengths. Try finding something to fit such as 'it was evening/stars glinting in the sky'. From the recapitulation this will turn into 'it was summertime then/and the air was soft and warm'. An unhurried pace – a crotchet pulse of around 76 – will help this detail to project naturally, with very small breaks in the line as though inserting consonants to show the shapes.

Peter Maxwell Davies is currently Master of the Queen's Music and is also well-known for founding the St Magnus Festival in the Orkney Islands, which is where he lives. Once a composer who sometimes shocked the establishment with his new works, he has more recently used stories from the Orkneys and a more accessible style in his music. His most famous piano piece is probably *Farewell to Stromness*, but he has written several smaller works for children. Apart from the *p* and *andante* indications at the beginning, and the plethora of phrase marks, this music is devoid of any other musical directions. To give a convincing performance a pianist will need to have a strong sense of the atmosphere behind the piece – the secret story in this song. Directors sometimes tell an actor a secret before they give a speech, knowing that this secret can change the way they deliver the lines. Try that here!

| Mayer | Marche Miniature | *Yorktown Music Press* |

It is unusual to find a march marked *misterioso* – is this a child playing with their toy soldiers way past bedtime? An unwilling recruit in a children's game? Or a march through the woods in the dark? This dotted rhythm on repeated notes sounds better – and more military – if well articulated, separating the semiquaver in sound from the following note, whilst keeping the rhythm absolutely precise. Because of this, a suggested metronome mark around ♩ = 112 would be most appropriate. The opening theme needs playing at a variety of dynamic levels; notice exactly how the hand and arm feel as you increase or decrease the level of sound, always keeping the wrist supple. As the music breaks into a *legato* G major melody, you will need more focus in the right-hand sound – more arm involvement. Remember to make the *crescendo* to *f* in the left-hand chords, adding weight and drama to this phrase, which suddenly deflates back to the opening *mp*. The quaver chords that occur in bars 3, 7 and elsewhere need voicing towards the top note. One way of practising this is to play that note loudly alone, then immediately afterwards playing all the other notes quietly. Make the gap between *f* top note and *p* chord smaller until they are playing at the same time. Absolutely no slowing up at the end. Whatever your storyline is, this soldier marches away into the distance in tempo.

| Monn | Minuet | *Peters* |

Monn was one of the many composers who succumbed to tuberculosis at a young age. He is little known today, although Schoenberg transcribed one of Monn's harpsichord concertos for cello and orchestra, keeping his name occasionally in the public eye. This minuet is in an early classical style, presumably meant for the *fortepiano* with its dynamic contrasts, and is perhaps a little over-dependent on sequences.

No repeats and, although you should prepare to play the *da capo*, it is possible that the examiner may need to stop you because of time. Notice the difference between the acciaccaturas, played quickly before the beat, and the one appoggiatura in the penultimate bar of the minuet, which you should play as a crotchet. It would be appropriate to end the trills with a turn and it is suggested to begin the D♯ trill on the note, as it is preceded by the E. The phrasing is very detailed; the slurs not only show the emphasis within the small phrases, but also imply detached articulation when they are absent. Keep the longer term shapes in mind, feeling where the harmony is leading, to avoid the lines sounding too fragmented. In the trio the first bar phrases towards the dissonance in the second bar, then gets quieter as it resolves. This is even more beautiful on its return, as the ascending scale makes a *diminuendo*. Bear in mind too the different character of each section: the minuet is more lively and direct, whilst the trio is more lyrical – less obviously dance-like. Not an easy choice, but the trio in particular is quite touching.

Oesten   Polka-Mazurka op. 155 no. 2   *Peters*

Berlin-born Theodor Oesten is known now only for his pieces for children, but the opus number of this *Polka-Mazurka* gives some idea of how prolific he must have been. You should observe the *da capo,* and the central F major section is so short that it needs to be repeated to balance the outer sections, which should be played without repeats both times.

All the details are in the music and the $\boldsymbol{f}/\boldsymbol{p}$ contrasts, neat articulation and accents should help capture the vitality and upright, rhythmic poise of this aristocratic dance. The $\boldsymbol{f}$ *legato* right-hand activity of the first two bars, the shaping helped by a flexible wrist, is answered quietly by a brisk triplet, a crisp *staccato* and the mazurkian second beat accent. Perhaps two dancers gesturing to each other? Be sure to hold the sustained basses in the central F major interlude. This section has more sense of *cantabile*, and there will be more weight and depth in these bass notes. Keep the chords light in the middle texture, always listening for a good balance with the lyrical top line. The whole piece fits beautifully under the fingers and is spirited rather than fast, around ♩ = 126.

Rodrigo   Canción del Hada Rubia   *UMP*

Joaquin Rodrigo revelled in the title of First Marquis of the Gardens of Aranjuez and, of course, it is his guitar concerto, *Concierto de Aranjuez,* that is easily his most well known work. He became almost blind after a childhood illness but went on to study in Paris, teach at Madrid University and bring a certain Spanish idiom into the mainstream repertoire. He died in 1999 at the splendid age of 97.

The pedal would help here to join the chords and enrich the sound. Most of the time you can hold the pedal throughout the bar – the melody notes being high enough to allow this – as long as they are played *cantabile*. But avoid the pedal when the moving line is in the left hand. Because of the absence of phrasing detail it is possible to miss the answering melodic lines in the bass. These begin in bars 17, 23 and 27, and it is especially these last two entries that will need a good focus on the top note of the fifth so that our ears are drawn to the left-hand melody. There is a famous poem by Heine describing the mermaid Lorelei sitting on her rock above the Rhein, combing her golden hair, and this golden-haired Spanish fairy sounds to me as though she is in a similarly relaxed mood. One in a bar, at around ♩· = 50 on the metronome, will be a good speed to manage the opening eight-bar phrase in one breath.

Zilcher   Wiegenlied   *Schott*

There's a lot of acting involved in playing the piano. Finding that state of mind in which you would sing a lullaby takes a leap of imagination – particularly in an exam situation! Have a picture already planned in your mind, and take a few moments to think of that before starting the piece. The rocking left hand, which is practically ubiquitous, does much to capture the mood of this tender lullaby and it will help to pre-hear this, as though it is already a sound present in the room, which you tune in to then join.

We are now well into the romantic period and the slurs indicate stresses and phrasing rather than precise articulation. Use the pedal throughout, perhaps varying the pedalling to suit the key. So in the central D minor section you may like a richer sound and use one pedal per bar, sustaining the chord. When using longer pedals it's doubly important to listen to the melody line, making sure that each note sings above the pedalled harmony. Think warmth for the $\boldsymbol{mf}$ phrases, adding more arm weight but not allowing an inappropriate edge into the sound. There is a sense of *tenuto* on the crotchet As in these places. Elsewhere keep the wrist flexible and let it help shape the hairpins, lifting to lighten the end of slurs. The silence towards the end is perhaps where you realise that the child has at last fallen asleep, and you creep out of the room in the final bars.

Zipoli	Versi (Fugetten) 1	*Peters*

An Italian composer and Jesuit missionary, Zipoli composed many works for keyboard which are ideal teaching material. Here the exercise is in part-playing, and the particular co-ordination needed to play and distinguish between two parts within one hand. Bars 8–9 in the left hand and 10–11 in the right hand are perfect for practising this technique. Play one part in each hand first, listening for the *legato* in each line, then play one line *forte* and the other *piano*, then the other way around. In performance we need to hear these as two different lines, rather than one line playing dotted crotchets, so making a dynamic difference will help this. Ultimately all three lines should be easily distinguishable, but at any point there will probably be one leading voice. So the top line will make a small *diminuendo* into the middle of bar 2, which is where the alto line comes to the fore with the fugal answer. Bar 4 is a linking bar, but in bar 5 the bass line steps into the spotlight. The general dynamic level remains relatively constant, but this shifting of importance between the parts, and allowing the contour of the lines to be reflected in the dynamic shading, will keep this musically alive. The last chord could be spread, with the bass on the beat.

Intermediate level

At Intermediate level (Grades 4-5), candidates will typically be able to support their intentions in performance by demonstrating a sound understanding of material, leading to a more personal and imaginative interpretation, in which there is a reasonably consistent application of developing technical skills. Performances will be clear and well-projected with appropriate volume, control of pace (including variations in speed), control of tone quality and appropriate application of instrumental colour (e.g. tone control) to support mood and character. Candidates will show evidence of sensitivity to and considerable control of material. Effective preparation and study will lead to a secure, accurate and sustained performance which will engage the audience. These features will be demonstrated through material which is substantial enough to convey some development, in terms of both the composer's intentions and the candidate's interpretation. Content will be sufficiently complex to provide some internal contrast and range (e.g. the preparation and achievement of climax, or a ternary form movement with a contrasting middle section). There will be a stylistic variety of musical language and form. Some subtleties of syntax will provide opportunity for a variety of approaches and interpretative choices (e.g. choice of articulation patterns in a movement from a baroque suite).

Grade 4

Group A

Handel	Allemande in A minor, HWV 478	Trinity Guildhall

Charles Jennens was an important librettist for Handel's oratorios. He was also a man of culture who collected and commissioned paintings and, most relevant here, collected manuscript copies of various works by Handel. These were passed on to his great-nephew, the third Earl of Aylesford, and are consequently known as the *Aylesford Collection*. It is from there that this allemande derives.

As the name suggests, the allemande was a German dance but, as the second movement in a suite, it lost some of its dance connotations and became more serious in character, with a semiquaver upbeat and a decorative melodic line. For much of the time the left hand plays the part of a continuo bass, with occasional semiquavers filling gaps in the solo line. Cellists playing continuo will frequently detach larger intervals, such as octaves, or use articulation to show the phrases, for instance gently releasing the middle C in bar 12 to begin a new phrase on the C♯. Meanwhile the interweaving of the two lines, quite playful in the final bar of each half, becomes problematic in bar 7, when right hand then left hand play the same note in quick succession. The smallest touch of strategic pedalling may hide this, but the left hand will need to relinquish the note sooner than would otherwise be ideal.

The alla breve time signature suggests a flowing tempo, and the frequent start of right-hand gestures after ties will need good listening to ensure the phrases begin more quietly and lead towards the next strong beat. The top part is instrumental, quite complex in its suggestion of two lines within one, and fingering will need to be planned and practised for comfort and security. Chords can be lightly spread, as though played by the continuo harpsichord, and ornaments should be neatly integrated into the line, both dynamically and rhythmically. Once this is in the fingers, it is a beguiling piece that almost plays itself in one long sweep, like pulling a loose thread and watching it unravel, creating captivating shapes on the floor.

Beethoven	Rondo (2nd movement from *Sonatina in F*, Anh 5)	Trinity Guildhall

This is the finale of a two-movement sonatina, with a lively main theme and two contrasting sections. It may only be a 'little' sonata, probably written in Beethoven's youth, but it has all the features that are expected of rondo form, including a small quasi-improvised cadenza before the final statement of the theme.

Beethoven marks *staccato* in the right hand and it is reasonable to assume that he would expect the left hand to match this. Keep the *staccato* in the left hand even when the right hand has longer notes, giving energy and buoyancy to the pulse. After the quiet oboe and bassoon duo of the opening a neat turn leads to a *tutti* outburst. Avoid digging in to those bass notes – keep the little finger rounded, playing on its tip, not its side. The arpeggiated chord in bar 8 is tricky; the secret is to ensure that the previous bass note is quickly released to allow it to be replayed. The first contrasting section is busy with semiquavers, but less grounded rhythmically as we lose the constant quaver pulse. Find an easy fluency in the right hand, helped by some lateral arm movement to enable the fingers to shape the notes and prevent tension. Remember to *crescendo* in the left-hand chords as well, and avoid any sense of over-forcing the right hand as you approach f.

The quaver pulse returns in the C section, but now the music is more lyrical and in the relative minor. Find a different balance between the hands here, with plenty of space in the texture for the melody to project. Notice the articulation detail, especially the string of two-note slurs, using a gentle 'drop-float' action for these. All composers of this period improvised and in the bars linking to the main theme, there is this sense of trying to find a way back from D minor to F major, and from a *cantabile*, expressive mood to the spirited fun of the opening.

Kuhlau	Allegretto (from *Sonatina in G*, op. 55 no. 2)	Trinity Guildhall

Friedrich Kuhlau, a contemporary of Beethoven, played an important part in the history of Danish music as both composer and concert pianist. He was part Danish, part German and, as you can hear in this sonatina, well-versed in the traditional classical style. He is rarely heard on the concert stage now, but pieces such as these are ideal teaching material and good preparation for the more complex sonata movements pianists will encounter later.

The opening theme is the more lyrical of the two, marked *dolce*, but the mood is light and flowing. The Alberti bass requires attention: keep the fifth finger well-rounded to balance the hand and allow a little rotary movement to help shape the figuration, keeping it dynamically well under the melodic material. A suggestion is to detach any crotchets that are not slurred, for instance in bars 2 and 7, avoiding any sense of heaviness. With a modulation to the dominant achieved by bar 8, the second subject material is playful as it *crescendo*s to bar 16, then quite virtuosic and extrovert as the scales cascade up and down the piano into the double bar – a mixture of energy and poise is needed here. To use D major scale fingering is logical, but there is an argument for re-thinking traditional scale fingerings and finding patterns that allow the fingers to pass over on to a black note. That would mean fingering left-hand D major 2-1-4-3-2-1-3-2 with the 4 and 3 crossing on to

F♯ and C♯. Whichever fingering you opt for, this section will need to be securely memorised; with such quick changes of position there is little time to look at the music.

After a few bars of development the opening returns, slightly extended, and with the scalic second theme in the tonic. Use the whole arm, right from the shoulder, to play the final *sforzando* exclamation mark.

Yuyama	Kaki-no-Tane	Trinity Guildhall

Akira Yuyama imagined all his favourite confectionary passing by on a conveyor belt, and made this the basis for a collection of pieces called *Confections: A Piano Sweet*. First published in 1973, the pieces were so popular that they went through 90 printings in Japan. Yuyama writes: 'to let the instrument sing and chatter fully and freely ... this is what I had in mind while composing them.'

Kaki-no-Tane (meaning persimmon seed) chatters more than sings, and is also stereotypically Japanese sounding, coupled with some quite complex rhythmic layering and vivid dynamics. Independence between the two hands is needed and it may be fun to explore this in different ways. Try playing scales *staccato* in one hand, *legato* in the other; play C major in one hand and E flat (i.e. a different fingering) in the other; set up a constant pulse in one hand and then play cross-rhythms in the other. You can also isolate the cross-rhythms without the notes, so playing the left-hand three-note groups in bars 11-17 whilst tapping the right-hand rhythm. Playing such games is very much in the spirit of this piece, which positively delights in capricious changes of mood and direction. Articulation plays an important part in this. The right-hand chords in bar 19 are strident, energetic, with bright, edgy glockenspiel notes on top (struck with a hard stick). The arms hover above the keys, making firm darts into the keyboard. But a few bars later the accents have disappeared and the dynamic is *p*; now the movements are smaller, the fingers closer to the keys. The articulation of the semiquavers in bar 5 and elsewhere is also very deliberate: there are three consonants in this bar (pa-a, pa, pa), not two (pa-a-a, pa). Above all, observe the *scherzando*. Learning this may take quite a lot of work, but ultimately it should sound playful and effortless.

Heller	Etude op. 47 no. 7	*Peters*

At least three editions of this study differ very slightly: a dynamic placed a quaver earlier (in bar 17 some have the *p* on the first note, some on the second – on the first is better); pedal markings added (almost definitely editorial and best to use common sense); and slurs extended in the chordal passages (use the pedal to join these and there is little audible difference). But most of the detail remains the same: the contrasted dynamics, the tight, crisp *staccato* and the accents.

Hungarian pianist Stephen Heller was a friend of Chopin and Liszt, and spent much of his life in Paris where many innovations in piano writing were being heard. In the 1850s and 60s he was quite famous, travelling to London to perform, but is now known almost exclusively for his pedagogical works. These are often strongly characterised, as is this one, being full of an undercurrent of excitement, with breathless flurries of activity and sudden *forte* eruptions.

It requires good control to be able to change the dynamics so quickly, and keep the fingers close to the keys for accuracy and speed in the *staccato*. In the longer unison *legato* lines just before the recapitulation and at the end, a small *crescendo–diminuendo* will help the shaping. Be very precise about the length of notes, especially at the ends of phrases. The tied dotted crotchet chords should release just before the start of the next phrase. Some final *staccato* chords are accented, some not. The difference should be in touch, not length.

Kember   Louisiana Two-Step   *Schott*

First of all, some practicalities. In bar 19 the last note in the left hand should probably be an E♮. An E♭ makes sense harmonically but jars in what is otherwise such a straightforward-sounding piece. Also questioned is the G in the left hand in bar 26; it sounds plausible, but is the only difference in what otherwise is a straight repeat of the opening, so B♭ is highly possible. Either of these alternatives will be acceptable in an exam performance. Lastly the tenths in bars 29, 30 etc: few young pianists will be able to reach these so it is perfectly legitimate to release the bass note in these places, or the tenor D in the case of the last bar. It would also sound appropriate to use the pedal in the very last bar to sustain these notes.

The Louisiana two-step is a dance move and a search on YouTube will give you some examples to look at and listen to. Those offbeat quavers in the left hand can be short and reasonably prominent – a good exercise for the thumb so try to ensure that it moves independently. In contrast, the bass notes should be sustained for their full length; this sort of co-ordination is a wonderful workout for the brain. The first four bars act as a 'take your partners' introduction and then the dance begins. Avoid any stabbing at those offbeat entries in the right hand; the mood is easy-going and relaxed. Notice the rests and hairpins in bar 29 onwards: each bar has a *diminuendo* then the next begins again at ***mp***, and make sure the last semiquaver does not linger into the following bar. Dynamic detail has been carefully marked and Kember's suggested tempo is quite brisk, but excellent, although around ♩ = 66 would also be acceptable for the exam.

Nichelmann   Allegro for Clavier   *Peters*

Christoph Nichelmann knew various members of the Bach family, at one time working alongside C P E Bach for Frederick the Great. He was himself a harpsichordist as well as a composer, and wrote several keyboard concertos as well as various smaller pieces such as this one. The style is early classical but maintains elements of the baroque, such as the largely linear writing and some of the ornamentation. The playing needs to be clean and clear, with precise rhythms and articulation.

The mood is lively (c. ♩ = 66) so the ornaments should be compact and neat. In bar 13 it is suggested to play the appoggiatura as a quaver, followed by quintuplet trill (with or without a turn). The mordents a few bars later can start on the note and be three notes long. The mordent and turn in the penultimate bar of the first half can be interpreted as a turn beginning on the note. The trill in bar 43 is inconsistent and a mordent here would be more logical. Articulation has been notated in much detail, some of which is probably editorial, and there are choices to make such as whether to play unmarked semiquavers *legato* or detached. The wedges in the opening bars imply a slight accent on those chords, whereas elsewhere it will be the first notes of slurs that are stressed. Note that in bar 23 it is the alto voice that takes the lead from the last semiquaver. 'Clavier' is an ambiguous term, but the dynamic markings suggest that Nichelmann may have had a clavichord or *fortepiano* in mind. This piece offers the opportunity to explore the repertoire of the period, and may also lead pianists to explore the wonderfully inventive music of Nichelmann's friend and contemporary C P E Bach.

Taggart   Smile   *Hunt*

The opening of this, with its play between C-A and C-Ab is reminiscent of Kabalevsky's *Clowns*, which twists between A-B-C and A-B-C♯. But whereas that uses a crisp, energised *staccato* on the downbeats, the mood here is more relaxed and nonchalant. The tune and rhythms are immediately catchy, and all of the musical detail is carefully notated in the score, but there are some more tricky details to master. However despite any difficulties, this piece should ultimately sound as though you are enjoying every moment.

The chord progressions are mostly straightforward, but it is well worth spending time on making sure they are understood. There are dominant-tonic cadences in various keys, but also some diminished and half-diminished chords to explain. Throughout, the bass notes are held until the *staccato* chord releases; this may cause some problems for small hands, for instance in bar 2, and one solution may be to take the middle C in the right hand. Alternatively a touch of pedal would help, but note that you cannot use this when the right hand is marked *staccato*. Be very sure of all upbeats – are they *staccato* or *legato*? Another slight conundrum is the articulation detail in bar 11; in the middle of the bar, the right hand should – theoretically – articulate the 4th quaver, whereas the left hand has a slur across. A small difference admittedly but worth noting, especially as it provides an opportunity to practise dealing with such co-ordination puzzles. In bar 24 the left-hand C will need to be quickly released before it is needed by the right hand on the next quaver (note here that the right-hand slur is longer than usual). At the end of bar 43 the left hand takes the lead for a few notes.

Voříšek   Rondo in G, op. 18 no. 1   *Bärenreiter*

Voříšek is one of two Bohemian composers to feature in this grade (see Benda's sonatina, page 36). After studying law alongside music in Prague, he made Vienna his home, learning with Hummel and initially working as a barrister before he was able to survive as a professional musician. Born 70 years after Benda, Voříšek was a friend and contemporary of Schubert, and this is clear in the more adventurous harmonic language of this piece. One point of similarity is the form but, whereas Benda is content to repeat his opening section, Voříšek makes numerous changes and builds elements of sonata form into the movement.

Looking at the differences between the three versions of the opening theme, one of the elements to notice is the dynamics. *Sforzando* is not an absolute, but should always be interpreted in context. So the **sf** within the soft opening will sound different from the **sf** after the double bar, within a more dramatic *forte*. The *crescendo* into bar 12 is relatively short; contrast this with the eight-bar *crescendo* from 40–48. Come down slightly into bar 43, beginning the next phrase **p** or **mp** to make the next *crescendo* work (just as happens later in bars 79–82). With all the articulation detail it is suggested to play most of this *senza ped.* but the *forte* bars, 12-14 and elsewhere, could benefit from a touch of pedal. The *rit.* into the pause on the last notes in bars 34-35 contrast with the absence of *rit.* and pause on the rest in bars 70-72. There is a wonderfully Beethovenian touch when you suddenly find yourself in A flat major on the last page. Do not lose tempo, but find a special sound for the secret delight of this moment before the dramatic plunge to C♯ and a return to the tonic. The final chords are emphatic, tightly spread and absolutely in tempo. One of the longer pieces in the syllabus, but a delight to play.

Group B

Mozart	Solfeggio in F, K. 393 (385b) no. 2	Trinity Guildhall

This work has an unusual provenance. It was originally an exercise for voice with a simple bass line accompaniment, probably to be treated as a figured bass. This explains the title, as 'solfeggio' used to denote an exercise in which singers would sing the 'solfege' names of the notes. During the same year, 1782, Mozart was working on the C minor mass and he used this solfeggio for the soprano solo entry in the Kyrie. Hearing the melody sung above a sustained orchestral accompaniment will help pianists imagine the right colours and mood for this sophisticated piece.

The correct tempo will prevent the opening from being too static, yet leave room to shape the semiquaver triplets later in the piece. The bass quavers could lead into and away from the beat – a subtle, unobtrusive *crescendo* and *diminuendo* that will prevent them plodding. Enjoy their solo linking moments in bars 2 and 5. The middle of bar 5 begins a varied repeat of the previous phrase leading into a cadenza. The trills in bars 5 and 6 can begin with an appoggiatura on the upper note and should be gentle, allowing the left-hand quavers to play a leading role before the melody rises to its highest note. The pauses would originally have given the voice an opportunity to improvise a small embellishment and, although Mozart has been specific about the notes he wants played here, they should still feel as though they are spontaneously added. The pauses need to be instinctive, not counted. Does the pause allow the intensity to subside? To heighten the drama? To take stock before the next coloratura moment?

As the music becomes busier in the last section it also becomes easier to shape, always keeping an elegance and poise in both the sound and the phrasing. The underlying harmonies are straightforward and the vocal line merely weaves arabesques around the chords, albeit with ever more expressive, chromatic appoggiaturas. This music should not feel effortful but it takes great art and many hours of practice to find that ease.

Schumann	Sicilienne (no. 11 from *Album for the Young* op. 68)	Trinity Guildhall

Given to his daughter Marie as a birthday present in 1848, Schumann's *Album for the Young* is a wealth of imaginative teaching pieces divided into two sections, for *Kleinere* (smaller) students and *Erwachsenere* (more grown-up) ones; this sicilienne comes from the former. Originally Schumann had the two sections more obviously separated and the title was *Two Siciliennes*, but he later merged them into one piece with a ternary structure. Here the repeats are necessary, but only the first time around.

The marking *schalkhaft* (mischievous) is very unusual. Is Schumann making a comment here on Sicilians? Laughing at his inclusion of a thoroughly un-sicilienne-like middle section? Or simply discouraging pianists from playing this too seriously? Whichever you decide, the mischievous nature has an effect on the dynamic levels. Much of the piece is played quietly, whispering well out of the earshot of adults. Quick *crescendos* lead to sudden *forte* outbursts, but we quickly return to *piano*. Schumann has also been very precise about the articulation; only play *legato* where marked. Accents abound in the second sicilienne and it is also important to notice their absence. So the accents on the right-hand Fs in bars 25 and 26 will be more effective if there are no accents on the other beats. The top hat accents in the first section are stronger but must match the general dynamic level – some are within p some within f. The timing in the second-time bar should be precise; the sudden falling on the dominant of A minor immediately after a cadence in G should be quite shocking, hence the pause for the tension to dissipate. This feels different from the pause at the end of the second section; here there is simply a stop, in silence, to catch breath before returning to the opening.

Kabalevsky	A Sad Story (no. 6 from *Thirty Pieces for Children* op. 27)	Trinity Guildhall

Dmitri Borisovich Kabalevsky was born in Russia in 1904, studying and then teaching at the Moscow Conservatoire, and later becoming well known as an expert on music education. In 1848 the Soviet state (under Stalin) accused several composers, including Shostakovich and Prokofiev, of 'formalism'. This term ostensibly implied a prioritising of form over content, but was applied to any music that the authorities did not like or understand. Kabalevsky had originally been one of a list of composers to be targeted but, due to strategic political connections, managed to have his name removed from the list.

It is perhaps surprising that Kabalevsky was initially accused, as his music has always been more accessible, less adventurous, than that of many of his contemporaries. This piece has much poignancy but this comes from its simplicity, slightly varied repetitions, the use of flattened harmonies, and an interplay between major and minor. The slurs in the left hand of the opening imply a relaxation of the sound on the second chord – a continual waxing and waning of intent. This contrasts with the climax where there is greater equality of the chords from bar to bar, reflecting the more impassioned music here. The melody, at times almost Phrygian with its flattened second, sixth and seventh, requires a true *cantabile* touch, with the weight of the arm transferring to the fingers through a flexible wrist. This use of weight will allow the many repeated notes, particularly at the *forte* outburst in bar 25, to be rhetorical, speech-like, maintaining the intensity of the line. Here the pedal is particularly necessary, both to link the melodic notes, but also to sustain the left hand as it moves from the middle range chords to the low open fifth. You can hold the pedal for a bar at a time, and even for the last three bars of F major, so that the low F continues to underpin the final chord.

Bullard	Tapping Heels	Trinity Guildhall

Tapping Heels comes from a set of miniatures celebrating musical styles from around the world. Be meticulous about following all the detail in this piece and listen to some other habaneras to absorb the style of this Cuban dance. The most famous of all is sung by Carmen in Bizet's opera and, although that is a far more sultry version, it gives this sense of controlled, held rhythm and also ends with an '*olé*' gesture. In fact it is only at the end that the two hands play together;

throughout the rest of the piece they share the notes, creating the illusion of a single line. This creates possibilities of redistribution and switching between hands will be less audible if made on the second semiquaver of a group, rather than the first, in bars 7–8 and 13–15.

Experiment with different fingerings in bars 31–33: using a thumb in the right hand places the whole hand further into the keyboard than using, for example, the third finger which makes the choreography of the hands more cumbersome. Similarly, try angling the left hand across the keyboard and playing all those black notes with the same finger (or even with two fingers) and see if that makes them more reliable. Everyone's hand is different and these are tricky climactic bars which need total security. The ensuing sudden return to *pianissimo* will show excellent control of tone. Avoid tension in the wrist for the f accents, helping with the arm instead, then for the pp keep the fingers close to the keyboard and take the arm weight out of play. It is the syncopation which really adds character to the piece, and it is fascinating to feel the difference of effect between tying over the second beat in the opening and replacing the tie with silence in the middle section. The first throws the tension of the bar onto the second beat – an appoggiatura onto the implied A minor harmony – whereas there is a more nonchalant, relaxed feel about the gesture in bar 17 with the dynamic flow being away from the dominant, the bass D. A highly effective piece.

Hammond	Never Too Late	Trinity Guildhall

The outer sections of this piece are laid out for four voices, whilst the middle section has only three. It remains in E minor throughout, so the change in texture will be important for providing contrast. The melody is always in the top part, sitting roughly within the confines of the stave and marked, with one exception, in two-bar phrases. The nature of the accompaniment is what changes and the broken chord figuration of the central section lends an extra fluidity and gentle forward momentum, helping to sustain and shape the melodic line. Elsewhere the chordal accompaniment anchors the music to the main beats, which is perhaps why the melody seems so contained, restricted in movement. This is not meant pejoratively – the effect of the moments when it reaches for something higher, as in bar 6 and again at the end, are very touching as a result.

Even though the parameters of the tune may be limited, there needs to be a freedom in the wrist to find an expressive sound quality, one that sings above the lower voices and can absorb the semiquavers into the *legato* without bumps. This is a piece for which good *legato* pedalling is indispensible and possibly taking some of the alto notes into the left hand will enable the top voice to find its best sound. The suggested fingering in bar 6 is not comfortable, whereas taking the C♯ in the left hand will give you freedom to find a right-hand fingering that will make the semiquavers easier to shape. A small *crescendo* to the mf in bar 18 works well. Enjoy the unexpected C minor harmony in the penultimate bar and then keep the pedal through the last bar, leaving the somewhat indecisive ending hanging in the air. *Never Too Late* is an intriguing title, and this piece speaks of both regret and hope.

Benda	Sonatina in G: Un poco allegretto	*Peters*

This sonatina movement is in rondo form and evokes the colours of a small chamber ensemble. The first eight bars are an elegant, one-in-a-bar dance ($\decrescendo$. = c. 52) with lightly released third quavers in the first bars, and then detached quavers in bars 6 and 7. This repeats with added double basses and perhaps horns making a richer sound; try using some pedal here. The violin then has a solo in the B section. Shape the viola line under the solo and notice that the bass here is tied for three bars, then re-strikes. The C section, initially in the tonic minor, features the solo violin again and, although both of these solos are marked *mf*, keep this sense of a single instrument in mind – very different in sound from the ensemble playing in the *tuttis* and also enabling a touch more flexibility in the phrasing.

Georg Benda is one of a group of classical Bohemian composers little heard today – and the second to feature in this grade (see Voříšek's rondo, page 33). Mysliveček, Koželuh and Dussek were also writing around the same time and their influence can be traced in Mozart and Beethoven particularly. Here, the phrasing of the rondo theme with five repetitive, slurred bars, balanced by the more quickly changing and energetic chords of the last three bars, is both unusual and musically satisfying. The writing in the violin solos is inventive, needing secure fingering and quick, adjusting movements to cover so much territory smoothly. Both the harmonic language and the piano writing are idiomatic for this period, and this will be a good stylistic study to prepare for the more interpretatively challenging Mozart.

Norton   Early Evening   *Boosey*

The pedal is indispensible here to capture the moody, 'cool', evening atmosphere of this piece from Norton's *Microswing*. You can hold it throughout bars like bar 4, where all the notes belong to the same chord, but elsewhere you will probably want to change it on the fourth quaver, or be slow to put it down at the beginning of the bar, allowing the first quavers to be clearly articulated. Clarity is always easier to maintain within the pedal the higher you are on the keyboard, but next-door notes in the bass clef, for instance in bar 7, may need more care. The melody moves into the bass at bar 5; find a warm, *cantabile* sound, listening to the balance with the right-hand chords as the bass line rises to touch the chordal accompaniment.

The seventh chords around which the opening is built – on C, D and E – are useful material for improvisation. Practically any white note sounds good on top, so you could play duets using these chords. They are also helpful to begin to think about voicing: if you were to add the third to the opening chord in the left hand, it would sound too dense. The voicing Norton uses, with the E a tenth above the bass, works perfectly. Most pianists will find the swung rhythms and syncopations easy to reproduce, but notice how few bars (only three) actually play on the third beat. This sense of suspension mid-bar is one of the elements, alongside the harmony, that give this piece its laidback evening ambience and performers will need to get into that relaxed mood to give a successful interpretation – not always easy under exam conditions!

Pärt   Für Anna Maria   *Universal*

Estonian composer Arvo Pärt radically changed his musical style in the 1970s, describing his new technique as 'tintinnabulation'. He wrote: 'I work with very few elements ... I build with primitive materials – with the triad, with one specific tonality. The three notes of the triad are like bells and that is why I call it tintinnabulation.' Pärt, now 76 and living in Berlin, has written several ostensibly simple pieces for piano, which use repetition and uncomplicated materials to highlight a meditative approach. He also often leaves many interpretative choices to the performer, as he has done here.

The first choice that needs to be made is over the mood. 'Happy' or 'thoughtful' are the options, with metronome marks to suit either choice. Whichever is chosen, notice that there is a clear difference in articulation between the sections marked by double lines. The first has a *tenuto* bass, implying weight but also separate bows, contrasting with the slurs in the second section which will need independent shaping, sometimes going against the right-hand patterns. At the start the right hand lifts the fourth quaver and adds a very slight extra stress to the fifth, resulting in a move towards the middle of each bar. This also changes in the second section. Pärt has indicated precise pedalling in two places, both where he wants the pedal to sustain harmonies over barlines and rests. These may just be exceptional cases and the suggestion is to use the pedal elsewhere in the *legato* sections. Fingering should be unfussy; there is no need to do anything complicated, simply lift the thumb and/or fifth finger at the ends of groups to move the hand to the next octave position. The choice of dynamic should reflect the overall mood, while observing Pärt's hairpins and avoiding any extremes or sudden changes. Once the mood has been chosen, aim for one *affekt* through the piece.

Wolf	Schlummerlied no. 3	*Schott*

Hugo Wolf was primarily a song composer, much loved for his settings of *Mörike*, *Eichendorff*, the *Spanish Songbook* and perhaps most of all, the delicate, romantic miniatures of his *Italian Songbook*. He lived life intensely, composing song after song in bouts of inspiration and then suffering severe attacks of depression. His death was a release from the torments of tertiary syphilis after several years in an asylum.

Although this is a reflective, peaceful lied, we can perhaps see elements of his personality in his marking of every nuance of dynamic – the sort of detail that would later become more systematised in the second Viennese school. Here it is purely for expressive effect and, without playing with excessive *rubato* (which Wolf hated) pianists will need to feel the ebb and flow in the phrasing that the hairpins imply; these need to be interpreted with much subtlety. Note too how the left-hand phrases are sometimes in canon with the right hand, meaning that the gentle increase in tone towards bar 2 in the right hand will be echoed in bar 3 in the left hand. Pedal will be necessary to achieve the *legato* Wolf asks for and listen to all the thirds, checking for a clean, synchronised attack. If performers cannot reach the ninth towards the end, the left-hand A can be taken in the right hand. Wolf often called his songs *gedichte* (poems) and nearly all his music was inspired by words. It may help to create a mental picture before starting this piece – of a child falling asleep, or perhaps of dozing on a warm afternoon.

Grade 5

Group A

Purcell	Prelude (from *Suite in C*, Z. 666)	Trinity Guildhall

As one voice after another proclaims the main theme of this prelude it seems to be unstoppable, building with an infectious energy firstly to the cadence in the dominant and then, after unwinding through a right-hand solo, towards the end. At its climax there are five parts sounding simultaneously and, although it begins more modestly with only two voices, they move so quickly across the keyboard that we seem to hear three or four lines. This complexity will take some choreographing and performers will need to make decisions on articulation and voice-leading.

This edition suggests detaching the two middle quavers in the first bar of the theme. Not the only possibility but, whatever you choose, you must be consistent. Sometimes the lower line should come to the fore, for instance in bar 3 and 6 when it has the theme, but also in bar 9 where its theme on C answers the right hand from the previous bar. At bar 12 the left hand reverts to an accompanying bass line for a while and the lowest G would resonate on early instruments. The part writing is not consistent in the final bars, but show the difference between the soprano and alto in bar 26 onwards, the lower voice perhaps being slightly softer than the top. This is particularly important in bar 31 when the soprano moves triumphantly towards the subdominant with her Bb, heralding the end of the movement.

The cadential trills start on upper notes (except for the very last bar). Avoid any tightness in the hand so that the trill is strong, clear and even. The joy inherent in this piece can easily take over in performance and lead to rushing. Guard against this, ensuring that you return to *piano* and a steady tempo after the central right-hand solo, in preparation for the second build-up.

| Arne | Minuet with Variations (from *Sonata VIII*) | Trinity Guildhall |

At the top of the first printed edition is written: 'The following Plain Minuet is not Mr. Arne's; but (at the Request of a Lady) he Compos'd the Bass, and Variations that follow, in Order to make it an agreeable Lesson for the Harpsichord.'

The original minuet is twice as long but somewhat plain and repetitive, so we have used the first half of the minuet only and made a realisation of the figured bass in the theme. Arne has written some delightful variations, cleverly giving pianists the opportunity to show off their prowess in neat ornamentation, hand crossing and virtuosic fingerwork.

The tempo should remain basically the same throughout the piece – a speed that helps characterise this rather elegant, unhurried dance. The increasing subdivisions of the beat will give a sense of growing virtuosity and excitement, although in reality the last two variations are relatively unproblematic, given secure fingerwork and a light touch. Some dynamics are suggested but allow a subtle dynamic shaping of the phrases to follow the shape of the figuration – totally appropriate on a modern instrument. In the second variation you will probably want to add some articulation in the left hand; slurring the second and third crotchets of bar 33, and the first and second of bar 35 would work well, adding lightness with the detached notes and throwing the main stress of the bars on to different beats.

The closeness of the two lines in the theme makes the sustaining of the D in bar 4 and elsewhere impossible. A touch of pedal can help, but the cello line in these places briefly takes our attention away from the melody. Again some articulation will help to achieve the dance character. The first variation concentrates on ornamentation, vital on the harpsichord to decorate the line and sustain longer notes. The downbeat stress in bars 17 and 18 allows a relaxation on to the third beat of the bar where the harmony changes. The turn must not interfere with this phrasing, so will need to be more lightly played to allow the *diminuendo*. Appoggiaturas are played on the beat and so will temporarily replace the top note of the chords in bars 3 and 8.

Haydn　　　　Allegro (1st movement from *Sonata in C*, Hob. XVI/1)　　　Trinity Guildhall

This opening sonata movement is full of energy. Aim for the upper metronome range and a sense of one in a bar, which fits with the rate of harmonic change. Haydn used the inverted turn sign interchangeably with the more common sign without the vertical line; he usually expected both to be played as turns that began on the upper note, but preferred to use the latter when it came in between notes rather than on them. Begin these turns on the beat and dispatch them as quickly and as neatly as possible – they emphasise the downbeat and powerfully launch the upward arpeggio. It is this strength that will provide a contrast with the second subject which is not at all the usual lyrical theme, but instead contents itself with small, broken and more elegant phrases. Both are accompanied by Alberti basses. Practise these first as chords and keep the hand balanced; the little finger should be rounded and the thumb plays towards the tip and not on the first knuckle.

The wedge *staccato* marks imply *staccato* with attitude. There is no other original articulation detail, but consider adding some to fit the mood of each section. A general rule of thumb would be to detach the quavers, play the semiquavers *legato* and sustain crotchets for their full length unless marked otherwise. Editorial dynamics have been added, but there is a continual sense of ebb and flow in such writing. For instance, there will be a natural *crescendo* towards the interrupted cadence in bar 16; the dominant to tonic progressions in bars 21-22 will imply a slight *diminuendo*; and the move away from, and back to, A minor in bars 24-26 will be reflected in the sound. Energy allied to absolute precision and a buoyancy in the rhythm are the keys to a successful performance.

Beethoven　　　　Bagatelle in G minor op. 119 no. 1　　　　Trinity Guildhall

Beethoven wrote this bagatelle at the beginning of the 19th century, later revising some of these early pieces and adding some new ones to make the op. 119 collection. Bagatelle is usually translated as a 'trifle' – something relatively small scale and whimsical – but there is both warmth and poignancy in this piece which defies this characterisation.

Allegretto is a qualified *allegro*, so there should be no sense of hurry; the string of suspensions in the varied return of the theme at bar 45 need space to be satisfyingly shaped with a good 'drop-float' action as each relaxes on to its resolution. Similarly the *staccato* on the opening crotchets needs thought – too short and the chords could sound clipped and edgy. Find an articulation that reflects the key and the mood; the *staccato* dot above or below a note was originally the opposite of a dot after a note (i.e. the latter added on half the value of the note, whereas the former subtracted half the value). Notice how Beethoven ends all the phrases in the first 12 bars on the dominant – both unusual and adding to the uncertain, almost hesitant nature of this opening.

Everything changes in the central E flat section. A warmer sound is required and the pedal will help achieve this. Make sure all the parts are audible as much of the expressiveness is in the chromaticism in the lower voices. The dynamic here remains a muted *dolce*. Let the left hand take over the main voice in bar 59, the right hand gradually resuming dominance towards bar 64. The return to $\boldsymbol{p}$ and the detached chords of the opening is sudden, and the gradual descent into the major has a Schubertian sense of resignation in which the major is more poignant than the minor. Repeats are to be played in the exam.

March, little soldier! (Marcha, Soldadinho!)

Pinto   (from *Scenas Infantis* (*Memories of Childhood*))   Trinity Guildhall

This is a character piece with some pianistically challenging moments. It needs a reasonably sized hand but these are toy soldiers and a sense of fun and delight in its virtuosity should project in performance.

The *glissando* will need practice: it is very light so move the arm quickly and avoid bedding the first note – this is likely to result in bruised cuticles! Use the third finger, or several fingers, and begin at quite an oblique angle, gradually bringing the hand into a more vertical position as you approach the top note. The repeated notes in bar 8 should be firm and rhythmically precise. Some pianists find finger changes work best for them while others may use the same finger with a wrist *staccato*, moving the hand inwards on the semiquavers. Notice the different articulations in bar 17 onwards: the short, *pizzicato* quaver chords move into the lower part of the right hand, whilst the left hand plays heavy bass drums and the trumpet sustains dotted crotchets on the top line. The triplets a few bars later may be stronger fingered 3-5-3, with a quick shift of position for the *legato* in the middle of the bar. Here too notice the held minims in the middle of the texture.

After the opening fanfare the whole piece is a gradual *crescendo* and *diminuendo* as the soldiers march into view and then away into the distance – all within an immutable tempo. Work on the left hand alone for a while, feeling how the arm becomes more involved as the music reaches *mp*, then *mf* and finally *f*. Making sure this supporting part also observes the dynamics will help to make them more effective. *Sforzandi* and accents are never absolute but relate to the general dynamic level – important in the last few bars.

Prelude in D minor, BMV 935 (no. 3 from

J S Bach   *Sechs kleine Präludien für Anfänger auf dem Klavier*)   *Wiener Urtext*

There is something immensely satisfying about such perfect two-part writing. A good edition will present a blank canvas without dynamics, articulation, tempo marking, and perhaps even fingering. Decisions will need to be made on all of these, but one of the most important initially will be the fingering. Even if the edition is already fingered, check that it really does suit the performer's hand. Sometimes sequences are most reliable when the same fingering is used for each pattern, in bars 13-15 in the left hand for instance. For smaller hands, large stretches may cause tension in the hand and be audible in the quality of tone. The Wiener Urtext edition has a sneaky solution for the last bar, suggesting that the left hand takes both dotted crotchets and the right hand crosses over to play the final arpeggio. It works well (even better if the left hand also plays the first note of the arpeggio) and as repeats are not required in the exam, it will not be necessary to cross back again.

Whilst thinking about fingering, it is worth having some idea of articulation. Most quavers are accompanying lines supporting the more melodic semiquavers, and will be non-legato. This is particularly valid when there are larger intervals, like the sixths and octaves in the bass. Consecutive notes, or those that are more melodic, can be played legato. The stream of semiquavers should be played relatively smoothly, although notice how often the phrase seems to turn around itself mid-bar. The first two bars are ambiguous: two or three in a bar? Play with this, feeling that the second half of the bar leads forward into the next, phrasing almost inaudibly from the fourth note. This will give a sense of flow and one-in-a-bar to the piece and avoid strong downbeats. An unhurried tempo, around ♪= 132, will give space to all the interesting details – the Ab in bar 18, the contrary motion duet in bar 21 and the similar motion duet, plunging to the low F# in bar 31. Notice when the left hand plays the lead role, particularly in bar 40. The trill in bar 4 will begin on the upper note and finish just before the end of the bar; for the ornament in bar 23 the suggestion is to play a quaver appoggiatura and then a turn.

Sanfter Vorwurf (Gentle Reproach)
Heller   (no. 2 of *Fünf Lieder ohne Worte*)   *Universal*

From a set of *Songs without Words*, this piece is a small, dramatic *scena* in its own right, full of imaginative detail, sudden changes of mood and rhetorical flourishes. One of Heller's studies is another alternative choice for Grade 4 and both works show that his teaching pieces are written to develop aspects of musicianship, and are not merely finger exercises.

Here the annoyance of the first bars gives way to a more 'gentle reproach', with an impassioned entreaty followed by conciliatory chords of agreement. The main theme comes in F, G minor, B flat and C, providing useful V⁷-1 practise in different inversions. Meanwhile the right hand plays two parts, sustaining a long note whilst playing accented quavers on top and then a *legato* line below. Notice that the left hand also plays smoothly in bar 4. The placing of the ***p*** in bars 3 and 7 on the second quaver may be deliberate, so allow the initial C to be struck loudly enough to be heard during the two bars, but later in the piece the ***p*** moves to the first beat – ambiguous! The pedal markings too are not wholly to be trusted: sustaining through the rest in bar 10 sounds good, but *legato* pedalling is needed in bar 14, not as marked. The *portamento* in bar 22 works well if weighted, detached notes are played, with pedal changes on each one. This phrase appears *legato* later but, on most pianos, pedalling through it, as suggested, will sound too blurred; hold the left-hand chord and pedal with the ears. Similarly chords that were smooth in bar 14 are marked *mezzo-staccato* towards the end. All of this changing detail, along with the various tempo directions – *con anima, slentando* etc. – are suggestive of an inner dramatic narrative, an attempt to capture something spontaneous. Performers will need to evoke this sense of improvisation in performance.

Despite his well-known friends (see *Etude* op. 47 no. 7, Grade 4), and his initial popularity in Paris, Heller became poor, ill and lonely towards the end of his life. It was the British who came to his aid – primarily Sir Charles Hallé, Lord Leighton and Robert Browning – who set up a fund to support him.

McCabe   **Sports Car (from *Afternoons and Afterwards*)**   *Novello*

Once all of the details are sorted out, playing this is enormous fun; it is such a witty and descriptive piece. But be prepared for a challenge as it could be easy to get the left hand patterns confused, or to take a wrong turning in the twisting right hand. In performance it is always best to keep going to maintain momentum and mood, and ignore small slips along the way – you can correct those at home later. Few people in the audience would notice whether you played a B or a G in the middle of the left-hand bars!

Look for the left-hand patterns and do not be afraid to mark things on the music if this helps. Some pianists find colour a useful tool to highlight tricky elements or changes – the eyes notice the colour far in advance. This bass line needs to be built into the muscle memory, but also intellectually understanding the patterns will make it more reliable. The direction is 'jovial' and the dynamic level is mostly around **mp**, so this is not a mad chase on the racing track but a genial trip through the countryside. Find an easy left-hand movement that separates the quavers without making them too jerky or crisp within the texture. From bar 35 the right hand can have fun with the syncopation, adding a slight emphasis to the seconds, then releasing the quavers.

There is no relaxation of the forward momentum (or 'drive') until just before the end, where the performer stops to admire the view for a few moments before putting the car back in gear with a loud revving of the engine. A few bars later there is an emergency stop, but keep the quavers in mind to make sure the tied note is exactly the right length. The suggested tempo is excellent but a couple of clicks below on the metronome would be acceptable.

Pleyel Sonata 1 B. 571, 2nd movement: Adagio *Doblinger*

Ignaz Pleyel was born in Austria and studied with Haydn in Eisenstadt, becoming one of the most prolific composers of his generation. He was working in France when the French revolution prompted his move to London. Haydn was here at the same time, as were many other pianist-composers such as Clementi, Cramer and Dussek. It was perhaps following in Clementi's footsteps that, on his return to Paris, Pleyel set up his own publishing company followed by a piano manufacturing business. It is for his pianos that his name is now remembered.

This *adagio* is in a pure classical style with musical interest maintained through its rhythmic variety, detail of articulation and instrumental textures. This is not a Beethoven *adagio*; here the harmonic language is simple with little chromaticism, and the style is light, charming and galant. Find a tempo that will accommodate the smallest notes and the ornaments whilst keeping a sense of two, not four, in a bar; around ♩ = 40 is good. The phrases are generally quite short, so look at the underlying harmony to work out the longer term shaping. As discussed in the Grade 5 Haydn sonata movement, the inverted turn sign was often used interchangeably with the ordinary turn and the latter is appropriate here − before the beat in bar 2 and on the beat in bar 9. Pleyel asks the performer to assume some articulation detail: bar 12 should be played as bar 10 and bar 23 as bar 22. Unslurred semiquavers (and quavers) can be lightly detached and notice the difference between demi-semiquavers and hemi-demi-semiquavers (e.g. bar 14 has both). The *fortissimo* in bar 24, after a total absence of dynamics elsewhere, is quite incongruous and most probably a mistake or a blot on the manuscript! Nevertheless, some dynamic contrast is needed and scoring this for a small ensemble will help the performer reflect the different textures. No repeats in the exam, but be prepared to play the *da capo*.

Zachau Vom Himmel hoch, da komm ich her *Peters*

Friedrich Wilhelm Zachau is now best known as Handel's first teacher. He taught the young boy various instruments, including the organ and violin, and contemporary sources tell us that he was fully conversant with the Italian style, which would have been an important influence on the future composer's many Italian operas.

However, the style of *Vom Himmel hoch* is most definitely German, with the original Lutheran carol in the top voice and the two lower voices weaving beneath the sustained notes of the melody. This is pianistically sophisticated writing and in order to play all these parts smoothly (and comfortably) some re-allocation of the middle voice to the left hand may be advisable. The one place where no solution is possible is the re-striking of the A over the barline between bars 21-22. Peters Edition have often fingered consecutive notes in the top part with the same finger. Ultimately the tone will do much to carry the line of the carol and give it a semblance of continuity, but *legato* fingering would also help and is possible with a little ingenuity and quick finger substitutions. This continuity of the top line will also determine the tempo: much slower than ♩ = 69 and it will be difficult to phrase this line. There is no need to vary the general dynamic too much but shape the lower lines, following their natural curves, and perhaps have a sense of *diminuendo* towards B minor and *crescendo* back towards the tonic. A sound practice technique is to separate out the voices, combining them in duos, perhaps singing in the carol so that they are heard linearly and not just in combination. Bach was fond of this carol, using it in several works and making it the theme of his *Canonic Variations* for organ.

Group B

Debussy Page d'album Trinity Guildhall

This is a late Debussy miniature, seeming to encapsulate the essence of what is so often called 'impressionism'. Debussy dismissed this as a 'useful term of abuse', but it represents that element of spontaneity, of capturing the moment, that is important here. These 38 bars contain 13 different tempo indications. Debussy is surely attempting to direct pianists towards a *rubato* – a gentle, organic ebb and flow of the pulse. Subdividing the beat is often useful for this; for instance, keep the quavers in mind as you slow down in bar 4, hearing in your head the gradual coming to a halt of the roulette wheel.

Pedalling, articulation, layering of the textures – all these elements demand much careful listening and fingertip control, particularly as so much of the piece is played in the lower dynamic range. Spontaneity comes into the picture as much will depend on the piano and acoustic on the day, which is why it is vital to keep listening to the sound and adjusting touch and pedalling as necessary. Knowing that the opening theme returns in *pianissimo*, it is sensible to play the opening in a firm *piano*, hearing the richness of the bass notes as they cadence with a *diminuendo* into F major. Pedal is employed throughout, to sustain bass notes and to enrich the sound. The quasi waltz from bar 4 has the bass notes marked *staccato*, but avoid any edginess in the sound. Think of a resonant cello *pizzicato*; just a touch of pedal perhaps on these, not to sustain them but to add body to the sound. The *staccato* on the chords in bar 23 onwards implies that they are played lightly, with less weight and importance than, for instance, the chord in bar 5. On top of this left hand, practise the middle-voice melody in the right hand alone, adding the upper chords lightly when you are sure of the phrasing and *rubato*. One of the things Debussy seems to be playing with in this piece is rhythmic stress: the cross rhythms in the opening, which are different when it returns; the varying of the main stress between first and second beats; and the suspension of pulse towards the end.

Cornick Last Summer Trinity Guildhall

This moody bossa nova needs subtle control of its sound world and a good ear for voicing. For instance, the left hand in bar 5: the bass note has to be rich enough in sound to sustain through the bar and to give the major 7th dissonance enough edge that the resolution on the fourth quaver will feel like a relaxation of tension (and dynamic). The next bar is similarly shaped, although at a lower dynamic level, but notice that in bars 7 and 8 the first third is released, throwing an accent on to the fourth quaver – a rhythmic trait typical of the bossa nova. Avoid any stress of the third beat in the main theme, instead phrasing the sixths as one gesture from the first chord. Voice these towards the top note and this is where a *legato* can be played between 3-4-5. The thumb needs to play quite lightly so that its need to detach each note is not obvious in the texture. There is a warm, downwards shift in the harmony at bar 15. Cornick has marked this *piano subito*, so you will need to be cautious about the preceding *diminuendo*. But the Db ninth adds a special colouring – prepare the fingers firmly enough so that the notes synchronise, then imagine releasing the whole arm on to a goose down duvet, feeling it slowly sink into the chord.

Another essential element of this soundscape is the pedal. Only at the end has Cornick been precise about exactly how he wants it used, so elsewhere you should follow the adage 'pedal with your ears', occasionally delaying very slightly the change of pedal, so that the harmonies subtly overlap before clearing. This is an enormously evocative piece and is ideal for thinking about these aspects of tone control and colour.

Milne	Vendetta	Trinity Guildhall

The steady but unchanging pulse of the Argentinian tango provides the undercurrent of excitement in this brooding piece. The title is perfect – no crime of passion here but cold-hearted revenge, and pianists will need a cool head to judge precisely those left-hand tenths, to balance the right-hand voices against the left-hand accompaniment, and to ensure that the differences between *mf*, *f* and *ff* are clearly audible. This is such an enjoyable piece to perform as well as to listen to but, as with tangos on the dance floor, there is some tricky footwork to sort out first.

The tenths will work best with the help of a gentle lateral movement. Try holding down the middle note (the B in bar 3) probably with finger 2 and feel an easy swing in the arm, keeping the elbows free as you pivot around the held finger to play the bass E and top G♯. For the two-part writing, for instance from bar 40, play the soprano and alto lines with two hands at first, beginning with the top part as the firmer main voice, then the lower part. Try the Kodály exercise of playing one voice and singing the other – excellent for checking that you can really hear these as two separate lines. Milne has been wonderfully meticulous in notating all the detail, from pedalling to articulation and dynamics. The last are often easier to judge if the various levels are associated with something else. Different moods are the most obvious, with the *mf* representing cool control, the *p* a threatening whisper and the brief foray into *ff* being the point at which you nearly lose your temper. Colours can also work well, perhaps with the *mf* as blue, the *f* as purple and the *ff* as red.

Nickol	Slink (no. 3 from *Night Thoughts*)	Trinity Guildhall

Night Thoughts was written in 2004 and is listed as being originally for clavichord. This emphasises the relative intimacy of this nocturnal image, disturbed by frightening accents and *sforzandi*.

Articulation is key. Notice the *tenuto* on the upbeat quaver in the bass; think *Jaws* with its ominous rising semitone and give the first note due weight. The *staccato* chord can be very short, keeping the hand close to the keys to avoid an accent, but then drop the weight on to the syncopated third. With the pedal securely holding the chord, use plenty of arm to scare the audience with the accented *forte* notes in bar 2. The *simile* at the end of this bar implies that all such two-note figures in the bass will be *legato*, although take care over the different rhythm in bar 9, with the quaver on the beat for a change. The 'sinister and bluesy' indication is reminiscent of the paintings of Edward Hopper – semi-deserted bars in the middle of nowhere, and often heavy with atmosphere, just like this piece.

Rodney Bennett   Two Turtle-Doves   *Bosworth*

The two turtle doves are surely the main love interest in the Christmas roll call, billing and cooing their way through all but the first verse. Richard Rodney Bennett depicts them moving together in thirds, only very occasionally breaking away from their close huddle. His warning to use only a little pedal is, I suspect, a caution against blurring the major/minor harmonies but, practically, quite a bit of pedal will be required to make the *legato* in bars 5 and 6, and linking the major seventh chords in one pedal is quite acceptable. Notice the *pochiss. sost.* and the f *ma dolce.* Bennett is cautioning subtlety in performance; these lovebirds have no wish to be in the limelight – that spot can be reserved for the five gold rings!

British-born Bennett is a somewhat chameleon-like musician, with successful film scores to his name (*Four Weddings and a Funeral*), more than 200 classical compositions, and a parallel life as a jazz singer and pianist. The cycle, *Partridge Pie*, from which this comes is deliciously inventive, both musically and pianistically. Interpret the slurs through dynamic shaping rather than leaving gaps in the sound, but also be aware of the longer shapes, for instance to and away from the subdominant in the first four bars. The left hand can do much to show this, making small *crescendi* as it moves from the fifth of the chord to the sixth and relaxing the sound as it returns. Ensure the few left-hand rests are audible, especially in the penultimate bars. Thirds need some help from the arm and good fingering for the *legato*. Do not be too rigid about the pulse – within the dotted crotchet beats there is room for a gentle ebb and flow. The written-in *rubato* of the arpeggiated chord and *tenuto* marks towards the end suggest these two lovebirds fall asleep leaning against each other.

MacDowell   Summer Song op. 7 no. 3   *Faber*

This feels like late summer with a tinge of melancholy at the thought of losing the warmth of the long evenings. A beautiful and subtle piece, needing a sophisticated ear for sound and voicing, and an instinctive sense of the *rubato* this style demands. Nothing over-stated; the suggested metronome mark is not slow and the *senza rit.* at the end also implies an avoidance of any sentimentality.

Edward MacDowell was born in New York and began his piano studies there, continuing in Paris and Frankfurt where he met and played for Liszt. He returned to America and became well known as a piano teacher and composer, primarily of piano works. Many of these are written on themes from nature and most pianists will at some point play the justly popular *To a Wild Rose*. Here too we sense an outdoor atmosphere, bathed in summer light and a sense of time pausing. Long melodic lines need careful shaping – feeling one-in-a-bar will help this, as will playing the top line alone, thinking of each phrase as one gesture, albeit with moments of tension and release largely conditioned by the underlying harmonies. Notice that the two *mf* bars lead to a *subito* *p* the first time, then to *subito* *pp* the second. The unhurried arpeggiated chords will look after the timing here, but a slight lingering on the top C in bar 43 will emphasise the pathos of this moment. The *staccato* bars need to fit in with the general mood, so find a cushioned articulation that just adds lightness and air into the texture. Elsewhere the pedal will change with the harmonies, occasionally holding through whole bars, never allowing the chromaticism of the inner voices to blur.

Shostakovich   Gavotte (from *Dances of the Dolls*)   *Boosey*

Famously, there are few photographs of Shostakovich that show him smiling, yet there are many works, such as this gavotte, that show much wit and humour. Shostakovich's *Dances of the Dolls* were originally movements from his *Ballet Suites* for orchestra, but are beautifully arranged for young pianists – all extraneous notes expunged – so that a clean, pseudo-classical texture is all that remains. This idea of mechanical dolls dancing makes the off-beat accents and sudden sleight of hand move into D flat all the more amusing.

Slurs are carefully marked and classically imply both an emphasis of the first note in the slur and a lifting of the last. Experiment with articulation elsewhere, perhaps finding a warmer, less clipped *detaché* (walking *en pointe* perhaps) for the opening crotchets and something altogether more crisp (a *battement?*) when marked *staccato* as in bars 17 and 18. There are one or two moments that would benefit from the sustaining pedal: the fourth beat accents in bars 36, 40 etc. to give added sonority and incongruity, and to help with the *legato* in bars 35 and 36. Once set, the tempo should be more or less constant but unhurried, poised, hearing space around the upbeats to new sections to allow the dancers to breathe and re-group (for instance in bars 8 and 16). Find a new colour for the A minor section, more muted shades and a heavier texture with the sustained drone-like basses. Only a slight slowing up at the end – this is no deflating Olympia, but a long-life battery-operated prima ballerina, ending with a final pirouette.

Süße Träumerei (Sweet Reverie)
Tchaikovsky   (from *Kinderalbum* op. 39)   *Weiner Urtext*

Tchaikovsky's op. 39 – his own collection of children's pieces modelled on Schumann's *Album for the Young* – has provided a rich source of pieces for various piano collections, including exam syllabuses. But despite the 'children's' label, there is much art in playing this reverie well; it demands an understanding of *cantabile* tone, a good ear for pedalling and a musical instinct for an appropriately romantic *rubato*.

There are small variations in editions. Some have no tempo marking whereas a Russian edition is marked *moderato*. A range of speeds could work, between ♩ = 66 and 80. 'With much feeling' is the direction on some; *espressivo* on others (the former perhaps unsurprisingly coming from the Russian edition), and there are small differences in the precise placing of dynamic marks (and their repetition in the reprise) and the division of slurs. Ultimately the details need to be fitted into an overall concept of the piece and there can be many satisfactory interpretations. Begin by learning the outer parts, ensuring that dynamics are followed in the cello line as well as the violin. Practise putting in the chords very gently, working out exactly where the pedal will need to be changed and where the sounds can be allowed to merge. Imagine separate swings on the bell for the accents in bars 21-22, followed by a long, smooth *diminuendo*. Finding a *cantabile* sound is partly about the transfer of arm weight from note to note, but also about the breathing needed in singing, the time needed to finish bar 8 and begin bar 9, or to give space to the climax in bar 14 – the accent here adding warmth, or interpreted as an agogic stress, rather than a hard-edged, forced sound. There are many recordings of Tchaikovsky's short pieces to help young pianists assimilate the style, and many of these deserve to be performed more often.

Advanced Level

At Advanced level (Grades 6–8), candidates will typically be able consciously to integrate their skills, knowledge and understanding in a secure and sustained performance which demonstrates mature grasp of the material. Along with confidence, a sense of ownership and self-awareness, this will result in a discriminating and sensitive personal interpretation that conveys complexity and control of shape (e.g. throughout a sonata movement), and awareness of stylistic interpretation. The performance will be grounded in thorough and relevant preparation, and will demonstrate authority and control. Candidates will combine skilful and appropriate command with imaginative response and flair to engage the audience wholeheartedly.

These features will be demonstrated through material largely drawn from the standard repertoire for the instrument. Overall length will be sufficient to enable variety and range of presentation to be demonstrated and sustained. Content will be substantial, with some depth and sophistication, enabling the candidate to engage with complex emotions and abstract musical thought. It will be such as to require analysis and reflection in the preparation, and present challenging physical requirements in one or more technical aspects. The musical language may demand considerable inferential understanding and thoughtful interpretation to reflect subtlety of meaning (e.g. contrapuntal texture, musical irony or humour).

Grade 6

Group A

	Allegro di molto	
CPE Bach	(1st movement from Sonata in F minor, Wq. 63/6)	Trinity Guildhall

C P E Bach's surviving letters relate mostly to business deals, efficiently carried through and giving no hint of the capricious and wildly passionate nature of his music, at which his father J S Bach would probably have winced. This sonata movement is one of 18 written to accompany C P E's famous *Versuch* (essay on keyboard playing) and – like his father's own teaching pieces – originally contained no written instructions for dynamics or articulation; pupils were expected to use their imagination. Clues lie in the texture and in C P E's other music, notably his 60 symphonies: imagine the vigorous opening played by a full string section (expressive violins throughout bars 5–8), contrasted later with the delicate *p* from a few *legato* woodwinds at bars 9, 11 and 13. Really skilful players may try to finish with the right hand *p* in bar 10 as the left hand enters *f* – vice versa in bar 11.

Spreading the left-hand chords in bars 1, 3 and 5 (and later) is quite acceptable, adding extra force as orchestral horns and a continuo harpsichord would: the cross-hand quavers in bars 2 and 4 could well go *staccato martellato*. The implied little-finger melody and bass amid the semiquavers of bars 21–22 is matched in equivalent bars 49–50. For extra strength in semiquavers (or to avoid exposing weak fingers), try starting bar 10 with left hand 4121 2131, ending bar 12 with 231 2131, and starting bars 29, 31 and 33 with right hand 2434. Keep bar 24's semiquavers strong, or else the previous chord may (wrongly) sound like the overall climax. Bar 28's quavers would surely have been written *8va* (matching similar passages elsewhere) if the keyboards of Bach's time could all have reached beyond high C. It is tempting to take the higher octave – some editions even print the notes this way – but probably safer to stick to what is written.

Dussek	**Allegro (1st movement from Sonatina op. 20 no. 6)**	**Trinity Guildhall**

If it was not for Jan Ladislav Dussek, we pianists might still all be performing in the old-fashioned way, with our backs to the audience. Dussek was so proud of his handsome profile that he insisted on sitting sideways – with the extra benefit that the raised piano lid then propelled the sound directly towards the audience. Like most 19th-century pianists, Dussek wrote a lot of music for himself to play and teach, including 28 sonatas and 15 concertos. This sonatina movement sounds like Weber, heightened by extreme changes of dynamics. These are not necessarily complete: for instance bar 2 could *crescendo* towards the *f* in bar 3, and bars 19-24 could perhaps drop below *ff* somewhere. Try an up-and-down *cresc./dim.* in bar 6, and *cresc.* without *dim.* in bar 8 (possibly in bar 30 too). Compare left-hand thumb shifts between bars 1-2 (after the third beat) and 3-4 (after the second); notice left-hand durations in bars 5-8 beneath the busy right hand, then compare bars 15-17 (slightly different); compare bar 35's fourth-beat harmony with bar 33's. Bar 19's *ff* is warm but not aggressive: save that emotion for the surprising key change at bar 37. Notice that left hand of bar 41 stays in the treble clef, and that Cb persists through bar 60. Try crotchet pedals on the third beats of bars 1-2, minim ones on the third beats of 3, 4, 6 and 8, and similarly throughout. Lift phrase-endings in bar 79 for a cleanly articulated finish.

	Menuetto and Trio	
Beethoven	**(3rd movement from Sonata in D, op. 10 no. 3)**	**Trinity Guildhall**

Here is proof that quick music can still be expressive: in fact, even before learning the harmony, play just the tune up to speed. This gives a better idea of the overall phrasing than the printed mixture of long and short slurs, important though these all are. Notice particularly how bars 7-8 should shade off (despite the isolated *sf*), as should the right hand in bar 31, and the tenor in bars 45-46 and 49-50. The alto F♯ in bars such as 1 and 4 must be *pp* to avoid overbalancing the tied treble note and sounding like superfluous melody notes themselves.

The *sf* markings in bar 7 and so on (particularly from bar 17, which looks loud but isn't) are simply the > accents of Beethoven's time, and do not imply any overall *f*. Bar 25's simultaneous tune and trill would be very tricky in one hand; playing the crotchets with the left hand works well if a whole-bar pedal sustains the bass. Carefully lift the right hand of bar 31 while the left hand ties over: notice the different articulation between bars 44 and 48 and – much later – in the left hand between bars like 55/6 (detached) and 70/1 (slurred). Pairs of slurred *f* crotchets from bar 70/1 may be pedalled for extra richness. The trio should really go no slower than the menuetto: triplets must be even and the sometimes surprising dynamics clearly observed, with no unwritten *crescendos* or *diminuendos*. Carefully count duplets after triplets in bar 67 (and lifted, over the sustained left hand). The trio ends abruptly with no *rall.*, the menuetto resuming innocently as if all that excitement had never happened.

Raff Romance op. 2

This pretty piece is permeated by a rising two-note figure first appearing in the left hand of bar 2. It is tempting to imagine this as yodelling; Joseph Joachim Raff was Swiss, after all. In any event, it should probably always be softer than the phrase preceding it: landing quietly in order to do this after the leaps in bars like 39 and 41 may require a fraction more time. This will produce a *rubato* effect, also appropriate elsewhere even when not required technically. Beware, however, of jerky stopping and starting through bars 45–51 and 58–9 as you hunt for the next bass note. The marking *quasi cadenza* in bar 34 implies free rather than strict time: one option is to lengthen the first notes of bars 34 and 35, and gather speed when moving off; another is to *accel.* and *cresc.* straight away so that bars 35–36 are brilliant (much faster than Tempo 1), then slowing down even earlier than marked, say from barline 36/7. Many other options are possible.

The opening *con ped.* instruction is deliberately non-specific. Choose pedalling that sustains each chord (and its released bass note) yet avoids blurring: for example, minim plus two crotchet pedals in bar 1, whole bar in bar 2; minim-tied-to-quaver pedals from bar 15, plus short dabs anywhere where fingers alone cannot make the top line *legato*; crotchet pedals through bars 20–21. Count carefully through bar 29 – easy to miscalculate once the semiquavers stop.

Two-part Invention no. 13 in A minor

J S Bach (from *Two-Part Inventions*, BWV 772-786) *Weiner Urtext*

Bach wrote his inventions (in two and three parts) as exercises in musicality as well as technique. 'Authentic' editions follow the composer and leave few if any clues to interpretation: older ones are freer in this respect, and their suggestions well worth considering. Many options exist (the piece may equally start f or p), and subtle clues lie in the music itself. Traditional performances may carefully articulate (*legato*) semis and (detached) quavers the same way in each hand, but the 'tension-relaxation' harmony in bars 9–10 may be heightened with *legato* quavers in the left hand and *staccato* in the right hand. Syncopated tied quavers (as in bars 3–5) may be accented, and/or preceded by a *staccato* quaver, as can the only crotchet in the whole piece (bar 1).

Tempo may vary widely from (say) ♩ = 76, but – as always with Bach – all semiquavers are melodic and never mere decoration. The first figure starts on the second semi, sometimes after a rest, elsewhere emerging without a break. Make noticeable fresh starts, e.g. in bars 1, 2 and 6 (left hand) but never with a bump: in fact a *crescendo* through seven semis to the next quaver always makes for a better flow. High left hand at bar 6 may imply f; high-pitched diminished seventh harmony at bar 14 can be p *subito*, while low-pitched growling bar 21 may be f. Join the right hand seamlessly to the left in bars 14–17; signal bar 18's 'reprise' with a *crescendo* to f. Master bar 19's tricky co-ordination with dotted rhythm and other practice, try bringing out rising tenor offbeats through 23, and make a *rit.* through bar 25 for a smooth rather than abrupt ending.

Brahms Waltz in E, op. 39 no. 2 (from *Waltzes* op. 39) *Henle*

This set of waltzes was originally written for piano duet and later transcribed for solo piano by Brahms himself. Easy with four hands to share the work, in solo form it becomes trickier, with many right-hand octaves (which should always sound effortlessly melodic) and wide skips in the left hand (which require gentle landings and careful pedalling). Repeats should be played: the first-time bars are numbered as 8a and 24a, the second-time bars as 8b and 24b.

The traditional dance music 'thump' on every downbeat sounds monotonous. The occasional printed *cresc./dim.* helps to avoid this. Try ♩ = 92, or any tempo that allows those bass dotted-minim chords to be clearly arpeggiated without snatching. (Even players with tiny hands can stretch these without having to break, so the written effect is obviously deliberate and should be clearly heard.) The right-hand quavers in bars like 1–7 and 9–12 (note the continuous D♯s here) are bare octaves, not full chords; enjoy the bass counter-melody from bar 9 and the tenor in bars 15–16 (where a *poco rall.* can be played the first time and a *molto rall.* the second). A strict tempo throughout is inappropriate: try the tiniest of *ritenutos* in bar 4, an equally tiny *accelerando* in bar 6, a more definite pull-back in bars 8 (both times) and 23. Stretching the tempo around barline 22/3 heightens the expression as well as making it easier to play. Bass-note lengths throughout provide exact clues as to pedalling, e.g. lift on the third beats of bars 15–16, and pedal 23–24's crotchets separately.

Sonata in C, Hob. XV1/35, 3rd movement: Finale

Haydn (from *Selected Piano Sonatas* vol. 1) *Henle*

This light, cheeky minuet has a sting, not in the tail, but in the trio, stormy and troubled. First, the bar count: the first section equals bars 1–8, of course, the second 9–25, and the third 26–53. Thereafter, editions disagree: Henle thinks the trio should crash in before the previous section has finished, and designates the last bar before the key change (bar 53) as a first-time bar. Most other editions (like Wiener Urtext) think instead that bar 53 should be played both times. In these notes this interpretation is adopted, so the trio is numbered bars 54–68 (the first-time bar is 60a, the second-time 60b), and the key change to three naturals comes at bar 69.

Haydn left few dynamics: only those in bars 17 and 85 (the pause bars), 22, 34, 68 and 90 are authentic, though the music itself demands other changes elsewhere. Try starting *f* (the printed *p* in equivalent bar 69 makes for an effective surprise), *p* at 9, *crescendo* to *f* through 16; *p* at 26, *dim.* in 39 to *p* at 40, *f* at 46; *f* again at 54, *f* at 73 (equivalent to bar 22 and authorised there), *p* at 77, *p* subito at 92, *f* at 93. Start with slurred two-bar phrases, just lifting the last two crotchets; similarly later except at obvious changes like all-*legato* bars 11–13 (right hand) and 30–32 (left hand). Avoid a choppy, broken sound in the trio's left-hand octaves by always slurring the thumb to the following fifth finger as well as the previous one. Make the three-part writing in bars 61–66 as smooth as J S Bach; conversely, cluck *staccato* through bar 87 (Haydn did like this farmyard sound) and be brilliant in 91 and 93. The very last three crotchets may go short-short-long, either with or without a *rit*.

No. 1 of Moments musicaux op. 94 D. 780

Schubert (from *Impromptus and Moments musicaux*) *Henle*

Here, as always with Schubert, every bar contains something to sing. The tenths in this particular piece can be spread, but the span of a ninth is a great help in bars like 31. It needs a cool head for the look-both-ways-at-once leap in bar 16. More importantly, it mixes duplets and triplets, sometimes simultaneously, though not always as written (see later, regarding bar 38). Most importantly, much of the piece, however busy (like bars 10–12), is marked *p*, and needs to sound effortless. Printed > accents are usually gentle: serious ones are marked either *fp* or *fz*. The breath (quaver rest) that ends bar 2 needs unpedalled silence (trickier so, in bars 23-24), as do the quicker (semiquaver-rest) versions in bars 13-21. A good starting tempo is ♩ = 100; the trio (bar 30) may go a touch faster, at say ♩ = 108.

Make bars 30-37 choral rather than an arpeggio exercise, pedalling the implied minim-crotchet melody in 30-31 and letting tenors sing as well as sopranos in bars 32-33. Scholars now think that Schubert semiquavers in bars like 38 and 40 should go together with, not after, the third note of the left-hand triplet. At a slower speed – like the Field nocturne in Grade 8, or Beethoven's *Moonlight* – it would be a different story. Notice the two-beat left-hand cross-rhythm persisting through bars 38-44/5, and in bar 66 take care to move off the crotchet A punctually. The pauses on the lower voices have to be printed on the beat for grammatical reasons, but they do not apply until after the treble G has sounded.

Group B

Dohnányi   Canzonetta op. 41 no. 3   Trinity Guildhall

Ernö Dohnányi (1877-1960) is famous for two pieces, the *Nursery Variations* op. 25 for piano and orchestra, and the solo *Rhapsody in C*, op. 11 no. 3. Both are rich in humour; Dohnányi is also famous (or notorious) for a book of distinctly tricky finger exercises. This canzonetta, however, is passionate in the style of gipsy music from his native Hungary: a feeling of heartbreak is never far away, and the tempo must never be metronomic. The mode is minor, but with many sharpened sixths easy to miss, like the E♮s in the G minor outburst from bar 15. Start the whole piece by singing out the top voice *legato* with careful fingering. Pedal sometimes in minims (bars 11-12 and first chord of 18, to sustain the bass), sometimes according to the tied notes (bars 6, 13, 20 and 28, plus bars 9-10 and 14-17: blurring here is probably harmless). Elsewhere use your judgment, especially in bars 1-4, where it may be difficult to hold down the tenths and necessary to choose between blurring the tune or losing some of the tied notes. All notes in bar 20 may go in the right hand except the first three: here, and in the other ripples (bars 6 and 13), the whole arpeggio may be free in rhythm yet should not really spread past the first beat, even at the very end. Notice B♭ throughout bar 17, D♭ through 18, and A and E♮s in the right hand of bar 19.

Bartók   Stamping Dance (from *Mikrokosmos* vol. 5 SZ107)   Trinity Guildhall

Bartók, though born only four years later than his compatriot Dohnányi (see above), always sounded far more modern. His six books of *Mikrokosmos* were intended mainly as teaching material, though many pieces in the higher-grade volumes work very well as short recital items. *Stamping Dance* is in, or nearly in, G, with many modal and chromatic inflexions which add colour to the basically simple folk-song melody. Most of the stamping occurs in the first four bars and must sound confident: players with small hands may detach the crotchets and leap to and from the bass – or else play the chords in the right hand. Bartók always marked his scores punctiliously (the closing stated duration is typical) so bars 13-20 – in default of any contrary instruction – remain ***f***: the grace notes in bars 15-18 recall catches in the voice or ornaments typical of bagpipe playing. The *crescendo* in bar 22 is one of this piece's many variations in level or tempo that are spread over a long time: here, the move is only from ***mf*** to ***f***. More remarkably, the later *poco a poco rit.* (from bar 45) and *accel.* (bar 55) spread over six bars each and move only between ♩ = 92 and 120 – tiny fluctuations indeed. The canon in bars 28-40 needs identical phrasing between the hands, of course: the following unisons (40/1-45) should lift off at each phrase-ending, as the quaver tails so carefully show. The tie to nothing after 46's bass note signals a very slight tying-over beyond the barline; the following *meno mosso* varies the opening theme (try fingering left hand at bar 58/9 with 2132/1), and leads to a stamping *coda* with scrupulously marked lines and accents to add colour. Lift the very last note punctually, with no pause.

Shostakovich   Prelude no. 8 (from *24 Preludes and Fugues* op. 87)   Trinity Guildhall

Henry David Thoreau said, 'The mass of men lead lives of quiet desperation'. Shostakovich was harassed by the Soviet authorities for most of his life, generally for not writing nice optimistic music that the least cultured person (or politician) could understand without effort. His world was one where you expressed an opinion at your peril. Despite its cheerful-sounding *allegretto* marking and light unpedalled texture, this prelude is anxiety-ridden, the long tune from bar 6 fretfully trying to escape the same few notes while the left hand ticks along remorselessly. The grace-note chirrups from bar 19 (play these very quickly, and very close to the main note) could be isolated chuckles, or more likely surreptitious but painful pin-pricks. The varied right-hand articulations are easy to focus on when above a consistently *staccato* left hand – less so over the moaning *legato* left hand from 25 (try thumb on G♮ over barline 27/8). Hold all dotted crotchets for their full length, particularly the throw-away high F♯ at 36. Bar 54's accented B♭ nudges the music towards its *coda*, the falling bass through 59-61 is all the more effective if done strictly *a tempo*, with no *rit.* at all. The wavering modulations may make you overlook the key signature: notice G♯ in bar 20, C♯ against E♭ to close bar 28, and C♯s through bars 41-5.

Headington   Prelude no. 2 (from *Five Preludes*)   Trinity Guildhall

Besides the *Five Preludes* of 1954, British composer Christopher Headington composed piano sonatas, string quartets, song cycles and a violin concerto. He was also a respected writer and broadcaster, and tragically died in a skiing accident. Parts of this prelude sound a little like Prokofiev or Poulenc. Keep the left-hand semiquavers even and smooth: crotchet pedals work well most of the way through, though some cunning (plus a light touch) is necessary in bars like 4-9 (where hands may collide) in order to sustain released long notes without excessive blurring. Pick up the tune in bar 5 with a calm rather than accented G♯. The end of bar 6 in the left hand may be fingered 5121 5121, and the same part of bar 9 with 5421 5121. Notice F♭ in the third beat of bar 10; the right hand is still in the bass clef over barline 14/5. The right hand at bar 18 is in a weak register and may need playing slightly louder than ***pp*** – a level that the left hand should not exceed. Exploit the closing *molto ritenuto* to the full, leaving ample time for a calm cadence with clear chord changes. Most of this piece would sound well as a flute, cello and piano trio.

Bonsor   Dreamy   Trinity Guildhall

Scottish composer Brian Bonsor here deserts his usual instrument – the recorder – for a comfortably swinging piano piece. Anyone uncertain of how to swing is kindly shown how to 'bend' the printed rhythm in the introductory note. A sustained (though out-of-reach) minim bass is implied whenever bar 1's left-hand rhythm appears (e.g. bars 3-6 and so on) and obviously needs minim pedalling in order to match the finger-held bass in bars like 2 and 7. Pedal the same way in bars 33-34 where non-swung quavers appear for the first time. The five notes of bar 2's third-beat chord are simultaneous, despite the printed alignment. Lift the right thumb in bar 6 to let the left hand sound. Play the tune alone once to see how it is phrased, noticing the chance for a breath and fresh start halfway through bar 4. It is F♯ before ♮ in bar 4, and D♮ before ♯ in bar 13. Bar 37's chromatic grace notes plus next note are in the left hand, of course, and notice F♯s lurking among the fourth-beat chord. Spread all left notes before any right to start bars 38 and 39, whose carefully placed dynamics mean a solo in the tenor. Bar 39's quaver D is played, not tied, all those printed downbeat ties merely indicating to sustain beyond the printed duration (with pedal).

Debussy   Jimbo's Lullaby (from *Children's Corner*)   *Bärenreiter*

Written for Debussy's daughter Chouchou, this lullaby is about her stuffed velvet elephant. The word 'lullaby' is most important: this piece must be gentle throughout – the very last note barely audible, so as not to wake any sleeping children. Start 'gently and a little clumsily' at around ♩ = 104: ensure bar 4's melody note is not weaker than the previous crotchet, unlike the specifically marked occasions like bars 8/9 and 27/8 where Debussy wants just such an effect. The composer generally signalled his famous pedal effects with long notes impossible to sustain with fingers alone, as in bars 59-62 and 78-80: bar 9's pedal mark is therefore untypical. Pedals should hold unchanged until barline 14/15. The middle-voice tune in bars 11-14 quotes the French lullaby 'Do, do, l'enfant do', recurring in whole-tone form at bar 39 and faintly recalled in 78-79. Fragments of another tune in bars 29-32 (check those different note lengths) coalesce into complete form from bars 47 and 54, and are counterpointed with the very first theme (and best left unpedalled for clarity) from bar 63. Whole-bar pedals work well in bars 21-28 and 67-69; barline 41/2 may need a dab of pedal to join the right-hand chords without blurring the left-hand *staccato*. Bar 26 may *crescendo* to more than *p*, which can be *subito* at 47. Some French instructions are easily guessable: others mean 'bring out a bit' (bar 21) and, most importantly, 'without slowing down' (bar 74).

Glass   Metamorphosis One (from *Solo Piano*)   *Chester*

Philip Glass (born Baltimore, 1937, to Lithuanian Jewish parents) has written music for films (*The Hours, Notes on a Scandal*) as well as concerts, and his *Metamorphosis One* featured in the 'Valley of Darkness' episode of the TV series *Battlestar Galactica*. He is usually grouped with composers like Steve Reich, Terry Riley and, to a lesser extent, John Adams – all labelled 'minimalists'. *Metamorphosis One* ticks this box: this four-page piece contains 13 different bars to learn which will need to be played with perfect accuracy. Tempi are metronomic, so the chord in bars 4-5 should be patiently held for its full length. Lean well over to the left in order to strike bar 8's crossed-hand octave cleanly and perfectly together. The tiny '8' touching the bass clef just before bar 8 and in similar places means play an octave lower. Play each recurring fragment exactly the same each time, as if inducing a non-Western trance: looking for varied interpretation is emphatically not what this kind of music is about.

Kabalevsky   Cavalryman (no. 29 from *Thirty Pieces for Children* op. 27)   *Boosey*

Unlike Prokofiev, Shostakovich and too many others, cultured artist and multi-linguist Dmitri Kabalevsky (1904-1987) managed to escape official Soviet censure during his career; a considerable achievement in an age of official paranoia and repression. He helped his cause by writing large quantities of optimistic music comprehensible to anyone: the well-known violin and third piano concertos are typical. *Cavalryman* rides like the wind, the opening left-hand whip-cracks prompting a tempo of at least ♩ = 144. Certain editions leave some dynamics unspecified. Bar 13's ***p*** *sub.* applies only to the right hand (*staccatissimo*, as always), so by analogy with bar 3 the left hand can be ***mf***. Yet in bar 46 (the last time this theme recurs) could probably – and excitingly – stay ***f*** in both hands. Switch carefully to straight quavers in bar 23, after two bars dotted; the offbeats in bars 24-25 are not in unison as you may expect; work on the different right/left articulations in bars 28-29 and enjoy the jazz-like bass crotchets hidden in bars 38-40. The final left-hand octave B♭ is by no means necessary if you are uncomfortable reaching it: a single-note thump is just as effective.

Peters   Wheeler Dealer (from *Ragtime Preludes*)   *Boosey*

Wheeler Dealer is the last of the set of *8 Ragtime Preludes*, published in 1994 and written by Greenwich-based composer Peter Wilson (pen-name Emerson Peters). The right style will come instinctively to natural swingers: more cautious players should note that not only are dotted-quaver-semi patterns swung into crotchet-plus-quaver triplets (as requested right at the start), but off-beat quavers like those in bars 3, 10 and 12 are swung too: they fall as the third notes of (unsounded) triplets, producing the odd effect of two notations in bars 10 and 12 (one for the first beat, the other for second and third beats), both sounding the same and neither of them exactly as written! Make the 'walking bass' in bars 26-28 heavy and detached; notice the right hand A, not B, just before the first-time bar 36a. Right/left synchronisation may be tricky in bars 37-41: practise away from the piano as a two-handed drum exercise to get comfortable with it. Read bar 51 carefully, noticing one A♮ amid the prevailing B♭⁷-A⁷ harmony. Do the D.C. in the exam but no repeats, going therefore from bar 52 back to 1-18, then straight to the coda. Positively no *rit.* at the end!

Scriabin   Prelude in E, op. 11 no. 9 (from *Scriabin: Selected Works for piano*)   *Schott*

The Chopin influence on the young Alexander Scriabin (1872-1915) is inescapable, so in addition to (for preference) big hands, players need an instinct for *rubato* sometimes too subtle to spell out in words. This no. 9 is typical of a set of 24 preludes, individually beautiful if rather enervating in large doses. Like Schumann, Scriabin often neglected to write the instruction *a tempo* after his *rit.* and *accel.* markings: here it could go into bars 11 (if not sooner) and 25. The tempo may – perhaps should – fluctuate elsewhere; for instance, bars 5 and 7 could push on a fraction, and 6 and 8 pull back. Use near-continuous pedal, carefully changing on every new harmony, not just when the bass moves. Bar 2, for example, needs one long pedal, but bar 4 needs three crotchet pedals. Low-pitched stepwise quavers in bars 13-14 should, however, be unpedalled (just pedal the third beats) and bar 24's C♮ be repedalled ultra-cleanly. Balance crotchet accompaniment ***ppp*** beneath quiet held notes as in bar 2. Bars 9-12 reprise bars 1-4 but with altered dynamics.

The overall violin-cello duet texture is heightened in bars 17-24, where 'cello' and 'violin' may predominate in alternate bars. Hold bar 30's pause unashamed, for a long time: no-one will get bored, or walk out before you have moved off. The final chord (where you spread all left notes before any right) is tricky if you cannot finger-hold the right hand G# to B: experiment with half-pedalling to try and lose the lowest E over barline 35/6 yet retain the G#.

Grade 7

Group A

	Courante	
J S Bach	(from *English Suite no. 2 in A minor*, BWV 807)	**Trinity Guildhall**

Grander than the French suites which they otherwise resemble, Bach's English suites usually open with a substantial piece that could stand alone in a short recital. Then, in English and French alike, follow a sequence of dances: this mostly two-voice courante is typical. Technically, its trickiest parts are bars like 5-6, 10, 18-19 and 22-23, where the left hand moves unpredictably against a busy right hand. Practising in a dotted-quaver-semiquaver rhythm aids co-ordination and emphasises the basic harmony clearly – a further aid to the ear. Alternative left-hand fingerings may suit: try starting bar 7 with 5 13 2312 1; try playing bar 14's A-G# with 12, and taking bar 15 with 1432 1432 1324. With no dynamic markings in sight, dig deep for clues to interpretation. Courante, the dictionary tells us, means 'running', a quicker dance than the stately allemande which precedes it in the complete suite. Rising treble may indicate *cresc.*, the natural tendency if sung. The following scheme is only one of many options: start *p*, *crescendo* in bars 5-6 towards bright C major and through high-pitched bar 7 to *f* at bar 9. Make a *dim.*, possibly, as bar 9 descends, *crescendo* through bars 10-11; bar 12 can be *f*. Start the second section (bar 13) either *p* (to copy bar 1) or *f* (to reflect bright C major), in which case *dim.* soon to underline the modulations. *Crescendo* through 16, cadence strongly in D minor (17-18). Try *dim.* from barline 18/19, *crescendo* through 21 and passionate bar 22, staying *f* to the end. Ornaments may go several ways and different options may be chosen when making the repeats, which should be played in the exam. The album and recording offer some suggestions, and the chords may arpeggiate either upwards or downwards.

Soler	Sonata in F, R. 8	**Trinity Guildhall**

'More Scarlattian than Scarlatti himself', is the usual reaction to the music of Padre Antonio Soler: less productive perhaps (only around 150 keyboard sonatas to Scarlatti's 555), but equally colourful and daring. The same style suited Soler all his life: maybe his monastic lifestyle shielded him from contemporary music elsewhere (he was still alive when Beethoven started composing). The Scarlatti fingerprints are all here: vigorous texture, sudden interruptions, and an exciting though unsettling atmosphere produced by irregular phrase lengths. Once located, they form vital clues to the momentum of the piece and its climaxes. Bar 20, for instance, interrupts a four-bar sequence and launches a fresh set of four-bar phrases, which end in not a four- but a five-bar phrase (32-36). Bars 50-51 interrupt another four-bar phrase structure: the later seven-bar phrase (60-66) repeats but is interrupted by a three-bar cadential finish (73-75). The very few printed dynamics are editorial and may be added to or even changed: try dropping to p at 9, resume f at 11/2, p again at 17, *crescendo* slowly from 22. Much further ahead, bars 111/2-114 could possibly echo 107/8-111, but the added thirds imply a richer (possibly louder) texture. The left hand from bar 24 (and 96) needs good control: if the printed fingering is troublesome try mixing in lots of repeated 42 42's or even 31 31's instead. Notice bar 53's Bb – easily missed after the previous stretch of C major. The texture around here is altered in the reprise (122-125); so are bars 135 and 142, the original high A's being replaced not by top D's (which just might have been off the top of the keyboard) but by Bbs whose hemi twiddles fail to conceal those consecutive octaves with the bass.

Hummel   Adagio and Allegro vivace (from *Caprice* op. 49)   Trinity Guildhall

Johann Nepomuk Hummel was in no way inhibited by his near contemporary Beethoven, either as concert pianist or composer, and produced many piano concertos and sonatas. The whole *Caprice* op. 49 is in six sections, the second being a longer version of this *Adagio* and the third starting like this *Allegro con brio* but in Ab, not F, and oddly notated there in $\frac{6}{8}$ rather than $\frac{3}{8}$. The exam *Adagio* looks short but at this tempo unwinds an immensely long melody, stretching – despite the rests and dynamic changes – right through to bar 11. Count bar 4 carefully in a slow four, the single semiquaver E therefore falling on 'three' and the two hemidemis quickly tucked in like grace notes. Turns in bars 6-7 may go demi, hemi triplet, demi, demi – fearsome-looking if spelt out in print, but in actual performance nearly slow enough to sing. Bar 10 is suddenly forceful, one of many mood swings in this piece best brought out by careful reading of all the printed dynamics, both here and in the *Allegro*. Lift the end of every slur from bar 11 for the required breathless effect: try adding *una corda* from bar 13' s pp if already too quiet.

Playing the *Allegro vivace* is rather like skating – comfortable provided you don't want to stop. Bear in mind those three quick right-hand leaps (bars 79/80, 88 and 96) when choosing the opening speed. Neat fingerwork is essential: practising the semiquaver bars in dotted rhythms is good for right-hand finger control and helps to bring out the quaver melodies buried among them. Check left-hand note values when the right hand is busy: the left hand alone has a pretty question-and-answer routine in bars 40-48, and from bars 97-104 makes a surprisingly good tune by itself. Finger lower notes of the octaves in bars 27-29 with 5-4-5 rather than blurring the right-hand scales with pedal. Pedal is scarcely needed anywhere, in fact, though it adds warmth to the crotchets in 31-37; the expressive (but still in strict time) chorale tune (52-59); and all six of the final chords, where the solitary crotchet (bar 118) and final dotted crotchet (plus essential pause) may each be *più f.*

Mendelssohn   Song Without Words op. 19b no. 1   Trinity Guildhall

The idea of tune and accompaniment on piano alone is ancient, of course, but Mendelssohn was one of the first to turn it into an art form, and here is the very first of them. The 'song' part of the title is obviously the top voice, but do not neglect the bass line, discreetly rising through bars 3-5, echoing the soprano in bars 9 and 10, and producing a calm deep bell effect from bar 44 to the end. All semiquavers should switch from hand-to-hand so smoothly that listeners cannot hear the joins, even if you rearrange the printed allocation. Taking all semis at bar 5, beat 3 in the left hand, as the album suggests, leaves the right hand free for the turn, and taking the B on beat 2 of bar 14 with the left hand makes it easier to reach the right hand's top D♯ (similarly in bar 43). The printed right-hand finger changing in bar 3 (similarly elsewhere) makes the top voice *legato*: enhance it with near-continuous *legato* pedalling on each crotchet and minim. Try taking bar 32's last two quavers with fingering 34. Bringing out the melody is a start: next, phrase it musically, avoiding bumps at phrase endings and being extra expressive in variant bar 32. Check the harmonic subtleties: for example, bar 2, beat 3 differs from bar 2, beat 2 in order to 'clear the air' for the imminent melody note, and bar 17 starts G-E minor not G-G. The expressive rising tenor in bars 26-27 may be gently brought out. The basic flowing tempo should not be metronomic: try lingering over bar 10's E♯; do not sag in bar 13 (the phrase does not finish for another two bars) but pull back the tempo from bar 48, beat 4, if not earlier. No repeat, by the way.

Ibert	La cage de cristal (from *Histoires*)	Leduc

This piece is available separately, in the complete album of ten *Histoires*, or in a selection of four that includes the best-known of them – *Le petit âne blanc* (*The Little White Donkey*). Like Debussy in his *Préludes*, Ibert puts the title at the end of the piece, almost as an afterthought, but it is an important guide to interpretation: *La cage de cristal* is cute, odd and fragile. Its first theme is subtly articulated: *legato* against the light right hand at first, then all *staccato* (both tune and accompaniment) from bar 5; nearly all *legato* from 9 and 21 (despite odd *staccato*s and quaver rests); and finally, from bar 28, like bar 9 though even softer, faster and with some easy-to-miss *tenuto* notes and one left-hand slur. Bars 7 and 30 sound comparatively coarse. Bar 7's single *rf* (oddly missing from equivalent bar 30) may mean just a downbeat accent or else is shorthand for 'loud all through'. Learn the chord-patterns in these bars by practising with grace notes compressed on to main notes, always watching for A♯s even in the second-beat grace notes. *En badinant* at bar 11 means 'jokingly' though this soon turns to expressiveness, carefully specified in bar 15. Count the demi runs carefully, not moving off tied notes until after the 'and' following each main beat. Try leaning the right arm inwards from bar 21 for extra weight to bring out the alto voice theme, as requested. Some vocabulary: *soutenu* means sustained; *léger* – light; *accentuez* – make accents; *doux* – sweet; *cédez un peu* – make a slight *rall*; *plus vite, et en pressant jusqu'à la fin* – quicker, and hurry through to the end.

Mozart	Sonata no. 5 in G, K. 283, 1st movement: Allegro (from *Piano Sonatas* vol. 1)	Henle

This popular piece is suitable for small hands and contains only two hazards: the quick leaps at bar 30 (and equivalent bar 97) and the trills against awkward left hand in 43-44 (and 110-111). Take your tempo from these, though anything much below ♩ = 116 may drag. The first theme's rests should not be obscured: avoid pedal and instead add richness to bars 1-3 by finger-holding the left hand's downbeat notes for a full bar. The *fp* in bars 5-6 are not really *f*, but accents within *p*: save a real *f* for bar 6/7. The three-quaver pick-ups to bars 17-19 could *crescendo* to add momentum without hurrying, and similarly where this rhythm recurs in bars 40-41.

Bar 25's Scotch snap rhythms risk slipping off the beat: avoid this by singing to bars 25/6 the words 'Ted-dy, Ted-dy, Ted-dy/ROOS-e-velt!'. Some editions advise ending bar 30's semis with the right hand, thereby exchanging a quick left-hand leap for a right-hand one over the barline.

Notice sudden *p*s and *f*s in bars 31-33, 38 and (with no *cresc.*) round barline 47/8. Check that the left hand in bars 43-44 is reliably controlled before attempting to add the trill, which may comprise as few as six notes (starting on the upper note, and with or without turn) though not as few as four. Count carefully through stop-start bars 53-60, adding *diminuendo*s through bars 55 and 59 to avoid lumpiness. Try pedalling the right-hand crotchets in bars 62-68 for richness, for in Mozart's time any left-hand *staccato* mark could also have meant 'accent'. Signal the recapitulation (bar 72) with an optional (and tiny) *rit*. Bar 80's appoggiatura may go as a quaver and bar 83's as a semi. The many octave displacements (bars 94, 98, 107, 111 and 115) need practice – and notice some differently voiced chords (compare bars 118-119 with exposition bars 51-52) during the sprint home.

Paradies   Giga in B♭   *Banks Music Publications*

Pietro Domenico Paradies (1707-1791) is most famous for the *Toccata in A* extracted from his 12 keyboard sonatas published in 1754. This giga may come from another of them though the most easily obtainable editions do not make this clear. His keyboard writing is a reminder of Scarlatti: in both men's music the printed dynamics may – quite legitimately – be changed, for few if any will be authentic. For instance, you could start *p* or *f*; be *f* at bar 4, beat 3; *p* at bar 7, beat 3; *meno p* at bar 8, beat 3; *più f* at bar 9, beat 3. Try an echo at bar 12, optionally staying *p* until bar 15, beat 2. Bars 26-29 could stay *p*; *f* bursting in with left-hand octaves at bar 30, beat 2. Try *meno f* at bar 32, beat 3; *p* at bar 34, beat 3; *mp* at bar 36, beat 3; *mf* at beat 36, beat 3; *f* at bar 38, beat 2 with echo at bar 39, beat 2; *p* at bar 41, beat 2; and *f* at bar 42, beat 2. The prevailing syncopations should never be gabbled, but the overall tempo should be no less than ♩. = 126.

Schubert   Sonata in A, op. 120 D. 664, 2nd movement: Andante   *Wiener Urtext*

Everything Schubert ever wrote for instruments – sonatas, symphonies, chamber music – always had the sound of the voice in mind: there is something to sing in every bar, and not just in the top part. Notice how the opening treble theme is sometimes doubled, an octave lower and equally expressively, in the tenor. Accented crotchets should all be gentle: in fact, given Schubert's notoriously ambiguous handwriting, they could equally mean *diminuendo* from first to second note. This is romantic music, verging on post-classical, where emotions run deep and tempos could fluctuate within a movement – some editions even suggest going slightly faster from bar 33 and a little faster still from 42 (Tempo 1 would resume from bar 50).

Demis in bar 7 should be tucked in without bumping. Bars 16-25 will gain richness without pedal, which might blur the right-hand quavers if the left hand plays with a *tenuto* touch (i.e. holding down most notes until they recur, rather than punctually lifting). Add pedal to any right-hand notes longer than a crotchet, except for bar 22's turn (four demis) which is better without. Bar 32's modulation always surprises listeners: ease the tempo slightly, rather than crashing into it in strict tempo. Rhythms in bars 37-39 are easier than they look, and some editions spell out what the right hand actually plays; notes after the dotted quavers go with, not after, the third notes in the left hand. Spread bar 56's downbeat (the left hand with, not before, the right) if necessary, catching bass with pedal. Super-confident players might like to bring out the second soprano tune (E-G-F♯-E) in bar 71 – in contrary motion to the tenor – and the similar one two bars later. The main first soprano tune lasts through to the final D, for the last two chords are part of the theme, not a quiet afterthought.

Schumann

Kind im Einschlummern
(no. 12 from *Kinderscenen* op. 15)

Henle

Kind im Einschlummern (Child Falling Asleep) can be a challenge to interpret, for the insistent rhythm could quickly become monotonous – maybe Schumann was trying to hypnotise a child into sleeping! A little *rubato* is essential, for example to close bars 4 and 8. The wide-looking left-hand stretches in this piece can all be pedalled over. The typical *ped.* marking simply means 'use pedal' and not 'hold down continuously without changing'. Crotchet pedals work well until bar 11, when the stepwise bass movement needs a cleaner sound. Sometimes, from here, a semiquaver pedal linking one chord to the next will be sufficient. Bar 9's second chord places the right-hand thumb across two notes: check the revised slurring when this recurs at 13/4. Bars 17–20 form a tricky finger-holding exercise: pause on barline 17/8 to check four notes are held, then lift the thumb as bar 18's high E is played; switch from 4 to thumb on the C♯ over barline 18/9; lift bar 19's F♯ as the E is played, then hold everything and add bar 20's A♯; and finally, lift bar 20's G♯ as F♯ is played. Count left-hand leger lines towards the close: bars 27–28 contain (in the left hand) B and A, not G and F♯.

Group B

Ravel   Assez lent (no. 2 from *Valses nobles et sentimentales*)   Trinity Guildhall

The complete set of *Valses nobles et sentimentales* was premiered without telling the audience who composed them. This no. 2 prompted some to guess Satie – the theme from bar 9 sounding very like a minor-key *Gymnopédie* – though the sophisticated harmonies before and after are quite outside Satie's sound world and need careful sight-reading. Ravel's sound world was often passionate, but always delicate.

The introductory chromatic yearnings recur three more times (bars 17, 33 and 49), higher and usually louder than before. To be recognisable as appoggiaturas they need careful handling: try pausing on third beats during practice to check that the correct notes are held in both hands (whether with fingers or pedal) and no others. Avoid blurring (especially the crotchet rests of bars 5-7) except in near-impossible places like bars 25, 28 and 29/30 (similarly in bars 57-62), where ideally the bass should sustain yet chords should be clear. Try half- or even quarter-pedalling here (pianos vary), though this is very tricky to get exactly right and no penalty accrues if this is not manageable. Carefully disentangle the ties in bars 33-36 to locate the one or two notes needing to be played. The *mystérieux* top voices from bar 41 should be ***pppp*** to avoid drowning the tune. Spread the left hand in bars 49-52 if necessary: do not omit any notes. Keep grace notes clearly ahead of the beats to clarify the different patterns in bars 26-28 and 57-59. Try finger-holding bar 63's left hand until beat 2 of bar 64 where repedalling will erase the unwanted A yet keep the whole harmony.

Poulenc   Assez modéré (no. 1 from *Trois mouvements perpétuels*)   Trinity Guildhall

The *Trois mouvements perpétuels* were published only a year after their composition, the act of a publisher confident of the then only 18-year-old Francis Poulenc (1899-1963). Strictly speaking, any of them could go on for ever (the repeat marks traditionally imply more than twice round), but one repeat in the exam is quite enough. Poulenc's music, even the mature stuff, is whimsical: its moods (and dynamics) change without warning. Over an unchanging bass (imagine a miniature *p* pinwheel rather than a clanking *f* water mill), we see pictures of Beethoven in bars 1-4, 9-10 (a theme from his song cycle *An die ferne Geliebte*), a merry-go-round (5-7) going off its spindle (10-11), tinkling bells (12-13, 18-19), something spilt on a cafe table and oozing through the slats (14-17) and finally a sphinx (24).

Hop down in bar 1 if the right hand cannot stretch the tenth, but land quietly; keep the alto quiet in bar 2 to let the minim through; crush grace notes closely to their main notes (10, 13-17); slow down hugely during 22-23 and pause where marked; sustain bar 24's pedal unchanged to the end for a mysterious four-octave reverberation. Remember naturals after the grace notes in bars 13-17 and on the very last A of the piece. Translations of the French: bar 1 – left hand generally expressionless; bar 5 – bring out; bar 12 – gently struck, or 'pinged'; bar 14 – colourless and staying *p*; bar 22 – slow down, bearing down on the right hand.

Copland   Sentimental Melody (Slow Dance)   Trinity Guildhall

Aaron Copland is considered by many the 'father' of American music: his *Fanfare for the Common Man* is an all-time favourite, with *Appalachian Spring* and *Billy the Kid* not far behind. The *Sentimental Melody* (1929) predates all of these and shows the pervasive influence of its time – jazz (it postdated Gershwin's *Rhapsody in Blue* by only three years). Unlike later jazz-influenced music, which used dotted-quaver-semiquaver notation (for example Brian Bonsor's Grade 6 piece), the characteristic swing rhythm is here carefully notated with triplet marks. Harmony is subtle, nearly bitonal in fact, with the left hand in F but the right hand favouring Db. Jazz players will instinctively smear all the grace notes: 18th-century precision is not part of the style. Minim pedals suit most of the piece, except for desolate bars 13-17, which would sound well on solo clarinet and bowed double-bass, part of a sound world Copland recreated for his equally jazzy clarinet concerto of 1947. Leave plenty of time for the out-of-reach grace note in bar 29, and carefully sustain the last chord with pedal while adding the closing high and low payoffs.

Henze   Ballade (no. 1 from 6 Pieces for Young Pianists)   Trinity Guildhall

Hans Werner Henze is one of today's most prolific composers, whose works include (at the time of writing) ten symphonies, 13 choral works, 63 works for orchestral and other large forces, songs, chamber and instrumental music. But his first love was the theatre, for which he has composed 54 works including the children's opera *Policino*, which immediately preceded *Ballade*. Henze's musical texture is often complex: this piece is simpler but needs strict counting, exact note-holding, and a good ear to detect the right notes in this challenging (atonal if not strictly twelve-tone) idiom.

Discords abound, not all of them confirmed with the reassuring accidentals (particularly naturals) expected in more traditional styles: the right hand of bar 13 has deliberate F and G naturals against sharps in the left hand; the left-hand B♮ persists through bars 15-16 against B♭s in the right hand. Bar 1 uses all 12 notes of the chromatic scale except G♯, whose delayed first appearance (at the end of bar 2) is thereby heightened – an unlikely though genuine similarity with Mendelssohn's *Song Without Words* (earlier in this grade). Similarly, the five beats from bar 13's *mf* contains all notes except C♮, saved in order to start the next phrase. The persistent rocking chords through bars 15-16 (only two different chords in each hand) contain all 12 notes.

This all sounds fiercely analytical but the falling two-note figure first heard closing bar 2, and pervading bars like 5 and 9, needs playing as expressively as if its harmony was tonal and romantic. Selective pedalling may add warmth to longer notes and are essential in those few places where Henze, like Debussy, writes notes unsustainable by fingers alone, as in bars 4-5. Distinguish between slurs and ties: play just the C♯ on the fourth beat of bar 7, for example, but play everything at the start of bar 12.

Paynter	Melting	Trinity Guildhall

John Paynter was an influential musical educator, encouraging children to think for themselves, like composers. He co-authored a pioneering book for teachers, *Sound and Silence* – controversial at the time (1970) but much respected now. Of *Melting* he wrote: 'This piece is both an image of the gradual melting of static snow-blocks and a melting and merging of the harmonies.' The word 'melting' also crops up in the important footnote about pedalling printed in the album. It is tempting to clip the long passages where almost nothing happens (bars 2-3, 12-13, 81-83, 91-93), but the apparent stasis is part of the intention. It is also tempting to change pedal with new harmonies (like bars 20, 50 and 59) but held pedals are vital and will produce a magical sound world. If a wrong note is played, keep the pedal down regardless: better a smudge than hasty repedalling to hide the mistake, thereby losing all the carefully built-up texture. The final effect of silently pressing the keys down then changing pedal to expose just the held-down chord is magical.

McGuire	No. 5 of 5 Miniature Pieces (from *A Century of Piano Music* Grades 5-7)	Bosworth

Edward McGuire (born in Glasgow, 1948) studied composition at the Royal Academy of Music with Ingvar Lidholm in Sweden. A flautist with the folk group Whistlebinkies, he wrote one of the few orchestral works ever to include the Highland bagpipes – the tone-poem *Calgacus* (1976). The last of his *Five Miniature Pieces* sounds like Lutosławski, and through him Bartók; its ingenious construction – in two keys at once – and sparse textures (particularly the thinned-out reprise, from bar 41/2) make it an effective piece. Imagine a folk dance in the right hand, continuing regardless of arguments (the opposing key in the left hand), interruptions (the gradually diminishing foghorn blares in bars 15-33) and occasional stumbles (the changes of time-signature). ♪=♪ as always in this style: the silences in particular should be counted carefully (two quavers to close bar 8, four – no more, no less – to close bar 45). Articulations are scrupulously marked: observe the *tenuto* right hand against the *staccato* left hand in bars 4 and 10, and the little *legato* whoops that launch bars like 15, 17 and 46, but not 50. In context, the closing B♭ against A is completely logical.

Milne	Wild Mushrooms (from *Pepperbox Jazz* book 2)	Faber

Elissa Milne was born in Australia in 1967, raised in New Zealand, and is now Sydney-based. At least six of her piano collections have 'pepper' in the title and all are jazzy. *Wild Mushrooms* is the tenth of 11 pieces forming *Pepperbox Jazz* book 2, a collection composed in 1999 and first published in 2006. The piece contains references to French waltzes (bars 12-23), Ravel (33-40), *Murder on the Orient Express* (41-44) and even the Sugar Plum Fairy (45-46). The markings 'swung' and 'straight 8's' are useful and refer to quavers, not octaves. The whole piece is player-friendly: bars 49–80 exactly repeat bars 1–32 and the closing scale is the easiest chromatic contrary, where black and white notes all coincide. Read the unpredictable harmonies of bars 36–39 carefully; finger bar 81 with right hand 123 123 123 (similarly later) and 89–91 with right hand 534 243 132/1 24 1/424 242 412. The final octave Ds are after the second beat, not on it – be wary of miscounting or making even the slightest *rall.* which could spoil the effect.

Prokofiev	No. 10 from *Visions Fugitives* op. 22	*Boosey*

Prokofiev was fond of irony: he even wrote some piano pieces called *Sarcasms* and the *Ridicolosamente* tempo marking of this *Vision Fugitive* ('Fleeting Glimpse') is typical. The marking, and the music itself, could perhaps suggest a red-nosed circus clown with a twisted smile. His harmony is quirky, requiring a keen ear for right (even if odd-sounding) notes, plus nimbleness between the hands to avoid their colliding. He exploits the augmented second integral to the B♭ harmonic minor scale: the spice it provides should be well brought out in performance, and he deliberately 'spoils' classical V⁷–I cadences by placing V⁷ a semitone too low (as in bars 20/1, 28/9 and 37/8). The opening p *sostenuto* does not contradict the *staccato* dots: it means 'left hand stay quiet'. Hold the left hand high in order to let the right hand under, and try to keep the right hand flattened even in bars 11–14 to avoid colliding with the left hand. Ignore the classical 'no thumb on black notes' rule and finger all the five-note runs (bars 15–16 etc.) with 54321. *Sotto* and *sopra* mean 'below' and 'above', and relate to hand positions, so flatten the left hand and raise the right for bars 19–20, fingering the right hand with 1 215/4 and, from bar 21, 4 (held) 3 23 13/2. The note F is deliberately omitted from bar 32 to avoid upstaging the left hand, just one of several clever points in this piece. Others include those out-of-key grace-note flourishes (bars 16, 24 and so on): they all avoid the following downbeat, thereby making it sound new and fresh. Hence the A♮s in bars 20 – A♯s would sound like, and pre-empt, the following B♭s.

	Water-Wagtail	
Scott	(from *A Century of Piano Music* Grades 5–7)	*Bosworth*

Although English born, Cyril Scott (1879–1970) studied composition in Frankfurt, teaming up with Percy Grainger and (now barely known) fellow students Roger Quilter, Balfour Gardiner and Norman O'Neill to form a group known for a while as the Frankfurt Gang. Scott's impressionistic piano pieces earned him the name of the 'English Debussy': his best known piece is probably *Lotus-Land. Water-Wagtail* (an alternative name for the pied wagtail) could become equally popular on account of its simple but rich texture (owing a lot to pedal) and its teasing switches between $\frac{3}{4}$ and $\frac{2}{4}$ time.

There may be some misprints: bass minim Cs in bars 57–58 should almost certainly be Es; bar 89's left-hand E should, conversely, be a C. The second, third and fourth melody notes of bar 100 should read G, B and D, forming a correct transposition of bar 3. Bars 5, 32 and 83 have F as their third left-hand note, while bars 12, 90 and 110 have C: this may be deliberate, and is certainly harmless. Some vertical slurs (meaning spread chords) may be missing from climactic bars 71–78.

Printed right-hand fingerings are not compulsory but are all worth trying. An opening tempo of around ♩ = 96 provides an easy flow while a single two-bar pedal, four whole-bar pedals and two crotchet pedals will add warmth and a suitable haze. The tempo may relax in bar 14, the momentarily more serious bar 15 resuming in tempo. The contrasting middle section (*a tempo poco più mosso*) is stealthy then urgent, pedal perhaps being reserved for the right-hand crotchets. Lifting the *una corda* (left pedal) helps to distinguish bar 51's **p** from the previous **pp**. In this warm English summerscape, the cascading chords starting in bar 63 could be a leaf falling from the topmost branch of a tree and slowly spiralling into the water. Non-*staccato* left-hand pulsations from bar 113 (compare bar 35) aid the calming down process towards the long-pedalled **pp** ending.

Grade 8

Group A

	Air and Variations in E	
Handel	(*The Harmonious Blacksmith*, HWV 430)	Trinity Guildhall

Few if any listeners would ever guess by ear alone that the famous tune actually starts on the second beat. Avoid making the point with inappropriate bumps on down beats: treat it instead as a hint to keep the music flowing, without sitting down as each suspension resolves. Read it also as a hint to *cresc./dim.* round stronger beats of the bar like bar 3 beat 3; bar 4 beat 1; bar 5 beat 3; and bar 6 beat 1. The overall phrasing will be clear if slight breaths are made (without disrupting the rhythm) after bar 2 beat 1; bar 3 beat 3; bar 4 beat 1; bar 5 beats 1 and 3; and bar 6 beat 1. The album's printed fingering (throughout) allows for an all-*legato* approach but may be changed. A few discreet hops between notes are harmless.

The variations (originally called 'doubles') should ideally go no slower than the theme, and may copy its phrasing and those optional *cresc./dim.* Variations go in pairs, the left hand of numbers 2 and 4 matching the right hand of numbers 1 and 3. Variations 2 and 5 start with written out repeats, filling four bars rather than just two. Take this as a cue to repeat the first halves of the other variations as marked – as the recording does – so that in performance all variations will be the same length. (Do not repeat any second halves in the exam.) Notice unpredictable repeated treble Bs in variation 4. Some recordings swing the semiquavers round barline 32/3 to blend in with the prevailing rhythm, but this is not compulsory. Show-off variation 5 may be basically **f** (and a full-blooded **ff** from bar 42, beat 2), with pealing and brilliant scales firmly supported by accented crotchets: check bar 41, beat 1, where hands do not quite go where expected.

	Più tosto allegro con espressione	
Clementi	(1st movement from Sonata in F♯ minor, op. 25 no. 5)	Trinity Guildhall

Muzio Clementi, composer, piano manufacturer and shrewd businessman, wrote much besides the iconic study book *Gradus ad Parnassum*. He made a sensational London debut as pianist and composer the very year Beethoven was born (1770). Clementi's 100-plus sonatas are far outshone by Beethoven's today, but the younger man much admired them. This particular sonata was a favourite of Horowitz: it is volatile and passionate – rather like C P E Bach at times – with many mood changes, all carefully marked with dynamics. Much pathos is generated by emphasis on the augmented second that forms part of the harmonic minor scale: this needs careful reading in places like bars 99-100, where the D♮s may be easily overlooked (similarly in bar 3). Both the exposition and recapitulation end quite emptily, in a mood almost of desolation.

Più tosto means 'rather' or 'quite'. The many short slurs are authentic but possibly incomplete: certainly unslurred semiquavers should not deliberately be played more detached than slurred ones, and in any event the overall phrase structure takes precedence. Notes on the upper stave but with stems down in bars like 2 and 4-6 are obviously intended for the left hand, hence the absence of rests beneath. The only three real stopping places in the whole first page come in bars 8, 12 and (despite the odd slur) halfway through bar 24. The first right-hand notes in bars 27 and 29 are dissonances, needing emphasis (and fading off) different from that in bars 2, 14 and 16 (in the same rhythm), where the harmony is less tense. Notice that the ripples in bars 36-38 (and equivalent bars 109-111) change harmony after four notes; replace the printed right-hand third finger with second if easier. Double check the rhythms in bars 41-42 and 45/6-48, and keep the right hand non-synchronised with the left hand. The trills in bars 65-67 go the same way as bar 5 (and its footnote) but may here be fingered 231 for firm articulation. Hold bar 85's right-hand durations exactly, and do the *tenuto*s of bars 118-128 with pedal as the hands cross.

Schumann	Romance in F♯, op. 28 no. 2	Trinity Guildhall

In six sharps, and laid out on three staves, this piece looks daunting at first, but most of it lies easily under the hands. It is highly suitable for sensitive players with a flair for *rubato*. A steady tempo will allow plenty of time to balance individual notes or even reach them, for even at wide-leap moments (left hand, bars 6-7) the semiquavers must always be more gentle than the long notes they accompany. The melody itself is in thirds (the thumbs of both hands), not just in the right hand: bringing it out is the first stage towards mastery and expressive shaping is the all-important second stage.

Schumann's generalised instruction *con ped.* means 'use pedal sensitively, changing where the harmony changes' rather than 'hold down throughout, regardless of blurring'. Check the ties in bars 9-12: the only thing actually played on the fourth quaver beat each time is the right-hand semi. Check the one immediately following (i.e. the eighth one of the whole bar), for some wrong notes actually sound harmless and could be missed: bar 9 should move onto a G♯, not another E♯, and in bar 11 onto F♯, not D♯. Penultimate melody notes of bars 13-14 will need a change of pedal despite the finger held bass; conversely, second (tied over) melody notes in bars 22-23 should leave the pedal unchanged, for the following bass notes are part of the same chords and lifting the pedal would break the melody line.

Sacrifice the held tenor E over barline 15/6 if out of reach, rather than blurring the changing harmonies with pedal. Schumann's odd layout round barline 25/6 imitates string quartet writing and deserves consideration, but an easier option (and one which sounds the same) is to take the top stave's last three semis plus the B♯ from the chord together in the left hand, leaving the right hand to complete the chord with D♯-F♯-D♯. Resume as printed from the second beat of bar 26 – the hands should already be in position and will avoid Schumann's awkward leap in both hands at once. Try taking the left hand's high F♯ in the right hand to allow more time to prepare the grace notes. Observe note lengths punctiliously at the very end, respecting Schumann's carefully notated fade out. No repeat in the exam.

Brahms   Intermezzo op. 119 no. 3   *Trinity Guildhall*

Brahms's late piano pieces, opp. 116-119, are largely the reflections of an old man, more like gentle conversations between friends than public outpourings. Nevertheless, they are not all dreamy: this C major intermezzo is light and sprightly, and needs a very agile left hand. Typically, this often comprises an octave stretch then a leap onto some middle register harmony, and is best fingered: 513131 (bar 1) and 512 512 (bar 4). Bars 23-37 are well worth practising with the left hand alone: the *staccatos* marked here are signs of Brahms striving, as always, for lightness and could generally apply throughout the piece.

The opening theme is in alto with the voices above usually synchronising with it, though not always: observe the held notes in bars 1, 3, 4 and 7 (and particularly 49), the single tied notes that close bars like 7 and 9, and the multiple ties through 11-13. *Sostenuto* in bars 10 and 12 should imply a slight *rit.* and is possibly also intended at bar 22. Notice F♮s in busy bars 23-24 and unexpected bass notes (a third lower than may be expected) closing bars 30-32: dotted crotchet stems here merely signify held notes, not a counter melody. Bars 44 and 48 are musical chuckles, becoming a shout of laughter through bars 62/3-64, where the tempo may resume three semiquavers earlier than printed. Practise the right hand of bars 66-68 *legato* to learn the unpredictable leaps. Very short pedals may add warmth to the chords in bars 65 and 69 (spread them as marked, even if they can be reached comfortably without) and to the occasional bass note. Mostly, though, this piece goes unpedalled even in tempting places like bars 66-68.

Prelude & Fugue in E♭, BWV 876

J S Bach   (from *The Well-tempered Clavier* book 2)   *Any reliable edition*

Old editions may suggest dynamics but Bach left none: ideas may be deduced from the texture. The style may recall *Jesu, Joy of Man's Desiring* but can go a little faster, say at ♩. = 76 or so. The appoggiatura in bar 2 may be an on-the-beat quaver or crotchet, but the alto F always goes with it (i.e. on the beat, not after). Build from ***p*** in bar 5, using tenor voice left-hand phrases for over-the-barline momentum. Bar 9's surging high treble implies ***f***, sustained to the seventh (not the first) note of bar 12. Bar 13-15's build-up may be less, and the modulation to C minor at bar 24 may be approached via a long *diminuendo*. Exploit question-and-answer phrasing from bar 25 – a whole bar each at first – then reducing to two beats each in bars 29-30 and one beat in 31. Three-bar sequences from 32 compress into two-bar ones at 38; bars 41-49 are intense and passionate. Make seamless joins from right hand to left in bars 57-60; slur downward-swooping bass lines from 63. Bars 67-68 may broaden to ***f***, with a quiet *coda* starting at 69.

Fugal analysis always helps interpretation in performance. Expositions and clusters of middle entries are usually grand, whether ***f*** or ***p***, while episodes normally relax. The scheme here is blurred, for the subject is rarely absent, Bach finding an infinite number of ways to play with it. A good tempo is ♩ = 72, a similar pulse to the Prelude but the totally different texture will avoid monotony. Complete the exposition ***f*** at 29/30 then drop the volume, as the two-part texture from bar 33 implies (one voice in each hand here – some editions may not make this clear). Let this rebuild during the approach to C minor in bar 45: the expected perfect cadence fails to materialise, however, and the volume may dwindle accordingly. The subdominant section (bars 54-58) may be sombre, brightening at the home key final section (bar 59 onwards). The fugue subject stays calm and smooth despite the crotchet rest, and without accenting the syncopated minims. Release bar 22's bass Bb if necessary, check for the held G over barline 40/1, and hold Eb over barline 68/9 while carefully lifting tenor C.

Beethoven — Sonata in F, op. 10 no. 2, 1st movement: Allegro — *Schott*

Volatile but endlessly rewarding, this popular piece needs a well-controlled left hand, some reliable counting in order to negotiate accurately the silences and sudden stops – like those in bars 41, 45–46, 54, 65 (with crotchet) and 70 (with quaver), and 129–130. It is necessary to be comfortable with the fast 6-against-4, and a right hand ideally large enough to play the chord A-C-D♯-A without strain, though smaller hands can get by with some discreet tweaking. At full speed (say ♩ = 88) the four demi turns in bars 38–39 are still easy: bar 72 is harder and if four hemis are impossible try leaving out the first C♯. Similarly, reduce bar 9's five-note trill to four notes by omitting the central Bb. Longer trills (bars 58, 62 and 64) may happily buzz in unmeasured notes: they are less important than the left-hand figures they accompany, which should be even and in tempo. Check right/left synchronisation round the first of them: bar 57's left-hand thirds together (not split); bars 59–61's right-hand thumb goes with the bass and 5th finger after it.

Avoid slow practising the 6-against-4 of bars 30–35 unless really helpless: practise at speed instead, firstly by compressing the left hand into crotchet chords, then with the left hand playing just first, fourth, seventh and tenth notes, then – as in diving – holding the nose and jumping in! Finish off by noticing the five *sf*, which are really only accents within ***p***. Compare the rhythm of bar 5 with 122 and 137 – any discrepancy is probably deliberate. Notice the right-hand second subject octaves (bars 19–22) recapitulated as full chords (145–148): here and elsewhere, a small right hand may omit one note per chord (generally the lowest but one) depending on the harmony. The printed dynamics convey all the intended drama; avoid blurring the changes with unmarked *crescendo*s or *diminuendo*s. Mark the key changes with humour (bars 117 and 136), for instance by delaying the D major entry theatrically, and acting as if lost (with a *rall.*) before leaving it.

Chopin — Valse in Ab posth. op. 69 no. 1 (from *Waltzes*) — *Henle*

Chopin frequently copied his compositions for friends, or new publishers, and like any creative composer took the opportunity to revise them while doing so. The Fontana version of this waltz is the one normally found in anthologies: unlike the alternative version it should close bar 1 with two even quavers (not dotted-quaver-semi) and the right hand of bar 7 should start with a crotchet rest; the right hand of bar 14 should be minim crotchet, not minim dotted quaver semi. Next, check the bar count: repeated section bars 33–64 closes with bars numbered 64a (first time) and 64b (second time); the rest of the piece is written out in full, unlike the alternative, which uses a lot of short repeats.

Many passages recur identically: both the merry-go-round of bars 65–80 and persistent rhythm of bars 81–87 (repeated in bars 89–113) can be hard to keep interesting. Changes elsewhere are subtle: compare bar 19 with similar (but not identical) bar 3; bars 18 and 20 (tenor) with bars 2 and 4; bars 41–42 with 33–34 – it is the version from bars 17–32 that recurs from bars 49 and 113. Small-note runs in bars 27 and 59 could be mathematically exact but are possibly more effective if unevenly divided and played *accel.*: try splitting into 6+7 notes or possibly 5+8; bar 123 may go 5+7 or 4+8 just as convincingly as 6+6. Finally, allow for some *rubato*: although this is dance music, a metronomically strict tempo throughout would be the wrong style altogether.

Haydn   Sonata in D, Hob. XV1/37, 1st movement: Allegro con brio   *Henle*

The correct sonata (sometimes confusingly numbered 50, 12 or even 7) among all those in D is the one starting on quaver Ds, with mordents on the fifth and seventh notes. Counting and ornaments are mostly straightforward; good left-hand technique is helpful in bars like 24-27, 46-50 and 67-70. Play the opening for laughs, with crushed grace notes, *staccato* repeated notes and slurred pairs of quavers with twiddles: a sprightly performance can sound like a fox in a hen house. If the left hand cannot copy this exactly from bar 41, then cheat and replace the twiddles with single grace notes. Right-hand semis from bar 9 contain a tune in duet with the bass (with optionally pedalled crotchets), which is well worth picking out. Bar 16's 'dum-da-daa' fanfare chords work best if played softer than the downbeat, but bar 40's similar one may benefit from extra volume. Notice A♯s through bars 19-20 which are often missed; the left-hand third note of bar 27 may be a sharp or double sharp depending on the edition, and the equivalent note in bar 90 may be a natural or sharp. Bar 34's trill may go as plain semis, as some editions suggest, but sextuplets are more arresting.

Haydn specified few if any dynamics. Try starting *f* (*meno f* in 3-4 and 7-8). Drop to *p* at 17, and try alternating half-bar *f* and *p* in 19-20, resume *f* at 21; drop to *p* for minor-mode bar 29, take bar 30 *f*, with optional *dim.* to *p* or even *pp* in 31, then *ff* subito at 32. Go *p* after 35's downbeat, resume *f* at 39. The development (bars 41-60) cannot possibly go all at one level, so try starting *f*, *dim.* in 46 to *p* at 47, *crescendo* through 51-52 to *f* at 53; *p* subito at 59, *crescendo* through 60 to bring in the recap *f* (bar 61), thereafter match the exposition, level for level. Notice, among other subtle differences, that exposition bars 9-12 now telescope into recapitulation bars 74-75.

Tchaikovsky   June: Barcarolle (no. 6 from *The Seasons* op. 37 bis)   *Henle*

This is from a set of pieces usually called *The Seasons* but named *The Months* in the original Russian (far more logically, given that there are twelve of them). June finds Tchaikovsky in a largely doleful mood though we are allowed glimpses of an energetic ballet *en route*. Technically, the piece needs comfort with quick chords (sample bars 40-51 before choosing), sensitive pedalling, and some instinct for natural *rubato*.

Editions vary and some of the arbitrary phrase endings (minims, crotchets or quavers, as in bars 4, 5 and 10) may be pasted over with long and inauthentic pedal marks. Tchaikovsky seems to have left no pedal marks himself, though the piece urgently needs them: try whole-bar pedals in bars 1-2, three beats in bars 3-4, and short dabs (if anything) in bars 5-6. Swell towards bar 11's tenor C, which should be heard to sustain before moving off a bar later. Bar 21's grace notes go before the beat; bar 22 may pull back while briefly trailing the extensive duet to come much later (bar 53/4 onwards). The *poco più mosso* (bar 32) may remind ballet-goers of Mother Gigogne from *The Nutcracker*, and the $\frac{3}{4}$ section (from bar 40) sounds just like music for big jumps: go slightly steadier here if accuracy would otherwise suffer. Check middle voices in each hand from bar 42; forcibly replace prevailing $\frac{3}{4}$ with heavily accented $\frac{2}{4}$ hemiolas from 47; bar 51 contains carefully counted crotchets, not two more quavers. Bar 53's Tempo 1 turns the initial solo (think oboe) into a love duet (think oboe and cello): the 'cello' part requires careful *legato* fingering. The *coda* (from bar 83/4) recalls the Mother Gigogne episode; overlapping phrases in bars 86–87 and 90 actually end on minims, possibly one note beyond the edition's printed slurs, similarly in bar 91's double bass solo. Bar 91/2 onwards is in real phrases albeit in detached chords: each phrase starts exactly where the left hand changes register, thereby producing two eight-chord phrases, two four-chord, and a final eight-chord phrase closing with the left hand sustaining alone and unpedalled, the right hand having carefully lifted off.

Group B

Beach	Scottish Legend (no. 1 from *Two Pieces* op. 54)	Trinity Guildhall

American composer Amy Marcy Cheney Beach started out as a child prodigy and pianist but after her early marriage (in 1885, at the age of 18) gave up public performance – or rather, limited it to one charity performance per year – and concentrated on composing. Her works include songs, piano pieces, a piano concerto, chamber music, and a *Gaelic Symphony* no. 2 (oddly, there seems never to have been a no. 1).

To judge from this *Scottish Legend*, she may well have had big hands: certainly they are almost essential in places like the quick chord after grace notes at bar 12, beat 2 and indeed most of the central major key section. The printed pauses are vital to the improvisatory feeling and must all be generously observed. The big chords, even when spread, should also be absorbed into the overall melody line without bumping – luckily the slow tempo marking allows time for this. The opening D and E grace notes of bars 8, 16 and 36 are both played with the thumb: the left-hand grace notes may start (and finish) together with the right hand despite the printed alignment. Bar 12's big grace-note run-up in bars 12 and 28 may be fingered L551 (or 512) R125, or with a spectacular hand-crossing LL RRR L. The even bigger one in bar 32 may go as printed (L5 51 R1 2415 and pause) or hand over hand: L L R R RR L L and pause. Despite the selective tied-note markings, the first grace note sustains the whole chord and must be caught with pedal, not lost. Bar 28's left-hand C♯ can be tricky to resolve without blurring and unless the bass A can be held, try half-changing the pedal on the C♯. The crossed right-hand voices in bars 31 and 35 do not match those in equivalent bars 11 and 15, but are not significant.

Medtner	Bird's Tale (from *Romantic Sketches for the Young* op. 54)	Trinity Guildhall

Nikolai Medtner was once rated on a par with his compatriot and near-contemporary Rachmaninov – particularly in England, where he settled in 1936 – but his copious piano music (which includes three concertos and 14 sonatas) is largely forgotten now. His naturally intricate style makes other pieces of this set more suitable for children to listen to rather than actually attempt, but *Bird's Tale* is an exception. The carefully marked opening is delicate and deliberately hesitant, but the **pp** of bar 8 should not be too faint to phrase the harmony 'strong-weak'. Stems up = right hand and stems down = left hand, regardless of stave or clef, right through to bar 17 where small hands could take the E♭ in the right hand. Disentangling the ties over barline 12/3 will reveal that only the A♭ plays. Carefully lift lower notes at barline 14/5, repedalling to sustain the held G as the left hand searches for the next chord. The nervy 'fluttering wings' demisemi pattern from bar 18 should never obscure the still gentle melody above, unusual in its occasional five-bar phrases (bars 34/5–44 – and notice the changing harmonies in bar 35). The quasi-Bach interlude from bar 44 needs crisp trills and no pedal. The left hand leads from bar 66: practise the left hand alone, expressively and with pedal, to discover the best phrasing for this very long melody (right through to bar 89). Notice that the very last minim of the piece (the middle C) should definitely sustain alone, after the final flutter has disappeared.

Messiaen   La colombe (The Dove) (no. 1 from *Préludes*)   Trinity Guildhall

Messiaen became famous for daunting rhythmic complexities and hard to read non-diatonic chord progressions, but these *Préludes* date from early in his career and the rhythms are much simpler. Chords can be tricky to read, often based on an octatonic scale (of alternate semitones and tones) and written in unconventional enharmonics: typically, the first top-stave chord of bar 1 comes out as B♭ minor. Take courage: this motif only contains four different chords and is the same each time. Some stretches are wide: the highest middle-stave semis of bar 19 may be easier if taken in the right hand, and bar 20's bass Bs may go as grace notes before the beat. For the closing bars on a piano with three pedals: the middle one sustains the minim chord unchanged to the end, which allows the printed rests above and below to be observed. Players unused to (or without) three pedals will unavoidably fill some rests in, but may salvage some of the intended effect by silently depressing the minim chord after the last quasi-*pizzicato* bass octave, then lifting the pedal. Incidentally, the sharps against naturals in bars 21–22 are no misprints but a calculated and subtle overtone effect that Messiaen much exploited in later works.

The balance can be tricky, especially on an unfamiliar piano. Do not start too tentatively, else the *ppp*s may not speak at all. More importantly, this is romantic music. The long middle stave melody needs expressive shaping, and the printed *rubato*s and *rall.*s may be generous. Tempos may be flexible even where not indicated: the seriously slow opening tempo is characteristic, but may increase along with the passion, to ♪ = 72 at bar 6, possibly, and even ♪ = 84 at climactic bars 9 and 19.

Dring   Blue Air (from *Colour Suite*)   Trinity Guildhall

Madeleine Dring trained as both actress and composer (as a pupil of Gordon Jacob and Vaughan Williams), writing many works for oboist husband Roger Lord and much music for television. As befits an admirer of Poulenc, her music is deliberately simple, light, and often jazzy: this *Blue Air* (dating from 1963) is typical, and is reminiscent of Gershwin, or Ravel. The dotted-quaver-semi pattern should be played as $\frac{12}{8}$-time crotchet-quaver swing, incidentally making the crotchet triplets of bars like 10 and 19–20 easy to synchronise (second triplet crotchet goes with the left-hand semi). The preliminary quavers should be kept straight and serious, with no hint of the fun to come. One or two enharmonics may be surprising: bar 8's G♭ could have been written as F♯, and bar 29 (briefly in C♯ minor) could have contained F𝄪 for G♮ and A♯ for B♭. The main melody from bar 3 is in the right-hand thumb, as marked, but that does not exclude bringing out other subtleties like the modulating bass line and scrunchy A♭ against B♮ of bar 6. Make bar 26's

surprising Bm⁷ chord expansive, sustaining the tone over the next barline. Check D♮ hidden among
#s in bar 30; notice that the very last note of bar 32 is still (G)♯, and that the left hand of long-
pedalled bar 53 starts in the treble clef.

Rorem	Barcarolle no. 1	Trinity Guildhall

Ned Rorem (born in Richmond, Indiana) is a prolific writer, not just of music but also words:
his caustic comments on the avant-garde, and personalities belonging in it, gained him much
notoriety. His own music is very traditional, and the Barcarolles are among his earliest works.
He composed them shortly after moving to Morocco, but there is nothing Arabic about them.
The apparently unending melody of this no. 1 may be difficult to shape convincingly at first:
characterise the opening three-note pick-up on each reappearance (as in bars 8 and 19) to signal
each new departure the theme then takes. The middle section similarly reuses a three-note
pick-up, this time in longer notes (bars 23b–24, 29–30, 39–40, 45–6 and neatly recurring much
later – bar 78–79 – to help close the piece). Stretch the tempo imperceptibly if time is needed to
negotiate the concerto-like climax of bars 52–54. Carefully sustain bar 58's tenor B while lifting the
right hand to observe the printed comma (almost a theatrical cut-off). Even Rorem's instrumental
music is vocal at heart – shape any interesting inner parts with as much enjoyment as if they were
the altos and tenors in a choir.

Andaluza (no. 5 from *Danzas españolas*)

Granados	(from *Album for Piano*)	*Schirmer*

This, one of Granados's best known piano pieces, is equally popular on the guitar – a tone colour
worth bearing in mind while playing. Accompaniments must be kept generally very soft, to let the
melody through without forcing. A sharp eye is needed to spot those hard-to-memorise differences
between similar patterns: bars 15–18 are like 79–82, but not like 27–30 or 91–94. The left hand
slips off the beat at bar 11 (as it does, much much later, in bar 95), and effectively plays three
consecutive semis over barline 11/12. Check that nothing plays on the half bar of 24, nor on the
downbeat of the final bar (96). *Rubato* should be flexible and instinctive: strict tempo throughout
is absolutely the wrong style. If stuck for ideas, try *tenuto*-ing bar 5's first quaver, more so in bar 8;
tenuto bar 13's dotted quaver, and *rit.* in the ⅜ bar; push on to the close of bars 15 and 16, but linger
over 17, and slightly delay the change to major at bar 18. Try an *allargando* through passionate bar
20 (and 21 ad lib.), resuming tempo at bar 22: notice here the p after $f\!f$ and the strictly speaking
ungrammatical minims (shouldn't they be dotted crotchets tied to quavers?) which act as a pedal
mark.

The central *Andante* should never rush, though its overall speed should be faster than
♪ = *Andantino* (⅝) ♪. Note-lengths in the accompaniment are unpredictable but should be
respected rather than tidied up. Bar 41's *meno* could mean less speed or volume, or both. Check
the right-hand thumb in bar 46, which is not the same as bars 40 and 42. Keep the audience
waiting on barline 64/5; crashing into the recapitulation could ruin the mood. Lift carefully at the
very end: the final tenor B should sustain unaccompanied.

Hindemith   **Praeludium (from *Ludus tonalis*)**   *Schott*

This was designed to launch an unbroken 40-minute cycle of *Interludes and Fugues* in all keys, and starts with bravura: later accurate finger-holding and -lifting (bars 16-31) is required, and a grasp of widely varied moods. Try taking the last four demis of bar 1 with the left hand for extra power; note the silence after the third beat of bar 2, and start bar 3 with unhurried *pesante* grace notes. Figuration in bars 4-12 (variously five to ten notes per beat) is pretty fast: small hands may go LL RRRRR LL in bars 5-6, while hands of any size may take bar 6, beat 2 with LL then R123 1235 L, and bar 6, beat 4 with LLL R21235 L. Bar 7's triplet spans two beats and ten notes, and may finish at more than *ff*; grasp bars 8-12 with the right hand compressed into chords. Bar 14/5 should start *espressivo* despite the unfamiliar hamony; notice E♮ in bar 18 and left hand B♮ in bar 31, both misleadingly surrounded by flats. Try the left hand with 1 2 3/51-slide-1 2 3 4 round barline 19/20, and abandon the unstretchable middle C over barline 23/4 rather than smear with pedal. Quavers in bar 33 may go LL RRR twice; start steadily after the pause (learn this in five- or six-note groups) and *crescendo* with the *accelerando*. Bar 37's dotted-crotchet beat equals bar 36's crotchet (imagine continuous $\frac{4}{4}$ time with triplets). The final C♯ is *pp* yet should be heard sustaining after the left hand F♯ has lifted. Ingeniously, Hindemith closes the entire *Ludus Tonalis* cycle with this very same *Praeludium*, but upside-down and backwards!

Joplin   **Fig Leaf Rag (from *Complete Rags*)**   *Schirmer*

'Don't play this piece fast', warns Joplin himself. A quick look almost anywhere in Section B (from bar 53) will endorse him: this chord-filled right-hand part is decidedly tricky, especially in this key, and may need to be mastered as bare octaves first before the middle notes are filled in. Section A is more straightforward, with the 'oom-pah' left hand warmed up by quaver pedals on the 'ooms'. It is fatally easy to rush: keep extremely steady, especially when approaching favourite moments. Accent the tied-over mini-climax chords in bars 7-8 but not the one in bar 11, which leads to a bigger climax a bar later. Notice that bars 33-34 are not in unison. Enjoy the blaring single notes with grace note every two bars from bar 69: a super-high trombone smear is what is wanted here, not clean baroque grace notes. Like many other Joplin rags, this ends in a different key from where it started. Do not assume that a D.C. instruction is missing.

Nos. 3: Sehr langsam, 5: Etwas rasch *and*

Schoenberg   **6: Sehr langsam (from *Sechs Kleine Klavierstücke* op. 19)**   *Universal*

Atonal but not yet serial, these tiny miniatures demand precision and concentration. Schoenberg aimed to distil all the moods of a long piece into the smallest of forms with all repetition and extraneous gesture removed. The punctilious dynamic, articulation and tempo markings seem to leave no room for individual interpretation, but a late-Romantic approach to each swiftly changing mood (expressive phrasing, extreme delicacy, rhythmic life) can humanise the whole.

The very slow no. 3 (say ♩ = 52) starts forcefully but ends *ppp*, with the opening chord transposed down a third. Schoenberg's footnote merely emphasises the printed dynamics (right hand *f*, left hand *pp*), a point therefore worth taking very seriously. Respect the Brahmsian printed left-hand octave fingerings, designed for maximum *legato* without relying on pedal.

Compare the (not always matching) right-hand/left-hand *cresc./dim.* in bar 5. Bar 7 is a mere whimper and the two final chords barely audible as the held G sustains between and beyond them.

The 'rather fast' (*etwas rasch*) no. 5 starts 'tenderly, but full[-toned]'; peaking exactly on bar 4's alto C♯ is quite easy at a suitable three-in-a-bar tempo, like ♪ = 116. Up- and down-stems in bar 3 may imply alto before the comma, treble after it; try finding a different timbre for each voice, say one pedalled, the other not. In writing an impossible *cresc./dim.* on one note or chord, Schoenberg wanted 'a very expressive but gentle *marcato, sforzato*': the one in bar 9 might be achieved by adding a quaver pedal a split second after striking the note. Bar 14's right-hand C♭ is tied to left hand's B♮ without re-striking.

The very slow no. 6, composed in memory of Mahler, features chords based on fourths that Schoenberg had already used in his first Chamber Symphony. Small hands may start by taking the A in the left hand. Bar 4 demands simultaneous release (high voice) and sustain (chord), possible with a middle pedal but tricky without, involving some soundless retaking of the chord then releasing the pedal. Third pedal would also make bars 5–6 possible without blurring, though 'ordinary' sustaining pedal is officially sanctioned. Bar 7 goes 'with very tender expression', bar 8 is 'strictly in time' and the piece, and whole set, ends 'like a breath'. The pause placed carefully between the last two quavers (rather than above one or the other) is an enigma.

Trinity Guildhall publications

All available from your local music retailer

Piano Syllabus 2012-2014

Including Accompanying (Grades 5-8) and Certificates (Solo, Piano Duet, Six Hands)
Free of charge. Also downloadable from www.trinityguildhall.co.uk/music
TG 009821.

Piano Examination Pieces & Exercises 2012-2014

Book only

Initial	TG 009005	Grade 5	TG 009050
Grade 1	TG 009012	Grade 6	TG 009067
Grade 2	TG 009029	Grade 7	TG 009074
Grade 3	TG 009036	Grade 8	TG 009081
Grade 4	TG 009043		

Book & CD

Initial	TG 009098	Grade 5	TG 009142
Grade 1	TG 009104	Grade 6	TG 009159
Grade 2	TG 009111	Grade 7	TG 009166
Grade 3	TG 009128	Grade 8	TG 009173
Grade 4	TG 009135		

CD only

Initial & Grade 1	TG 009746	Grade 5	TG 009784
Grade 2	TG 009753	Grade 6	TG 009791
Grade 3	TG 009760	Grade 7	TG 009807
Grade 4	TG 009777	Grade 8	TG 009814

Teaching Notes 2012-2014

Initial-Grade 8   TG 009227

Piano Scales & Arpeggios

Initial-Grade 5   TG 006103
Grades 6-8   TG 006110

Piano Sound at Sight (2nd series)

Book 1 (Initial-Grade 2)	TG 009180	Book 3 (Grades 5-6)	TG 009203
Book 2 (Grades 3-4)	TG 009197	Book 4 (Grades 7-8)	TG 009210

Piano Sound at Sight (original series)

Book 1 (Initial-Grade 2)	TCL 002648	Book 3 (Grades 6-8)	TCL 002679
Book 2 (Grades 3-5)	TCL 002655		

RED MEAT

Also by Max Cannon:

a collection of RED MEAT cartoons

MORE
RED MEAT

the second collection of RED MEAT cartoons

from the secret files of Max Cannon

BOXTREE

First published 1998 by St. Martin's Press, New York

First published in Great Britain 1999 by Boxtree
an imprint of Macmillan Publishers Ltd
25 Eccleston Place London SW1W 9NF
and Basingstoke

Associated companies throughout the world

ISBN 0 7522 1708 9

9 8 7 6 5 4 3 2 1

A CIP catalogue record for this book is available from the British Library.

Printed and bound in Great Britain by The Bath Press, Bath.

Visit the official **RED MEAT** website at www.redmeat.com

This book is respectfully dedicated to all
the young men and women who selflessly
went to their rooms without any dinner,
so that inappropriate comedy might live.

©1998 MAX CANNON WWW.REDMEAT.COM

7

rotten egg incubator

I got me a mail-order certificate that says I'm a real minister, and it cost me only ten bucks.

I ain't married no people yet, but I practiced on some pigeons in the park the other day.

Now God is gonna kill me for sure.

©1998 MAX CANNON WWW.REDMEAT.COM

9

11

©1998 MAX CANNON   WWW.REDMEAT.COM

13

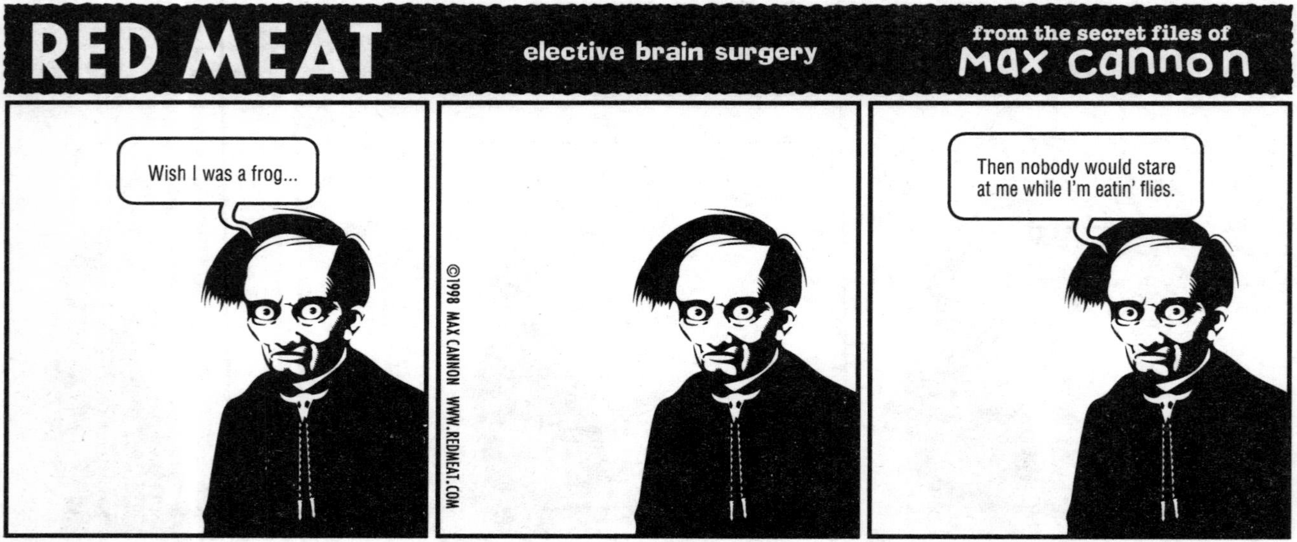
RED MEAT
elective brain surgery
from the secret files of
max cannon
Wish I was a frog...
©1998 MAX CANNON WWW.REDMEAT.COM
Then nobody would stare at me while I'm eatin' flies.

17

19

Milkman Dan, my bike is broke. Will you help me fix it?

I'd like to Karen, but I'm afraid I can't. The regulations prohibit it.

You're lyin'. There aren't no regulations.

I'll let you in on a little secret, Karen. You see, Milkman Dan, like most adults, lies to kids whenever he feels like it. And, like it or not, there's precious little you can do about it.

You're a dumb dodo-bird.

©1998 MAX CANNON WWW.REDMEAT.COM

I wish I could find some of those rubber tips that you put on the ends of chair legs.

Oh yeah...beautiful, curvaceous, naughty little brown rubber tips.

22

well, if the turkey is in the highchair, where's the baby?

Dear Lord, we thank you for this meal we are about to eat—which I, incidentally, paid for—and it's not like I expect any kind of gratitude for the sacrifices I make for this family on an excruciatingly regular basis...

©1998 MAX CANNON WWW.REDMEAT.COM

All I ask is that you smite my children (who have all grudgingly attended this family gathering) with a hideous and incurable pox that they might also know what it means to truly suffer as I have.

Way to go, Dad. I was gonna try to be cool for one night, but screw it...you suck, man!

Let him be the first afflicted, Lord.

25

26

28

This guy I knew lost all his teeth and he didn't have no money to buy dentures, so he figured out a cheap way to make his own fake teeth.

He'd buy a box of peppermint Chiclets every day and push 'em into the empty sockets in his gums. It only cost him thirty-five cents a day and they looked all perfect and white.

Except on holidays though, when he would buy the fruit-flavored kind with all the colors.

29

30

31

©1998 MAX CANNON

WWW.REDMEAT.COM

32

33

Here's some advice to young folks who are in love. If you are gonna carve both your initials with a plus sign and a heart around it, make sure you do it on a tree.

©1998 MAX CANNON WWW.REDMEAT.COM

And also, make sure that tree is not a fat lady in a brown dress.

34

36

milk toast for pantywaists

Ted, sweetheart...could you please go and smoke that smelly cigar out on the porch?

Sorry honey, but no can do. It's all part of my brand new macho image.

You're just going to have to get used to having a real man around the house.

©1998 MAX CANNON WWW.REDMEAT.COM

Well...I guess that means there's really no point in asking you to take the "naked lady" mudflaps off of the station wagon.

No dice, sweets. Those babies are testosterone city.

38

40

RED MEAT

humor so badly disfigured, that it could only be identified from its dental records

from the secret files of
Max cannon

One of the guys was telling me that before you had the tobacco shop you used to run some kind of zoo. Is that really true, Wally?

Yes, it is.

It was a petting zoo, you know...for kids. I did a darn good business for the first couple of years, but then things got pretty tough.

Toward the end, I was forced to rent the animals out to sailors for private parties and that kind of thing. Know what I mean?

That was you?

41

43

RED MEAT

the unmistakable splatter of rotten melons

from the secret files of

Max cannon

Honey...wake up. You were having a bad dream.

Mmph...oh Ted, I was having an awful dream that I was in a prison.

I know that dream. Women incarcerated under inhuman conditions. Forced to wear only ultra-short cutoff bluejeans and denim halter tops... all the time suffering the most unspeakable indignities at the hands of their sadistic captors.

©1998 MAX CANNON

And of course, the grand finale...a sweaty catfight breaks out in the cell block and the guards have to turn the fire hoses on the prisoners to break it up.

You're a very sick man, Ted.

WWW.REDMEAT.COM

44

squirming grubs in the
dank dirt of destiny

from the secret files of
Max cannon

My god, Ted. Are you going to wear that satin wrestling mask to bed again tonight?

Yes I am, honey.

I had fun last night, so I thought we'd do it again.

Alright, but let's establish a few ground rules: standard ten-count on the pin, no headlocks, and you leave your toolbelt on the bedstand.

Fair enough.

the business side of the doublewide

I took it easy today. I just pretty much laid around in my underwear all day.

Got kicked out of quite a few places, though.

©1998 MAX CANNON WWW.REDMEAT.COM

48

49

RED MEAT

the official pace car of the apocalypse

from the secret files of
Max Cannon

I don't get it, Ted...why were the people of this town so afraid of me that they had to drive me out like some awful monster?

Well John, you were a convenient scapegoat for our narrow-minded fear of that which is different from ourselves. It was just instinct.

©1998 MAX CANNON WWW.REDMEAT.COM

So the ritual livestock mutilations I did had nothing to do with it?

Get real John, we all have our little "episodes."

50

The flies in my apartment are drivin' me crazy...there's a million of 'em.

©1998 MAX CANNON WWW.REDMEAT.COM

I should probably clean up the kitchen.

I guess it's time to bury Aunt Sally, too.

51

RED MEAT something strange in the squirt gun from the secret files of **Max Cannon**

Sweetheart, why are you lying on the floor without any clothes on?

I'm sorry, honey...

I ate way too much at dinner, and I'm just trying to get comfortable.

©1998 MAX CANNON

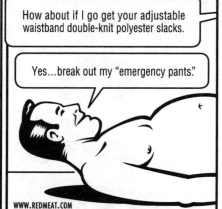

How about if I go get your adjustable waistband double-knit polyester slacks.

Yes...break out my "emergency pants."

WWW.REDMEAT.COM

52

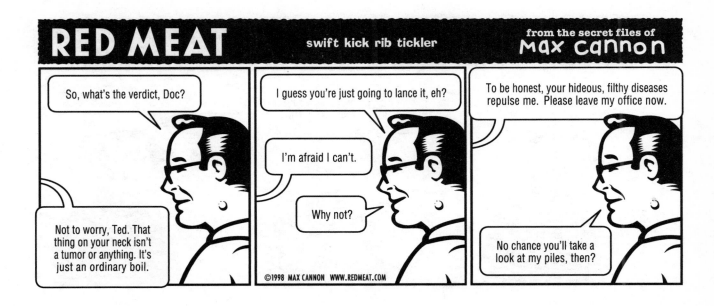

53

sucker punch in the gut bucket

The other day, there was this loud argument out in the hall between these two guys in my apartment building while I was tryin' to sleep.

I went out there and told 'em that they'd better knock it off or I was gonna have to use some "Kung Fu." That scared 'em off.

Plus, I was totally nekkid and I had a gun.

54

55

RED MEAT

frying bacon in the bedpan

from the secret files of
Max Cannon

It's true…no man is an island.

But if you take a bunch of dead guys and tie 'em together, they make a pretty good raft.

RED MEAT

non-prescription pep remedy

from the secret files of
Max Cannon

Say, Mr. Postman...those are some mighty cute shorts you're wearing, but why do you guys all sport those ugly dark knee socks?

You ladies at the dairy wouldn't understand. These shorts allow for total leg mobility, while the socks protect shins against teeth marks.

From dogs?

No...from humans. You see, when you're crushing a man's windpipe with your knee, you can be sure he will attempt to bite you.

I've noticed that.

©1998 MAX CANNON

WWW.REDMEAT.COM

57

RED MEAT

ball bearings in the butter tub

from the secret files of
Max Cannon

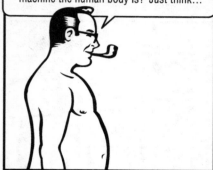

Honey...have you ever stopped to ponder what a marvelously complex and sublime machine the human body is? Just think...

Its tiniest components are more advanced than the most powerful computer. Every cell capable of storing the blueprint for life.

I don't care what you say, Ted. You're not getting me to come in there to "check out" your "chiseled Greco-Roman butt" again.

©1998 MAX CANNON WWW.REDMEAT.COM

58

RED MEAT

naptime on the railroad tracks

from the secret files of
Max Cannon

You know, Karen, a little child like yourself shouldn't be playing so far away from home.

I'm not very far away. My house is only one street away from here.

Yes, only one street away…but that would give your mom ample time to pack up a few things and move away to a brand new life, unburdened by the weight of motherhood.

She wouldn't do that.

©1998 MAX CANNON

Don't take it so hard, little lady. Why, I bet you could keep yourself alive for a couple of weeks at least by eating out of garbage cans and sleeping in storm drains at night.

You're lyin', Milkman Dan, and you'd better shut up!

If you hurry, you might still be able to catch her.

WWW.REDMEAT.COM

RED MEAT

spinning turrets of pure spite

from the secret files of

Max Cannon

I took some stuff down to the recycling place today, but they only took the styrofoam boxes.

©1998 MAX CANNON WWW.REDMEAT.COM

I guess they don't recycle pigeons.

60

When I was ten, my mother put this painting of a chihuahua with big scary eyes up in my bedroom, and I begged her to take it down.

She said she couldn't...or the devil clown under my bed would kill her.

©1998 MAX CANNON WWW.REDMEAT.COM

62

You know Johnny, you're the best salesman I've ever had working for me. In fact, the store is more successful than ever before.

That's great, Vern.

I'm also in your debt for administering CPR to me last week when I had the heart attack, but unfortunately, I still have to let you go.

B-but why...?

©1998 MAX CANNON WWW.REDMEAT.COM

Because when you talk, little pools of spittle foam form at the corners of your mouth...and it drives me up the wall.

I can wipe, sir.

Hey Ted, my wife and I are getting rid of some nasty-ass old furniture. We were wondering if you might want any of it.

I don't mean to be rude…but why would I want some "nasty-ass old furniture," Don?

I don't know…maybe it'll match the nasty-ass lime green color you painted your house.

©1998 MAX CANNON

Oh. So, in this case, "nasty-ass" would be a good thing, then…?

WWW.REDMEAT.COM

64

65

66

67

bitter mug of nether nog

Son...your mother tells me you don't believe in Santa Claus. Is that true?

That's right.

©1998 MAX CANNON WWW.REDMEAT.COM

I'm not going to pretend I believe that junk, just because it makes you and mom happy.

Welcome to adulthood, son. Hope you enjoy playing with pants and socks, because that's all you'll be getting as presents from now on.

scabrous skivvy scrapings

from the secret files of
Max Cannon

I asked my landlady how old she is, and she wouldn't tell me. "That's okay," I says...

"I'll just wait until you go to sleep tonight... then I'll cut you in half and count the rings."

©1998 MAX CANNON WWW.REDMEAT.COM

The cops didn't think it was funny, neither.

RED MEAT

shipwrecked voyage of discovery

from the secret files of
Max Cannon

You know, Karen, before I became a milk man, I was a high school science teacher for many years...until the district fired me.

How come you got fired?

Because of the rabbits. You see, one of my favorite in-class demonstrations every year was to dip live rabbits in liquid nitrogen, then give them a good whack on the counter top.

What happened, then?

They were so remarkably frozen that they'd shatter like glass.

That's awful! You're mean, Milkman Dan!

Hmm...I guess you don't want to hear about the time I imploded kittens in a vacuum tube, then?

WWW.REDMEAT.COM

71

Every time I go to the diner, I grab a handful of them little jellies out of the basket and take 'em home with me.

Yesterday, I took all them little jellies out of my cupboard and counted 'em…I got more than twenny-four thousand of 'em.

©1998 MAX CANNON WWW.REDMEAT.COM

Bow down before the "king of jellies."

72

RED MEAT

bendy-straw for spitoon guzzlers

Good golly boy, I'll tell you what…there's sure nothin' that tastes as right as that first dang ol' cigarette as the sun's a'pokin' up.

But hell's bells, it surely does get a might lonesome around here sometimes. Shoot, I'd give my best heifer for some company.

Well…I reckon I can always go pick some more methamphetamine out'a the chicken feed, so's them crazy voices'll start talkin'.

©1998 MAX CANNON WWW.REDMEAT.COM

73

74

75

half-hearted sips from the sagging udder of boredom

from the secret files of
Max Cannon

A few years ago, I used to sweep the floors at this country and western bar. There was this big glass aquarium behind the bar that was full of a bunch of real live rattlesnakes.

Part of my job was to feed them snakes two times a week. But the owner fired me when they all went crazy and got loose.

I probably shouldn't of gave them snakes candy bars.

77

You know, Ted...I thought retirement would be kind of pleasant after running a business for forty years, but it's more like a slow death.

I'm sorry to hear that, Wally. Maybe you're not used to having time on your hands. Do you have any hobbies or anything like that?

Hmm...

©1998 MAX CANNON   WWW.REDMEAT.COM

Does a beard count as a hobby?

Hoo-boy. You're a dead man.

78

dump truck motorcade

from the secret files of
Max cannon

My neck is stiff 'cause I slept on it funny.

If you call layin' unconscious in a garbage can all night "funny."

impromptu saliva bath

The guy who lives in the apartment next door to me is kind of a wierdo.

©1998 MAX CANNON WWW.REDMEAT.COM

He was in the war, and I guess it made him crazy because he's always nervous and he screams every time he hears a loud noise.

Too bad…because I got a lot of hammering to catch up on.

82

83

RED MEAT

snapped axle on the wonder wagon

from the secret files of
Max Cannon

84

RED MEAT the flat tire on your inner journey

Hi there, Ted...do you have an extra ventriloquist dummy I can borrow?

That's a strange thing to ask me for, Don. What makes you think I even have one?

©1998 MAX CANNON WWW.REDMEAT.COM

Don't mess around with me, man. Do you have an extra one or not?

Well, yeah...I guess so.

Damn...my wife was right. White people really do have ventriloquist dummies.

I'd..uh...appreciate it if you'd keep this to yourself, Don.

85

I got a bunch of ideas for movies they could make. For one of them, this guy gets all shot up by some crooks, and the only part of him the doctors can save is his spine.

©1998 MAX CANNON www.REDMEAT.COM

So the spine has to go and get revenge on the crooks. It's called "Spinal Justice."

Of course, they'd have to figure out a good special effects way so's the spine could hold a flame-thrower.

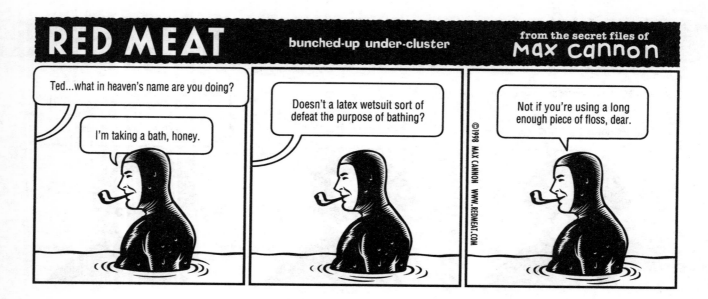

88

89

high-strung herald of the haphazard from the secret files of Max Cannon

Hey there, Wally...whaddaya know?

≋ BE-E-E-E-L-L-LCH!! ≋

Judging from the smell of that, I'd say you know of a pretty good place to get rancid nine-year-old corn dogs.

90

91

Look, Milkman Dan...this is absolutely the last time I'm going to talk to you about the unacceptable levels of bottle breakage on your delivery route. Next time you're fired.

But, sir...

It's like I told you last week...I just need a little time to get the hang of that new truck-mounted "milk catapult" I invented.

I have an idea...

©1998 MAX CANNON

How about if you just walk up to the porch and set the milk down like a normal person?

Oh come on now, sir...I'm usually far too drunk to walk.

WWW.REDMEAT.COM

92

My poor cat died a couple days ago from chewin' on an electrical cord.

©1998 MAX CANNON WWW.REDMEAT.COM

Kind of a stupid thing to do...

Considerin' as it was the only thing holdin' her on to that helicopter blade.

93

94

RED MEAT

bite-mark festoonery

from the secret files of
Max Cannon

A couple days ago my girlfriend got fired from her new job, so I thought I'd try to cheer her up. Now she's all mad at me.

I don't get it...

That chimp was alive when I put it in her bedroom closet.

95

flamenco-style fingernail removal

Coach...I-I think I broke my leg. Is it okay if I sit out the rest of the game?

Good idea.

Why don't we all just quit...you send the rest of the team home, and I'll go down to the principal's office and turn in my resignation.

©1998 MAX CANNON WWW.REDMEAT.COM

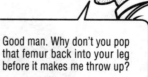

I get the point, Coach. I guess I should finish out the game.

Good man. Why don't you pop that femur back into your leg before it makes me throw up?

96

RED MEAT
hell-bent for naugahyde
from the secret files of
Max Cannon
Ted...are you going hunting again today?
That's right, dear. Why?
I can't understand what you get out of it. Don't you ever feel like it's wrong to kill poor, defenseless animals for kicks?
©1998 MAX CANNON WWW.REDMEAT.COM
I'd hardly call a chihuahua defenseless, sweetheart. It may be small in size, but it can tear a man's sock right off his foot.

massive otter spill at the oil refinery

Ted, are you still in the bath tub? You've been sitting alone in there for two hours.

Oh, I'm not alone. I've got over a hundred live goldfish in here with me, also. I'm attempting to teach them our language.

That's pointless. Fish don't have any vocal cords.

I'm well aware of that, sweetheart. I was referring to the "international language."

pinking shear tracheotomy

If I could be somebody besides myself, I would like to be Tarzan.

©1998 MAX CANNON WWW.REDMEAT.COM

Then maybe the cops would think twice about arresting me for being up in a tree at the park, butt-nekkid and screaming.

99

pungent unguent for stump-itch

Well, son...time to hit the sleeping bags. It's been a long day in the great outdoors.

But, Dad...it's startin' to rain.

That's not rain, it's bat urine. These night skies are teeming with millions of bats.

Bats...?! What if they bite us?

©1998 MAX CANNON WWW.REDMEAT.COM

Don't worry, they won't fly down here... those bats are just as afraid of the giant mulch ticks and pine leeches as we are.

Dad...I don't like camping.

No time for whining, son. We still have to check our sleeping bags for spiders.

100

101

102

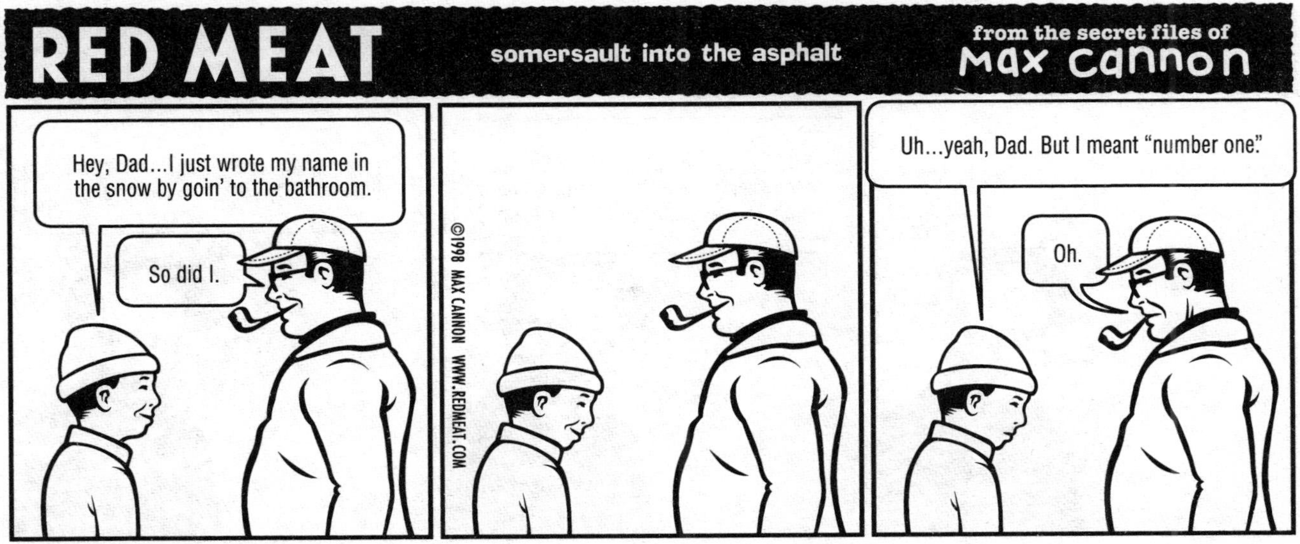

RED MEAT

somersault into the asphalt

from the secret files of Max Cannon

I took my grandmother to the park today, 'cause she likes to go feed the pigeons.

©1998 MAX CANNON WWW.REDMEAT.COM

She fed them pigeons for awhile, but I took her home after I seen that them birds started squirtin' out white foam.

I don't know what pigeons usually eat, but I'm pretty sure it ain't alka seltzer.

104

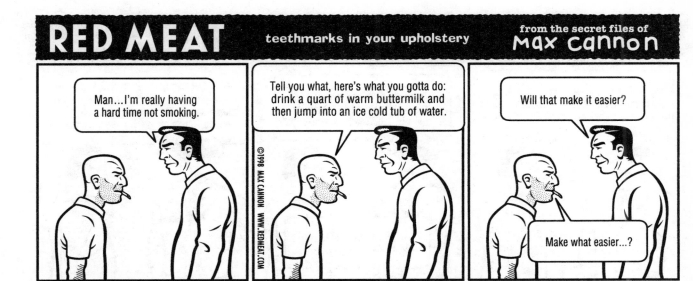

105

You know, Dan...you might want to be careful. There've been a few muggings around the neighborhood this month.

I know, but I'm not too worried. You see, I carry a little something I like to call "The Peacemaker."

Hmm. I never figured you for the type to carry a gun.

I don't...I was referring to your son. If I'm attacked, I just hold him up in front of me like a shield...his screams eventually draw enough attention to scare the mugger off.

©1998 MAX CANNON WWW.REDMEAT.COM

106

quarter-ton bumpercar

Can you help me? I'm a magic talking hand puppet from the Neighborhood of Pretend, and I seem to have lost my way back home.

©1998 MAX CANNON WWW.REDMEAT.COM

PTUI!

I'm just going to go ahead and assume that's "magic find-your-way-home" spit.

I got this job doin' face painting on kids at the street fair, but the guy who owns the booth fired me after only one day.

He shouldnt've yelled at me, though. I mean, he told me I could paint them little kids' faces any way I wanted to.

©1998 MAX CANNON   WWW.REDMEAT.COM

Still...I guess I prob'ly should have brought more colors of spray paint than just brown.

109

Honey, I'm having a problem at work. The boss has been making lewd sexual advances toward me. He also touches me...sometimes several times a day, in inappropriate ways.

Gee, sweetheart...as of an hour ago at lunchtime, you were self-employed.

So you see the difficult predicament that I'm in. Still, I can't help but think I'm somehow responsible. Just look at what I'm wearing... it's a veritable carnival of lurid man-flesh.

If you don't put your pants back on and go back to work, I'll touch you in some inappropriate ways with a frying pan.

110

THE
FOURTH
REICH

and Operation Eclipse

PATRICK DELAFORCE

FONTHILL

Fonthill Media Language Policy

Fonthill Media publishes in the international English language market. One language edition is published worldwide. As there are minor differences in spelling and presentation, especially with regard to American English and British English, a policy is necessary to define which form of English to use. The Fonthill Policy is to use the form of English native to the author. Patrick Delaforce was born and educated in England and now lives at Brighton therefore British English has been adopted in this publication.

Fonthill Media Limited
Fonthill Media LLC
www.fonthillmedia.com
office@fonthillmedia.com

First published in the United Kingdom and the
United States of America 2015

British Library Cataloguing in Publication Data:
A catalogue record for this book is available from the British Library

Copyright © Patrick Delaforce 2015

ISBN 978-1-78155-400-5

Typeset in Sabon 10.5/14
Printed in the USA

MIX
Paper from
responsible sources
FSC® C011935

THE
FOURTH
REICH
and Operation Eclipse

Contents

Foreword

The Fourth Reich and Operation Eclipse is the last book of a trilogy. *Monty's Rhine Adventure* and *Invasion of Hitler's Third Reich* were the first two, published by Fonthill Media.

In the first book Patrick Delaforce fought and was wounded in Holland, and in the second book he was wounded on the banks of the River Elbe. In this book the division in which he fought, 11th (Black Bull) Armoured Division corralled the Fourth Reich in Flensburg and then, when four key parts of Operation Eclipse had gone to plan, their Hussar Comet tanks and the armoured infantry of 1st Herefords and 1st Cheshires completed the capture of the Fourth Reich along with many of Hitler's élite.

It was absolutely vital in May 1945 that the appalling Reichministers of Norway, with 400,000 undefeated troops, Denmark, with over 200,000 undefeated troops, the malevolent German governors of the Netherlands, with 130,000 troops including Dutch SS, plus the great city of Hamburg should surrender to the British and not prolong the war by another three or four months with consequent heavy casualties. Adolf Hitler's Berlin bunker edict, Operation Nero, meant turning all the surviving pieces of his dying Third Reich into a wasteland—absolute Armageddon.

Delaforce also spent three weeks in Flensburg and, aged 21, was a judge/jurist for the regional War Crimes Tribunals of Hamburg in 1945 and Oldenburg in 1946 and witnessed Mr Alfred Pierrepoint hanging 13 war criminals in Hameln in December 1945.

CHAPTER 1

Planning the End of the Third Reich

It is doubtful whether the great commanders of the past, Julius Caesar, Marlborough, Wellington, Napoleon, and certainly not Adolf Hitler, thought through and planned thoroughly in great detail how the resulting peace might be won after their many shattering victories.

> War claims the lion's share of a government's attention and resources. Its demands are immediate, involving life and death, victory and defeat. Peace may be only a *dimly* perceived destination, lacking immediacy, low on the list of priorities. Nonetheless, inadequate preparation for the peace may jeopardise the victory gained by arms.

So wrote Basil Liddell Hart, the famous war historian of a bygone era. Carl von Clausewitz, the great Prussian thinker, wrote:

> The political object is the goal, war is the means of reaching it and means can never be considered in isolation from their purpose.

And later Liddell Hart expanded his theme:

> The object of war is to attain a *better* peace. Hence it is essential to conduct war with constant regard to the peace you desire. If you concentrate exclusively on victory with no thought for the after-effect, you may be too exhausted to profit by the peace [at the end of the Second World War, the UK was exhausted and bankrupt] while it is almost certain that the peace will be a bad one, containing the germs of another war [exactly as happened immediately after the end of the Great War]. Statesmen bear responsibility never to lose sight of the post-war prospect in chasing the 'image of victory'.

The Battle for Britain, mainly fought in the air, helped defeat Hitler's Operation Sealion. Goering's Luftwaffe had failed to destroy the RAF and bombed all the main cities—the Baedecker raids—instead. Hitler's army and navy showed no enthusiasm, so Barbarossa was unleashed and Britain breathed again.

Winston Churchill wrote in October 1941:

> We were still hard-pressed and our only ally Russia seemed near to defeat. Nevertheless I had resolved to prepare for an invasion of the Continent when the tide should turn. First we had to increase the intensity and scope of our raids and then translate all this experience into something much more massive. To mount a successful invasion from the United Kingdom new engines of war must be contrived and developed, the three fighting services must be trained to plan and fight as one team, supported by the industry of the nation and the whole island converted into an armed camp for launching the greatest seaborne assault of all time.

This assault came to pass three years later—[Operations Neptune and Overlord].

Hitler had declared to the German people 15 weeks into Barbarossa, on 3 October 1940, 'The final drive for Moscow is the beginning of the last great decisive battle of the war'. So certain was he of victory that he had ordered the Army High Command to disband 40 infantry divisions and return their ranks to industry!

In May 1942 Churchill set up the 'Combined Commanders' to plan for new offensive tactics with Earl Mountbatten in charge, promoted to Vice-Admiral. Combined raids on Norway, Bruneval, St Nazaire and the costly defeat at Dieppe in August 1942 followed. But major Anglo-American amphibious assaults were more successful in the North African and Mediterranean offensives.

In January 1943 Lieutenant-General Frederick Morgan, Chief of Staff, Supreme Commander (COSSAC), was initially responsible for three tasks:

a) Plan deception operations designed to reduce pressure on the Soviets by pinning the maximum number of German divisions in the West. For most of the war Hitler was convinced that Britain would launch attacks, even invade Norway, and accordingly kept there almost half a million troops (submarine bases, aircraft bases and a dozen harbour/port garrisons). From the initial COSSAC plans emerged Operation Solitude and Operation Fortress.

b) Plan the invasion of Europe, the basis for Neptune and Overlord.

c) Plans for an immediate return to the continent in case German resistance unexpectedly ended. Operation Rutter, then Jubilee in August 1942 followed the brilliant and audacious April raid on St Nazaire. These brave efforts worried the German defenders in France and perhaps proved to Stalin that the Allies were trying to help.

At that stage Morgan judged 'the sum total of all the various factors now operating cannot be far off from that of the factors which caused the [Great War] collapse in 1918'. But he received no guidance. His committees operated in a vacuum. No civil affairs structure existed in the USA or UK—the post-war world was largely unexplored territory.

A draft of Operation Rankin appeared for the Quebec Conference of August 1943 and was submitted to Churchill and Roosevelt. It was a plan 'to occupy, as rapidly as possible, appropriate areas from which we can take steps to enforce the terms of unconditional surrender imposed by the Allied Government on Germany and in addition to carry out the rehabilitation of the liberated countries'. Rankin tried to estimate the number of divisions necessary to carry out the occupation of identified strategic areas. The specified spheres of responsibility—British in the Netherlands (1), Denmark (2), the Ruhr (6), the Rhine valley (11), NW Germany (5)—totalled 25. The Americans would be responsible in Belgium, France, Luxembourg, and the Rhine valley, south of Dusseldorf (the ports of Bremen or Hamburg would be utilised by the US and UK respectively, plus Antwerp). The primary tasks would be disarmament of German troops, establishment of military government in the occupied areas in order to preserve law and order and to ensure that the Force Commanders' instructions in regard to security disarmament were all carried out. It was urgent for a Civil Affairs staff to be appointed to carry out the plans. Rankin was divided into three 'cases': 'A). A rapid German collapse and then early execution of Overlord. B). Contraction of German forces into pre-war borders. C). Unconditional surrender.' The planners thought Rankin C was the most likely. Thus the seizure of all airbases in France was vital to support future operations. Next, the occupation of the Siegfried Line. Finally, Allied forces would occupy designated areas of Germany including Berlin in order to establish control at the earliest possible moment over the industrial, political and communication centre of Germany. Only British and American zones of occupation were specified, side-lining the issue of Stalin's intentions and success on the Eastern Front.

Rankin C was designed for an unopposed movement into Germany. The plans failed to specify what to do with the German armed forces after disarmament, how to treat German police and paramilitary forces, repatriation of Allied prisoners of war (POW) and displaced personnel (DPs).

In January 1944 Major General C. A. West, Deputy G 3 of COSSAC, noted, 'We cannot wait for policy to be laid down by the United Nations. Need for studies on Armistice terms, sanctions, disarmament, DPs, POWs, martial law, disposal of captured war material, co-ordination of movement and transport.' By April 1944 there were no fewer than 72 staff studies under way for the post-conflict subjects. [CCS/551 vested the Commander's authority and responsibility for governing occupied territories.]

In July 1944 after the success of the D-Day landings, the first part of Overlord, a new post-war plan called Talisman dealt with German surrender, disarmament of German forces in the West, occupation of strategic areas in Germany, established conditions under which United Nations agencies, such as UNRRA, could assist in the relief and rehabilitation of the liberated countries, and de-nazification through counter-intelligence operations. Talisman assumed that military occupation would be a brief interlude prior to civil control. In August 1944 SHAEF, the final successor to COSSAC, outlined a plan that needed 39⅔ divisions, increased from 25. Talisman 2 appeared and was approved at the Second Quebec Conference in September 1944, but on 30 October the Talisman codeword was compromised and planning reverted to Eclipse.

SHAEF published the Eclipse Outline Plan on 10 November 1944, to take effect when Overlord was accomplished. It included surrender procedures, labour policies, handling POWs and DPs, disarming German armed forces and guidance for military government. Some of the key Eclipse files can be seen at the National Archives at Kew as WO 219/2460:WO 219/2461: WO 219/2544.

Recently we have seen what happened at the end of the successful war to topple the dictator in Iraq and the near civil war between Shia and Sunni *jihadists*. Almost certainly the same tragic sequence will follow in Afghanistan, when the American and British forces retreat hoping against hope that the Taliban will refrain from their usual terrible mayhem....

But the joint senior Allied planners in the Second World War pre-thought and pre-planned the end of the huge, complicated battle ground in Europe and the ultimate demise of the Third Reich. And it all went according to plan, despite the increasing animosity of the Soviets.

The top-secret Operation Eclipse is rarely mentioned in post-war histories, none of the great commanders nor the great military historians have written about it, apart from Alan Moorehead who used it as a title for his marvellous wartime reports.

It was a large amorphous umbrella and encompassed the end game which started on Victory in Europe Day in early May 1945. 500 copies of the Eclipse plan were sent to SHAEF missions in France, Holland, Belgium and Norway, and the majority to Sixth, Twelfth and Twenty-First Army Groups. It was signed and sent by Lt General W. B. Smith, Chief of Staff US Army, and included in great detail the probable form of the German collapse, the definition of zones of occupation, but excluded two areas. In Norway the first plan was Operation Apostle (German surrender) or Aladdin (German withdrawal). If in the event it was not Aladdin, then Apostle would be phased into Eclipse. In the Channel Islands the initial Operation Nest Egg would be blended into Eclipse. And, most importantly, the race to reach the Baltic before the Russian army was an Eclipse operation. Twenty-First Army Group under Field Marshal Bernard Montgomery would be responsible for the British zone and the US Sixth and Twelfth Army Groups would be responsible for the American zone.

The Yalta Conference in January 1945 agreed the post-war policy in Eclipse: 'inflexible purpose to destroy German militarism and Nazism and to ensure that Germany will *never* be able to disturb the peace of the world ... and supervise complete disarmament of Germany and extract reparations.'

CHAPTER 2

The Other Side of the Hill

All planning for the peace that might emerge in the future assumed that Overlord would be completely successful and that Stalin's Cossacks could continue their powerful drives towards Berlin. Tacitly everything was done to supply armaments to the Russians. Stalin might have made peace overtures to Hitler, which, if accepted might have prolonged the war by several years.

Bletchley Park closely monitored the thousands of daily messages sent by the German Enigma coding machines, but once the Allies had total command in Normandy, the greatest impediment for the Ultra organisation came from the use of telephones. But two Ultra decrypts on 22 June 1944 between Adolf Hitler and General von Schlieben authorised the latter to defend Cherbourg: '... your duty to defend the last pill-box and to leave the enemy not a harbour but a field of devastation ...' Ultra continued to produce invaluable information about Wehrmacht plans and intentions. On 3 August a vital order to General von Kluge from Hitler was picked up and a complete dialogue followed.

What Ultra could not eavesdrop on was the Hitler conference with three of his senior generals on 31 August shortly after his armies had suffered 400,000 casualties, killed, wounded and taken prisoner, and lost 2,200 AFVs, 2,200 vehicles and 1,500 field guns.

General de Gaulle was striding majestically down the Champs Elysées in Paris, whilst General Eisenhower's HQ at SHAEF on 26 August stated: 'Two and a half months of bitter fighting ... have brought an end of the war in Europe within sight, almost within reach.' And General Eisenhower said to Winston Churchill: 'By Christmas we shall be on the Rhine.' Hostages to fortune ...

Hitler declared:

The time hasn't come for a political decision. It is childish and naïve to expect that at a moment of grave military defeats the moment for favourable political dealings has come. Such moments come when you are having successes ... But the time will come when the tensions between the Allies will become so great that the break will occur. All the coalitions have disintegrated in history sooner or later. The only thing is to wait for the right moment, no matter how hard it is. Since the year 1941 it has been my task not to lose my nerve, under any circumstances; instead, whenever there is a collapse, my task has been to find a way out and a remedy in order to restore the situation. I really think one cannot imagine a worse crisis than the one we had in the east this year. When Field Marshal Model came the Army group centre was nothing but a hole.

I think it's pretty obvious that this war is no pleasure for me. For five years I have been separated from the world. I haven't been to the theatre. I haven't heard a concert and I haven't seen a film. I live only for the purpose of leading this fight, because I know if there is not an iron will behind it this battle cannot be won....

If necessary we'll fight on the Rhine. It doesn't make any difference. *Under all circumstances* we will continue this battle until as Frederick the Great said, one of our damned enemies gets too tired to fight any more. We'll fight until we get a peace which secures the life of the German nation for the next 50 or 100 years, and which, above all does not besmirch our honour a second time, as happened in 1918....

Things could have turned out differently. If my life had been ended [on 20 July] I think I can say that for me personally it would only have been a release from worry, sleepless nights, and a great nervous suffering. I am grateful to Destiny for letting me live....

So Hitler revitalised all his comrades in arms—Goering, Himmler, Goebbels, Bormann, even Admiral Doenitz, an outsider to the Berlin group.

Joseph Goebbels closed theatres, cabarets, drama schools and disbanded all orchestras except those needed for radio broadcasting. Only scientific, technical, school books and specific political works could continue to be published. The working week was extended to 60 hours. Many citizens were forced to dig trenches for defence of towns and air raid. Originally the Nazi state specifically excluded women from politics, from the army and from the administration of justice, but from 1936 the *Bund Deutscher Madel*, the girls' Hitler Youth Movement, became popular, and three years later a year's labour service for *all* unmarried and under-25-year-old women was compulsory. By the end of the war seven and a half million girls were thus mobilised. They worked on the farms, in auxiliary military units, signals, AA units or services office work. The other side of the coin was that by late 1944 there were four concentration camps for women: Moringen, Lichtenburg, Ravensbrück and Bergen-Belsen.

On 3 September 1944 Field Marshal Walter Model, the 'Führer's fireman', now C-in-C of Army Group B, issued an order to his men:

> We have lost a battle, but I tell you—we shall still win this war. I cannot say more now although I know that there are many questions burning on the lips of every soldier … do not allow your faith in Germany's future to be shaken … This hour will separate the real men from the weaklings.

Model hoped that Hitler's secret weapons of new, more powerful rockets and jet aircraft might avert defeat. By March 1945 over 10,000 V-1 flying bombs had been fired, half to the London area, half to Antwerp, causing 24,000 casualties. The V-2 rockets, 1,050 by 27 March 1945, fell in southern England, killing 2,700 Londoners.

Hitler received some unexpected help from the Allies. In September 1944 Henry Morgenthau, the secretary of the United States Treasury drew up a plan which was rashly circulated quite widely. On their defeat the Third Reich would have its industrial base and capabilities destroyed and instead there would be an agricultural economy. It was proposed at the Quebec Conference and gave Joseph Goebbels the opportunity to present it in Germany as unconditional surrender. Goebbels declared that the Allies intended the extermination of a considerable proportion of the German people. Berlin Radio proclaimed 'The Jew Morgenthau sings the same tune as the Jews in the Kremlin.' In their journals both Albert Speer and Admiral Doenitz mention how the Morgenthau Plan frightened the German people so that there seemed no alternative but to continue to fight.

Thanks to Speer, German armaments production had not been crippled by the Allied bombing intensity. Factories had been dispersed or built underground, so supplies of Luftwaffe fighter planes and assault

SP guns and the sinews of war appeared miraculously. The emergence of tens of thousands of lethal one-shot Panzerfaust, hand-held anti-AFV bazookas, gave the Allies a difficult time. Very young Hitler Youth schoolboys could destroy Sherman or Comet tanks at close quarters—and did.

Colonel-General Heinz Guderian, Chief-of-Staff OKW (High Command of the German Armed Forces) reported to his post-war Seventh US Army interrogators, that after the 20 July 1944 bomb conspiracy:

> Hitler's mistrust now reached extremes and the miracle of his survival gave him greater faith than ever in his mission. He shut himself up in his bunker, engaged in no further private talks and had every word of his conversations recorded. He lost himself more and more in a realm of the imagination which had no basis in reality. Every free expression of opinion and every objection to his frequently incomprehensible views evoked an outburst of rage on his part. He lost his capacity to listen to a report to the end. His criticisms became stronger and his actions more drastic, with every passing day. He felt that he along had the right to hold opinions upon which decisions would be based. He was convinced that he *alone* possessed clear perception concerning all fields of human activity. Accordingly he condemned generals, staff officers, diplomats, government officials and towards the end even Party and SS leaders as armchair strategists, weaklings and finally as criminals and traitors.

Goebbels predictably propagated the theme that 'the Führer had been preserved to save the German people from being engulfed by Slavic Bolshevist hordes'.

As a result of the awful retribution throughout Germany, the humiliation by the Nazi party of the Army hierarchy was complete.

CHAPTER 3

Churchill's Dilemmas

Winston Churchill was a control freak. His six-volume *The Second World War* contains scrupulous post-war considerations, plans, defeats and victories in the main text. In the considerable Appendices are the little nuggets with dates, names of people and subjects which are perhaps not important but are of paramount interest. Not necessarily in order of importance he had to deal with the War Cabinet (usually via the CIGS, Field Marshall Allan Brooke or General Ismay), with President Roosevelt, the Foreign Office, Lord Cherwell (special adviser on scores of arcane subjects), Mr Bracken (Minister of Information), Home Secretary, Foreign Secretary, Minister of Food and Production, First Sea Lord, Colonial Secretary (the ape colony on Gibraltar etc.), Secretary of State for India, Paymaster General, etc.

Once both Russians and Americans had come into the war, not necessarily to help Britain, but because Hitler had been stupid enough to declare war on them, he knew that victory was on the horizon. The atomic bomb research, code-named Tube Alloys, was of course known to him, but not its date of delivery nor even its baneful power. Nevertheless he was determined to prevaricate to obtain a firm date for the cross-Channel invasion. Certainly not in 1942, nor in 1943, which Stalin and Roosevelt wanted, but in 1944.

In May 1942 Churchill had set up a group known as the Combined Commanders, which included Vice-Admiral Earl Mountbatten, Chief of Combined Operations. In August they studied the cruel lessons learned by the costly failure of the Dieppe one-day raid. In January 1943 at the Casablanca Conference they were ordered under Lt-General Morgan to prepare a detailed plan for summer 1944. In early August 1943 on board the giant liner *Queen Mary* on his way to meet President Roosevelt, Churchill took three members of the COSSAC team to reveal initial plans for Operations Neptune and Overlord.

I had reserved the interlude which a five days voyage presented for the consideration of our long-wrought plans for this supreme operation of crossing the Channel. Plans on an ever-expanding scale had gone forward since the struggles on the coasts of Norway and France in 1940; we had learned much about amphibious war.... We were still hard-pressed and our only ally [in October 1941] Russia seemed near to defeat. Nevertheless I had resolved to prepare for an invasion of the Continent when the tide should turn. First we had to increase the intensity and scope of our raids and then translate all this experience into something much more massive. To mount a successful invasion from the United Kingdom new engines of war must be contrived and developed; the three fighting services must be trained to plan and fight as one team [British, Americans, Canadians, Poles and Free French], supported by the industry of the nation, and the whole island converted into an armed camp for launching the greatest seaborne assault of all time.

Few people realised that during the Great War, early in 1915, Churchill had proposed:

... steam tractors, fitted with bullet-proof coverings inside which men and weaponry could be stored, utilising 'caterpillar tracks' to allow the vehicle to cross the rugged terrain and trenches of the battlefield.

This was a design plan for the first tank to be used on 15 September 1916. In July 1917 he produced a scheme for the capture of the Frisian islands of Sylt and Borkum to circumvent the deadly trench warfare. Fifty tank-landing lighters fitted with wire-cutters in their bows. A shelving bow or drawbridge would allow the tanks to land under their own power and force a way through barbed wire towards the enemy defences—a prototype for the 1943–44 Landing Craft Tanks. And his second plan was to create an artificial island in the shallow waters north of the two islands. A number of flat-bottomed barges or caissons made of concrete would float when empty of water and be towed across to the site of the artificial island. On arrival sea cocks would be opened, the barge would sink to the bottom and gradually fill with sand. Churchill specified their size: from 50 feet × 40 feet

× 20 feet, to 120 feet × 80 feet × 40 feet. They would become an artificial atoll, a weatherproof harbour with regular pens for Royal Navy destroyers and submarines. This brilliant concept was developed 27 years later as the famous Mulberry harbours, which were towed across the Channel in 1944 to provide (fairly) safe havens. Churchill listed with COSSAC:

> ... the question of where the first lodgements and landings should be made, the type of beach, tides, weather, sites for constructing airfield, length of voyage, nearby ports to be captured, provision of cover by home-based aircraft, enemy dispositions and their minefields and defences.

So Brigadier K. G. McLean and the two other officers of General Morgan's staff came to Winston Churchill who lay in bed in his spacious cabin. They showed him a large-scale map. 'The whole project was majestic.'

Earlier, in the summer of 1943 Churchill had set up the European Advisory Committee, initially in London, composed of Mr J. G. Winant, the American Ambassador, M. Gousen, the Soviet Ambassador and Sir William Strang of the British Foreign Office. The purpose of this committee was to begin work on the political and administrative problems which might arise in Germany when Hitler's Third Reich was on the point of collapse. Proposals were discussed, mainly relating to the initial disarmament of the Nazi military machine, and partitions of Germany by the Allies (Berlin as a separate joint zone, the British in NW Germany, the Americans in the South and Southwest, and the Russians to the East). The belligerent Morganthau Plan was sent to the 'Three Wise Men' for their views.

Churchill had also in that same summer set up a Cabinet Committee under Clement Atlee, Lord President of the Council, to study Eclipse plans for the Allies to occupy Germany in concert with the Chiefs of Staff. Their recommendations were also sent to the 'Three Wise Men'. Churchill wrote:

> At this time the subject seemed to be purely theoretical. No one could foresee when or how the end of the war would come. The German armies held immense areas of European Russia.... The proposals of the European Advisory Council were not thought sufficiently pressing or practical to be brought before the War Cabinet....

In those days a common opinion about Russia was that it would not continue the war once it had regained its frontiers, and that when the time came the Western Allies might well have to try and persuade it not to relax its efforts. The question of the Russian zone of occupation in Germany therefore did not bulk large in the Anglo-American discussions.

On 10 September Churchill wrote to Stalin:

> With regard to the meeting of Foreign Office representatives we defer to your wishes that Moscow should be the scene. [On the] Agenda. His Majesty's Government declares itself willing to discuss any and every subject with its Russian and United States Allies ... This meeting of Foreign Office representatives seems to me a most important and necessary preliminary to the meeting of the three heads of Governments ... I wish to tell you that on this meeting of the three of us [Stalin, Churchill and Roosevelt], so greatly desired by all the United Nations, may depend not only the best and shortest method of finishing the war but also those good arrangements for *the future of the world* which will enable the British, American and Russian nations to render a lasting service to humanity.

Later, on 11 October 1943, on his return from the Quebec Conference, Churchill briefed his Foreign Secretary, Anthony Eden, on the forthcoming meeting in Teheran:

> 1) Great Britain seeks no territory or special advantage for herself as the outcome of the war which she entered in pursuance of her obligations and in defence of public law.

> 2) We hold strongly to a system of a League of Nations, which will include a Council of Europe, with an International Court and an armed Power capable of enforcing its decisions. During the Armistice period [Eclipse] which may be prolonged, we hold that the three Great Powers, the British Commonwealth and Empire, the United States and the Union of Soviet Socialist Republics, with the addition of China, should remain united, well armed, and capable of enforcing the Armistice terms and of building up the *permanent* structure of peace throughout the globe.

> 3) We consider that states and nations that have been subjugated by Nazi or Fascist violence during the war should emerge at the Peace conference with their full sovereign rights, and that all questions of final territorial transference

must be settled at the peace table, due regard being paid to the interests of the populations affected.

4) Re-affirms the principle of the Atlantic Charter.

5) Welcome any agreement between Poland and Russia.

6) Resolved that Nazism and Facism be extirpated in the aggressor countries.

7) Future structure of Germany subject to an *agreed* policy among the three Great Powers of the West.

8) Disarmament and prevention of the guilty Powers from an armed menace to the peace of Europe.

9) Free all European nations from subjection.

10) Authority by victory of the three Great Powers in order to serve the general good and the cause of human progress.

The three Foreign Secretaries met in Moscow. The Americans had four suggestions, Great Britain no fewer than twelve, but the Russians single-mindedly wanted consideration of measures to shorten the duration of the war against Germany and her allies in Europe. Mr Eden, Ambassador A. D. Kerr, Sir William Strang (Foreign Office), and General Ismay represented the British.

Winston Churchill had told Stalin that:

> ... the British divisions being put into Overlord and beyond were the most that could be provided by a country with a total population of 45 millions. Those divisions could be kept up to strength in the line but the number could not be increased. It would have to be left to the United States who had a large number of reserve divisions to broaden the front and nourish the battle.

In fact 19 American divisions were deployed in Normandy, plus three Canadian when Overlord took place.

On 25 January 1944, four months before Overlord started, Churchill also minuted:

It is to my mind very unwise to make plans on the basis of Hitler being defeated in 1944. The possibility of his gaining a victory in France cannot be excluded. The hazards of battle are very great. The reserves of the enemy are capable of being thrown from point to point with great facility. All my information from the interior of Germany goes to show that Hitler and his government are still in the fullest control and that there is no sign of revolt as a result of the bombings. In all our contacts with the German troops, such as we see in Italy, their quality, discipline and skill are apparent.

And four weeks later, to General Ismay and the Chiefs of staff:

In the event of Overlord not being successful it would perhaps be necessary to adopt flanking movements both in Norway, from Turkey and the Aegean in the winter 1944/5.

The great Allied conference in Yalta took place in the Yusupon Palace, with huge delegations from all three countries. Joseph Stalin was the host and every possible situation was discussed, including the dismemberment of Germany, a French zone in occupied Germany, reparations by the Germans, liberation of Poland, and membership of a 'World-Instrument for Peace'. Stalin said towards the end:

All of us want to secure peace for at least fifty years. The greatest danger is conflict among ourselves, because if we remain united the German menace is not very important. Therefore we must now think how to secure our unity in the future, and how to guarantee that the three Great Powers (and possibly China and France) will maintain a united front. Some system must be elaborated to prevent conflict between the main Great Powers.

The Yalta Conference lasted from 4 to 8 February and Churchill did some informal horse trading about respective interests in the European countries still to be freed including Poland and Greece. Poland was discussed at seven of the eight plenary meetings of the Yalta Conference. By the time Churchill left the Crimea on Sunday 11 February he was under the strong impression that all the key points between the three Allies had been resolved.

As the weeks passed after Yalta it was clear that the Soviet Government was doing nothing about the agreed plans to broaden the Polish Government to include all Polish parties in a democratic fashion. President Roosevelt was seriously ill and his strength had faded. The Soviets were suspicious that the Allies were making secret peace arrangements behind Stalin's back and Stalin accused Roosevelt and Churchill in April. Churchill wrote:

> We separated in the Crimea, not only as Allies but as friends facing still a mighty foe with whom all our armies were struggling in fierce and ceaseless battle.

But two months later he wrote:

> Hitler's Germany was doomed and he himself about to perish. The Russians were fighting in Berlin. Vienna and most of Austria was in their hands. *The whole relationship of Russia with the Western Allies was in flux.* The agreement and understandings of Yalta, such as they were had already been broken or brushed aside by the triumphant Kremlin. New perils, perhaps as terrible as those we had surmounted, loomed and glared upon the torn and harassed world.

After the Yalta Conference Churchill wrote to his daughter Sarah:

> I do not suppose that at any moment of history has the agony of the world been so great or widespread. Tonight the sun goes down on more suffering than ever before in the world.

CHAPTER 4

Dying Days of the Third Reich: Eyewitness Accounts

This author was much involved in many of the key battles that decided the fate of Hitler's Third Reich. First there was Operation Veritable to break the Siegfried Line, then Operation Plunder, Monty's huge all-arms forcing of the mighty Rhine. Less well known are the vicious battles to cross the Dortmund–Ems Canal and clear the Teutoburger Wald, followed by the Rivers Weser, Aller and Elbe via the appalling concentration camp of Bergen-Belsen. Every day there were savage rearguard actions by determined last-ditch SS, Panzer Grenadiers, General Student's paratroops, Doenitz marines, sturdy Wehrmacht and scores of juvenile delinquents, the Hitler *Jugend* whose one-shot bazookas destroyed Comets, Shermans and Churchill tanks at close quarters.

It was the end of a five-year war and Britain's civilian army was determined, but also understandably cautious, to avenge friends killed or missing, to free thousands of prisoners of war and, unwittingly, to race Stalin's Cossack armies to the Baltic ports.

So history should take note of the names of Frank Gillard, Wynford Vaughan-Thomas, Chester Wilmot, Matthew Halton, Richard Dimbleby, Ian Wilson, Robert Dunnett, Edward Murrow, Denis Johnston, Robert Barr and many others including the incomparable Alan Moorehead, author of *Eclipse*.

Arnhem

Frank Gillard, 27 September 1944:

It was not a defeat. This operation must be viewed as a whole, though naturally we all of us became preoccupied with the fighting of our beleaguered troops in and around Arnhem. In those few days from 17 September onwards, the Second Army swept forward over no less than five major obstacles, the Wilhelmina Canal, the Dommell river at St Oedenrode, the Zuid Willemsvaart Canal at Veghel, the great bridge over the Maas at Grave and the Dutch Rhine itself, the Waal, at Nijmegen.

Rhine Crossing

Stewart Macpherson, 29 March 1945:

Standing on the bank of the Rhine one can look down on one of the great sights of the war. Stretching across the bridge, and as far as the eye can see, were hundreds of tanks, lorries, carriers, bulldozers, ammo wagons, vehicles of every conceivable type, flooding across the river. Overhead, squadrons of Spitfires, Typhoons, Tempests and Mustangs took their turn in patrolling—giving constant protection to our ground forces, just in case the Luftwaffe should dare interfere.

Liberation

Chester Wilmot, 30 March 1945:

Today I've been with our armour east of the Rhine, roaming over the rolling farmlands of Germany's great north-western plain. The leading tanks are now far beyond the area which slashed and torn by our shellfire. We've left behind that belt of Germany where every village was in ruins, every house had its scars of shell or bullet, every field was pitted with craters or scored with tank tracks. We saw the German peasants standing by the roadside with their white flags in their hands. As the traffic streamed by they began waving and smiling ... In some of the villages there were other people who were waving in real welcome. They were foreign workers and prisoners of war who had been liberated at last. Today we passed hundreds of them: French, Belgians, Poles, Czechs and Russians. You could pick the prisoners out because most of them still wore tattered uniforms of their own armies.

'Swanning'

Wynford Vaughan-Thomas, 7 April 1945:

Our armour is now 'swanning' as they say in the British Army or, in American parlance 'the rat race is on'. 'Swanning' means that our tanks are having an almost free run, and it's the strangest possible experience to follow in their wake …This is the road into the Reich—the most exciting and impressive sight you could hope to see … Everything is moving at speed. So now rolling past us goes this astonishing spectacle of the power and weight of the second Army … It's overwhelming.

Dreams

Matthew Halton, 12 April 1945:

But the great sensation these days is exhilaration. How often we've dreamed of this. In the long dark nights of the London Blitz, in the shelling on the road to Damascus, in the jungles of Burma, in the dreary sandstorms or blinding heat of the Libyan desert, in the white dust of Sicily, and in the cold bloody winter on the Moro river in Italy. And then in Normandy when it seemed that the SS divisions would never crack, I've looked forward to this day, and now we go through the ruins of Germany.

Demons

Matthew Halton, 12 April 1945:

The rich farmlands and pleasant villages have escaped destruction. Germany's a beautiful country, spacious and massive. You can drive for a hundred miles through open country and forests. You see no obvious need for more 'lebensraum'. It's clean, well-ordered country, the buildings are solid and strong. And you think what a great people the Germans could have been if they hadn't had a demon in them. And to see them now you wouldn't think they had a demon in them ... I've seen women on their knees, tears running down their cheeks as British tanks rolled past and they knew they were free ...

Stalag 11B

Chester Wilmot, 16 April 1945:

This afternoon, at Stalag 11b [reached by 8th Hussars, Desert Rats Division at Fallingbostel] I saw some of the 20,000 Allied prisoners of war and learned from padres, doctors and NCOs how they'd been treated. There were 4,256 British troops and 2,428 Americans prisoner of war. Of these 6,700 more than 1,000 are in hospital suffering from wounds, injuries or starvation. In this camp I saw clear evidence of the German neglect and wanton disregard for the lives and health of their prisoners. The Germans marched 2,500 British prisoners here from Poland lest they should be set free by the Russians. Ten days ago 3,000 other British and American prisoners made the terrible trek from Poland, but when the Second Army crossed the river Weser, the Germans sent these 3,000 POW back towards the Russians, because they were airmen and paratroops. All this German oppression and brutality and starvation hadn't been able to kill the spirit and self-respect of these men of Arnhem, men of Crete, of Dunkirk and Calais, men of Bomber Command and the Eighth US Air Force ... This afternoon they had the supreme pleasure of watching their German guards being marched away to our prison cage, and as they watched, they cheered.

Belsen

Richard Dimbleby, 19 April 1945:

In the shadow of some trees lay a great collection of bodies. I walked about them trying to count, there were perhaps 150 of them flung down on each other, all naked, all so thin that their yellow skin glistened like stretched rubber on their bones. Some of the poor starved creatures who were there looked so utterly unreal and inhuman that I could have imagined that they had never lived at all. They were like polished skeletons, the skeletons that medical students like to play practical jokes with. At one end of the pile a cluster of men and women were gathered round a fire: they were using rags and old shoes taken from the bodies to keep it alight and they were heating soup over it ... I have never seen British soldiers so moved to cold fury as the men who opened the Belsen camp this week, and those of the military police and the RAMC now on duty trying to save the prisoners who are not too far gone in starvation.

This author witnessed some of this horror from his Sherman tank at mid-day when his battle group passed very slowly through the camp.

That autumn he and two other officers tried 30–40 camp guards in a Hamburg court room.

Norwegian Defiance

Vidkun Quisling, Minister President of Norway, met Adolf Hitler in January 1945. Later Quisling testified that he hoped **a last-ditch stand in Norway** [*author's emphasis*] would provide a way out for him as well as the remainder of the Wehrmacht and the Third Reich. 'Having smashed Germany, the Western Powers would face two alternatives—to sacrifice much blood and money in overpowering strongly entrenched positions at the same time destroying Norway, or to negotiate a Norwegian peace that allowed the Germans to remain and form the backbone of a Nordic defence. In any future East-West war Scandinavia would then be able to **muster two million men** [*author's emphasis*] and the Northern flank against Russia would be definitely secured. (Source: *The Bitter Years* p. 350).

Blackmail in Holland

In General Eisenhower's Report 1944–45 he wrote:

In western Holland no further ground advances were made [after 2 May 1945] across the flood barriers behind which the German twenty-Fifth Army lay entrenched ... Even had we been able to launch an offensive against western

Holland the enemy would have opened the dykes to flood the whole country, ruining its fertility for many years to come and bringing further miseries to its people. We warned general Blaskowitz, the German commander, that the opening of the dykes would constitute an incredible blot upon his military honour and that of the German Army. Meanwhile Seyss-Inquart, the Nazi commissioner for Holland, offered a solution by proposing a truce. If the Allied forces were to continue to stand on the Grebbe Line as at present, **no further flooding would take place and the Germans would cease all repressive measures against the Dutch** [*author's emphasis*] at the same time co-operating in the introduction of relief supplies.

CHAPTER 5

Speer and the German Wastelands: Operation Nero

When the citizen armies of Britain, America and Canada had smashed their way into the Third Reich early in 1945 they could see for themselves the awful wastelands. The fifty great cities and towns had been destroyed by years of attritional bombing. In his book *Eclipse* Alan Moorehead describes what the British Army encountered as they entered their enemy's heartlands:

Like ants in an ant-heap the people scurried over the ruins, diving furtively into cellars and doorways in a side-track with their bundles only to be blocked by debris and then turn irresolutely back, shoving and bumping against one another. Everyone was on the move, and there was a frantic ant-like quality about their activity. Life was sordid, aimless, leading nowhere. Every house in every unbombed village was stacked to the roof with city refugees living on soup and potatoes. From the Ruhr across Germany an occasional factory chimney smoked, but ninety per cent of the country's industry was at a standstill. No trains ran. Every family was bereaved or broken up. The housing situation was impossible and likely to get worse. A very large part of the population was simply wandering on the roads with the millions of foreigners. And to these was now added the German army itself. A mass flight from the Russians towards the Elbe and the Anglo-American lines began. Officers stripped off their uniforms and begged or stole civilian clothes from the near-by houses. Mass fear had gripped them so greatly that when aircraft appeared in the sky the shout went up: 'The Russians! The Russians!' and the mob would break out in panic across the countryside.

In the British zone of combat and occupation Bremen and Hamburg were the two key cities. Wynford Vaughan-Thomas, the intrepid BBC reporter, noted on 26 April:

> I am in the centre of the city of Bremen if you can call this chaotic rubbish-heap in which our bulldozers are working ... There are walls standing, there are factory chimneys here and there, but there's no shape and no order and certainly no hope for this shell of a city that was once called 'Bremen'. It is the sheer size of the smashed area that overwhelms you. These endless vistas down small streets to the houses leaning at drunken angles and this inhuman landscape of great flats with their sides ripped open and the intimate household goods just blown out into the bomb craters ... There is hardly a house intact in which these people could live. Everybody has gone into giant air-raid shelters, these great blocks of almost solid concrete that are dotted all over the ruins.

And a few days later:

> Hamburg, the city that Lord Haw-Haw [William Joyce] made notorious, we found a completely and utterly bomb-ruined city. Hamburg was devastated. Whole quarters have disintegrated under air-attacks. There are miles upon miles of blackened walls and utterly burnt-out streets and in the ruins there are still nearly a million people and 50,000 foreign workers living in the cellars and air-raid shelters. The docks are even more devastated than the town, the great shipyards of Blohm and Voss are a wilderness of tangled girders and in the middle of this chaos fourteen unfinished U-Boats still stand rusting on the slipways. Work on them finally stopped two months ago: after that date was a dead city.

A few weeks after V-E Day this author sailed on the charming Alster Lake, listened to Hans Schmidt-Isserstedt and the Hamburg Rundfunk orchestra playing divine classical music in a partly ruined theatre. But the streets had been cleared and some of the utilities still worked. The British Army of the Rhine turned the large intact Atlantic Hotel overlooking the lake into a first-class British officers' club with excellent Wehrmacht-looted wines and delicacies. And in another repaired theatre he was the junior member of the trio of officers of the first War Crimes Tribunal who dispensed British-style law, justice (and retribution) to dozens of thoroughly guilty SS camp guards, later despatched by the busy Mr Albert Pierrepoint, the last British hangman.

But the appalling wastelands of the Third Reich, awful as they were, could have been even worse.

Adolf Hitler spent the last few months of his life in his Berlin bunker surrounded by his evil court. Martin Bormann (1900–45) became Hitler's shadow and dealt with the Führer's money and property affairs but worked his way to become Party Minister in charge of Nazi Party HQ. He thus controlled access to Hitler, even blocking access to Goering, Goebbels, Himmler and Speer. Hitler ran the war. Bormann became indispensable and was thoroughly trusted by the Führer. Albert Speer (1905–81) became Reich Minister for Armaments and Production in 1942–45 in succession to Dr Fritz Todt who died in an air crash. Because he had been a professional architect he became Hitler's almost-friend. Speer was a brilliant administrator and worked miracles to keep German armaments, from Tiger tanks to U-boats and 88 mm AA guns, all in production despite the continuous bombing. In January 1945 he recalled the scene in the Berlin bunker:

Night after night Hitler sat with Goebbels, Robert Ley [a dedicated, brutal, vulgar, anti-semitic follower of his boss] and Bormann for a few hours. No one was admitted to these gatherings. No one knew what they were talking about, whether they were reminiscing about their beginnings, or talking about the end and what would come after it. They grasped at every straw [Morgenthau Plan, Roosevelt's death etc.]—yet they were in no way prepared to regard the fate of the entire nation as nearly as their own. 'We will leave nothing but a desert to the Americans, English and Russians.' This was the standard close to any discussion of the matter. Hitler agreed. Later it turned out that Hitler was more radical than any of them. While the others were talking he concealed his attitudes behind a pose of statesmanship. But it was he who issued the orders for smashing the foundation of the nation's existence.

'We'll not capitulate. Never. We can go down but we'll take a world with us' Hitler stated after the failure of his Ardennes gamble. A Wagnerian end implicitly beckoned—Valhalla it would be. Berlin, Hamburg, Bremen, the 50 cities of the Third Reich in flames and burning. Hitler said to Speer at midnight on Speer's 40th birthday, 18 March 1945, in an icy tone:

If the war is lost, the people will be lost also. It is not necessary to worry about what the German people will need for elemental survival. On the contrary it is best for us to destroy even these things. For the nation has proved to be the weaker and the future belongs solely to the stronger eastern nation [Russia]. In any case only those who are inferior will remain after this struggle, for the good have already been killed.

On 19 March 1945 Hitler issued a protocol about *Nerobefehl*, Operation Nero: 'Demolitions on Reich Territory Decree'. It was prepared for his Führer by Colonel Gundelach, Chief of staff to the Commanding General of the Army Engineers.

The struggle for the very existence of our people forces us to seize any means which can weaken the combat readiness of our enemy and prevent him from advancing. Every opportunity, direct or indirect, to inflict the most lasting possible damage on the enemy's striking power must be used to the utmost. It is a mistake to believe that when we win back the lost territories we will be able to retrieve and use these transportation, communications, production and supply facilities that have not been destroyed or have been temporarily crippled; when the enemy withdraws he will leave us only scorched earth and will show no consideration for the welfare of the population. Therefore I order:

1) All military, transportation, communications, industrial and food-supply facilities, as well as all resources within the Reich, which the enemy might use either immediately, or in the foreseeable future for continuing the war, are to be destroyed.

2) Those responsible for these measures are: the military commands for all military objects, including the transportation and communications installations; the gauleiters [gau was a region] and defence commissioners for all industrial and supply facilities, as well as other resources. When necessary, the troops are to assist the gauleiters and the defence commissioners in carrying out their task.

3) These orders are to be communicated at once to all troop commanders; contrary instructions are invalid.

On 27 March 1945 Hitler issued specific implementation instructions:

Communications facilities are to be destroyed by dynamiting, fire or demolition. Items to be rendered totally unusable are: telephone, telegraph and amplification stations and centrals (wire lead-in points, switchboards, junction boxes, pylons and if sufficient time is available above-ground lines and long-distance cables); stocks of telegraph equipment of all types, cables and wiring, factory records (cable layout plans, wiring diagrams, descriptions of devices etc.); the major radio facilities (broadcasting and receiving) stations; towers, antennas. Efforts should be made to remove beforehand especially valuable parts ... Special orders follow for the national capital and its immediate environs—the radio stations in Naüen, Königswusterhausen, Zeesen, Rehmate and Beelitz.

Albert Speer was absolutely horrified and protested vigorously by letter and face-to-face meetings. He wrote in his memoirs:

I came to the decision to eliminate Hitler ... At the moment of the regime's doom I was on the point of receiving from Hitler himself, of all people [they had worked closely together for several years—as architect, almost-friend and Minister] the moral impulse to attempt murder against him.

He planned to insert poison gas down an air filter into Hitler's bunker, but the practical problems deterred action. Hitler later told his situation conference, on 27 April, 'Failure to obey my orders would mean immediate annihilation, a leap into the void for any party leader', a specific threat to Speer.

Speer wrote:

Hitler's message was the death sentence of the German people; it called for the application of the scorched earth principle in its most sweeping form. The decree further stripped me of all my powers, all my orders for the preservation of industry were explicitly revoked. Now the gauleiters were put in charge of the programme of destruction. The consequences would have been inconceivable. For an indefinite period there would have been no electricity, no gas, no pure water, no coal, no transportation. All railroad facilities, canals, locks, docks, ships and locomotives destroyed ... No storage facilities, no telephone communications—in short, a country thrown back into the Middle Ages.

To his infinite credit, Albert Speer drove at high speed to visit the key players and persuade them not to follow Hitler's draconian edicts. Field Marshal Albert Kesselring, Commander-in-Chief West, was 'a pure soldier, not inclined to discuss Hitler's orders'; SS General Paul Hausser in Heidelberg was more sensible; Gauleiter Stöhr of the Palatinate and the Saar had no intention of obeying the Führer's Nero Order; Field Marshal Walther Model in the Westerwald avoided all discussion about safeguarding the Ruhr industries. Some of the gauleiters visited by Speer said 'Let the enemy march into a burned and deserted city'.

But the intrepid Speer had previously hindered the implementation of Operation Nero in the destruction of French industry. Now he persuaded Colonel-General Heinrich (Upper Silesia) and Colonel-General Guderian (the *entire* eastern front) that all installations vital to the German economy should be spared destruction wherever possible. The three gauleiters of the Ruhr region, however, were determined to carry out Hitler's Nero orders. Speer had an urgent conference with Dr Walter Rohland at Landsberg castle, then met the gauleiters. Florian of Düsseldorf blamed not Hitler but the German people, but Gauleiters Hoffman and Schlessman were more reasonable.

Speer then again met Field Marshal Model who was more receptive and promised to keep the fighting away from industrial areas. And General Siegfried Westphal, Kesselring's chief of staff, promised to interpret Nero 'in a merciful sense'. He visited Gauleiter Wagner of Baden and Württenberg and managed to sabotage the Nero written orders before they reached Wagner. Speer talked to Mayor Neinhaus of Heidelberg, his native city, and asked SS General Hausser to declare the city a hospital zone to be abandoned without a fight. At Würzburg he visited Gauleiter Hellmuth and convinced him not to destroy the Schweinfurt ball-bearings industry factories.

On 28 March Speer returned to Berlin and had a dramatic confrontation with his Führer. It was a very tense meeting with the ailing, once powerful ruler of most of Europe, who eventually allowed Speer overall responsibility for implementing all measures for the destruction of his Reich. This took the key decisions out of the hands of the gauleiters. Hitler knew, of course, that his brutal Operation Nero would be diminished and diluted to avoid the destruction he had ordered.

Nevertheless Hitler then told his secretaries:

If anything happens to me, Germany is lost, since I have no successor. Hess has gone mad. Goering has squandered the sympathies of the German people and Himmler is rejected by the party.

On 29 March 1945 Operation Nero was transmitted through General Alfred Jodl, Chief of Wehrmacht Operations Staff and forwarded the next day by the Reichsleiter Martin Bormann to the reichsleiters and gauleiters. All enumerated in the Geheime Reichssache, the classified information sheet on 30 March giving the Ministry of Armaments and War Production (Speer) responsibility for implementing Operation Nero. Speer now boldly again went on his frenzied pilgrimage to save the Reich infrastructure from being destroyed, meeting Gauleiter Kaufmann of Hamburg and the evil Seyss-Inquart of Holland, who promised to prevent the large-scale flooding which Hitler was planning.

On 3 April Speer sent out orders forbidding the blowing up of sluices, locks, dams and canal bridges. To all industrial enquiries he ordered that the factory or works be *temporarily* crippled. For instance to Gauleiter Uiberreither of Graz he ordered 'According to the Führer's orders of March 30 1945 there is to be no scorched earth ...'

Speer stayed close to Hitler in that crucial period: 'Every absence furnished cause for suspicion.' And in his memoirs he wrote:

In the nineteen days between March 18 and April 7 1945 no less than twelve contradictory decrees had been issued on the question [implementation of Operation Nero].

When the British, American and Canadian armies fought their way through the Third Reich to victory they encountered desolation, shattered cities, bomb damage everywhere, but it would have been appalling if Hitler's Operation Nero had been carried out.

CHAPTER 6

Operation Eclipse
Winning the Peace—Avoiding Chaos

On 18 April 1945 Prime Minister Churchill wrote to President Truman:

> The occupational zones of Germany were decided rather hastily at Quebec in
> September 1944 when it was not foreseen that General Eisenhower's armies
> would make such a mighty inroad into Germany. The zones cannot be altered
> except by agreement with the Russians. But the moment that V-E [Victory
> in Europe] Day has occurred we should try to set up the Allied Control
> Commission in Berlin [and Vienna] and should insist upon a fair distribution
> of the food produced in Germany between all parts of Germany ... We poor
> British are to take over the ruined Ruhr and large manufacturing districts
> which are, like ourselves, in normal times large importers of food.

When Victory in Europe had been agreed and signed once by the
Allies (Americans, British and Canadians) and with diplomatic tension
high, ratified a day or so later by the Russians. The excellent planning
by the European Advisory Commission (EAC) established in early 1944
forecast that:

> ... in view of the chaotic conditions to be anticipated in Germany, whether
> a capitulation occurs before division or after invasion and consequent
> establishment of military government, an initial period of Allied military
> government in Germany is inevitable and should be provided for.

Winston Churchill followed events closely in the now peaceful Third
Reich. On 6 May 1945 he wrote to Field Marshal Montgomery:

The formidable mass of helpless German civilians and wounded in this area [particularly in Schleswig-Holstein] must be a great problem to you. Do not hesitate to address me direct if ordinary channels work too slowly.' But to the Foreign Office on 14 May Churchill was brusque, even rude: 'I deprecate the raising of these grave constitutional issues [technicalities about the Fourth Reich in Flensburg] at a time when the only question is to avoid sheer chaos. The orders seem to be to get the Germans to do exactly what we want them to do. We will never be able to rule Germany apart from the Germans, unless you are prepared to let every miserable little German school-child lay its weary head upon your already overburdened lap.

And on 16 May to the UK Minister of Agriculture:

If all the Germans are put to work to grow food on the land what are the crops that can be started if they begin to dig on June 1st? Have you any reports on the state of their tilth?

Fortunately Field Marshal Montgomery had very able staff officers: Major General Francis de Guingand, Major General Gerald Templar and Major General Miles Graham. And so did the defeated Wehrmacht with General Eberhard Kinzel, Chief of Staff to Field Marshal Ernst Busch. Kinzel wore an eye-glass and a magnificent grey great-coat with scarlet and was extremely efficient and helpful.

The general policy was to make use of existing German Headquarters to control and administer German troops. In the British Zone of Occupation there were 1.4 million: 120,000 from Holland, 160,000 from Denmark, 340,000 from the Wismar region, 75,000 from East Prussia, 134,000 from South Schleswig-Holstein, 250,000 from North Schleswig-Holstein, 100,000 from north of the Elbe, and 220,000 already in the area. They were corralled into five main areas: the Wismar cushion 569,000; NW Hamburg 410,000; West Hamburg 260,000; Emden area 180,000; Magdeburg Bulge between Hannover and the Elbe 300,000. From these areas speedy disbandment took place, separating the sheep from the goats. The latter included the SS, camp guards, Gestapo etc. In all areas full documentation of all the enemy soldiers took place. The SS troops were then isolated on Nordstrand Island, guarded by the Royal Navy NW of the Kiel Canal. There were also 200,000 German prisoners of war held in areas situated in the lines of communication captured during the invasion of the Third Reich. The grand total was almost one and three-quarter million German troops.

So hard on the heels of the British and American troops fighting through the 50 ravaged cities came Allied Military Government (AMGOT) civilian officers (in the British Zone there were many 'bobbies'—policemen) who moved in to take control. AMGOT's task was to set up administrations to restore law and order, to secure water, food and fuel supplies and shelter. AMGOT directed Germans to dig, build, and clear wreckage (this author saw the cleared streets in Hamburg and Kiel shortly after V-E Day), insisting that only by work could they feed and shelter themselves. They had expected some hostility but found that most Germans were willing to co-operate. The arrival of a military government signified the true end of the war. Local mayors, preferably of anti-Nazi sentiment, which was difficult to assess, were reappointed or appointed to get basic services going. AMGOT provided tent camps for thousands of displaced persons (DP) and wherever possible made Germans feed them—four million were repatriated in three months. Despite Speer's valiant efforts to ensure that Hitler's appalling Operation Nero was not put into action the breakdown of local government, transport and communications was almost total. Field Marshal Montgomery, head of the British Zone and AMGOT, launched Operation Barleycorn and half a million German soldiers were released promptly from their cages to bring in the 1945 harvest.

AMGOT were determined that the Germans who had ransacked Europe for food and supplies should not now have more to eat than the newly liberated peoples. So they drew up calorie rations and scales that were deemed fair and realistic. Ordinary people were rationed to 1,550 calories a day, men doing heavy work to 2,800 calories. A daily ration of 12.7 ounces of bread and 10.5 ounces of potatoes was set but in practice many people had less. Riots took place in cities such as Hannover and Osnabrück—total anarchy—mainly inspired by violent DPs expressing their freedom. The wretched Russian DPs were unfortunately doomed to be repatriated and deemed to be traitors for surrendering to the Allies, so would be sent to gulags to rot and die. Inevitably black markets soon thrived and the Allied military police were kept very busy.

The Potsdam Agreement of 2 August specified the tasks of the new Allied Control Council (ACC) based on the 14 November 1944 meeting of the three great powers in London. The *Alliierter Kontrollrat*, also referred to as the Four Powers or *Vier Machte*, was based in the handsome Kammergerich in the Kleistpark in Berlin- Schöneberg. France had been added later to the trio but had no duties.

The initial members of the ACC were Marshal Georgy Zhukov for the Soviet Union, General Dwight Eisenhower for the USA, Field Marshal Bernard Montgomery, and General Jean de Lattre de Tassigny for France. Churchill had to persuade Stalin to accept a French seat on the ACC.

In 1945 the five key issues were thus addressed.

War Criminals

Directive No. 9, 30 August and Law No. 10, 20 December.

The legal division of ACC was charged with ensuring the provisions of the London Agreement of 8 August on the prosecution of German war criminals were carried out. Each occupying power to have its own legal system independently of the International Military Tribunal sitting at Nüremburg. [In the British Zone there were military tribunals in Hamburg and Oldenburg. This author was a judge/jurist in two trials.]

Dissolution of the German army and government agencies

Order No. 1, 30 August prohibition of the wearing of uniform by the German army which now did not exist.

Directive No. 18, 12 November dissolution of all German army units and then Law No. 8 of 30 November. Within 3 months 2 million military had been disarmed and demobilised.

Restoration of order into German hands

Law No. 4, 30 October re-established the German court system according to German legislation before Hitler's rise to power.

Directive No. 16, 6 November German police forces could have 'light weapons' to combat crime.

De-nazification and eradication of militarism

Law No. 1, 20 September repealed most of the strictly Nazi laws enacted under the Third Reich.

Law No. 2 10 October provided for the total dissolution of the National Socialist Party.

Directive No. 23 prohibited any athletic activities done as part of military training.

Expulsion of German-speaking minorities residing outside Germany from Czechoslovakia, Hungary and Poland to the four occupation zones of Germany

Another key, but difficult problem was that of fraternisation with the enemy which from V-E Day was extremely strict. The ACC, on 20 September, formally issued an order. The only exception was marriage or when a military governor decided to billet his soldiers with a German family. However *de facto* every British and American service unit employed locals in half a dozen fairly essential roles and certainly by Christmas it had been rescinded. In mid-summer 1945 this author played hockey for his brigade against the German police and suffered a smashed kneecap, needing hospital treatment. The police seemed to be sympathetic!

Almost top of the list in priorities was Eclipsegator, the codeword for the airlift repatriation of prisoners of war. SHAEF were responsible for 1,054,000 POW, of which 105,000 were British, 29,000 American, 360,000 Soviet and 200,000 other Allied. The Soviet Zone repatriated a further 80,000 British, 44,000 American and from Austria came 14,700 British and 4,400 American. The evacuation rate was 12,000 a day. A Lancaster plane could take 25, Halifax 20, B-17 40, B-24 32 and C-47 28. Of the total 60 per cent needed emergency rations to be dropped from the air. The RAF had a thousand Bomber Command Lancaster and Halifax planes as airlift resources and the USAAF had 1,800 B-17 and B-24 bombers available. In the early days after V-E Day emergency rations, two pounds weight per man, were dropped by the Allied air forces to 950,000 Allied POW still in their camps, to 2,000,000 foreign workers and 3,000,000 for the relief of Holland. The Allied POW camps were instructed to lay out strips of white material 12 feet by 2 feet, plus smoke signals to attract pilots. A single strip mean 'All's well'; parallel strips meant 'Camp in danger'; a cross shape 'Medical supplies urgently needed'; and a large L shape 'Starving'.

In August 1945 President Truman ended the generous lease-lend programme with Britain—50 elderly destroyers in exchange for useful harbours, but vital supplies of armaments of all kinds, which had the effect of bankrupting the recipients! United Nations Relief and Rehabilitation (UNRRA) programme was founded in November 1943 and once Europe was at peace again it sent 20 million tons of aid to the starving countries. The equivalent of 2,000 full cargo ships were sent across the Atlantic, a brilliant humanitarian crusade.

But in January 1946 after nine months of peace, Churchill wrote:

What is the plight to which Europe has been reduced? Over wide areas a vast quivering mass of tormented hungry careworn and bewildered human beings gape at the ruins of their cities and homes and scan the dark horizons for the approach of some new peril, tyranny or terror. Among the victors there is a babel of jarring voices; among the vanquished a sudden silence of despair.

The harvests of 1945 and 1946 were very poor and the winters exceptionally severe. Later that year Churchill wrote:

Christmas 1946 a vast high pressure area began to form near the Arctic Circle. Rolling across Norway the front settled over Britain bringing ferocious winds and a biting cold. By dawn on 6 January 1947 snow began falling in London. Western Europe experienced the most punishing weather in living memory, snow piled as high as 20 feet. The Thames froze. Unemployment skyrocketed six-fold during the crisis. In Berlin 19,000 inhabitants were treated for frostbite. On the walls of the bombed-out Reichstag parliament building were scrawled the words 'Blessed are the dead for their hands do not freeze'.

At the same time the fragile partnership with Stalin and the USSR degenerated as the barriers went up all over Europe, and Poland was left to suffer again for another decade or so.

Germany's division into four zones at the end of the war had given the German industrial heartland which lay in the west, to Britain, France and America. The agrarian east fell into Russia's zone. The German invasions of Russia had caused them to demand $10 billion worth of reparations. They hoped that by taking industrial equipment out of Germany as war reparations would repair some of the damage. If that happened revival of the West would not occur. The German occupation by the British Army of the Rhine soon became an intolerable financial burden on the British economy, but Germany, perhaps partly due to Albert Speer who had openly defied Hitler's Nero decree, had 80 per cent of its industrial capacity surviving. Indeed thanks to Speer, German industry had actually expanded during the war, despite Bomber Harris's best efforts.

Britain and America were soon pouring aid into Germany and they certainly had no intention of seeing this being beneficial to Russia after Churchill's Iron Curtain was in place. France wanted ownership of the great centres of German mining and heavy industries: the regions of the Ruhr, the Rhineland and the Saar. General Lucius Clay, in charge of the American occupation zone, consistently blamed the French more than the Russians for obstructing plans for the German recovery. In late 1945 Stalin was 67 years old and had been in power for 23 years. A tyrant who held half the world in thrall, who had butchered 20 million of his own peoples, he was a disarmingly frail man in the flesh: small, paunched, party-faced, with a shock of white hair, pock-marked face, and bad teeth, but with a calm confident manner. The extraordinary thing was that he could charm people like Churchill, Presidents Roosevelt and Truman and many key politicians who visited him in the Kremlin.

At the end of the war Stalin had an army of 175 divisions. The *US News & World Report* noted: 'Russia's armies and air force are in a position to pour across Europe and into Asia almost at will'. Since Leningrad, Kiev, Minsk and Kharkov had been almost totally destroyed production of steel was down to 50 per cent of the pre-war level, and agricultural production was down to 60 per cent. In 1946 and 1947 European harvests were devastated by drought and in Russia agricultural machinery was very scarce.

However the governments of all four occupied zones of Germany were unanimous—they did not want a strong, centralised German government that could rise like a phoenix from the ashes with renewed aggressive power.

The Americans, to their eternal credit, spent almost two years of political manoeuvres involving Russia, France and the UK putting together the magnificent Marshall Aid Plan. It was in everyone's interests to make Europe once again prosperous, and peaceful, even for Greece, Turkey and other relative minnows. The only exception was the USSR who, early in 1948, had destroyed the independence and democratic character of a dozen European countries in the Soviet bloc. President Truman and General Marshall had worked tirelessly to put a financial package together that would save Europe from an agonisingly long recovery.

America, with a population then of 150 million, produced $300 billion-worth of goods a year. Europe, with a population of 260 million, was collectively producing 'only' $150 million-worth of goods. The United States was thus committed to at last becoming a truly great international power.

Soon 150 American ships would be carrying Marshall Plan cargoes of wheat, four, cotton, drilling equipment, automobile tyres, aircraft parts, borax, tractors, synthetic resin, even tobacco and horse meat to Europe.

The economic miracle in Germany (*Wirtschaftswunder*) was astonishing. The volume of foreign trade doubled in 1949 and 1950. Unemployment, rampant in 1946–1947, fell from 8 or 9 per cent to 0.4 per cent. In 1946 2.5 million tons of steel were poured in Germany, and three years later, 9 million tons. Coal production doubled. New autobahns and bridges were built and car production soon produced exports of Volkswagens and Opels. This despite the fact that near-starvation diets of 1,000 calories a day were the norm for millions.

CHAPTER 7

The 'Chain of Deception'

Two key members of Hitler's ministry survived the war and wrote considerable autobiographies. Albert Speer, Hitler's original architect, became a powerful minister and was almost a friend of his Führer. Grand Admiral Karl Doenitz, the formidable naval and U-Boat fleet commander, became the unlikely successor. For a few weeks he was Führer of the Fourth Reich based in Flensburg, until this author's division surrounded and captured most of the key political survivors of the Third Reich. The chapter is arranged in diary form.

On 30 March 1945 Admiral Doenitz defied Hitler's Operation Nero, so that no demolitions in dockyards or harbours could be carried out without Doenitz's specific orders.

On 10 April 1945 when the Russian advance to the middle Oder at Küstrin and Frankfurt, and the American thrust threatened to cut Germany in two, Hitler issued a provisional order vesting authority for the northern half of Germany to Doenitz. Gauleiter Paul Wegener of Bremen and General Eberhard Kinzl were appointed to assist Doenitz, the former for civil affairs, the latter for military. Later at Flensburg Kinzl became the official link with the British Army.

22 April. Just before the Russians entered Berlin, Doenitz and staff went to Ploen in Holstein. The next day there was a conference with the gauleiters of Mecklenburg and Schleswig-Holstein but Kaufmann of Hamburg refused to attend. Doenitz knew that the defence of Hamburg city was vital if large numbers of civilians facing the Russians in the East

were to be rescued. If the river Elbe–Trave canal was closed by British forces more than seven million Germans would be at the mercy of the Russians.

18–23 April. Commander Cremers' U-boat crews in field grey uniforms destroyed about 40 tanks of the 7th and 11th Armoured Divisions outside Hamburg.

23 April. Hitler decided to remain in Berlin but the Army Supreme HQ moved to Rheinsberg under Generals Kettel and Jodl. Doenitz visited on 28 April and met Himmler who clearly expected to be Hitler's choice as the new Führer.

23 April. Doenitz was informed that Goering had attempted a coup d'etat and Hitler had relieved him of all his responsibilities. General Ritter von Greim was appointed C-in-C of the Luftwaffe. All key communications from Hitler's bunker HQ came from and were signed by Martin Bormann, Hitler's faithful 'controller'. For instance on 30 April a radio signal in naval cipher arrived: 'Fresh treachery afoot. According to enemy broadcast Himmler has made offer to surrender via Sweden. Führer expects you to take instant and ruthless actions against traitors—Bormann.' Doenitz realised that Himmler's control of the SS gave him total protection.

On the evening of 30 April a secure naval cipher message from Berlin arrived:

> Grand Admiral Doenitz. The Führer has appointed you Herr Admiral as his successor in place of Reichsmarschall Goering. Confirmation in writing follows. You are hereby authorised to take any measures which the situation demands. Bormann.

Later Speer told Doenitz that he had recommended the Grand Admiral as Hitler's successor. Doenitz in his autobiography claimed that he was totally surprised:

> For some considerable time it had been my constant fear that the absence of any central authority would lead to chaos and the senseless sacrifice of

hundreds of thousands of lives ... the ensuing chaos would spread too, to the countries which we still occupied and particularly to the Netherlands, Denmark and Norway. Uprisings by the populations of those countries would be met with counter measures by the occupying German troops and would lead to more fighting and bloodshed ...

At midnight on 30 April Himmler arrived by invitation at Ploen, Doenitz's HQ, accompanied by six armed SS officers. Lüedde-Neurath, ADC to Doenitz, received them:

I offered Himmler a chair and myself sat down behind my writing desk, upon which lay hidden by some papers, a pistol with the safety catch off ... I handed Himmler the telegram containing my appointment.... I watched him closely. As he read an expression of astonishment, indeed of consternation spread over his face. All hope seemed to collapse within him. He went very pale. Finally he stood up and bowed, 'Allow me to become the second man in your state.' I replied that that was out of the question. There was no way I could use any of his services. He left at one o'clock in the morning. That same night I ordered Field Marshal Keitel and General Jodl to come to Ploen.

1 May 1945, 3.18 pm. Grand Admiral Doenitz (Top Secret. Only via officers):

Führer deceased yesterday at 3.30 p.m. Testament of April 29 appoints you Reich President, Minister Goebbels Chancellor, Reichsleiter Bormann Party Ministry, Minister Seyss-Inquart Foreign Minister. On the Führer's instructions the testament sent out of Berlin to you and to Field Marshal Schörner to assure its preservation for the people. Reichsleiter Bormann will try to get you today to orient you on the situation. The form and time of announcement to the troops and public are left to you. Confirm receipt. Goebbels. Bormann.

By chance Albert Speer was present when this fateful radio message was delivered. The day before he had met Himmler who was convinced that:

Goering is going to be his successor now. We've long had an understanding that I would be his Premier. Even without Hitler, I can make him chief of state ... You know what he's like. Naturally I'll be the one to make the decisions. I've already been in touch with various persons I mean to take into my cabinet.

Keitel is coming to see me shortly ... Europe cannot manage without me in the future either. It will go on needing me as Minister of Police.

Albert Speer wrote ruefully in his autobiography:

This was the last link in a chain of deceptions, betrayals, hypocrisies and intrigues during those days and weeks. Himmler had betrayed his Führer by negotiations [with Count Bernadotte, the Swedish red Cross representative]. Bormann had carried off his last great intrigue against Goering by playing on Hitler's feelings. Goering was hoping to strike a bargain with the Allies. Kaufmann had made a deal with the British. Keitel was hiring out to a new master while Hitler was still alive.

And I myself, finally in the past months deceived the man [Hitler] who had discovered me and furthered my career: I had even at times considered how to kill him. All of us felt forced to these acts by the system which we ourselves represented—and forced also by Hitler, who for his part had betrayed us all and his people.

On this note the Third Reich ended.

William Shakespeare could have written a marvellous drama—a mixture of Macbeth, Hamlet and Othello.

CHAPTER 8

Speer and the Fourth Reich

Karl Doenitz, the new Chief of Staff, was still caught up in the idea of the National Socialist Regime, just as I was, and more than either of us imagined. For twelve years we had served that regime: we thought it would be cheap opportunism now to make a sharp turnabout. But the death of Hitler broke that mental bind which had for so long warped our thinking. For Doenitz this meant that the objectivity of the trained military officer came to the fore. From the moment he took over [as Führer], Doenitz held that we should end the war as quickly as possible and that once this task was done, our work was over.

On that very 1 May 1945 one of the first military conferences took place between Doenitz as the new Commander in Chief of the armed forces and Field Marshal Ernst Busch. Busch wanted to attack the superior British forces advancing on Hamburg [7th Armoured Desert Rats Division, 15th Scottish and 53rd Welsh Divisions], while Doenitz was against any offensive measures. All that should be done, he said, was to keep the way to the West open as long as possible for the refugees from the East. Columns of them were blocked near Lübeck: a delaying action by the German troops in the West should be continued only to allow the flow to continue, Doenitz said. Busch made a great to-do about the Grand Admiral's no longer acting in Hitler's spirit. But Doenitz was no longer moved by such exhortations. The day before in a dispute with the new Chief of State, Himmler [Commander in Chief of the Army Reserve Ersatz Armee, and still head of the dreaded, sinister Schutzstaffel, the SS, which made him the most powerful man in the Third Reich after Hitler], had been made to understand that there was no place for him in the new government [the Fourth Reich in Flensburg].

So Doenitz, Speer and Himmler had dinner together. It transpired that Gauleiter Kaufmann intended to surrender Hamburg to the British without a fight, and leaflets were being printed addressed to the populace. Doenitz was angry that Kaufmann was taking unilateral action without consultation, and that this would free up more British troops and thus block refugees from the East arriving. Speer then visited Hamburg as the Doenitz herald. However Doenitz soon agreed to a peaceful surrender of that great ruined city, visited in mid-May by this author.

Speer continued:

> Burning oil trucks and automobiles shot up only minutes before lay by the side of the road [out of Hamburg] as I drove back to Eutin Lake. In Schleswig the traffic was heavier, a jumble of military vehicles, civilian cars, columns of people on foot, some soldiers, some civilians. When I was occasionally recognised, no one said anything angry. There was an air of friendly, regretful constraint about the way people greeted me. I arrived at the HQ in Plon on the evening of 2 May.
>
> Doenitz had already moved to Flensburg to evade the rapidly advancing British troops [11th Armoured Division and 6th Airborne with looted transport]. But I met [General Wilhelm] Keitel [Chief of Staff of the OKW, High Command of the armed forces who soon organised the surrender of the German army before his arrest] and [General Alfred] Jodl [who soon signed on behalf of Admiral Doenitz the unconditional surrender of Germany to Field Marshal Bernard Montgomery], who were on the point of leaving to join their new master. Doenitz had taken up quarters on the passenger ship Patria [moored on Flensburg lake]. We had breakfast together in the captain's cabin and there I presented him with an Edict prohibiting the destruction of any facilities, including bridges. He promptly signed it [technically the end of Operation Nero], thus I had achieved at last every point of the programme I had demanded of Hitler on 19 March—although it was now far too late.

Doenitz then agreed that Speer should make a radio speech from the Flensburg studio, hooked into German forces radio in Copenhagen and Oslo, urging the German people in the area already captured by the Allies to turn all their energies into reconstruction and:

> … counteract the lethargy which had come over the people as a result of the paralysing horror and the immeasurable disillusionment of recent months.

Speer had to show the draft of his speech to Graf von Schwerin-Krosigk, the new Foreign Minister, who was a member of the old German nobility, a Rhodes scholar at Oxford who in March 1945 urged Goebbels to help make peace perhaps via the Pope or the League of Nations. All this time Himmler with a large bodyguard of SS troops was scurrying around urging Doenitz and Speer that valuable territories in Norway, Denmark and part of Holland were:

> ... pledges for our security. These were of sufficient importance to the enemy so that we could negotiate concessions for ourselves in exchange for the assurance that we would surrender them intact [without fighting].

On 5 May Doenitz had personally rejected similar suggestions from Joseph Terboven, Hitler's governor in Norway. On 6 May Doenitz signed an order prohibiting demolitions of any kind in the still occupied territories, parts of Holland, Czechoslovakia, Denmark and Norway.

Doenitz resisted suggestions from Himmler and others to remove the Fourth Reich HQ to Denmark or Prague. 'An old Imperial City, Himmler urged, was more fitting as the HQ of a government than historically insignificant Flensburg.' Doenitz realised that such a move would take the HQ from naval protection into a city in the power of the SS.

Speer noted how senior gauleiters, Koch of East Prussia, Lohse, Rosenberg and others, appeared demanding flights or voyages by submarine to South America. Arthur Seyss-Inquart, Reichskommissar for Holland and responsible for a wicked brutal regime:

> ... rode a PT boat through the enemy blockade at night to confer with Doenitz and me, but he refused the chance to remain at the seat of government [in Flensburg] and returned to Holland in his PT boat. 'My place is there' he said mournfully, 'I'll be arrested immediately after my return'. He was, was tried at Nuremburg and there hanged on 16 October 1947.

On 7 May the armoured infantry troops of 11th Armoured Division arrived and encircled Flensburg.

> There was now only a tiny enclave in which our government still had executive authority. The Control Commission for the OKW under Major General Rooks installed itself on the Patria and soon began functioning as a liaison office to the Doenitz government. To my mind, the capitulation meant that the Doenitz government had done its job in bringing the lost war to an end.

But Wilhelm Stuckart, State Secretary of the Ministry of the Interior (to Himmler), wrote a memorandum to all the ministers of the Fourth Reich stating that Doenitz as Chief of State and Hitler's legitimate successor, had no right to surrender his position. The continuity of the German Reich should be preserved and the legitimacy of future governments would not be imperilled. Doenitz then agreed with Stuckart.

It must sound absurd that this pathetic little bunch of once-powerful men, who had held sway for many years over Hitler's huge evil conquests, most of Europe—and now holed up in a pretty little town with no Wehrmacht, no Luftwaffe, no Navy, should consider affairs of state in such detail. But to Major General Rooks US, and Brigadier Foord UK the issue was clear. If Doenitz encouraged or ordered his Reichkommisars in Norway, Denmark and Holland to fight on, and several hundred U-boats to torpedo every vessel they encountered, there would be utter chaos with several hundred thousand lives at risk. Operation Eclipse could only start its business of reconstruction in the destroyed Third Reich when all of the occupied territories totally surrendered themselves and all their weaponry.

Speer, an astute observer of the government, noted: 'The first British and American newspapermen arrived in Flensburg on 7th May'. Alan Moorehead, as recounted in his excellent book *Eclipse,* beat the whistle. On Saturday 5 May he flew into Copenhagen with the armed airborne troops, General Dening and an Admiral, with their staff. A day of splendid liberation followed and then on the 7th he and Alexander Clifford flew into Oslo. The amazing trinity of the British Navy, Army and Air force swept into Norway, Denmark and Holland and seized control of those three important countries without denial.

Back in Flensburg Speer observed that by magic all SS uniforms vanished; overnight Gauleiter Paul Wegener (Bremen) and now Reichkommissar for civil affairs, and Wilhelm Stuckart, SS Obergruppenführer Otto Ohlendorf became 'civilians'. Dr Karl Gebhardt, Himmler's intimate, transferred himself into a Red Cross 'general', and Ernst Backe and Julius Dorpmüller, both ministers in Doenitz's new cabinet, simply vanished in a plane towards General Eisenhower's HQ. Field Marshal Wilhelm Keitel, still Chief of the German High Command, was taken prisoner. Most of the 5,000 German troops were allowed to carry side arms.

> We composed memoranda in a vacuum, trying to offset our unimportance by sham activity. Every morning at ten, a cabinet meeting took place in the Cabinet Room, a former school room.

Speer was probably the most important Reich survivor from the Allied point of view. For four days he was interviewed by the United States Strategic Bombing Survey (USSBS) team on Eisenhower's staff in the sixteenth-century Glücksburg castle several miles from Flensburg. On 19 May Chairman d'Olier, Vice-Chairman Henry Alexander, assistant Dr Galbraith, Paul Nitze, George Ball, Colonel Gilkrest and Williams systematically went through various aspects of the air war and the effects of the bombing. Amongst Speer's outstanding talents was the way the many key elements of the Reich factories went underground outside the main cities, thus allowing a very high rate of production to continue.

On 23 May back in Flensburg:

> I could see that many anti-tank guns [of the 11th Armoured Division] were trained on Glücksburg Castle. Shortly afterwards the Reich war flag, which had been raised every day at the naval school, was taken down by the British.

Later at the great Nüremburg Trials Speer pleaded guilty and was sentenced to 20 years' imprisonment for his use of slave labour in his many production programmes. If the courts had been fully aware of his efforts and considerable success in neutralising Adolf Hitler's Operation Nero appalling edict to destroy all the Third Reich infrastructure, he might have been given a lighter sentence.

He was released from Spandau prison in Berlin in 1966 and died in 1981.

CHAPTER 9

The Race for Berlin

For nearly 60 years the Allied failure to capture Berlin *before* Stalin's armies in April–May 1945 has been controversial.

Field Marshal Montgomery brusquely informed SHAEF on 24 March 1945 what he intended:

> I explained my plan of moving up to the [river] Elbe line and drew on the map the right boundary that I suggested for 21 Army Group, i.e. between me and Bradley. The only comment made by Ike was that he though Magdeburg (on the Elbe) should be inclusive to Bradley ... I at once agreed and Bradley agreed also. No other comment was made.

Monty assumed that he had authority to cast caution aside and strike deep into Germany with Allied armour and close air support.

On 27 March he sent the following signal to Eisenhower:

> My intention is to drive hard for the line of the Elbe using [the American] Ninth Army and [the British] Second Army. The right of the Ninth will be directed on Magdeburg and the left of the second Army on Hamburg ... I have ordered Ninth and Second to move their armoured and mobile forces forward at once and to get through to the Elbe with the utmost speed and drive. The situation looks good ... My Tactical HQ moves to an area 1033 NW of Bonninghardt on Thursday 29th March. Thereafter the axis on which my TAC HQ will move will be Wesselmunster-Wiedenbruck-Herford-Hannover—then via the Autobahn to Berlin I hope.

From a military point of view the Western Front at the end of March was wide open, for General Model's armies in the Ruhr were encircled by 18 American divisions. They created a 200-mile breach which Kesselring or any other commander could not possibly close—yes delay of course, but ahead of Montgomery there were no prepared defences, apart from five river barriers, nor any field armies; no physical barriers that could not be quickly broken, although the Ibbenburen 30-mile ridge, brilliantly defended, caused some delay. The main resistance would come from the remnants of General Student's Paratroop Army and Admiral Doenitz's Marine divisions. With Bradley's Ninth Army, Montgomery had 60 divisions, huge stocks of petrol and stores, well forward on the Rhine and ample transport to move them eastwards 300 miles towards Berlin. Chester Wilmot wrote in his book The Struggle for Europe:

> Eisenhower's administrative resources were more than adequate to carry his armies to Berlin in irresistible strength [author's emphasis].... Politically, too, the way was clear for though the German capital lay in the centre of this area which was to be occupied by the Soviet Union after the war, it had never been suggested that the military forces of one power should not enter the occupation zone of another in pursuit of the common enemy. Nor was there any agreement that Berlin was to be captured by the Red Army. At the Yalta conference this question had not even been discussed ...

However, cables between the President and Stalin were misinterpreted and the latter gained the impression that the Allies were negotiating unilaterally for peace. In effect he accused their leaders of treachery.

Eisenhower was on record as having asked General Omar Bradley 'how many casualties do you thing the capture of Berlin from the west (i.e. the Allied armies) will cost us?' Bradley recalled that in the Ardennes Battle of the Bulge in December 1944–January 1945 the American casualties had been about 100,000, and produced this figure for Ike. This figure would be totally unacceptable to his commander in Washington, General C. G. Marshall. In a political voting year the electorate in the USA would be horrified at such a casualty count.

The relationship between Bradley and Montgomery had been soured by humiliations in Normandy and in the Ardennes. So, like Iago, he persuaded Ike to withdraw his US Ninth Army from Monty's control.

At the same time in late March 1945, Eisenhower and the senior members of SHAEF had become convinced that Hitler himself or one of his senior generals would conduct a major defence of the so-called 'Southern Redoubt'. This area centred around Hitler's Berchtesgaden, a small town in the Bavarian Alps. The Obersalzberg 'Eagle's Nest' was one of Hitler's command centres 6,400 feet above sea-level. The Redoubt was an area 240 miles in length and 80 miles in depth and comprised the western half of Austria. Eisenhower wrote post war in his 'D-Day to V-E Day 1944/5':

> Evidence had been received that the [Hitler] government were preparing to evacuate Berlin and move southward, ultimately perhaps to Berchtesgaden in the National Redoubt.

Bradley too was convinced that Hitler would make a last stand in his Eagle's Nest with all surviving troops. It would take 'an army' to subdue them. So, unilaterally, without apparent consultation with anybody else, Eisenhower sent a personal message to Joseph Stalin in Moscow on 28 March 1945:

> My immediate operations are designed to encircle and destroy the enemy forces defending the Ruhr etc. etc.

No mention at all of an advance on Berlin. He made sure that Montgomery was informed:

> ...Ninth United States Army will revert to Bradley's command. The mission of your army group will be to protect Bradley's northern flank.

Monty said to his staff, 'All very dirty work, I fear.'

On 29 March 1945 Major Hansen, ADC to General Bradley, Commander of the US Ninth Army, wrote in his diary:

> In the Third Army sector, the 4th Armoured Division is continuing north towards Kassel to complete our first phase of the battle for Berlin.

Initially Churchill was horrified and very angry that the Supreme Commander, without consulting him or Montgomery, should make such a major decision, compounded by sending it as a personal message to Stalin. By now Stalin was reneging on previous agreements, particularly in regard to Polish elections. Churchill remonstrated quite strongly with Eisenhower and on 5 April sent a serious message to President Roosevelt:

> There is very little doubt in my mind that the Soviet leaders, whoever they may be, are surprised and disconcerted at the rapid advance of the Allied armies in the West and the almost total defeat of the enemy on our front, especially as they [the Russians] say they are themselves in no position to deliver a decisive attack before the middle of May. All this makes it the most important that we should join hands with the Russian armies as far to the east as possible, and, if circumstances allow, enter Berlin.

So on 7 April Churchill notified the Chiefs of Staff including General Ismay:

> If we crossed the Elbe and advanced to Berlin, or on a line between Berlin and Berlin and the Baltic which is all well with the Russian zone we should not give this up as a **military matter** [author's emphasis].

What then happened?

The Nazi Southern Redoubt was a hoax. There was no defiant Götterdämmerung of any kind. Montgomery's British Liberation Army reached the River Elbe at Lauenberg on 19 April 1945. This author was Forward Observation Officer with the battle group 4 KSLI/3 RTR and was the first British officer to reach that river and start firing his self-propelled guns at targets across the river.

Berlin was less than a hundred miles away.

But Stalin's armies under Generals Zhukov, Konev and Rokossovsky totalling 2.5 million men, 6,250 tanks and 42,000 guns, aided by hundreds of planes, smashed their way 235 miles to swamp the German defences around Berlin. The Red Army had 352,425 casualties with over 100,000 dead. So Eisenhower was perfectly sensible in declining the honour of capturing Hitler's citadel.

CHAPTER 10

Racing the Russians
to the Baltic

It had taken Lt General 'Bubbles' Barker's 8th Corps a month to advance from the Rhine in Operation Plunder to reach the river Elbe. It had covered more than 200 miles and on the way captured 700 German officers and over 30,000 men. 11th Armoured Division had led for most of the way, although the 6th Airborne, having recovered from their mauling in Operation Varsity, kept up at an astonishing rate. The author's battle group, 3rd RTR/4th KSLI, were the first to see the great river on the morning of 19 April. The long metallic railway bridge across into the town of Lauenburg was within 200 yards of the leading 3rd RTR Comets when it was blown up in their faces.

In the meantime, Prime Minister Churchill was having a heated exchange with Marshal Stalin over the fate of fifteen Polish diplomats sent to Moscow to try to negotiate future boundaries with the Russians. Eventually, true to form, a show trial on 18 June meant that the leadership of the Polish Underground Movement was liquidated. President Roosevelt, ailing for months, died on 12 April, which of course inspired Hitler in his Berlin bunker and depressed Churchill. Anthony Eden, British Foreign Secretary, was in Washington to meet President Harry Truman, newly elected. Churchill sent Eden a telegraph message on 19 April:

This is for your eyes alone. It would seem that the Western Allies are not immediately in a position to force their way into Berlin [despite Eisenhower's unilateral message to Stalin on 28 March]. The Russians have two and a half million troops on the sector of the front opposite that city. The Americans have only their spearheads, say 25 divisions, which are covering an immense

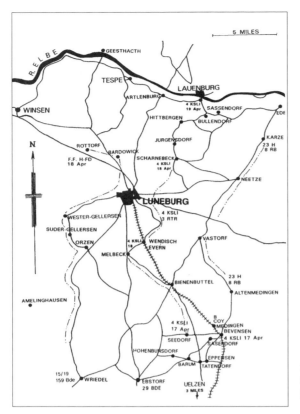

11th Armoured Division drive to reach the Elbe opposite Lauenburg.

front and are at many points engaged with the Germans ... It is thought most important that Montgomery should take Lübeck [key port half way between Hamburg and Wismar], as soon as possible, and he has an additional American Army Corps to strengthen his movements if he requires it. Our arrival at Lübeck before our Russian friends from Stettin would save a lot of argument later on.

There is no reason why the Russians should occupy Denmark, which is a country to be liberated and to have its sovereignty restored. Our position at Lübeck, if we get it, would be decisive in this matter.

Churchill also wanted the Americans to check the region south of Stuttgart: 'In this region are the main German installations connected with their atomic research and we had better get hold of these in the interests of the special secrecy attached to this topic [known as Tube Alloys]'.

Captured German Kampfengruppe troops. (*Imperial War Museum*)

The last remnants of the German Army move on to Luneburg to surrender.

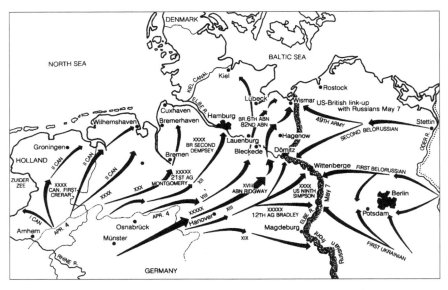

The Allied dash to the Baltic, reaching Wismar before the Russians was vital.

'Hitler's Nuclear Option', relates how the 'Thieving Magpies' flew into action with some success.

Montgomery now had to choose how to get the British Liberation Army across the Elbe and corral the two million Germans, many of whom were wounded in hospitals, and end the war. He still hoped that Eisenhower and SHAEF would allow him to advance on Berlin despite the latter's embargo. He thought, on 19 April, that Bremen and Hamburg would need serious attacks and he genuinely believed that he could not launch Operation Enterprise—the forced crossing of the Elbe—quickly. Then Eisenhower recalled the US 9th Army, which was still nominally under Monty's control!

In his official account published in *The London Gazette* on 4 September 1946, Montgomery wrote: 'The main drive to the Elbe continued towards Lüneburg, which was reached on the 18th [April] and our forces began to line up on the southern bank of the river masking the city of Hamburg. The Elbe was crossed on 29 April and spearheads made straight for Lübeck in order to seal off Schleswig-Holstein peninsula.' There is no mention of what his great army did for the days 19–29 April. No mention of the urgency that Churchill in particular wanted to get to the Baltic *before* the Russians.

Right: Captain Graham Scott, A Squadron 3 RTR, marking up his map. (*Les Slater*)

Below: A Squadron 3 RTR Comets on the move north towards the river Elbe. (*Les Slater*)

General Eisenhower's report, written on 13 July 1945, 'D-Day to VE Day', spelt out his and SHAEF's policy:

> In the north a route lay across the North German Plain towards the Baltic and Berlin. Berlin was the symbol of victory before the eyes of every Allied soldier from the day we set foot in Normandy, but other gains would spring from an advance to the northern sector, gains which were at least as important as those to be derived from capture of the German capital. By a thrust to the Baltic we should cut off from the main enemy armies those elements which were located in Denmark, Norway, northwest Germany and Holland, at once depriving them of supplies and preventing their *coming to the assistance of the forces in the center of Germany.*
>
> Furthermore we should gain the north German ports [Bremen for the Americans] and thus deny the enemy use of his naval bases and ship-building yards, bringing to an end the activities of the submarines and other craft which had for so long preyed upon our supply routes. Finally we should link hands with the Russian forces sweeping across Pomerania to the north of Berlin.

The American 9th Army, under Montgomery's command for Operation Plunder, reverted to General Bradley. When Montgomery complained that the British Liberation Army was not strong enough to force a crossing over the Elbe (see Chester Wilmot's report below), he was allocated the US 18th Airborne Corps to help:

> 30 April 1945. Here in the north, there's still an army to be reckoned with; an army whose fighting power Himmler [he had been appointed C-in-C Home Army, after the 20 July plot] may still regard as a bargaining weapon. We have smashed the German Army as a whole and its Air Force; but we haven't yet broken the power or the spirit of the German Navy. And it's now fighting hard in defence of its great ports and naval bases in the north. Even though the navy has never been thoroughly pro-Nazi, it has been unquestionably loyal to the German High Command. In Kiel, Wilhelmshaven and the northern ports there are more than 100,000 German naval personnel—most of them with some training in the use of weapons, and they're being put into the land battle. We're meeting marines, sailors, and even submarine crews, and they're fighting well.
>
> Moreover, when Field Marshal Busch became Commander-in-Chief North-West, he took over an area where the organisation and discipline behind the lines was still good, because the navy still had the situation firmly in hand.

Busch also found that in addition to the troops fighting south of the Elbe he had four other divisions that he could bring from Denmark. He thus had the core of a force to protect the naval bases, and the navy was determined that he should use it to do so. This combination of circumstances has provided the 2nd Army with the immediate task of isolating and smashing this force, and of seizing the naval bases behind it. We can't afford at this stage of the war to pause in the task. So long as there are any pockets of resistance as well organised as this one, the Nazis may be encouraged to fight on elsewhere. And so here in the north the 2nd Army is striking at what amounts to Himmler's last hope.

Eisenhower's report continued:

Although it was not conceivable that resistance could long be maintained in the north German plain, it was possible that some withdrawal might be attempted into Denmark and Norway with a view to make a last stand in those countries while 'Fortress Holland' would also continue to hold out behind the water barriers. The prevention of such a withdrawal by means of a *rapid* [author's emphasis] Allied advance to the Baltic, thus became the primary objective of our operations in the northern sector. For the subsequent reduction of Norway, in the event that the German garrison there [nearly 400,000] continued to hold out, a task force was assembled in Scotland under the command of Lt General Sir Andrew Thorne.

Eisenhower and SHAEF certainly made sure that Montgomery's 'orders' were to be a very rapid drive, come what may, to the Baltic, including Kiel, the whole of Denmark and the remainder of Holland.

Operation Enterprise was a slow, thorough, methodical assault plan to gain two bridgeheads over the river Elbe, in the Alamein and Rhine crossing style, for the assault. Montgomery chose 15th Scottish Division to make the main attack; they were christened 'The Crossing Sweepers' after the Seine, the Escaut, the Rhine and now the Elbe. The Commando Brigade would be tasked to capture the town of Lauenburg, and 11th Armoured and 6th Airborne would set off north to thwart Marshal Konstantin Rokossovsky's 2nd Belorussian Army, which was making rapid progress through Mecklenburg and heading west.

For a week, very complicated plans were being drawn up for the assault crossing of the river Elbe. 8th Corps was given the honour of establishing a bridgehead, initially 1,500 yards deep and 2,500 yards wide. This would be the responsibility of 15th Scottish with 1st

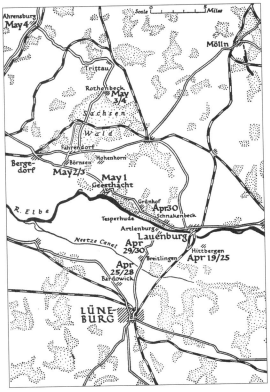

Above: Prisoners being interrogated after the capture of Zeven, among them youths, only fourteen years old, from the Volksturm.

Left: The final battlegrounds beyond the Elbe, Operation Enterprise.

Operation Enterprise: 10 HLI troops have crossed the river Elbe, 19 April 1945.

Commando Brigade under command. And 11th Armoured would then pass through and thrust north for Lübeck, Kiel and the Danish frontier.

The complications arose because the northern bank of the river Elbe is a substantial steep escarpment, which would make Buffalo or DUKW landings difficult. Moreover, enemy observation points had clear observation of the southern bank activities for several miles. No vehicle movements were allowed in the forward positions during daylight. The Elbe in April is about 300 yards in width in the Artlenburg-Lauenburg stretch and flows at about two knots. There was only one road into Artlenburg, a small town with narrow side streets with gardens and woods, and another from Scharnesbeck to Lauenburg. Enemy strength was estimated at about nine battalions of very mixed provenance with about 100 guns, and rather surprisingly supported by daring Luftwaffe jet plane attacks.

The final plan for Operation Enterprise was for a two-brigade attack at 0200 hrs on 29 April, under 'Monty's Searchlights', supported by a substantial barrage from seventeen artillery regiments.

1st Commando Brigade was tasked with a crossing west of Hohnstorf, to capture Lauenburg from the rear. 44th Brigade, led by the Royal Scots and RSF on board the LVTs of 11th RTR, would attack through the Grünhof forests to capture Schnakenbeck, starting from just west and east of Artlenburg.

Colonel R. Foster, Commander of 11th Army Group Royal Engineers, who had masterminded the complex Rhine crossing so successfully, was in charge of the plan for the Elbe crossing. This included suitable DD tank and LVT approaches; river entries and exits; a DUKW crossing; two 12-person assault boat ferries, at the Lauenburg crossing a Class 9 raft ferry and a Class 9 bridge of folding-bridge equipment; for the Artlenburg crossing a Class 40 raft ferry and a Class 40 Bailey pontoon-bridge. Colonel Foster also had to provide boom protection above and below the crossing places.

The follow-up plan was for 46th Brigade to go through the Commando bridgehead, and for 227th Brigade through 44th Brigade. The Recce Regiment would land its armoured cars and carriers in the van of the assault and push out patrols to the north, west and east. The bridgehead was a country of field and farm, deer forests and lakes, lonely castles, villages and little country towns, and west, along the Elbe, the outskirts of the sprawling mangled port of Hamburg.

Operation Enterprise went well. The courage of the sappers who built the pontoon bridges regardless of damage or casualties was beyond all praise. The immense fire plan fell on the German 245th Wehrmacht Division strongpoints. At exactly 0218hrs the huge black Buffaloes of 11th RTR, with the 77th Assault Squadron RE AVRE bombards, carried the 8th Royal Scots and 6th RSF across from two crossing points: Hohnstorf opposite Lauenburg and Artlenburg on the left. At 0330hrs the Argylls and KOSB crossed, as did the Seaforths on the Commando front. Altogether Hobart's 'Funnies' made 1,139 lifts during Enterprise, of infantry carriers, jeeps, scout cars, Weasels, anti-tank guns and trailers.

15th Scottish took a different centre line over the Elbe at Lutau, where the Glasgow Highlanders had a fight, Royal Scots met enemy SPs in Kollow. KOSB sent patrols into Gülzower Holz wood, took many prisoners and found two long-range 12-inch guns, which had shelled the Enterprise bridgehead, then Grünhof and Tesperhude. The HLI reached Wiershop, the Argylls Krummel and the Gordons Hamwarde. On 1 May Geesthach and its garrison surrendered over the phone to Brigadier Colville. In the town was a store of V-1 rocket fuel and ammunition and a dangerous stock of poison gas containers. 15th Scottish were joined by 53rd Welsh and also 5th British Division (arriving from Italy) to clear the huge forest to the west of Sachsenwald. The KOSB captured the Prince and Princess von Bismarck in the schloss of Friedrichsruh. The sixteen-eighteen-year-old cadets from the Flak school in Hamburg had a bitter last battle with the HLI in Hohenhern and Neu Bornsen. In deep hillside gulleys, east of Bornsen, they used their 20 mm light A/A guns to good effect until artillery and tanks dealt with them.

The Recce Regiment in Elmenhorst noted: 'We were checking the amazing procession of the defeated German forces along the Hamburg road. They were coming from the east and the north. There were men on foot, men on bicycles and men in carts. There were wheezing, massive dilapidated lorries dragging three or four or five trailers, all piled high with passengers and baggage. When stopped, some of the lorries managed to start again. Many did not. Looking at this motley collection, one wondered how the German Army had managed to resist so long.'

The endless stream of uniformed jetsam poured along every road: Luftwaffe, Flak units, marines, panzergrenadiers, U-boat crews, town police, Volksturm, a few Hitler *Jugend*, a few SS (some were still fighting in the Forst Segeberg). However, their fierce discipline and allegiance to their now-dead Führer kept them going indomitably. The Allied air forces ruled the skies. The Allied tanks and AFVs and artillery forces outnumbered the Wehrmacht by ten to one, and the writing was on the

6th Airborne paratroops meet Russians at Wismar. (*Imperial War Museum*)

wall during Overlord and the irresistible Russian advances. However, it was not until all the German towns were crammed with dead and wounded, with red crosses painted on the hospital roofs and the survivors penned into Schleswig-Holstein that there was a final surrender. And that was mainly due to the death of Hitler in a sordid Berlin bunker.

The Commandos rapidly cleared Lauenburg and captured the road bridge over the Elbe-Trave Canal. On the same day the Scots Greys Sherman tanks of 4th Black Rat Armoured Brigade teamed up with two brigades of 6th Airborne Division, and crossed over and reached Boizenburg in the evening. Early on 2 May the Scots Greys and Airborne troops covered the 70 miles to Wismar in about 8 hours. Lt Edmiston's troop were followed by Lt Colonel D. N. Stewart, the Greys' CO in a scout car, followed by the CO of 3rd Parachute Brigade riding pillion on a despatch rider's motorcycle! Wittenburg was passed, despite meeting towed 88mm guns. They went through Lutzon and Gladebusch with minor actions on the way. Eight miles short of Wismar, B Squadron destroyed five trains laden with German soldiery and equipment. At 1300hrs the Greys' recce troop reached Wismar and their eleven Honeys (small fast tanks) discovered an aerodrome north-east of the town on the

The British 6th Airborne Division's first contact with Russian troops at Wismar.

seashore. Some shooting took place and 200 Luftwaffe troops marching in threes in perfect step came out of the hangers and surrendered. During the evening Russian troops, male and female, drunk and sober, appeared in 'White' scout cars, fraternised for half an hour shaking hands and drinking vodka, then withdrew eastwards and erected a monster road block, the first instalment of the Iron Curtain! By late evening the whole of 3rd Parachute Brigade had taken control of Wismar.

The 11th Armoured Division in two mixed brigade battle groups crossed the Elbe in the early evening of 30 April and by the evening of 1 May had reached Sandesneben and Gronwold. On the next day they had occupied Bad Oldesloe and Reinfeld and liberated a POW Luft camp containing RAF personnel, near Kastorf. At 1530hrs the 2nd Fife and Forfars' Comets with 1st Cheshires' infantry entered Lübeck while 23rd Hussars and 8th Rifle Brigade headed towards Travemünde and Neustadt. By evening the naval installations and airfields were taken and reported to be in good condition. Between 2 and 4 May the division captured 70,000 prisoners and no fewer than twenty-five generals and admirals, and freed hundreds of Allied POWs. Major General Pip Roberts, the dashing GOC of the Black Bull Division, had one final task. He took a Comet tank squadron and infantry to Flensburg on the Danish border to tell Grand Admiral Doenitz, Hitler's reluctant successor, and Field Marshal Keitel, head of OKW (German Armed Forces) with the Supreme HQ of OKW, that pending the arrival of a special mission from SHAEF, they were under 11th Armoured orders.

A day or so before the Fife and Forfars entered Lübeck a terrible disaster had taken place. The German SS concentration bosses at Neuengamme KZ had decided to liquidate the remaining 10,000 prisoners before the British arrived. The camp was just outside Hamburg and over the last seven years 40,000 mainly Jewish men, women and children had been murdered there. The SS guards numbered 800 and Rothenburgsort, a Hamburg suburb, was a killing centre. An uprising by Russian prisoners was savagely put down. As the BLA approached Hamburg over 7,000 prisoners were marched or were sent by train to Lübeck and herded into two large passenger liners, 2,000 into the *Deutschland* and 5,000 into the *Cap Acona*, both used as prison hulks. Nine Typhoon fighter bombers of the RAF 198th Squadron, led by Squadron Leader Martin Rumbold, saw the tempting target of four ships in Lübeck harbour. In their attack over 3,000 POWs were burned

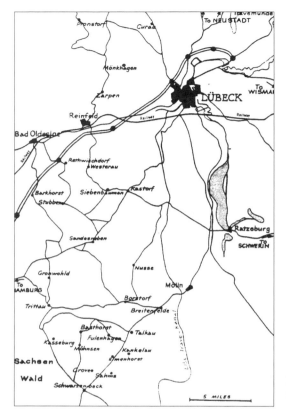

The route to Lübeck and the end
of Operation Enterprise.

Lübeck harbour: 11th Armoured
Division Cromwell tank.
(*Imperial War Museum*)

British soldiers interrogating members of the staff of the German State Railway HQ, captured near Lübeck while they were trying to leave the country.

to death on the *Cap Acona*, and many others, including Poles, Czechs, Norwegians and many Russians died.

Major Anthony Hibbert was Brigade Major of 1st Parachute Brigade and was taken prisoner at Arnhem, but he escaped. Having broken his leg in a car accident he was unable to rejoin the Paras in an active role, so in March 1945 he was appointed the co-ordinating officer for an airborne operation to seize the vital port of Kiel. He reported to Lt General Browning's AA HQ. Apparently Eisenhower had requested plans in December 1944 for an operation to seize Kiel. However, T-Force personnel had to be included, with a Royal Naval officer as second in command. As the British Liberation Army advanced so swiftly into the heart of Germany, the airborne drop was not needed. Hibbert then joined his friend Brian Urquhart, the intelligence officer in Market Garden whose advice went unheeded. Both were therefore key members of T-Force and tasked with investigating 150 targets in Kiel (compared to 75 in Hamburg). With a T-Force of 500 strong, they had to confront the Kiel garrison of 40,000 kriegsmarines with their slave army of 420,000 foreign labourers.

One key problem was that General Dempsey's order from Montgomery's HQ 10 minutes after the 4 May surrender said: 'No advance beyond

The Hamburg-American Line's 27,000 ton *New York* after being bombed during an air attack on Kiel.

this line to take place without orders from me.' All four Corps were to stand fast on the line Dömitz, Ludwigslust, Schwerin, Wismar, Neustadt, Bad Segeberg, Wedel, Stade, Bremervorde and Bremen. So Kiel was in *verboten* territory. Another problem was that T-Force, although a law unto themselves, had no written authority to advance to Kiel.

Urquhart told Hibbert that it was possible that the Russians contained at Wismar could launch an amphibious commando operation to seize the port of Kiel, which was an ice-free port with easy access to the North Sea. The prime target for T-Force was the Walterwerke factory and its chief designer, Dr Hellmuth Walter, whose new developments for U-boat design were important. Brigadier G. H. C. Pennycock, the OC T-Force and Lt Colonel Ray Bloomfield, the senior staff officer, concurred: '... advance to Kiel and investigate the specified targets'.

Besides the 5th King's battalion of infantry, there were detachments of the Special Boat Squadron (SBS), the Special Air Service (SAS) and Royal Marine Commandos in this T-Force battle group. D Squadron 1st SAS Regiment led in jeeps from Bad Segeberg at 0800hrs on VE Day [Ref. WO 285/12]. In Neumünster the jeeps of 30th Assault Unit Royal Marines with their White Ensigns fluttering surged into the lead. Later there was controversy about the first unit to enter Kiel: SAS/SBS/30th Assault? Over 80 per cent of the city was in ruins, the cathedral in pieces, the railway station shattered and 40 per cent of T-Force targets had been obliterated. Hibbert headed for the Naval Academy under Kapitan Wilhelm Möhr, who was sceptical that 200 assorted British had authority to ask for surrender [Ref. WO 205/1049]. A phone call to Admiral Doenitz in Flensburg achieved his agreement to the surrender. Among the vessels in the port were the *Prinz Eugen* and *Admiral Hipper*, two powerful heavy cruisers. The King's men secured most of the port, quays, wharfs and docks. The three intrepid majors, Hibbert, Gaskell and Lambert, issued orders from the city's police HQ at 2.30 p.m. German troops for the time being could keep their weapons, while the freed slave labourers were forbidden to carry arms. The latter were told in French, English and German that they would be returned to their homes as soon as possible. 30th Assault unit soon 'captured' Dr Walter, a heavy, flabby, black-haired Nazi. He was an important find and soon a posse of high-powered Royal Navy scientists under Commander Aylen arrived to supervise investigation of Dr Walter's microfilms, machinery and plant. T-Force targets included ELAC, whose Dr Fisher was an

German POWs in Lübeck. (*Imperial War Museum*)

outstanding torpedo designer, Krupp Germania, where a complete Type XXIII submarine was discovered, and Deutsche Werke, where small U-boats were being built. Eventually, two days later, a Guards unit of 8th Corps arrived to organise a Victory Parade. Hibbert was officially in disgrace. Lt General Barker arrived in Kiel and told him that Admiral Baillie-Grohman, whose powerful naval squadron had 'liberated' Copenhagen, now intended to 'liberate' Kiel. Nevertheless, Hibbert and Urquhart had shown splendid initiative. After the war the grateful citizens of Kiel awarded Hibbert the 'Great Seal of Kiel' for his role, along with 500 commandos and paratroops, in capturing the port-city, which prevented the Russians from invading Denmark.

Guards Armoured were tasked with clearing up the rectangle west of Hamburg and the Elbe, which included Bremervörde, Stade, Himmelpforten, Hechthausen and most importantly, the naval port of Cuxhaven. After liberating the camps of Westertimke and Sandbostel, they found eleven enormous craters, 60 feet across and 40 feet deep caused by sea mine explosions around Bremervörde. Every army bulldozer for miles around was co-opted and within 24 hours eight of the craters were filled up.

A whole battalion of 351st Marine Division was guarding the Hamme-Oste canal bridge and 51st Highland Division was asked to take them on. The Guards moved east to tackle Stade, also protected by giant craters. A Coldstream battle group managed to find a way round cross-country. Stade, with five hospitals containing over a thousand German wounded, surrendered without a fight. The Irish battle group then took Elm and Oldendorf after the news of the deaths of Hitler and Goebbels was heard on the radio. It must have demoralised many local listeners. Bremervörde then capitulated unexpectedly.

Major General Allan Adair, in his history of the Guards Armoured details the complicated negotiations of the days just after the Armistice was signed. The German General Goltzsch, commander of Corps Ems in the Cuxhaven peninsula, General Erdmann, GOC 17th Parachute Division, and two well-known kampfgruppen COs, Colonels Grassmel and Hardegg, were all involved in surrender negotiations. The Royal Navy sent a detachment under Captain Lawford RN, as Cuxhaven was a great port. The 101 ships in the harbour included a destroyer, nine submarines and eleven minesweepers. In the middle of the night five more destroyers arrived from Norway, anxious to surrender. The 7th

Tank dozer pushes an enemy tank off the Bremervorde road, 1 May 1945. (*Birkin Haward*)

Assault bridge laid by 82 Assault Squadron RE in final action at Bremevorde, 2 May 1945. (*Birkin Haward*)

Field Marshal Montgomery meets General Rokossovsk at Wismar.

Parachute Division under Colonel Menzel was paraded on the captured airfield and surrendered with great dignity. They ranked among the very finest troops in the German Army and refused to surrender to any unit except the Guards Armoured.

On 11 May the Guards provided a company of Scots Guards plus sappers from 615th Field Squadron to accompany and guard Rear Admiral Muirhead-Gould RN on an expedition in four minesweepers to accept the surrender of Heligoland, an island 50 miles north-west of Cuxhaven in the North Sea. The admiral's flotilla rendezvous was off the island of Neuwerk at the end of the Elbe estuary. There were 7,000 kriegsmarines on Heligoland, plus 2,000 TODT workers kept busy repairing the continual damage done by the RAF over the years. The artificial manmade harbour had space for two large 'basins', a huge submarine pen, barracks and other military buildings. But cut deep in the rock was a naval town, offices, power stations, torpedo rooms, food and wine stores, hospitals. The whole garrison could live there in complete safety. It was the German Rock of Gibraltar.

Montgomery signalled the War Office in London on 3 May as soon as he knew that 6th Airborne had made contact at Bunz, 7 miles east

The Baltic round-up by the British Liberation Army.

The author (right) in Kiel, early May 1945.

of Wismar: 'There is no doubt that the very rapid movement from the Elbe bridgeheads north to the Baltic was a very fine performance on the part of the troops concerned. There is no doubt also that we only just beat the Russians by about 12 hours. All's well that ends well and the whole of the Schleswig peninsula and Denmark is now effectively sealed off and we shall keep it so ... the flood of German troops and civilians fleeing from the approaching Russians is a spectacle that can seldom have been seen before.'

It was indeed a close-run thing. The Russians vigorously attacked and held the Danish island of Bornholm, 57 miles from the mainland. It was a German naval base occupied by the kriegsmarines since 1940, commanded by Commander Kamptz. Prime Minister Churchill signalled Anthony Eden, then in San Francisco: 'The British Naval Attaché in Stockholm reported that the Russians may have dropped parachutists a few miles south of Copenhagen and that Communist activities have appeared there.'

Field Marshal
Montgomery
decorates Marshal
Zhukov.

CHAPTER 11

Capture of Hamburg

7th Armoured Division had been tasked with the capture of the great city of Hamburg, which lies 60 miles north-east of Bremen. The Desert Rats' 'swan' from the Rhine had taken them through Hoya and Verden, both defended small towns astride the river Weser, then east through Barven, Wagenfeld, Diepholz, Bassum and Twistringen. They encountered the flank guards of 15th Panzergrenadier Division, whose assault SP guns and several Tigers caused grief. Indeed the panzergrenadiers counter-attacked rather vigorously around Syke, Wildeshausen and Harpstedt. By the time the division had arrived, 3 miles south of Bremen, the Desert Rats in four days had taken 1,700 prisoners from 18th Ersatz Battalion and 15th Panzergrenadiers. Bypassing Bremen they were ordered to make tracks for Hamburg via Walsrode, and Fallingbostel of course, and Soltau, where in close country amid beech woods and thick pine trees, assault SPs, Panthers, Spandau and bazooka teams caused casualties to 8th and 11th Hussars. The tracks through the woods resembled appalling peat bogs. On 18 April around Todtglusingen, the enemy, with 88mm anti-tank guns and SPs, were so strong that 'Limejuice' calls for Typhoon support were frequent. North of Soltau were the far-ranging moors and forest of Luneburg Heath, full of scratch kampfgruppen from the resident training centres. The last remnants of General Student's 1st Parachute Army were escaping from Bremen to get to Bremervorde and the river Elbe crossings and ferries.

For two weeks the division was occupied in clearing up a vast salient pointing towards Hamburg. It had a frontage of some 60 miles, and was 25 miles wide. Two entirely unrelated battles were being fought: in the north to mop up the area around the great autobahn from Bremen to Hamburg, and to the south to defeat a large pocket of enemy resistance east of Soltau.

Desert Rats captured Soltau near Lüneburg Heath.

Postcard of Hamburg before 'Bomber' Harris had fire-bombed the city.

Several infantry divisions post-Bremen were involved in the two weeks of mopping up, including the 53rd Welsh and 15th Scottish. The 43rd Wessex Wyverns and Guards Division were tasked with clearing the Cuxhaven peninsula, a large square area bounded on three sides by the river Elbe, Bremerhaven, 40 miles north-west, and Cuxhaven, some 60 miles due north. There were many sea mines and many carriers and armoured cars were blown to pieces with their crews. WASP flame-throwers were used frequently. There were often vile, cold days with drenching rain, and the rearguards of 15th Panzergrenadiers were certainly dying hard. Unbelievably, every village and hamlet was still bitterly defended and all the contestants knew that the war would finish—soon. The German Naval HQ for the North Sea was an enormous institution in Buxtehede, a series of modern barracks planted in the green countryside. It harboured among the kriegsmarines 500 female 'WRENs' in 'grey mouse' uniforms, who stood up during their lunch of hot potatoes and glared at their British captors. At the end of the barracks was a Nazi chapel with no religious emblems, or paintings, or altar. On the walls were ethereal paintings of Hitler and other Nazi leaders, surrounded by the swastika and the Nazi invocations to faith and war where one could worship the Führer—quietly and with deep conviction.

The German Commandant arriving at Cuxhaven at the mouth of the Elbe, in order to surrender the town.

Air Marshal 'Bomber' Harris organised Operation Gomorrah, the mass bombing of Hamburg. It was planned on 27 May 1943. On 24 July 2,300 tons of high explosive were dropped and in the Blitz week that followed the USAAF made 1,672 daylight sorties and 1,500 civilians were killed. The RAF used 'window' bales of ten-inch strips of aluminium foil to confuse German radar. On 28 July, a 43-minute firestorm was created when 2,326 tons of bombs were dropped on a warm night with low humidity and by dawn 42,000 civilians had been killed and 48,000 buildings destroyed. One-third of the damage was in the central districts of Hamburg, a flourishing Hanseatic commercial and cultural centre with a population of about one and a half million, including the suburbs. In the dock area were acres and acres of rubble, which had once been houses. Whole streets were buried. The majority of buildings still standing were gutted by fire or badly damaged and uninhabitable. The ruined buildings had comprised 275,000 apartments or 61 per cent of Hamburg's total living accommodation. A further 109,000 homes were damaged. No trams ran, there was no running water, no electricity, no gas, no radio, no postal service and no telephone.

A million people had fled the city and were homeless. The targets for the bombing raids were eighty military installations, twelve bridges, 112 Nazi party offices and 3,785 industrial plants, all of which were destroyed or badly damaged.

In his book *Inside the Third Reich*, Albert Speer recorded the bombing of the magnificent city of Hamburg: 'On 25 July [1943] shortly after midnight, 791 British planes attacked Hamburg and on the 25th and 26th daylight raids by 235 American bombers followed on 27th by the second night raid, staged by 787 British planes, and a third by 777 British planes on 29 July. This succession of heavy attacks ended on 2 August with a mission flown by 750 British bombers.' Speer often gave his Führer advice. He advocated a pinpoint bombing strategy on a limited number of carefully selected strategic targets, i.e. not mass bombing:

While I was trying to convert Hitler and the General Staff of the airforce to this policy, our Western enemies launched five major attacks on a single big city— Hamburg—within a week. Rash as this operation was, it had catastrophic consequences for us. The first attacks put the water supply pipes out of action, so that in the subsequent bombings the fire department had no way of fighting the fires. Huge conflagrations created cyclone-like firestorms: the asphalt of the streets began to blaze; people were suffocated in their cellars or burned to death in the streets. The devastation of this series of air raids could only be compared with the effects of a major earthquake. Gauleiter Kaufman teletyped Hitler repeatedly begging him to visit the stricken city. When these pleas proved fruitless, he asked Hitler at least to receive a delegation of some of the heroic rescue crews. But Hitler refused even that. Hamburg had suffered the fate Goering and Hitler had conceived for London in 1940.

Hamburg had put the fear of God in me. At the meeting of Central Planning on 29 July I pointed out, 'If the air raids continue on the present scale within three months we shall be relieved of a number of questions we are at present discussing. We shall simply be coasting downhill smoothly and relatively quickly.'

On 19 March 1945 the Führer issued an appalling order to every gauleiter in the remains of the Third Reich. In effect it was for Götterdammerung, the self-inflicted destruction of 'all military, transportation, communications, industrial and food-supply facilities. All resources within the Reich that the enemy might use immediately or in the foreseeable future for continuing the war, are to be destroyed by dynamiting, fire or demolition.' Albert Speer very bravely issued his own directive countermanding much of Hitler's 'Wagnerian' edict. Speer then *forbade* the destruction of locks, sluices, dams, drawbridges and harbour installations.

Gauleiter Kaufman asked Speer to visit Hamburg urgently as the navy was preparing to demolish all the port installations and shipyards. Speer and Kaufman prevailed diplomatically.

On 1 May a conference between Admiral Doenitz, the new Commander in Chief of the German armed forces, and Field Marshal Ernst Busch took place concerning the fate of Hamburg. Busch wanted to attack the superior British forces advancing on the city, while Doenitz was against offensive plans. Moreover Himmler then brought the news that Gauleiter Kaufman intended to surrender Hamburg *without* a fight. Kaufman told Speer that if necessary he would mobilise the masses to active resistance against the defenders of the city. Speer then phoned Doenitz: 'I told him of the threat of open rebellion in Hamburg.' An hour later Doenitz agreed to the surrender without a fight.

On 1 May the 2nd Argyll and Sutherland Highlanders of 15th Scottish Division and supporting Coldstream Guards tanks were patrolling

The opening of surrender negotiations for Hamburg, by officers of the 2nd Argyll & Sutherland Highlanders. From left to right: Major Vyvyan Cornwell (with flag), Major McElwee, Lt Colonel Russell Morgan and the Recce troop leader with the German colonel.

Major General Barber, GOC 15th Scottish, and intelligence officer interview the German Chief of Staff, Marshal Busch, prelude to the surrender of Hamburg, 2 May 1945.

vigorously from Bergendorf towards Hamburg. In the midst of an action to subdue Spandau posts, two German officers walked towards the battle group. Waving their white flag they were the forerunners of a surrender delegation. By stages it went to Majors Cornwell and McElwen, to Lt Colonel Morgan and eventually to Major General 'Tiny' Barber, GOC 15th Scottish Division. The German chief of staff to Marshal Busch started the surrender talks.

Admiral Doenitz and what was left of the German navy were trying to rescue seven million Germans—civilian and military—in the east, who were hoping to be shipped to the west. The rescue convoy was bringing back some of the refugees freezing on the open beaches and docks, and it was vital that the ports and harbours of Schleswig-Holstein be kept open. Hence the Hitler order to Major General Alwin Woltz, who had become the Town Commander of Hamburg on 15 April, to keep on fighting hard to delay the Allied advance towards the Baltic ports. Woltz's garrison included the Training (Ersatz) Battalion of the SS Hitler Jugend Division, a number of Volksturm battalions, a garrison regiment, many Flak battery gunners and Lt Commander Cremer's tank-distribution unit of U-boat crews.

So Woltz wanted war and Gauleiter Kaufman wanted peace. Major General L. O. Lyne, GOC 7th Armoured, sent a polite but threatening letter to Woltz on 29 April mentioning that famous German generals Joseph Harpe, GOC 5th Panzer Army, Fritz Bayerlein, GOC 53rd Corps, and many others had already surrendered—and above all that Reichsführer SS Himmler had already made an offer of unconditional surrender to the Western Powers. Lyne was only 'economical with the truth' when he mentioned that Bremen fell in 24 hours, instead of six days! Woltz sent back a polite answer on 1 May, suggesting a rendezvous 'for discussion'. However, on the same day Woltz received an order from General Keitel initiated by Doenitz that Hamburg could be surrendered on the afternoon of 3 May. General Lyne sent Woltz and his delegation to General Dempsey of 2nd Army at the Lüneburg HQ.

The gallant Cherry Pickers under Lt Colonel Bill Wainman arrived in the Rathausplatz and 1/5th Queens Infantry rolled over the two great iron bridges in stately Kangaroos of 49th APC and their adjutant raised the regimental flag over the city's Rathaus. And Colonel Wainman was busy in the Rathausplatz feeding the pigeons!

In spite of the awful damage, the streets were full of Germans walking about with purpose. The children looked at the Tommies with great

Hamburg, May 1945.

curiosity but were kept well back by their mothers in case they might be kicked. Most of the women—and who can blame them—looked at the khaki-clad invaders with hate in their faces, but the men looked more cowed and ashamed. There were still 600,000 civilians living in the ruins.

Wynford Vaughan-Thomas, the BBC correspondent, was at Lauenburg on the river Elbe, 12 miles south-east, where this author, FOO with the 3rd RTR/4th KSLI battlegroup, had just been blown up. This is what Wynford Vaughan-Thomas saw:

3 May 1945. Since two o'clock this morning this endless stream of transport has been pouring through this town, under the white flags hung over the shattered houses by the inhabitants who are standing in the streets looking dumbfounded at this wreckage of the Wehrmacht that's going past us. For, make no mistake about it, this army we see going by us is the most curious collection of wreckage you ever saw—improvised cars with people riding on the bumpers, half-track vehicles, thousands of them going through in a steady stream, and to make matters even more fantastic they've got their own traffic

policemen directing them, under British orders, standing on the corner waving listlessly on, as the thing goes steadily by us.

These people are defeated soldiers—you can see it in their eyes. In the middle of them there comes a much more joyous note. We see a charabanc full of RAF released prisoners, cheering as they go by, and the Germans on the half-tracks looking glumly on.

The next day the correspondent was in Hamburg where he broadcast from the station of the infamous, but unwittingly very funny 'Lord Haw-Haw', William Joyce:

I wonder what Lord Haw-Haw's views on the news are now? For Hamburg, the city he made notorious, is this evening under the control of the British Forces, and we found a completely and utterly bomb-ruined city.

We thought Bremen was bad, but Hamburg is devastated. Whole quarters have disintegrated under air attacks. There are miles upon miles of blackened walls and utterly burnt-out streets, and in the ruins there are still nearly a million people and 50,000 foreign workers living in the cellars and air-raid shelters. Today you don't see a single civilian on the streets; as soon as we came in we imposed a 48-hour curfew, and there's a Sunday quiet over the whole city; all that stirs in the streets is a British jeep or an armoured car, or a patrol of British Tommies watching that the curfew is strictly enforced.

The docks are even more devastated than the town, the great shipyards of Bloem and Voss are a wilderness of tangled girders, and in the middle of this chaos 14 unfinished U-boats still stand rusting on the slipways. Work on them finally stopped two months ago; after that date Hamburg was a dead city.

Rummaging through Lord Haw-Haw's desk we found a revealing timetable he drew up for his work, for 10 April 1945, and at the end of it is the glorious item: "1450–1510 hrs a pause to collect my wits." Well—he and the citizens of Hamburg have now got plenty of time to collect their wits, for tonight the sturdy soldiers of the Devons, the famous Desert Rats, are on guard over Haw-Haw's studios, the Allied military authorities are now running his programme, and instead of "Germany Calling" the colonel in charge gives you now the new call-sign of "Station Hamburg". This is Radio Hamburg, a station of the Allied Military Government.

The 'Thieving Magpies' had identified 100 targets in the Hamburg area for inspection and possible seizure. The first target was of course the city's

Ruins of Hamburg, May 1945.

1/5 Queens enter Hamburg greeted by cheerful German troops. (*Imperial War Museum*)

radio station, which was handed over to military government and named British journalists. The Phoenix Rubber Works in Harburg, a suburb in the south, making rubber protectors for U-boats, with technicians working on a 'stealth' or 'invisible' submarine, was a prime target. Other factories inspected were Electroacoustic and Germaniawerke. Scientists and specialists detained included Dr Karl Badstein (super-gun project); Johannes Engeike (guided aircraft-to-aircraft missiles); and Dr Dohler (spark plug pulse generator). 30th Assault Unit spent much time in the U-boat pens and Blohm and Voss shipyards examining submarine prototypes.

Major General 'Bobby' Ross, 53rd Welsh Division, entered Hamburg on 4 May to assume responsibility and garrison the city. The general sent his two key administration officers, Joe Grimond and Jim Cooper, into Hamburg the day *before* the surrender. Divisional HQ and the officers' mess was in the Hotel Atlantic. The 2,000-seat Schouspielhaus Opera was taken over for showbusiness, and a cabaret had to be arranged for the general's splendid victory dinner in the Atlantic Hotel. A large German naval marine warehouse contained hundreds of cases of Angus Mackay Scotch whisky, which Divisional HQ collared by

Desert Rats tanks in the centre of Hamburg.

The shattered centre of Hamburg.

Hamburg after its fall. Here submarines litter the dockyard at the great Blohm and Voss works.

quickly sending twenty-four troop carrying vehicles (TCVs) to collect and distribute them—probably fairly!

Fairly soon after VE Day, the author got to know Hamburg city rather well. The top-class Atlantic Hotel was quickly repainted and re-civilised and became a very smart officers' restaurant and hotel. It overlooks the charming Alster lake, where he sailed. In the evening Herr Schmidt-Isserstedt, the conductor of the well-known Norddeutsche Rundfunk radio orchestra, emerged from the ruins and played scintillating opera and concert *musik* to the well-behaved troops of the British Army of the Rhine, as the British Liberation Army became known. The author had some serious business in Hamburg too as the junior officer on a war crimes tribunal. His division held a German *Gau* with a very large chunk of Schleswig Holstein, mainly agricultural, which was reasonably undamaged. There he became Intelligence Officer of 3rd Regiment Royal Horse Artillery in the Desert Rats Division.

CHAPTER 12

Admiral Doenitz's 'Fourth Reich'

By the middle of April there were three main groups of power remaining in the Third Reich. Firstly, the Berlin garrison headed by Hitler, Goebbels, Bormann (deputy Führer) and General Krebs. Secondly, the Oberkommando der Wehrmacht (OKW) comprised Keitel, Jodl, Friedeburg and Doenitz. They abandoned Hitler in the capital and moved or were pushed steadily north-west until the little cluster arrived at the port of Flensburg on the Danish frontier. Hamburg was the last remaining big city under their control. Thirdly, part of the OKW was operating with the armies in the south. Hitler had sacked Goering on the 15 April and only Himmler was capable of liaising with the OKW. He had visited Bremen to threaten and bluster, trying to force General Becker to keep on resisting. For a week until 24 April, Himmler had been in touch with the Swedish Count Bernadotte, trying to elicit an answer to the question, 'Will America and Britain accept our unconditional surrender *now*, and allow us to concentrate all our remaining forces fending off the Red Army?' Just outside Hamburg was Bismarck's ancient castle, the Friedrichsruh, the HQ of the International Red Cross where Himmler carried out his hopeless talks.

Grand Admiral Karl Doenitz was commander of the German navy from 1943 and was Führer of Nazi Germany for twenty-three days in May 1945. His U-boat warfare in the Battle of the Atlantic had nearly brought Britain to its knees. The Royal Navy and RAF, helped by Bletchley Park's Ultra detection, eventually got the upper hand. Since the declaration of war in 1939, 863 U-boats had gone out on operational patrols and eventually 754 had been sunk or damaged beyond repair. The losses of U-boat crews, officers and men killed in action, totalled 27,491, but they had sunk 2,800

Sketch of Doenitz's HQ, Schloss Glücksberg.

Allied merchant ships and 148 Allied warships. Doenitz continued to be one of Hitler's favourites, particularly since exciting new stealth techniques and fast mini-subs promised future miracles. He was described as having a cold, expressionless face with a piercing gaze, and had the nickname 'The Big Lion'. Even when the British troops were on the river Elbe, 50 miles from his HQ at Ploen, he declared: 'Europe will realise that Adolf Hitler is the only statesman of any stature in Europe.' When Hitler committed suicide in the Berlin bunker on the afternoon of 30 April, by default Doenitz was destined to succeed him. Goering had decided to leave the bunker, claiming urgent tasks in southern Germany. When he telegraphed Hitler offering to take command of the surviving German forces, Martin Bormann, Hitler's poisonous shadow, interpreted this to his master as a treasonable act. Goering was ordered to be arrested and stripped of all offices and honours. Hitler's last will expelled him from the Nazi Party. Hitler had got wind of Himmler's secret peace negotiations, so he was blacklisted. Bormann was not acceptable as the next Führer, so that left Doenitz, who remained the logical candidate. On 1 May, he became Führer and appointed his first cabinet. Goebbels was dead, Bormann was missing believed killed, Goering banished, Ribbentrop and Thierach (Minister of Justice) were ignored. So Schwerin-Krosigk became Foreign Minister and State Secretary Stuckardt became Minister of the Interior. Himmler turned up and tried hard to join but was rejected immediately. At his first conference in Flensburg Schoener, Army Group Czechoslovakia, Frank, Reich Protector of Bohemia, Seyss-Inquart, the Overlord of Holland, Lindemann, Governor of Denmark, and Terboren, political leader in Norway, were either present or communicated their views. Their main object was to save their people and troops in the east from capture by the Red Army, which would be followed by imprisonment and gulags in Russia. This was clear in Doenitz's mind. German newspapers appeared on 2 May with black borders. One of these newspapers, soon to fall into the hands of the advancing British, bore the three-word headline: 'Unser Führer gefallen'. By implication, 'our Leader' had fallen *in battle*, presumably during the Russian onslaught on Berlin.

Admiral Karl Doenitz and Albert Speer, Hitler's architect and Minister of Armaments, Buildings and War Production, had long worked closely together on naval issues, building of U-boat pens, and U-boat production. They had a healthy respect for each other. Speer wrote *Inside the Third Reich,* a fascinating and more or less warts-and-all book. When Doenitz became the new Chief of State, Speer wrote: 'For 12 years we had served the ideas of the National Socialist regime ... But the death of Hitler broke that mental bind which had for so long warped our thinking. For Doenitz this meant that the objectivity of the trained military officer came to the fore. From the moment he took over, Doenitz held that we should end the war as quickly as possible and that once the task was done, our work was over.' On 1 May, the first military conference between Doenitz as the new Commander in Chief of the armed forces and Field Marshal Ernst Busch took place. Busch, in effect, wanted Götterdämmerung attacks on the superior forces advancing on Hamburg. Doenitz did not agree. He said: 'All that should be done was to keep the way to the West open as long as possible for the refugees from the East.' Columns of them were blocked near Lübeck. A delaying action by the German troops in the West should be continued only to allow the flow to continue. Busch made a great to-do about the Grand Admiral no longer acting in Hitler's spirit, but Doenitz was no longer moved by such exhortations.

At thirty-seven minutes past ten o'clock on the night of 1 May, Doenitz broke the news to the German nation by the following announcement over Radio Hamburg:

German Wehrmacht! My comrades! The Führer has fallen. Faithful to the great idea of preserving the peoples of Europe from Bolshevism he had consecrated his life, and died a hero's death. One of the greatest heroes in German history has passed away. We lower our flags in proud reverence and sorrow. The Führer had appointed me to succeed him as Head of the State and Supreme Commander of the Wehrmacht. I take over the command of all branches of the German Wehrmacht in the determination to continue the struggle against Bolshevism until the fighting troops and the hundreds of thousands of families in Eastern Germany have been preserved from enslavement or destruction. I must continue to wage war on the British and Americans in so far and for so long as they hinder me in the prosecution of the fight against Bolshevism. The situation demands of you, who have already accomplished such great historical feats and now long for the end of the war, further unconditional service. I demand discipline and obedience. Only by the unquestioning execution of my orders can chaos and the downfall of Germany be avoided. He who now shirks his duty, thus bringing death and enslavement upon German women and children, is a coward and a traitor. The oath pledged by you to the Führer now applies for each one of you to me as the successor appointed by the Führer.

German soldiers! Do your duty! The life of our nation is at stake!

Intense negotiations followed between Doenitz, his various emissaries, and Field Marshal Montgomery and SHAEF. On 5 May all German forces in Holland, north-west Germany and Denmark surrendered to Monty. At 1427hrs that afternoon, the newly appointed German Foreign Minister, Count Schwerin von Korsigk, broadcasting from Flensburg, the headquarters of the German government, announced that Germany's fighting troops had surrendered and that the war was over. His words, although couched in the rhetoric of untarnished pride, were unambiguous:

German men and women, the High Command of the German armed forces, on orders of Grand Admiral Doenitz, has today declared unconditional surrender of all German fighting troops. As the leading minister of the Reich government, which the Admiral of the Fleet has appointed for dealing with war tasks, I turn at this tragic moment of our history to the German nation.

After a heroic fight of almost six years of incomparable hardness, Germany has succumbed to the overwhelming power of her enemies. To continue the war would only mean senseless bloodshed and futile disintegration. The government, which has a feeling of responsibility for the future of the nation, was compelled to act on the collapse of all physical and material forces and to demand of the enemy cessation of hostilities. It was the noblest task of the Admiral of the Fleet and of the government supporting him, after the terrible sacrifices which the war has caused.

Chester Wilmot reported on the BBC:

8 May 1945. I don't think you can realise the completeness of the German defeat until you've been to Flensburg, the present seat of the Doenitz government and of Keitel's High Command.

In the streets civilians were going about their normal business with expressionless faces, but the crowds outside the food shops were much larger than those gathered to read Doenitz's proclamation about the end of the war in the northwest. Neither the civilians nor the ordinary troops any longer care.

All this wasn't surprising, but I did expect that somehow the atmosphere at the High Command Headquarters would be different; but this was the scene. A rather dirty Marine barracks housed the headquarters and the government; outside it, 18 scruffy sentries, as dirty and dishevelled as the troops in the town. In the car park beyond the gate there were a dozen big staff cars, replicas of those great sleek black Mercedes in which the Nazi leaders have swaggered through the capitals of Europe. And now, here they were in the last bolt-hole, their shining black surfaces hastily camouflaged with paint that had just been slashed on, and with branches of trees tied on so that they looked like Macduff's men who carried Birnam wood to Dunsinane.

Here in these cars was the end of Nazi glory. The only evidence that this was the High Command's Headquarters was a small sign painted in black on the torn-off bottom of a camouflaged boot-box. It bore the letters 'OKW' [Oberkommando der Wehrmacht—High Command of the Armed Forces].

British officers who had been inside told me that the interior is just as dirty and decrepit. It has the same atmosphere of defeat and despair. Yesterday a British officer tried to deliver a message to Field Marshal Keitel. He found him in a poky room at the end of a long passage, no sentries outside the door— three Germans lounging at the window at the end might have been sentries. He went in through an outer office, pushing his way past typists and clerks, through a small door and into Keitel's office, a room 20 feet by 15. Keitel sat at a small table in full uniform with his Field Marshal's baton beside him. Behind his chair was a photograph of Hitler. On the wall in front was a large school map of Europe, which Hitler conquered but couldn't hold down. Here in this miserable little room, a far cry from the great chancelleries of Europe where he so often laid down terms, sat Keitel himself. Here and in Doenitz's office, the German Führer and Chief of the High Command had come to the fateful decisions of the past few days. The power and glory of the greater Reich, the pomp and pageantry of Hitler's empire, had been reduced to this. Only the glittering uniforms remained. During yesterday afternoon Keitel was handed the text of the surrender terms which Jodl had signed at SHAEF, a document which meant not even peace with honour but defeat with humiliation.

When Doenitz himself broadcast from Flensburg on 8 May, his reference to the Soviet occupation of the eastern half of Germany was oblique: 'The German people should walk in defeat "dignified and courageous",' he said, 'in the hope that our children may one day have a free, secure existence.' He was able to announce one change that the Allies considered essential in any future Germany. All connection between the German state and the Nazi party had been severed. 'The Nazi party has left the scene of its activity,' he said. A few hours later Flensburg radio announced that the Nazi salute 'Heil Hitler!' was abolished. That same day the German navy, which the new ruler of Germany had commanded at the height of its powers, suffered its final humiliation, as all U-boats, which had caused such enormous losses to Allied and neutral shipping and to the lives of sailors and merchant seamen, were ordered to surface and to report for instructions to the nearest Allied commanders.

The German Operation Rainbow in the final week of May ordered submarine commanders in port or harbour to scuttle their craft, so fifty-six did in Flensburg, thirty-one in Travemünde, twenty-six in Kiel, fifteen in Wilhelmshaven and ten in Hamburg. Finally the British Royal Navy in Operation Deadlight ordered all U-boat commanders at sea to surface and fly a black flag or pennant. More than 100 were then taken out into the Atlantic and sunk in deep water west of Ireland. Presumably their crews were taken off first!

Winston Churchill sent a memo to the Foreign Office on 14 May:

It is of high importance that the surrender of the German people should be completed through agencies which have authority over them. I neither know nor care about Doenitz. He may be a war criminal. He used submarines to sink ships … the question is has he any power to get the Germans to lay down their arms and hand them over quickly without any more loss of life? We cannot go round into every German slum and argue with every German that it is his duty to surrender or we will shoot him. There must be some kind of force which will give orders which they will obey. Once they obey we can do what we like to carry through unconditional surrender.

At Flensburg, Grand Admiral Doenitz had continued to act as if he were the head of the German government. Every morning since VE Day, wearing his admiral's uniform, he had been driven in the armoured Mercedes, which Hitler had given him, from his living quarters to the nearby naval school in which his government was housed. Each day he had held a meeting of his cabinet. On 21 May, as this masquerade continued, a British naval mission reached Flensburg by air. This mission was accommodated on board the Hamburg-Amerika liner *Caribia* in Flensburg harbour. Berthed on the opposite side of the pier was the liner *Patria*, in which was accommodated the Allied Control Commission, established by Eisenhower, under the command of an American, General Rooks. A Russian military mission was also present, with Eisenhower's authority to interrogate members of the German government.

'As might be expected,' the head of the British Naval Mission, Commodore G. R. G. Allen, wrote in his official report, 'the political atmosphere was somewhat confused; on the one hand the German naval authorities were ready to co-operate under the terms of the capitulation, and to discuss matters of naval policy and technical matters quite freely. The German armed forces, both naval and military, appeared to be in good shape with good morale and well disciplined. The naval ratings were smart and well turned out, and there was no visible sign of demoralisation. The civil population were evidently well fed and appeared reasonably contented, self-confident and relatively indifferent to events happening around them. On the other hand, General Rooks told me that Admiral Doenitz himself had recently stated that the conditions were likely to deteriorate sharply in the near future if the Western Allies insisted upon maintaining their present policy of non-co-operation with the Germans in the occupied areas.'

On the afternoon of 22 May Doenitz's adjutant received a telephone call summoning Grand Admiral Doenitz, General Jodl and Admiral von Friedeburg to meet the head of the Allied Control Commission, General Rooks, on board the liner *Patria* at 0945 hrs. the next morning. When he was told this, Doenitz said curtly, 'Pack the bags.'

Jodl, Speer and Doenitz are arrested at Flensburg by troops of 11th Armoured Division during Operation Blackout.

Commodore Allen was on board the *Patria* on the morning of 23 May when the arrest of Doenitz and his government took place. Allen reported to London:

General Rooks had confined all officers to the ships during this event to prevent any untoward incident, and a British brigade with tanks was deployed in the town to maintain order. Admiral Doenitz conducted himself with much dignity; the other two appeared nervous. Rooks told them, 'Gentlemen, I am in receipt of instructions from Supreme Headquarters, European Theatre of Operations, from the Supreme Commander, General Eisenhower, to call you before me this morning to tell you that he has decided, in concert with the Soviet High Command, that today the acting German government and the German High Command, with several of its members, shall be taken into custody as prisoners of war. Thereby the acting German government is dissolved.'

After General Rooks had announced what was in effect the final end of the Third Reich, Doenitz commented that 'words at this moment would be superfluous'. All German naval officers at Flensburg were confined to their quarters. A detachment of British troops surrounded the police buildings in Mütvik where Doenitz and the members of his

Speer (in the raincoat), Doenitz and Jodl under arrest at Flensburg, the final seat of the government of the Fourth Reich, May 1945.

administration were brought under guard, each of them permitted one suitcase of personal belongings.

Operation Blackout took place on 23 May. At 1000hrs the 1st Cheshires and 1st Herefords with 15/19th Hussar Comets of 11th Armoured Division swooped on the barracks, the government buildings in Flensburg and the Hamburg-Amerika liner *Patria*. A naval patrol of two destroyers cruised along Flensburg Fjord to ensure there was no escape by sea for the Doenitz government and the town garrison. A very well-planned attack on the massive Schloss Glücksburg on the lake took place, although no shots were fired. By 1130hrs, 5,000 prisoners had been taken, including Grand Admiral Doenitz, General Jodl, Generals Reinbecke, Dethleffsen and Reich Minister Alfred Speer (Admiral von Friedeburg committed suicide). The VIPs were escorted to 159th Brigade HQ, thence to Flensburg aerodrome and into captivity. Nuremberg loomed for the VIPs and prison camps for the rest.

The day ended with the Hussar Comets thundering noisily through the narrow cobbled streets of Flensburg.

Doenitz's 'Fourth' Reich had come and gone. Ahead lay death for Jodl, 20 years in Spandau Prison for Speer and 10 years for Doenitz.

CHAPTER 13

Final Surrender: Operation Eclipse

The situation in Germany at the very end of April 1945 was frankly chaotic. It was beyond comprehension that this proud, dominant country known as the Third Reich, destined as its leaders thought to last for a thousand years, had not just crumbled but completely collapsed. Fifty great cities, including Berlin, Hamburg, Bremen and those in the Ruhr, were in ruins. Some of the photographs in this book, such as those taken by the author in shattered Hamburg, bear witness to this. Many cities had no electricity, gas or clean running water. The national government had disintegrated and Doenitz's Fourth Reich in Flensburg was just a comic opera. Alan Moorehead wrote:

> Like ants in an ant-heap the people scurried over the ruins, diving furtively into cellars and doorways in search of loot. Like ants you would see women scuttling down a side-track with their bundles only to be blocked by débris and then turn irresolutely back, shoving and bumping against one another. Everyone was on the move, and there was a frantic ant-like quality about their activity. Life was sordid, aimless, stacked to the roof with city refugees living on soup and potatoes. From the Ruhr across Germany an occasional factory chimney smokes, but 90 percent of the country's industry was at a standstill. No trains ran. Every family was bereaved or broken up. The housing situation was impossible and likely to get worse. A very large part of the population was simply wandering on the roads with the millions of foreigners. And to these was now added the German army itself. A mass flight from the Russians towards the Elbe and the Anglo-American lines began. Officers stripped off their uniforms and begged or stole civilian clothes from the nearby houses. Mass fear had gripped them so greatly that when aircraft appeared in the sky

The Third Reich—completely collapsed.

the shout went up: 'The Russians! The Russians!' and the mob would break out in panic across the countryside.

Negotiations for surrender started on the Italian front. In the last week of April Bologna fell and the Allies reached the river Po; on the 26th Milan was taken by partisans. Colonel General Heinrich von Vietinghoff, the commander in chief of all German forces in Italy—after Hitler had recalled Field Marshal Kesselring to try to stem the Allied advances in the west—had lost 150,000 men as prisoners, taken in less than three weeks. Waffen SS General Karl Wolff's efforts to make peace with Allen Dulles, the American head of the OSS in Switzerland, on behalf of all the German troops in the Mediterranean, had come to naught. The Allies would only accept unconditional surrender, so no progress was made. But on 29 April, the day before Hitler committed suicide, von Vietinghoff and Wolff *unilaterally* agreed to the unconditional surrender of the one million Germans in Italy. Cessation of hostilities took place on 2 May. This started the rot!

General Patton's armoured cohorts had sealed the fate of the 'last redoubt' in Bavaria, no doubt much to Eisenhower's relief. Goering and many OKW officers were captured. The Third Reich was now effectively split in two.

Mass
surrender of
the Wehrmacht
north of
Hamburg.

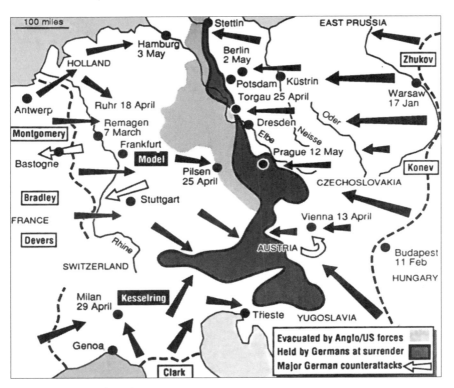

The end of the Third Reich, May 1945.

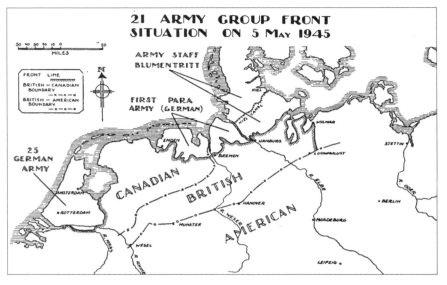

21st Army Group Front situation on 5 May 1945.

Chester Wilmot reported the situation:

3 May 1945. The general surrender of the German forces opposing the 2nd British Army may now come at any hour; except in the pocket west of Bremen there is no longer any real opposition on General Dempsey's front, and pilots today reported that there are white flags flying from the houses 50 miles behind the nominal enemy line.

It's been a day of surrender and negotiation for surrender by German officers ranging from commanders of regiments to commanders of armies. Last night two German divisions surrendered intact. Early this morning the commander of the Hamburg garrison, General Wolz, agreed not only to hand over unconditionally Germany's greatest port, but also personally to lead the 7th British Armoured Division into the city this evening. During the morning the 11th Armoured Division received word that the garrison of Neumünster, 35 miles north of Hamburg and only 30 miles from the great naval base of Kiel, was ready to give in. The Neumünster garrison also said that other troops on the Kiel canal itself were anxious to surrender.

But the biggest news of the day was the complete break up and the attempted surrender of two of the German armies in Army Groups Vistula, the group which has been opposing Rokossovsky and was defending the area north of Berlin. These armies had retreated about 150 miles since the Russian breakthrough on the Oder last month, and yesterday our columns cut right through the area where they were vainly trying to reorganise. Their fighting spirit was already broken, and they disintegrated at once.

Today, their commanders, General Manteuffel of the 3rd Panzer Army and General Tippelskirch of the 1st Panzer Army, offered to surrender their complete forces to Field Marshal Montgomery. This was refused, though we have accepted the personal capitulation of the two generals and many senior officers of Army Group Vistula.

The official British attitude is that as these two armies are still engaged in fighting the Russians, we can't accept their surrender, and in any case their commanders are in no position to hand over the armies to us. And so tonight in the woods and villages between the Baltic and the Elbe there are tens of thousands of Germans from Army Group Vistula vainly trying to find someone who will accept them as prisoners. Their commanders have surrendered, their staffs have disintegrated; only those units still in direct contact with the Russians continue fighting—fighting rather than yield to the Red Army.

The fact is that at all costs the Germans want to avoid surrendering to the Soviet troops. They know how great are Germany's crimes against Russia, and they know that the Russians won't forget.

Field Marshal Busch, commanding the Schleswig-Holstein area, and General Lindemann, the commander in Denmark, sent an emissary to Stockholm to say that when the British Army reached the Baltic *before* the Russians they would surrender. On 3 May therefore, they asked to surrender the 3rd Panzer, 12th and 21st Armies. The delegation appeared at Field Marshal Montgomery's HQ, under Admiral von Friedeburg, who had replaced Grand Admiral Doenitz as head of the German army.

The 2nd Army Report of Operations describes in very sober words the events of those exciting days:

Meanwhile conversations were held at the Headquarters of 21st Army Group with the delegation headed by General Admiral von Friedeburg. He stated that he had arrived from Keitel to negotiate surrender of the German forces (in the North) to Field Marshal Montgomery. He stated that they were extremely worried about their soldiers and the valuable people being savaged by the Russians. He further requested the passage of civilian refugees moving back from the Russian sectors to safety through our lines, stating that he had been trying to get the population fleeing from the Russians back into Schleswig Holstein. He added that a considerable number had already been moved into that province, that conditions were fairly chaotic and that food would last for only 14 days.

The General Admiral suggested that, to allow the occupation to keep pace with the enormous administrative tasks, 2nd Army should agree to advance bound by bound. This would give the Germans time to organise their administration and to hand over something workable.

The commander of 21st Army Group stated that under no circumstances would he agree and that first of all von Friedeburg must surrender. After that it would be the duty of the staffs to work out the most suitable ways and means of enforcing the act.

The German high command knew that if they could drag out the negotiations, probably more civilians and military fleeing from the Red Army would be able to surrender to the more benevolent Allies.

On 4 May von Friedeburg had received permission from Doenitz and Field Marshal Keitel, the chief of the German high command, that unconditional surrender of all German armed forces, land, sea and air in north-west Germany, Holland, Schleswig Holstein and Denmark could be signed and agreed. General Eisenhower wrote in his report, 'D-Day to VE Day': 'I had instructed Field Marshal Montgomery that a capitulation covering these areas *might be regarded as a tactical matter* and, as such be dealt with by him. It was arranged that a Russian officer should be present to accept the German submission on behalf of his government. The instrument of surrender was accordingly signed on 4 May and it became effective at 0800hrs on 5 May.' On 4 May, Chester Wilmot reported:

Hallo BBC, this is Chester Wilmot speaking from Field Marshal Montgomery's tactical headquarters on a high windswept hill on the wild Lüneburger Heath near the river Elbe.

It's ten minutes past six on Friday 4 May: the hour and the day for which British fighting men and women and British peoples throughout the world have been fighting and working and waiting for five years and eight months. The commanders of the German forces opposing Field Marshal Montgomery's 21st Army Group have come to this headquarters today to surrender. To make unconditional surrender. The plenipotentaries are General Admiral von Friedeburg, Commander-in-Chief of the German Navy, who succeeded Admiral Doenitz in that post when Doenitz became the new Führer. With

Above: Field Marshal
Montgomery signing the
Instrument of Surrender.
(*Imperial War Museum*)

Right: The front page of the
Sunday Graphic showing
General Kinsel signing
unconditional surrender.

3 MORE GERMAN ARMIES MAKE TOTAL SURRENDER

Norway C.-in-C. Also Reported 'Ready To Capitulate'

FINAL GERMAN CAPITULATION WAS BROUGHT NEARER LAST NIGHT BY THE UNCONDITIONAL SURRENDER OF THREE MORE GERMAN ARMIES.

All three armies fell to the group commanded by General Devers—two to the Americans and one to the French—and with them probably another 400,000 men passed into Allied hands.

At the same time there were unconfirmed reports from Stockholm that General Boehme, Nazi Commander in Norway, had decided to capitulate; that a British military mission had arrived in Oslo; and that Terboven, Nazi Governor in Norway, had resigned.

The day's surrenders in the South—apparently ordered by Kesselring—meant almost an end to the fighting on the American fronts except in Czechoslovakia.

There Patton's Third Army captured the German 11th Panzer Division in a new offensive over a 110-mile front in which they took 12,000 prisoners.

Simultaneously the Russians attacked from the East, while Czech Patriots wirelessed for help, saying German tanks were advancing on Prague.

Despite the Cease Fire at 8 a.m. yesterday, fighting broke out in Denmark, and Copenhagen was shelled.

FULL STORY ON BACK PAGE

SURRENDER

'*Sunday Graphic*' cameraman Reginald Clough records Field-Marshal Montgomery's greatest triumph as General Kinsel, German plenipotentiary, signs unconditional surrender. — *Full Picture Story and Document on Middle Pages.*

Instrument of Surrender

of

All German armed forces in HOLLAND, in

northwest Germany including all islands,

and in DENMARK.

1. The German Command agrees to the surrender of all German armed forces in HOLLAND, in northwest GERMANY including the FRISIAN ISLANDS and HELIGOLAND and all other islands, in SCHLESWIG-HOLSTEIN, and in DENMARK, to the C.-in-C. 21 Army Group. This to include all naval ships in these areas. These forces to lay down their arms and to surrender unconditionally.

2. All hostilities on land, on sea, or in the air by German forces in the above areas to cease at 0800 hrs. British Double Summer Time on Saturday 5 May 1945.

3. The German command to carry out at once, and without argument or comment, all further orders that will be issued by the Allied Powers on any subject.

4. Disobedience of orders, or failure to comply with them, will be regarded as a breach of these surrender terms and will be dealt with by the Allied Powers in accordance with the accepted laws and usages of war.

5. This instrument of surrender is independent of, without prejudice to, and will be superseded by any general instrument of surrender imposed by or on behalf of the Allied Powers and applicable to Germany and the German armed forces as a whole.

6. This instrument of surrender is written in English and in German.

   The English version is the authentic text.

7. The decision of the Allied Powers will be final if any doubt or dispute arises as to the meaning or interpretation of the surrender terms.

B. L. Montgomery
Field-Marshal

4th May. 1945
1830 hrs

28. The 'instrument of surrender', signed by Field Marshal Montgomery and the German command – Friedeberg, Kinsel, Wagner, Polleck and Friedel – on 4 May 1945. *(Supplied by John Frost)*

Instrument of Surrender signed by Field Marshal Montgomery. (*Imperial War Museum*)

him are General Kinzel, Chief of Staff to Field Marshal Busch, Rear Admiral Wagner who is Chief of Staff to von Friedeburg; and another staff officer.

They came here yesterday hoping to parley—to talk terms. But they were told to go back and return today with power to make unconditional surrender. They have come back through the lines again today, to make that surrender. And now we're waiting for them to come through the trees that surround Field Marshal Montgomery's headquarters. And here they are now. General Admiral von Friedeburg is leading with Colonel Ewart, of Field Marshal Montgomery's Staff; with him is the General of Infantry Kinzel … Rear Admiral Wagner, and they're now walking up to the caravan which the Field Marshal uses for his HQ in the field …

However, on 5 May Admiral Friedeburg arrived at Eisenhower's HQ 'wishing to clarify a number of points'. He was sent packing but he and Field Marshal Alfred Jodl, on behalf of Admiral Doenitz's 'Reich', turned up again on 6 May procrastinating and asking for more time. Eisenhower remained very firm and at 0241hrs on the morning of 7 May the Act of Surrender was signed by Jodl, by Eisenhower's Chief of Staff, Bedell Smith, and by Major General Ivan Suslaparov for the Soviet High Command.

It was all over—at long last.

But in fact it wasn't!

Hugh Lunghi, in Moscow with the British Military Mission, later recalled:

On Monday May 7 we received the news that Eisenhower at his Reims headquarters had in the early hours of that morning accepted General Jodl's total capitulation of all German armed forces with a cease-fire at midnight on May 8. A General Susloparov had signed the surrender document on behalf of the Soviet Command. Again the Soviet media ignored the historic event.

Instead of congratulations, we received a curt communication addressed to the then Head of our Military Mission, Admiral Archer, copied to the United States Head of Mission General Deane, from the Soviet Chief of Staff, General Antonov. He demanded that what he called the 'temporary protocol' signed in Reims should be replaced by 'an act of general unconditional surrender' which would be drawn up and signed in Marshal Zhukov's headquarters in Berlin on the following day, May 8.

Stalin, it was obvious, intended that the only 'real' surrender should be to a Soviet commander. Years later we learned from Soviet generals' memoirs that Stalin had been furious that a Soviet representative had added his signature to the Reims surrender: 'Who the hell is Susloparov? He is to be punished severely for daring to sign such a document without the Soviet government's permission.'

Marshal Joseph Stalin was not at all happy that the surrender would take place at Reims with just one relatively unimportant Russian general present. It gave the impression to the outside world that the Western Allies had won the war, whereas Russia had made the most spectacular victories in driving the German hordes out of his country, and as from 2 May the capital, Berlin, had been conquered and captured by his Red

THE MOMENT OF DEFEAT General Jodl signs, above, the unconditional surrender of German forces at Reims on May 7. "With this signature, the German people and the German Army fall, for better or for worse, beneath the victors," said Jodl. On his left is Admiral von Friedeburg, and on his right the Luftwaffe representative, General Oxenius. General Jodl was later sentenced to be hanged

THE MOMENT OF VICTORY General Eisenhower's headquarters, Reims. The Russian, American and British, above, celebrate Jodl's capitulation. From left: Generals Susloparoff, Morgan, Smith and Eisenhower. On the right, Air Chief Marshal Sir Arthur Tedder. Eisenhower holds the pens used for the signatures.

Newspaper cuttings from the time of the surrender.

Army. He had a point! He demanded a final formal ratification in Berlin, under Russian arrangements, in the early hours of 9 May. Marshal Zhukov signed for the Russians; Air Chief Marshal Tedder for SHAEF; Field Marshal Keitel for Germany; and General de Lattre de Tassigny witnessed on behalf of France.

And that was that.

At the end of the First World War in 1918 the German army claimed correctly that it had not been beaten. It was political problems behind their lines that led to the Armistice. In the Second World War, the Germans could not make the same claim. The vast majority of their armed forces had been smashed, encircled and made prisoner. However, there were seven outposts of the Third Reich, which still had not been beaten: in Norway 360,000 troops; Denmark almost 250,000; north-west Holland 120,000; Dunkirk 40,000: the Channel Islands 40,000; and Lorient 30,000. The British Liberation Army, with the Royal Navy and RAF, had to tackle Norway, Denmark and north-west Holland (with the Canadians). There was a distinct possibility that the Führer's die-hard gauleiters might wish to stage their own Götterdämerung and fight to the end.

Map showing the four zones of occupation—Russian, American, French and British. There were 23 million demoralised Germans in the British zone re-named 'British Army of the Rhine'.

113

Once the Allied armies entered the Third Reich as the British Liberation Army early in 1945, Operation Eclipse came into force. It was designed to embrace the complete destruction of the German war potential. The initial stage consisted of herding the troops into compounds where they were disarmed. The sheep were separated from the goats! The SS and every unit considered to be violently Nazified were sent at once to prisoner of war camps such as Westertimke. There they would be closely identified and potential war criminals would be set aside for possible trials. The majority were concentrated under titular command of their own officers before being released to work on the farms or to other vital but peaceful work essential to keeping the German community alive. The most efficient were, of course, members of the Nazi party, and this made for difficult judgements.

Major General Francis de Guingand was Chief of Staff to the 21st Army Group, soon to be renamed the British Army of the Rhine (BAOR). He was given the responsibility to enforce the terms of surrender, i.e. to implement Operation Eclipse. The first very large conference took place on 8 May with representatives from Army Group HQ, the new military government, the chiefs of staff of the 2nd and Canadian Armies, the naval liaison officer, and Air Vice Marshal Groom of 2nd Tactical Air Force. Once they had agreed upon a firm plan to carry out the first stage of Eclipse, they herded and shepherded the huge German armies into captivity. General Kinzel, Chief of Staff to Field Marshal Busch who commanded the German Army group opposing 21st Army Group, was a brilliant conduit. He was an efficient staff officer, who sported an eye-glass and wore a magnificent field grey greatcoat with scarlet lapels, in every respect the typical Prussian General Staff Officer. He would carry out all of de Guingand's orders.

This was the prisoner state at the middle of May:

In the Wilhelmshaven-Emden Peninsula
Already in the area 60,000
To be moved from West Holland 120,000
Total 180,000

In the Cuxhaven Peninsula
Already in the area 160,000
From the area north of the Elbe 100,000

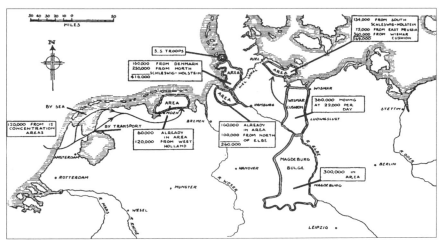

Map of the Concentration Plan for the captured forces of the Reich.

Total 260,000
In south-west Schleswig Holstein
From Denmark 160,000
From north Schleswig Holstein 250,000
Total 410,000

In south-east Schleswig Holstein
From south Schleswig Holstein 134,000
From East Prussia 75,000
From Wismar Pocket 360,000
Total 569,000

TOTAL 1,419,000
Not including the Magdeburg Pocket (from USA) 300,000

In the British zone of occupied Germany there were about 23 million people. In addition there were 200,000 German prisoners of war behind the Allied lines already in camps. All the sinister SS troops would be isolated on Nordstrand Island for security reasons.

There were reputed to be 130,000 Allied prisoners of war: British, Belgians, French, Yugoslavs, Poles, Italians and others, plus two million desperate Russians.

Finally there were 925,000 displaced persons either west- or east-bound—the former slaves of German industry and agriculture. And there were hundreds of thousands of sick and wounded German military and civil casualties in hospitals in the area.

General Templer was head of the Allied military government organisation and he was in charge of this extremely complex situation.

Once the million and a half soldiers of the Third Reich were safely behind barbed wire, each was carefully investigated.

Lt General Horrocks, GOC 30th Corps, found that he was responsible for the Hanover corps district. He wrote:

> Monty laid down the priorities as (1) food and (2) housing; he then, as always, gave us a free hand to look after our own districts until such time as proper military government could take over from us. It was a fascinating task. I found myself to all intents and purposes the benevolent (I hope) dictator of an area about the size of Wales. At my morning conference, instead of considering fire plans and laying down military objectives, we discussed such problems as food, coal, communications, press and so on. I soon discovered the merits of a dictatorship. I could really get things done quickly. One day in the late autumn a staff officer reported that the output of coal was dropping every week in our corps district. This was very serious with winter approaching. The reason, I was informed, was that the miners lacked clothes. I immediately ordered a levy to be carried out in certain nearby towns to provide adequate clothing for the miners, and sure enough a few weeks later the graph showing coal production began to rise.

Montgomery produced a series of operational 'civilian' orders to help keep the traumatic situation in Germany under reasonable control. Operation Barleycorn would demobilise German soldiers who volunteered to work on the land and bring the Westphalian harvests in. Operation Coal Scuttle was a scheme for German soldiers to gather fuel or work in the mines. Montgomery had many sensible, practical ideas for the future of his huge bailiwick. He ordered that the workers of Wolfsburg should be encouraged to produce the first post-war Volkswagens, the people's very cheap and reliable car.

To the victors, the spoils! Despite the barely concealed hostility of Stalin's obvious ownership of Berlin, a public relations operation ensured that Winston Churchill and the new US president, Harry Truman, should arrive together on 16 July 1945 to participate in a series of post-war meetings and rather grand victory parades. Churchill visited the Chancellery and the Russian guides took his entourage to Hitler's air raid shelter. Churchill was convinced that his late opponent's death 'was much more convenient than the one I had feared. He could have flown to England and surrendered himself saying, "Do what you will with me, but spare my misguided people!" I have no doubt that he would have shared the fate of the Nuremberg criminals.' On 18 July he lunched alone with President Truman: 'We had now emerged from the war with a great external debt of three thousand million pounds.' Truman, to his great credit, answered: 'If you had gone down like France we might be fighting the Germans on the American coast at the present time.' That night the indomitable Churchill dined with Stalin, and Majors Birse and Pavlov, the interpreters. Stalin told Churchill that the Russians had mobilised 12 million men, and 5 million of those were lost, killed or missing. The Germans had mobilised 18 million! During his stay in Berlin, Churchill learnt that the atomic bomb tests had been positive.

This is a description of the unique Victory Parade in Berlin: 'The first parade took place on 6 July. The Union Jack was hoisted in the Grosse Stern at the foot of the Franco-Prussian War memorial and Lt General Sir Ronald Weekes inspected the 1st Battalion Grenadier Guards (borrowed for the occasion), 1/5th Queens, 2nd Devons and the Canadian Composite Battalion (also borrowed). 5th RHA arrived on 10 July and moved into Kladow barracks and Divisional HQ on the 18th. Field Marshal Montgomery arrived on the 12th to invest the three Russian commanders, Marshals Zhukov, Rokossovsky and General Sokolovski. They all gave each other colourful and appropriate medals! This time the Grenadiers and 8th and 11th Hussars lined the route as Guard of Honour.'

Captain Bill Bellamy, 8th Hussars, recalled: 'We travelled the length of the Charlottenburger Chaussée as far as the Brandenberger Tur, the great triumphal Gate, marking the divide between British and Russian zones. Then the Tiergarten (zoo) and the Siegessaule. The trees in the parks on both sides of the avenue were stripped of their leaves—the aftermath of a First World War battle. The fighting must have been horrific.'

On 13 July the first full-scale Divisional Parade, a rehearsal for the Victory Parade, took place. Two days later the delegates for the Potsdam Conference started to arrive, including Prime Minister Winston Churchill, Anthony Eden and Clement Attlee. This was followed by

Watched by thousands of German civilians, Major General L. O. Lyne takes the salute as the Desert Rats enter Berlin on 4 July 1945.

Field Marshal Montgomery and Russian Marshal Zhukov inspect the Grenadier's Guard of Honour in Berlin.

All that was left of Joseph Goebbels' Propaganda Ministry. 310 bombing raids reduced Berlin to what Roosevelt called 'a second Carthage'.

Ruins of Anhallen Station, Berlin, destroyed by the RAF and the US 8th Air Force.

Left: Bitburg—devastated.

Below: Comet tanks approaching the saluting base at the Victory Parade.

7th Armoured Division enters Berlin. Major General Lyne taking the salute.

another frenetic week of last-minute rehearsals and flag poles and stands being erected for the great day—Saturday 21 July. The bands were provided by the Royal Marines, 11th Hussars and 2nd Devons, and the troops on parade were found from 3rd RHA, 5th RHA, 8th Hussars, 11th Hussars, 1st Battalion Grenadier Guards, 1/5th Queens, 2nd Devons and representatives from the Navy, RAF and RAF Regiment.

3rd RHA fired a nineteen-gun salute in honour of the Prime Minister and Field Marshals Montgomery, Alan Brooke and Alexander. Tom Ritson recalled: 'A few days later Mr Churchill was dismissed by the electorate and Mr Atlee returned to Potsdam in his place.' Vernon Besley, 1/5th Queens, wrote: 'We were all ready, the Queens right in front of Churchill waiting to start when there was a cascade of motor bikes escorting President Truman, with their sirens sounding, and the parade started.'

Captain Bill Bellamy observed:

The Russians outnumbered the British. They were quite smart in their loosely cut service dress, flat hats, gold or silver epaulettes, and polished jack-boots and they all had so many medals! As we approached the saluting base, being leader of the 8th Hussars column I had a very clear view. Mr Churchill stood slightly to the fore wearing a light coloured service dress and a peaked dress hat. He was standing, looking directly up the Chaussée and saluted us in answer to the colonel's salute. Standing next to him was Mr Atlee in civilian clothes and bareheaded. Then Field Marshals Alan Brooke and Montgomery with the tall bare-headed figure of Mr Anthony Eden to the left. General Lyne was standing to the PM's left, together with a senior naval officer. I also spotted Mr Morrison. Then it was all over and we were past.

The new Winston Club for 7th Armoured Division Other Ranks was later opened formally by Winston Churchill, where he made the famous speech that included:

Now I have only a word more to say about the Desert Rats. They were the first to begin. The 11th Hussars were in action in the desert in 1939 and ever since you have kept marching steadily forward on the long road to victory. Through so many countries and changing scenes you have fought your way. It is not without emotion that I can express to you what I feel about the Desert Rats.

Dear Desert Rats! May your glory ever shine! May your laurels never fade! May the memory of this glorious pilgrimage of war which you have made from Alamein, via the Baltic, never die!

It is a march unsurpassed through all the story of war so far as my reading of history leads me to believe. May the fathers long tell the children about this tale. May you all feel that in following your great ancestors you have accomplished something which has done good to the whole world; which has raised the honour of your own country and which every man has a right to be proud of.

When Field Marshal Montgomery eventually signed the Articles of Surrender by the various officers at the end of the Third Reich, he and the splendid British Army had, in just over the four months of early 1945, rescued and liberated from captivity nearly 20 million souls: the populations of Holland, eleven million; Denmark, four million; Norway, three million; two million displaced persons; and many hundreds of thousands of prisoners of war. And at least two or three million German citizens would be happier now their years of misery were over.

Nevertheless, by May 1945, the British forces in north-west Europe were the junior partners to the Russians and Americans in the great 'end game'.

On 13 May 1945 five years almost to the day since he became the King's First Minister, Winston Churchill spoke of the task ahead:

On the continent of Europe we have yet to make sure that the simple and honourable purposes for which we entered the war are not brushed aside or overlooked in the months following our success and that the words 'freedom', 'democracy' and 'liberation' are not distorted from their true meaning as we have understood them. There would be little use in punishing the Hitlerites for their crimes, if law and justice did not rule and if totalitarian or police governments were to take the place of the German invaders ... It is the victors who must search their hearts in their glowing hours, and be worthy by their nobility of the immense forces that they wield.

Architect of victory: Field Marshal Sir Bernard Montgomery

CHAPTER 14

Fourth Reich Timetable

Monday 30 April 1945. 15.30
Hitler and Eva Braun commit suicide in Berlin command bunker. His will expelled Goering and Himmler from the Nazi Party and from all offices of State. He appointed Admiral Doenitz President of the Reich, Minister of War and Supreme Commander of the Armed Forces. His other specific cabinet nominations were ignored by Doenitz. Goebbels and Bormann made unsuccessful efforts to negotiate with the Russians. Doenitz met Himmler in Lübeck.

Monday 30 April
Admiral Doenitz urged Gauleiter Kaufmann of Hamburg and his forces to defend the river Elbe positions against the Allies 'with utmost tenacity' to save the German race from Bolshevism 'and vital military operations without reservation'. Previously Doenitz had organised 50,000 naval ratings to fight on the eastern and western front lines.

Monday 30 April
Bormann from Hitler's Berlin bunker sent a naval cipher: 'Fresh treachery afoot ... Himmler has made offer to surrender via Sweden.' Doenitz visits Himmler at police barracks in Lübeck. Doenitz's HQ still in Ploen. Midnight visit by Himmler and six armed SS officers.

Tuesday 1 May
Doenitz powerful radio broadcast: 'The Führer has nominated me as his successor. The military struggle must continue to thwart expansion of Bolshevism in Europe.' Doenitz issues orders to arrest Goebbels and Bormann.

Tuesday 1 May
Doenitz issues Order of the Day to the German Armed Forces 'continue the fight until our troops and hundreds of thousands of German families in our Eastern Provinces have been saved from slavery or destruction'. Ribbentrop visits and asks for 'legal right to be appointed Foreign Minister'. Negative answer.

Wednesday 2 May
Graf Schwerin-Krosigk becomes Chairman of the Cabinet. Various conferences with top generals Keitel, Jodl, von Bock and von Manstein. Two officers each day provide a report on the military situation.

Wednesday 2 May
Heinrich Himmler, SS leaders Otto Ohlendorf, Rudolf Hoess with armed staff of 150 in Flensburg. Many hundreds of POW arrive at Flensburg by ship and train from Sachsenhausen and Neuegamme concentration camps guarded by SS teams in civilian clothes.

Wednesday 2 May
Doenitz sends for Reichskommissar Terboven and General Boehme from Norway, Frank the Reichsprotektor for Czechoslovakia, Seyss-Inquart, Reichskommissar for the Netherlands, and Dr Best and General Lindemann of Denmark.

Thursday 3 May
Doenitz and entourage at 2 a.m. reach Muerwik naval base, a northern suburb of Flensburg. He orders Admiral von Friedeburg to contact Field Marshal Montgomery in Hamburg re a cease-fire in Germany. All the SS and Gestapo in Flensburg are now dressed in naval uniforms with false pay books. Himmler and Hoess order key SS personnel to escape into Denmark and go into hiding. The small ship *The Ruth* arrives in Murwik with 1,000 POW from Stutthof concentration camp after 8 days at sea. Half died on the voyage, the rest ill and verminous without hope. Frank, Protector for Bohemia and Moravia visits.

Thursday 3 May 7.30 p.m.
Radio station Flensburg Reich operates from the main Post Office. Albert Speer broadcasts message to all Germans to prevent a collapse of

public life. 10.30 p.m. Allied bombing raid on Flensburg, 56 killed.

Friday 4 May
Flensburg declared an 'Open City' to prevent military and air force activity on the town. The steamer *Rheinfelsstrasse* from the Strength through Joy programme, with 1,600 POW and 100 SS guards arrives and more cattle railcars from Hamburg Neuengamme concentration camp with all desperate for water. Three sailor saboteurs are court-martialled on the destroyer *Paul Jacob*. Doenitz's special train arrives at Sörup station, Fensburg.

Friday 4 May
General Friedeburg reported on surrender meeting with Montgomery, who was prepared to accept the surrender of north Germany but demanded the inclusion of Holland and Denmark. He also demanded the simultaneous surrender of all warships and merchantmen. Doenitz was torn between naval honour and the need to provide transport for 300,000 German refugees and the prospect that refusal would mean more air raid and great loss of life. So finally he instructed the Chief of Naval Staff to ensure that the signal 'Regenbogen', code word for the sinking of warships and U-boats, should *not* be issued. A few U-boat commanders unilaterally blew up their craft on the night of 4–5 May before the armistice came into force. At mid-day on the 4th Doenitz ordered immediate cessation of the U-boat campaign: 'You have fought like lions, not defeated, heroes' he told them.

Saturday 5 May
Vice Admiral Rogge orders the execution of three sailors on the ship *Exelutionspeleton*. Himmler presents plans at police HQ of the re-formed Nazi administration in Schleswig-Holstein. Doenitz starts daily cabinet meetings with von Krosigk, Speer, Dorpmuller and Stuckart. The Social Democrat/Communist Committee of 46 Flensburg workers is formed. The British troops of 11th Armoured Division arrive in the night with 1st Herefords, 1st Cheshires and Inns of Court armoured cars. The town is surrounded but there is no fighting.

Sunday 6 May
Major General Rooks, USA, and Brigadier Foord, UK, and the Control Commission for the OKW arrive in Flensburg and install their office on the Sud-America *Patria* ship as liaison unit to the Fourth Reich.

Sunday 6 May

When Seyss-Inquart arrived at night by ship from Holland Doenitz made it clear that under no circumstances should there be any demolitions or inundations of dykes and polders. An attempt to bring about a separate surrender was mooted. The Danish Dr Best and General Lindemann vouched for the fighting efficiency of the German troops. [Two divisions had recently left to join the defenders of Hamburg and Cuxhaven.] Dr Best warned against continuations of hostilities on Danish soil. Doenitz had several conferences with Terboven and General Boehme. Himmler appeared with Gruppenführer Schellenberg, the Chief of the German Foreign Security Service. The latter suggested surrendering Norway, not to the Allies, but to Sweden, and allowing the 400,000 German troops there to be interned. Doenitz and Schwerin-Krosigk said that British concurrence would have to be obtained. At 5 p.m. Doenitz, in effect, fired Himmler.

Sunday 6 May

General Kinzel arrived at Doenitz HQ in Muerwik with news that General Eisenhower in his HQ in Reims, France, had refused categorically to accept any separate surrenders, it was all or nothing! And the opposite to the surrender to Montgomery on 4 May (effective 5 May signed and agreed by Friedeburg, Kinzel, Wagner, Pollek and Friedel). So Jodl flew to Reims for more negotiations.

Monday 7 May

Major General 'Pip' Roberts, commander 11th Armoured Division, controlling the Flensburg area, visits with Interpreter Lieutenant Hector Munro and Lt Peter Heath ADC in a huge Mercedes escorted by Inns of Court armoured cars. They :

> ... meet Field Marshal Keitel (a portly, fishy-eyed old gentleman in operetta resplendent uniform). All German troops to be disarmed, no more Nazi Hitler salutes, strike down all flags, evacuate the neighbouring Luftwaffe barracks to make room for the British Herefords and Cheshire troops (159 Brigade). Encounter Doenitz (tall, stiff and worried looking), noted offices for von Ribbentrop, Foreign Minister, Reichminister Speer, Reichminister Funk, Economic minister, Reichminister Rosenberg, Nazi philosopher and Minister for Occupied Territories, Count Schwerin von Krosigk, Finance Minister and Colonel-General Jodl, Chief of Staff to OKW.

Roberts' two junior officers made several more visits dispensing English cigarettes, obtaining information from Speer and Vice-Admiral Strauss.

Monday 7 May
Schwerin von Krosigk broadcast the message: 'Unity, Law and Justice must guide values of the "new" Germany', but the Hitler salute continued when the Wehrmacht greeted each other.

Monday 7 May
Intense negotiations continued in Reims between Eisenhower, General Jodl and Ike, Chief of Staff Bedell Smith was helpful and the second Instrument of Surrender was signed in Reims at 2.41 a.m. on 7 May. And repeated for the Russians by Marshal Zhukov in Berlin-Karlhorst the next day, witness by General Keitel, Stumpff and Admiral von Friedeburg. Air Vice Marshal Tedder signed for the British.

Monday 7 May
Brigadier Churcher, Commander of 159 Brigade, visited the Doenitz HQ and confronted Jodl (pink-faced and agile, the brains of the OKW) to shift urgently the 200 German troops from the barracks designated for the British troops. They arrived in force on 10 May. Noted that Doenitz used a large Mercedes car, once owned by Hitler, to ferry him 500 yards from home to office and back; and a photographer from Heinrich Hoffman's famous studio appeared to photograph the new Cabinet.

Tuesday 8 May
Herr Clausen, school teacher, notes:

> ... streets full of people, refugees, soldiers (without weapons) queuing in long lines outside bakers, butchers, vegetable shops and tobacconists. Order maintained by troops with white armbands, also unarmed.

Wednesday 9 May
Colonel Peter Andrews with three other British officers visit and inspect area.

> We experienced no open hostility. Reichssender Klaus Kahlenberg takes 20.30 p.m. church service. Since midnight silence on all war fronts, nearly six years of heroic struggle is over.

Then a 3-minute silence. The sixteenth-century moated castle of Glücksburg, several miles NE of Flensburg, owned by the Duke of Holstein was taken over by the USSBS and Eisenhower's staff temporarily to interview Speer and other government officials.

Thursday 10 May
On the ship *Gazelle* another court-martial took place.

Friday 11 May
Harbour master reported about 250 commercial vessels berthed in the harbour and inner fjord bringing 25,000 wounded German soldiers, refugees and POW from a concentration camp.

Sunday 13 May
British troops occupy Flensburg city and General Wilhelm Keitel is arrested. A Russian envoy, Ruskov, joins the Control Commission team and complains sharply that the co-operation between Doenitz cabinet and C.C. is too great.

Monday 14 May
Allied flags hoisted at police HQ and other key places. Doenitz orders all portraits of Hitler to be removed. The last refugee ship arrives in the harbour and the senior naval officer and staff do all they can to help them.

Monday 14 May
Churchill to Foreign Office:

> It must be remembered that if Doenitz is a useful tool to us that will have to be written off against his war atrocities for being in command of submarines. Do you want to have a handle with which to manipulate this conquered people, or just to have to thrust your hands into an agitated ant-heap.

Tuesday 15 May
British put the Mayor and Police Chief in gaol. Allied Nations Supervisory Commission orders German soldiers not to sing songs when they are marching. General Eisenhower wants Doenitz removed in the interests of friendship with Russia.

Wednesday 16 May
All German soldiers and sailors in the Muerwick town and naval barracks arrested.

Friday 18 May
Nazi ideologist Alfred Rosenberg arrested at Naval Academy Hospital. Since 8 May 2,000 former Gestapo Nazi official now wearing Wehrmacht uniform arrested.

Saturday 19 May
John Galbraith and George Ball, US ministers, arrive by plane, are quartered on *Patria*, Hamburg-America liner. Speer still quartered in Glücksburg Castle.

Wednesday 22 May. Pentecost
Von Friedeburg dons full dress uniform with all medals and commits suicide.

Thursday 23 May
Allied Military and Naval units move all valuable equipment out of Flensburg. Doenitz and Jodl told they are now prisoners of war and will be flown out of the country with only one suitcase each. 420 senior officials and staff are captured. Dozens of photographers arrive from Paris.

The American *Time* magazine reported:

The German Reich died on a sunny morning on 23rd May near the Baltic sea port of Flensburg.

CHAPTER 15

The ADC's Story

In September 1944 Kapitan Walter Lüdde-Neurath, a 30-year-old experienced commander of torpedo boats and destroyers in the German Kriegsmarine, became personal adjutant to the Commander-in-Chief, Grossadmiral Karl Doenitz. His memoir was published in 1948 under the title (translated) of *Unconditional Surrender*, since the highly secret Allied Operation Eclipse had become known and appeared in the OKW (Armed Forces High Command) War Diary of 10 April 1945, pages 1233 and 1494. Lüdde-Neurath accompanied Doenitz for the first time to Führer Headquarters (FHQ) in mid-September 1944 under the code name Wolfsschanze (Wolf's Lair) near Rastenburg between the East Prussian lakes. In his first few days he met Hitler ('shorter than pictured, walked with a stoop, fumbling and unceremonious') and had personal audiences with Goering, Himmler, Generals Keitel and Jodl, the sinister Martin Bormann and Albert Speer. Where the Admiral went, Lüdde-Neurath followed. He wrote:

Behind the decision to hold out at all costs was the enemy demand for 'unconditional surrender'. Since the Casablanca Conference of January 1943, this was the spectre which throttled all German peace initiatives at birth and was the best foundation possible for 'total war' … FHQ had a captured map from the British Operation Eclipse in which the frontier between West and East was etched in that same prominent manner which would become later bitter reality as the Iron Curtain. The effects of the predicted occupation, division and strangulation of the nation were painted very darkly with regard to the biological stock in which a reduction of the population by twenty to thirty million a generation was foreseen. Here was the reason why no stone

131

had to be left unturned in the effort to avert such a catastrophe ... There was an obligation to the population of the Eastern Provinces, if the Soviet advance could not be held, to evacuate the people to the West ... to have abandoned the refugees and soldiers in the East to the mercy of the Russians at the capitulation would have been criminal.

Throughout most of April 1945 Doenitz and his faithful adjutant attended the daily situation conference at the Reich Chancellery in Berlin and retired at night by a special train Auerahn to the Kriegsmarine HQ at Bernau, north of Berlin, code-named Koralle, country barracks hidden on the edge of a wood. On the 19th, with Russians on the outskirts of Berlin, Doenitz moved his HQ to Berlin-Dahlem, and two days later had his final meeting with his Führer, who was described on his birthday in the bunker:

His speech and eyes were as expressive as always. His mental powers seemed intact. He was by no means a 'lunatic' in the normally understood sense, but physically he was a beaten and broken man; bloated, bent, feeble and nervous.

On the 20th Hitler had appointed Doenitz Commander-in-Chief North with 'power of plenipotentiary to issue orders to all centres of the State, Party and Wehrmacht in the Northern Region.' On the 22nd Doenitz moved his HQ to Plön/Holstein where it stayed until 2 May. The OKW Generals Keitel and Jodl and their staffs transferred from Berlin, which was surrounded by the Russians, to Rheinsberg by the 24th.

The scorched-earth policy in Germany, for which Hitler had ordered the destruction of all military and economic property, caused feelings to run high amongst Doenitz's naval associates and Doenitz and General Alfred Jodl, head of OKW, both tried to moderate the effect of the Führer edict. Speer was the only one of the most senior ranks with the courage to criticise it face to face. Nevertheless Doenitz ordered the Kriegsmarine to make preparations for destroying German ports, blowing up quays, mine-laying and blocking navigable channels as had been done with all the Channel ports. The ports of Memel and Gdynia (Poland) were destroyed to hinder the Russian advances, but not Hamburg and the harbours at the western end of the Baltic. Lüdde-Neurath wrote that Speer by now in Doenitz's close circle reminded him frequently about stopping the destructive measures.

The secret code word for the order to scuttle the U-boat fleet, kept by the signals staff aboard each boat, was 'Regenbogen'. It was never issued but nevertheless 215 U-boats were sunk or blown up by their crews in May 1945 and another 153 were handed over to the British.

Another secret code word was 'Werwolf', the order for the underground resistance movement which was brought into operation in April, was cancelled on 5 May. Doenitz considered it counter-productive as he was negotiating terms of final surrender with the West. Lüdde-Neurath of course had a strong loyalty to Doenitz and wrote:

Adolf Hitler capitulated on 29 April 1945. Not before the world, but before himself and history. On that day he appointed his successor who learned that the Hitler Testament was now in force ... the military situation was hopeless... fighting to the last shell did not enter Doenitz's thinking. When Berlin fell the death of Hitler and the occupation of most of the Reich convinced him that the time had come for the German leadership to bear the consequences of their total defeat. He was ready to face up to it himself ... He saw his primary task to end the war as quickly as possible to spare further pointless sacrifice for friend and foe alike in a manner worthy of the unique heroic struggle of the German people, and above all to save as many as he could from the horrors of Bolshevism ... the fighting against the Russians had to continue and no proposals for capitulation were offered to them.

By careful procrastination Doenitz's efforts succeeded—between 23 January and 8 May 1945 2,022,602 Germans arrived safely from the East.

There was a dangerous loose cannon around. Heinrich Himmler as Chief of Police, Commander in Chief of the Ersatzheer (Replacements Army) and C-in-C of Army Group Vistula, had expected after Herman Goering's disgrace and Hess's absence as a POW in England, to become Hitler's successor. But Hitler had heard of Himmler's secret negotiations for surrender talks and immediately dismissed him. On 26, 27 and 30 April Himmler and Doenitz met at Schwerin, Rheinsberg and Lübeck. The former was 'playing the Crown Prince' according to Lüdde-Neurath, but Doenitz's nickname of The Lion ensured a stiff, uneasy relationship. On the 30th Doenitz met Himmler face to face and confronted him with the Bormann telegram confirming the Admiral as Hitler's successor. 'He went pale. He thought about it. Then he rose and congratulated me ...'

Doenitz wrote, but he had a Luger on his desk, just in case. A few days later Himmler, disguised as a village policeman, was captured by British military policemen and committed suicide.

Another key issue was the extent to which the members of Doenitz's small government, Generaladmiral von Friedeburg, Albert Speer, Graf Schwerin von Krosigk, Generaloberst Alfred Jodl and Generalfeldmarschall Keitel, were aware of the full horror of the extermination and concentration camps such as Auschwitz (1940), Dachau (1933) and Buchenwald (1933). It does now seem hard to believe the more prominent were unaware of the appalling 'Final Solution'. However in mid-May a prison ship arrived in Flensburg with concentration camp inmates, overloaded and with acute food shortage. The crew and guards had decamped. Doenitz acted swiftly. He ordered Kapitan zur See Lüth, the senior coastal station officer, personally to bring medical care and immediate relief supplies to the hundreds of camp prisoners. Then through Graf Schwerin von Krosigk, the Foreign Minister, on 15 May an ordinance was published in which the (Fourth) Reich Court was declared the competent authority for the investigation and prosecution of all excesses in the concentration camps.

CHAPTER 16

Liberation of *Festung* Holland

After his panzers and Luftwaffe had devastated Poland in late autumn 1939, Hitler planned his next, even more audacious move. His intentions were more or less described in *Mein Kampf*. The destruction of his old First World War enemy, France, and its huge army was irresistible. The only two ways of bypassing the redoubtable Maginot Line were either south through the Belgian Ardennes, or north through neutral Holland and Belgium. Hitler sent his main *schwerpunkt* through the former and his airborne army into the latter. Holland was a peaceful country with a population of about 11 million, prosperous with a well-established monarchy. Hitler could see many advantages to the capture of Holland: an excellent agricultural system; a Luftwaffe base; a kriegsmarine base for E-boats and U-boats to harass the Royal Navy and Allied convoys in the North Sea and English Channel.

Early on 10 May General Kurt Student unleashed 4,000 of his 4,500-strong parachute army to drop and secure the key bridges at Rotterdam, Dordrecht and Moerdijk before the Dutch could blow them up. His light infantry division of 12,000 men was landed on captured airfields in transport aircraft. The Dutch army put up a strong resistance in Rotterdam and Dordrecht and captured 1,000 German paratroopers, who were promptly shipped by sea to England for safe keeping. The German 9th Panzer Division raced through a gap in the southern flank and on the third day linked up with the paratroops.

The French 7th Army intended to move into Holland to help, but were too late. After Rotterdam was heavily bombed on the 14th killing 900 civilians, Goering threatened to bomb and destroy Utrecht, so inevitably the Dutch army surrendered. German casualties were 11,000, and 3,000

Aspects of war in Holland. (*Michael Bayley*)

civilian deaths were incurred in the Luftwaffe deluge of bombs. The Dutch army had 9,300 casualties. Queen Wilhelmina, her family and parliament reached London safely; she then appointed Pieter Gerbandy as her new prime minister. He was a more aggressive man than Dirk Jan de Geer.

Hitler then promoted a fellow Austrian Nazi, Arthur Seyss-Inquart (1892–1946) to head the country as civilian governor (Reichskommissariat Niederlande). Two other key appointments were the Dutch renegade Anton Mussert (1894–1946), who founded the National Socialist Movement in the Netherlands, and Hanns Albin Rauter, another Austrian, who became the SS commander and police chief in the country. Between them this terrible triumvirate brought the proud, peaceful country to the edge of destruction. All key aspects of life fell under Nazi control. There was food rationing and ration cards, and the press, radio, labour unions and political parties were controlled by selected Quisling-style collaborationists. Complete factories were dismantled and shipped into Germany to be reassembled there. Cattle, food, metals, machinery and textiles were sent over the border to reinforce Hitler's war efforts. Almost half a million Dutch people, mostly men of eighteen to forty-five years of age, were sent as slave labourers into the Third Reich factories. Many thousands were conscripted (*Arbeitseinatz*) to build parts of the gigantic Atlantic wall along the Dutch coastline. Some towns including Scheveningen were evacuated: 20,000 homes were abandoned and 65,000 people were forced to move.

In 1941, the persecution of the Jewish race started and the first batch of Jews was sent to a concentration camp at Mauthausen. In May 1942, all Jews were forced to wear the Star of David, and Dutch concentration camps were built at Vught and Amersfoort. The Dutch resistance groups—the Order Service of ex-army officers, the Council of Resistance, and the LKP—tried their best, but the German Gestapo and the OKW (Oberkommando der Wehrmacht) headed by Wilhelm Canaris, Herman Giskes of the Abwehr, and Joseph Schrieder of the Sicherheits Polizei, aided by informers, kept a stranglehold over any efforts to resist Hitler's henchmen. Nearly 50,000 young Dutchmen were recruited to form two renegade SS units: the 34th Grenadier Brigade Landstorm, which fought vigorously against the British and Canadians in 1944/45, and 4th Panzergrenadier Brigade Nederland, which was sent to fight alongside the Wehrmacht on the Eastern front.

Martin Bormann, the Führer's devoted Head of Secretariat recorded Hitler's table talk for several years. The book, *Hitler's Table Talk*, edited by Hugh Trevor-Roper, contained three curious extracts:

27 February 1942. I need a man for Belgium. The difficulty is to choose the man. No question of sending there a North German, somebody brutal, a martinet. I need an extraordinarily clever man as supple as an eel, amiable—and at the same time thick-skinned and tough. For Holland I have in Seyss-Inquart a man who has these qualities … Seyss has succeeded in encouraging in Holland a movement that is numbering more and more adherents and is waging war against Wilhelmina without our having to put a shoulder to the wheel. The idea of German solidarity is making more and more impression on the minds of the Dutch.

5 April 1942. [the Reichsführer SS Himmler talked to Hitler.] What struck me is that Anton Mussert is trying to get back his Dutch legion which at present is fighting on the Eastern front. For territorial defence he has no need of a Federal Dutch Army.

6 September 1942. What a fine race the Dutch are! The girls are splendid and very much to my taste.

Hitler regarded the Dutch people as part of his Aryan Herrenvolk who were forced to take part in his *Gleichschaltung* (enforced conformity). This meant that gradually all political parties were *verboten* except for the NSB.

German brutality was everywhere. In February 1943 General Lt Hendrik Seyffard, a Dutch renegade charged with the recruitment of Dutch volunteers to the Waffen SS, was assassinated in The Hague. SS General Rauter ordered the killing of fifty Dutch hostages as a reprisal. Further war crimes followed in 1944 after the German garrison of the village of Putten was attacked. The entire male population of 552 was deported to the camps, and only forty-eight survived. Each time the trade unions carried out a strike about conditions, the SS would execute the leaders and associates. In February 1941, 17 Dutch were killed in Amsterdam. In April 1943, a national strike ended with 150 civilians executed. A total of 2,800 were murdered by the Nazi regime.

A battle-scarred road to 's-Hertogenbosch.

Anxious civilians in Eindhoven, scared that the 'Moffen' might counter-attack and return. (*Imperial War Museum*)

After the sad failure of Operation Market Garden in September 1944, the entire population of Arnhem was forced to abandon their homes and leave the town because they might have helped the British paratroops. In March 1945, after a minor skirmish at De Woeste Hoeve, General Rauter ordered the execution of 250 hostages. By the·time of liberation in May 1945, after systematic hunting and purging, no fewer than 105,000 out of the original 140,000 Jewish population of Holland were murdered in the camps. This was the highest percentage of any Western European country. Only 20,000 Dutch Jews survived the war.

Market Garden and 'Dolle Dinsdag' ('Mad Tuesday') on 5 September 1944 had encouraged high hopes of a complete Allied victory. By the autumn of 1944, much of North Brabant, Nijmegen and Eindhoven had been liberated. Zeeland and Walcheren were painfully captured by the Canadians, the Scottish 52nd Lowland Division, many squadrons of Hobart's Funnies, a Royal Marine commando, and a powerful Royal Navy squadron. In early winter, in Operation Aintree, the British army captured all the Peel countryside around Venlo and Overloon. But sadly, the more densely populated cities in the north had to endure the *Hongerwinter* of 1944/45. To make things worse, the RAF bombed many towns, seeking V-weapon sites, submarine and E-boat depots and

A Coy 4 Lincolns pass a wrecked German A/TK gun in Willemstad.

2nd Troop A Squadron 15/19th Hussars in Geldrop.

'Dolle Dinstag' or 'Mad Tuesday', and news of possible freedom.

Gestapo HQ. In the process, unfortunately, many Dutch civilians were killed. Nijmegen alone lost 500 of its citizens who were killed in air raids. The Netherlands Red Cross begged the British to reconsider air attacks on Dutch cities, but not to much avail.

For his bravado attack in the Ardennes in December 1944, Hitler had created no fewer than twenty-five Volksgrenadier divisions, recruited mainly from reluctant industrial workers, convalescents, 'difficult' veterans and distinctly middle-aged conscripts. Their discipline and zeal for fighting was third class, compared to the élite SS and Waffen units. Major General Gerhard Franz commanded 256th Volksgrenadier Division in Holland and issued this order to his troops:

256 Volksgrenadier Division Commander Headquarters
11 October 1944

Certain events among units have impelled me to point out that discipline and *esprit de corps* among the troops must be raised in the shortest possible time. For this, all formation commanders, in particular company commanders, will be held personally responsible to me ...

It cannot be tolerated that a formation commander should get drunk, then wander about the woods at night shouting and firing his pistol at the sentry ...

It shows little discipline in a company when members of the company call each other 'cheats' during a discussion about captured loot ...

A unit shows little *esprit de corps* if a soldier can declare that owing to difficulty in walking he can no longer serve with the artillery since he could not escape quickly enough if the Tommy arrived. Such a statement is a basis for defeatism and this case should be dealt with by courts-martial.

It shows lamentable carelessness if one soldier while cleaning his arms injured four comrades by sheer negligence and in such a way that they will be unable to do any duty. Before cleaning weapons, in particular new weapons, sufficient instruction must be given in stripping and assembling so that everyone who may have to use these weapons is fully conversant with their use ...

During the last eight days no less than 11 desertions have been reported, seven of whom went over into enemy lines ... Reports about desertions are lamentable and generally arrive too late. In one particular case a soldier deserted his unit on 29 September 1944, and the official report was not made until 10 October 1944 ...

FRANZ

On 5 March 1945, Colonel General Blaskowitz of Army Group H doled out death for stragglers:

General Johannes Albrecht Blaskowitz (1883–1948)

As from midday 10 March, all soldiers in all branches of the Wehrmacht who may be encountered away from their units on roads or in villages, in supply columns or among groups of civilian refugees, or in dressing stations when not wounded, and who announce that they are stragglers looking for their units, will be summarily tried and shot ...
BLASKOWITZ
Colonel General

In early April 1945 Hitler designated the Netherlands as *Festung* Holland, to be defended at *all* costs.
In *Defeat in the West,* Milton Shulman wrote:

... the Nazi chiefs resorted to harsher and more terrifying methods as the end loomed nearer and nearer. Fear was still the weapon that was most effective in cowing the masses, and Goebbels wielded it with abandon. The bogy of Bolshevism was raised everywhere to frighten the nation into submission. On 16 March 1945 the following directive was issued to the National Socialist indoctrination officers of 15th Army in Holland. These officers performed a similar function in German units to the role carried out by Communist commissars in Russian units, but with far less success. This document

Infantry with Churchill tanks in Holland.

illustrated the propaganda line to be adopted in talks to the men and consisted of a series of warnings of catastrophes that would befall the German people 'in the event of capitulation'.

'As a natural consequence of the reparations demanded by the Reparations Commission in Moscow,' it reads, 'the whole German agricultural potential is to be at the disposal of Moscow, and hunger, calculatingly produced, will be applied as a means of oppression, at any time.

'German labour will be used as "reparations production"; as a natural consequence Moscow will deport German slave labour to Siberia by the million. German industry will then profit only Germany's enemies.

'Moscow will tear asunder all families by deportation, slave labour, etc. forever, with the full intention of destroying the family as the basis of the life of the race ...

'The German women will be raped by beasts in human guise, dishonoured and murdered ...

'German children will be torn from their parents by force, deported and brought up as Bolsheviks.

'The German people as an organic community will be literally murdered. Germany will become a vast graveyard. Whoever survives has nothing more to hope for in this life ...

'The want and suffering of the present war situation are nothing compared to the aims of extermination by our enemies. These will be carried out in the event of capitulation. The entire German people has risen against this fate and fights as a single armed Nazi army.'

Sporadic negotiations for surrender were taking place all along the various fronts, usually at a divisional or even lower level. But as long as Hitler still lived and dominated his Third Reich surrender was impossible. Except for those who had been forced to surrender in the Ruhr, no officer commanding an army or an army group was yet prepared to follow von Vietinghoff's example in Italy. Typical of this stubborn, unthinking, automatic adherence to a code was the behaviour of Colonel General Blaskowitz in Holland. A man of sixty-two years with a flattened, frog-like jaw, broad nostrils and thinning hair, Blaskowitz was a sterling product of the German General Staff. His forces in Holland had been pushed back to the Grebbe Line by the Canadians and British and were obviously incapable of resisting much longer. However, Blaskowitz and his superior civilian authority, Arthur von Seyss-Inquart, still held one trump card in their hands. They controlled the dykes protecting the Netherlands from the waters of the North Sea and the Zuider Zee.

On 14 April 1945, the Canadians reached the North Sea and took Leeuwarden and captured the last of the many V-1 and V-2 sites. Alan Moorehead reported:

> The last rocket and flying bomb had fallen on England. All around on the line of march we came on stranded trains filled with the V-weapons; V-2s packed with rounded wooden struts and wickerwork but so large that each projectile overlapped by half its length into the truck ahead. And in the railway yards there were many great drums of explosives and strange steel cranes and scaffoldings were latticed over with the branches of trees and there was evidence that they travelled only at night. But it made no difference. They lay there either broken by the RAF or sabotaged by the retreating Germans themselves, or simply abandoned in the cuttings by the wayside stations, a series of weird tossing shapes among the spring wheat, a brutal warning of what might have happened had the war continued another year.

Hobart's Funnies had been integrated into the Canadian Army for many months. At Leeuwarden, in Friesland, Crocodile flame-throwers of the Fife and Forfars helped 8th Canadian Infantry Brigade while 7th RTR Crocodiles assisted the Canadians to capture Deventer on 19 April. The Buffaloes of 11th RTR and 49th APC carried 2nd and 3rd Canadian Infantry divisions into the Zutphen and Appeldoorn areas.

William Hitchcock's book *Bitter Road to Freedom* details most of the grim suffering that the four million Dutch people in the main cities endured in the *Hongerwinter* of 1944/45: 'Starvation kills slowly. Thousands of Dutch people during the early spring of 1945 knew this only too well. While the Allied powers dithered thousands of people in western Holland simply wasted away. The average diet fell to about a thousand calories per day [the Allied troops enjoyed about 4,000 calories per day] and for the poor and elderly it often slipped below that.' One resident of Amsterdam wrote: 'The city is Oriental. Garbage heaps piled against tree stumps. Starved dogs, warped with hunger, tails between their legs, pawing at the heaps. Barefooted people, grey-haired people, sitting or lying in doorways and begging children with hunched up shoulders and gunny sacks under their arms.' People went very slowly on hunger walks into the countryside trying to barter goods for dairy products and vegetables.

The pressure applied by Queen Wilhelmina's court and government, Prime Minister Gerbrandy, and the Red Cross on Eisenhower, Churchill and Montgomery was intense. Unless the Allies invaded and drove out Seyss-Inquart and the 25th German Army garrisoning Holland, the Dutch population would suffer irrevocably. Over 3.6 million inhabitants were starving. But, and there were two great 'buts', Seyss-Inquart could destroy Holland by deliberately flooding 70 or 80 per cent of the country by destroying dams, dykes and all the polder-bunds. He made sure the Allies knew that. Also every week that delayed Operations Eclipse and Plunder meant that the German defenders could strengthen the many barriers in front of the Allies. Time was vital for Hitler and his generals. The alternative rendition of north and north-west Holland would take time and cause very heavy Allied and civilian casualties. The British Liberation Army had taken a bloody nose in Market Garden and subsequent operations: Aintree, the Battle of the Bulge, Blackcock, Veritable and Blockbuster had met fanatical and skilled defensive actions by Hitler's generals.

And one more 'but', which was not necessarily known at the time: all of Hitler's twelve or fifteen extermination (not necessarily concentration) camps were slaughtering the inmates in the gas chambers and other means, including starvation (vide Bergen-Belsen). Of the two million or more Russian prisoners of war in Germany, a very high percentage were dying of deliberate starvation.

Eisenhower pressed on with his strong attacks over the Rhine, across the river barriers, as fast as the deliberate Montgomery and the more rapid American generals could manage. However, the intense Dutch pressure on the Allies for succour caused Operation Manna to take place, after considerable negotiations with Seyss-Inquart. Eventually, four months later, on 25 April, 3,000 British RAF bombers parachuted 6,000 tons of supplies to the Dutch behind German lines, mainly around Rotterdam and The Hague. In late January, a small Swedish-inspired relief operation sent two ships, the *Noreg* and *Dagmar Bratt,* with 3,000 tons of flour, margarine and cod-liver oil to Delfzyl in northern Holland. By April they had sent 20,000 tons of provisions to help feed the starving millions.

Eisenhower had ordered 109,000 tons of various foodstuffs and medicines to be made available for Holland, and the great depot at Oss used by Germans and British (not necessarily at the same time) at

Operation Manna. (*Ken Dillon*)

Three Dutch children in battered Arnhem clutch Red Cross parcels after months of privation.

one stage had 30,000 tons available. The Germans deliberately put up excuses for delay week after week, but by mid-April even the die-hard Seyss-Inquart realised that some co-operation on humanitarian grounds was possible, so a local truce brought some more relief.

On 29 April Lancaster bombers flew over The Hague and other districts, dropping supplies to cope with the threat of starvation among Dutch civilians until land transport could be got through to them. The editor of the Netherlands News Agency flew in one of the Lancasters and described the mission:

The grocer called on the people of The Hague today—for the first time for years. True, it was Sunday, but this was definitely a case of 'the better the day, the better the deed'. He called at Rotterdam and Leyden as well. It was closing day too—not only because it was Sunday but also because the shops have had no food to sell for a long time.

I was with the RAF delivery men on their rounds. We travelled in a Lancaster bomber, and as a result of the day's activities rations were provided for thousands of starving Dutch people, many of whom had not had a square meal for months. Our squadron, for example, carried sufficient food—42 tons of it—to feed one-fifth of the population of The Hague for one day. But there were other squadrons as well.

Each of our aerial delivery vans carried food with which first-class meals can be produced. There were flour and yeast for bread-making, tins of meat and bacon, with pepper and salt and mustard to taste. The Dutch love for vegetables was met by tins of dehydrated potato, as well as bags of peas and beans. Sugar, margarine, dried milk, cheese, dried eggs and chocolate completed the order. Weeks of preparation and experiment had gone into the scheme, including the devising of special slings to ensure that in place of huge 12,000-pounders, each aircraft could drop 355 20-pound food bombs.

We crossed the North Sea on our mercy mission shortly after midday and approached The Hague at a very low level. Our target area, the Ypenburg civil airfield south-east of the town, was clearly visible. It had been marked out by Pathfinders with green flares, and in the centre was a white cross surmounted by a red light.

From the moment we crossed the Dutch coast, people in the fields and roads, and in the gardens of the sad little houses, waved frantically. But it was not until we were actually flying over The Hague that we saw what this manna from heaven really meant for the Dutch. Every road seemed full of

The famous Delft ceramics
celebrated the relief of Holland.

The river Grebbe was the unofficial boundary between occupied and free Holland.

people waving flags, sheets, or anything they could grab. The roofs of tall buildings were black with Dutch citizens welcoming us. On a barge we saw the Dutch tricolour bravely hoisted; across a large flat roof an Orange flag was colourfully stretched.

The people were certainly overjoyed to see these huge bombers emptying their bomb bays one after another on the target area, as thousands of food bombs fluttered out like confetti from a giant hand. And along the roads leading into The Hague were carts, perambulators and bicycles as the populace seemed to race to join in the great share-out. Unfortunately, owing to the recent spell of bad weather, we were just too late to give them their Sunday dinner, but with amazing enthusiasm the RAF aerial grocers today certainly delivered the goods.

'These were the best bombs we have dropped for years,' said Flight Officer Ellis, the bomb-aimer of our aircraft.

By 18 April the Canadians, British and the Polish Armoured Division had battered their way to the shores of the Zuider Zee. As a result the bulk of the German 25th Army was cut off from its home base and penned into the Grebbe and Eem lines enclave in the west and north-west. Eisenhower's staff received messages indicating that a truce, perhaps a surrender might be negotiated, so he and Bedell Smith instructed Major General Francis de Guingand, Chief of Staff 21st Army Group, to have preliminary talks. These took place on 28 April with Ernst Schwebel, commander of Zuid-Holland on behalf of Seyss-Inquart and Blaskowitz. De Guingand described the talks: 'My opposite number across the table—Schwebel—was one of the most revolting men I have ever seen. A plump sweating German who possessed the largest red nose I have ever seen, the end of which was like several ripe strawberries sewn together. With him he had Naval, Air and Army representatives as well as a food expert.' De Guingand had Lt General A. Galloway, who was head of the organisation to feed Holland, plus senior Canadian and SHAEF officers. Meeting No. 1 was an exchange of views. Meeting No. 2 on the 30th at the Hotel de Wereld in Wageningen was larger and included Prince Bernhard of the Netherlands, C-in-C of the Dutch troops in 21st Army Group. Bedell Smith came, as did Seyss-Inquart. The arrangements for food relief had been agreed but it was Admiral Doenitz in Flensburg who had to make the final decision about surrender, which took place at 0241hrs on 7 May.

One curious feature of the German surrender was the appearance of a group of Russian officers led by General Ivan Susloparov. They were of course interested in repatriating all Russian prisoners of war released by the Allies.

Since January 1945, SHAEF had been working with the Netherlands military administration—the provisional Dutch military power in the liberated part of Holland—to prepare fifty-one medical feeding teams to be rushed into the west and north-west of the country. Each team included a doctor, six nurses, five social workers and other staff. All had received Red Cross training and were supplied with special emergency rations. Overall they treated 279,000 patients in the early summer of 1945. SHAEF separately delivered 189,000 tons of supplies. On 5 May ships arrived in Rotterdam and the bulk came in by truck, then barge, to the target area. Within two weeks the Allies were able to offer the Dutch people a daily ration of 2,000 calories. For a week, food convoys poured through the Polar Bear lines and through the still heavily armed German troops on the river Grebbe truce lines. Lt Brian Lott of the 55th Anti-tank Regiment returned from leave to rejoin his unit at Ede. He recalled:

> We were involved in a humane role helping to feed the Dutch who in the towns and particularly Amsterdam, were starving. I was given a platoon of trucks and we moved to Bilthoven. The trucks travelled to Utrecht each day where food was being flown in by the RAF. We distributed the food from Bilthoven. The people were very grateful. Once I took a motor cycle and rode into Amsterdam. It was incredibly quiet and a terrible smell of death hung over the city. I did not see any Germans. I think I may have liberated Amsterdam on my own!

On 3 May much activity was noticed in the small shattered town of Wageningen. The Kensingtons saw many staff cars in the square outside a small hotel and an imposing array of red tabs. There was a BBC mobile recording van there as well. General von Blaskowitz, GOC of the German army in Holland, his face a grey mask of defeat, had just signed the unconditional surrender. The Lincolns noticed Lt General Bedell Smith of SHAEF, Prince Bernhard of Holland, the GOC of the 1st Canadian Corps and also, for the opposition, Seyss-Inquart.

Just two days later, Major S. Jacobson MC, second in command of the Recce Regiment, was sent to the HQ of an SS battalion beyond Utrecht to negotiate their surrender. He recalled:

> I went off in my jeep with Private Hall my driver, a Dutch Resistance interpreter (with a Sten) and a German SS officer as guide. It was a queer drive through an area not yet occupied by Allied troops. The villages seemed deserted except for armed German sentries. But as we drove through curtains were drawn aside, windows flung open, flags put out ... The SS colonel and adjutant had

A Squadron, 49th Recce Regiment, arriving in Dam Square, Utrecht, 7 May 1945. (*Monty Satchell*)

obviously just bathed, shaved and put on their best uniforms. I was in rather tired battle dress.

[When the capitulation papers were signed, he continued:]

We were faced by an amazing sight. Piled high with flowers, the jeep was hemmed in on every side by men, women and children, all perfectly quiet. But when I came out with the bit of paper in my hand, something snapped. They cheered, laughed and cried. I made a speech. It was funny, exciting, deeply moving. The war was over.

On the evening of the 4th came news that all German troops in north-west Germany, Denmark and western Holland had surrendered unconditionally, to take effect from 0800hrs on the 5th. On 6 May Major General Rawlins, GOC the Polar Bears 49th Division, met the commander of the German 88th Corps to arrange the occupation of north-west Holland and the disarming and concentration of the enemy. All units took part that day in Thanksgiving church parades, and there were double rum issues that night.

Amsterdam in early 1945.

Lt Colonel C. D. Hamilton of the 7th Dukes recalled:

> The plan was for the 49th Division to disarm the three divisions holding the
> Grebbe Line based on Hilversum and Utrecht, while the following day the
> Canadian 1st Division went on to the Hague and Rotterdam to put the coastal
> divisions behind the wire of their own defences. Our customers were our old
> opponents of 4 December, the 6th German Parachute Division, who had found
> us in the way when they tried to take the Nijmegen bridge.

Somewhere between 150,000 and 200,000 assorted soldiery of the Third
Reich were trapped inside the Grebbe and Eems river enclave. Inside were
several million half-starved Dutch men, women and children, mainly in
the cities of Amsterdam, Rotterdam, The Hague, Haarlem, Delft, Leiden
and Amersfoort. The enclave was 60 miles wide at its southern point,
narrowing to a triangle between the North Sea and Ijsselmeer.

The Canadians and British were tasked with the swift 'peaceful' entry
into the enclave, keeping their fingers crossed that *all* the German forces
would accept the terms of *immediate* surrender. General Blaskowitz was
ordered to seize and disarm all the renegade Dutch SS soldiers under
his command. This was accomplished slightly reluctantly, and soon

8,000 were arrested. Moreover the 120,000 German troops who had surrendered on 5 May were ordered to build their own barbed wire enclosures in lieu of camps, as a prelude to being shipped out east to the camps in Schleswig Holstein. For the time being they were allowed to keep their small arms, but they were forced to clear all the minefields they had set up.

Almost undamaged by war, the great city of Amsterdam had waited for liberation longer than most European cities. On the morning of 7 May, German forces were still present in large numbers in the centre when armoured cars of the Polar Bear Division arrived.

B Squadron of the 49th Recce Regiment achieved fame in the *Daily Express* of 8 May 1945 under the headline NAZIS CLEAR WAY. According to the reporter John Reffern, the first troops into Amsterdam produced: 'the greatest liberation scenes I have know. The hated Grunepolizei, German security police, were made to clear a way for them through the rejoicing crowds.'

Leonard Marsland Gander, a journalist at the *Daily Telegraph*, was also there wearing a British uniform and red beret. He remembered:

> The Dam Square was a wild sea of celebration within a ring of sullen German troops. We clawed our way through with difficulty, dispensing cigarettes, more in demand than food. After we left, the scene erupted. Attempts were made to disarm a German officer. German marines in De Groote Club fired into the crowd and at least 20 civilians were killed. Scattered fighting broke out until the Dutch Resistance leader arranged a truce. Our small troop was reinforced and a column of ten armoured cars returned to the centre of Amsterdam.

On 31 August 1944, SHAEF had set up the Dutch Forces of the Interior (Nederlandsche Binnenlandsche Strijdkraft—the NBS) under Prince Bernhard, who reported direct to General Eisenhower. By April 1945, there were 9,350 armed resistance members of the NBS organised in six zones and fourteen regions under Major General Koot.

On 7 May, the Recce Regiment in Otterloo led the advance into western Holland. A Squadron was directed on Utrecht, B Squadron on Hilversum and Amsterdam and C Squadron on Baarn and Amersfoort. The Germans fulfilled their surrender conditions with correctness. The only impediment was the Dutch civilians. The vehicles could only just get through the enthusiastic crowds. B Squadron was at Otterloo

Tony Van Renterghem, Chief of Staff, South Amsterdam Resistance District, April 1945.

and on the morning of the 7th, two troops were detailed to proceed to Amsterdam: No 1 Troop (two heavy and two light recce cars) under Lt George Bowman MC and No 4 Troop (six Bren gun carriers) under Lt John Rafferty. Trooper Percy Habershon was the gunner operator in a heavy armoured car commanded by Sgt Dai Davis, the driver of which was Lance Corporal Seagrove. Percy Haberson recalled:

The route was via Hilversum and once we started moving through the villages the reception was tremendous. National flags and Orange banners were hanging from all the buildings. At one of the bridges on the outskirts of Amsterdam we were met by a Dutch Resistance officer [Lt Tony van Renterghem], the liaison officer of the local Resistance group. He led us through the suburbs into Dam Square in front of the Old Royal Palace. Several thousand people had turned out but eventually two heavy armoured cars managed to get to the main doors of the palace where Lt G Bowman posted a notice regarding the surrender. The situation was becoming very volatile. There were fully armed German soldiers on the streets and Resistance fighters brandishing Sten guns were appearing. We then moved to a building some distance away at the side of a canal, the HQ of the German occupational forces. Lt Bowman and Lt van Renterghem went

Rotterdam port in early 1945.

inside. We were near a local hospital and a large crowd of nurses descended on us. Being 20 years old I lost interest in military matters until we were rescued from a fate worse than death by Lt Bowman who told us we were to move to a RV outside the city. What a shame!

Utrecht, a large prosperous city, was entered by the 4th Lincolns on the 7 May. They arrived in style, debussed on the outskirts and, led by their regimental band, marched in to scenes of indescribable enthusiasm. The battalion HQ was in the Hotel Terminus. Armed German troops looked on apathetically and were completely ignored by both Dutch and British. The Polar Bear vehicles were swamped by the numbers of people who clambered all over them. In the evening a band concert, the Dutch and the Lincolns, played all the nostalgic tunes, including of course the Dutch National Anthem 'Wilhelmus', followed by 'God Save the King'. Peter Stursberg, a journalist on the *Daily Herald* wrote an article on 8 May. The headline was DUTCH BEAT ALL FOR CHEERS:

The Dutch, whom we have always thought a stolid people, have outdone the Belgians and the French in their wild welcome to our troops during their victory march into Holland. The sound of cheering is still ringing in my ears as I write this in a hotel lobby here. I arrived in this ancient city with the first

British armoured cars. All the way from our starting point on the Grebbe line we drove through lines of people, but it was not till we got to the outskirts of the city that we were almost mobbed.

There had been some shooting in Utrecht between Nazis and Resistance men, and we stopped for a moment on a wide boulevard. A cheering, singing crowd descended on us and took over our vehicles. My coat was almost torn from my back, and I found that there was no room in the jeep for me except on the spare tyre. A girl had her arm round my neck, and a man was sitting on my knee. There were between 40 and 50 persons on the jeep and trailers, and more got on as we entered Utrecht.

This is the greatest liberation and the strangest, too. On our way up Germans drove past us in army cars and Volkswagens, and for a time, as we slowly edged our way through the crowds, two Germans cycled beside us. They had machine pistols slung over their backs, and might have been our escorts. The Dutch just ignored them. The girl who had her arm round my neck stuffed golden tulips into my raincoat. Our jeep and trailer load—by now a full chorus of 60 voices—broke into 'The Orange' as we passed a German headquarters.

The effect of starvation is noticeable in the pinched faces of the people. Some are so weak from hunger that they can hardly wave to us. I talked with the leader of the Resistance Movement here, and he told me that there was so little food that people were going round from house to house begging for a potato.

Other Polar Bear units took part in the official capture of Utrecht. The 1/4th KOYLI left Ede at 1300hrs on the 7th. Rex Flower recorded: 'The whole Bn in troop carriers along the road to Utrecht, as we came to the outskirts, everyone was out. There were thousands lining the streets. The convoy had to slow down. The people were absolutely going mad! They were ecstatic! It was definitely our best welcome of all. First we had children jumping on the vehicles, then a few young ladies. (We were not complaining.) It was fiesta time in the staid city of Utrecht. Poor semi-starving children clustered round the cookhouse. Everyone gave up part of their meals; the cooks gave them all leftovers. Doug, Jim and I were plied with drinks all day.'

The Hallams also 'fought' their way into Utrecht. The column was a splendid sight. Tulips bloomed in every rifle barrel, while hundreds of girls walked arm in arm with the Allied soldiers as they eventually marched in triumph through the town.

Above: Dutch SS troops interned after Holland's surrender.

Right: In Utrecht, Dutchmen shoulder welcome boxes of food and supplies shipped in by Allied forces in the days following the German surrender.

On 8 May, a thanksgiving service was held in Utrecht Cathedral and on Sunday 13th there was a victory parade followed by a service attended by the Burgomeister and Lt General C. Foulkes, GOC the 1st Canadian Corps.

On 9 May, the 4th Leicesters moved to Maarssen, six miles north-west of Utrecht, to disarm German troops. The battalion pioneer officer, Lt Daykin, arranged for the enemy working parties to blow up all dangerous ammunition.

Lt Colonel C. D. Hamilton of the 7th Dukes recalled:

The German paras first passed completely equipped through our 'sausage machine'. They dumped personal small arms, binoculars and watches in one house with A Company, then passed on to the open fields where their larger weapons, steel helmets, anti-gas kit and all the other multitudinous impedimenta of the division was stacked. For two days roads were blocked by hundreds of horse-drawn carts, the platoon trucks of one of the crack German divisions. Afterwards the Germans marched into a large wood where we guarded them for a week as they made themselves fit for their long march back to prison camps in northern Germany. I had one exhausting day inspecting every unit of two enemy brigade groups.

On the same day the Dutch newspaper *Het Parool* published a letter in English from Maurice Western, a journalist: 'We know that a dark nightmare has been lifted from your hearts and minds. While Germans in the end would have been driven from Holland regardless of any decisions which General Blaskowitz could make, most of us feared that the country would have been ravaged by the grimmest kind of war before freedom was secure again. Now as if by a miracle your dreads and ours are banished for ever and you have expressed your joy in rousing demonstrations that literally swept us off our feet and off our jeeps.'

Lt Tony van Renterghem, a key Resistance leader in Amsterdam wrote:

25,000 Dutch civilians had already died of hunger and thousands more were on the point of dying, particularly newborn babies and the very old. We were down to a diet of 330 calories a day, down from 1,200 calories in the summer of 1944. Even the German army in Amsterdam was down to 1,000 calories a day. The SS and Gestapo (unlike the Wehrmacht who were ready to surrender) still executed large numbers of the Resistance, Jews and hostages before the arrival of the Polar Bears. There was no electricity, gas, fuel of any kind. The sewage system had stopped pumping. There was no soap, no hot water. Meanwhile the Resistance was trying to feed 70,000 people who had gone underground such as Jews in hiding, or like myself, people who had been condemned to death, but were hiding. They had to stock up food for some 10,000 Resistance fighters who were called up to fight a guerilla war as soon as the Allies were near enough, and ordered us to attack the Germans from the back. Even more important was the protection of dykes and canal locks

Right: The Polar Bear monument on the Kade, Roosendaal, Holland. (*Bill Hudson*)

Below: 49th Division memorial, Utrecht, Holland. (*Bill Hudson*)

which the fanatical SS wanted to blow up to flood and destroy Holland. I was chief of staff of the South Amsterdam Resistance District. My main task at liberation was to prevent any fighting in my district between the trigger-happy Resistance and die-hard German army or SS, until a large enough Allied force was present. On 3 May the German Command finally allowed the Allied Air Force to drop food near the big cities, but collection and distribution without vehicles would take at least two weeks. Lt Bowman, out of radio contact, was advised by the Resistance CO when the shooting in Dam Square started, to withdraw to the town outskirts. Back at the bridge he called in reinforcements and Major H Taite joined him there with the main force a little later. At City Hall Major Taite met the German CO, Lt Kolonel Schroeder, a 'good' German who had long co-operated with the Resistance. The main Canadian force arrived the next day, 8 May, to take over military control of Amsterdam.

A new brigade of division artillery was formed with most of their guns laagered behind the lines. They concentrated at Doorn to start supervising the notorious 34th Landsturm Nederland SS Division. The Kensingtons formed part of the new brigade and, their historian wrote, rounded up: 'the avowed Nazi SS and all foreign Fascist volunteers, notorious in occupied Holland for their brutality. We received a rapturous welcome by the inhabitants of Doorn when the SS officers were evicted from the best houses.' On 10 May, the Kensingtons disarmed the 84th SS Regiment of 77 officers and 1,415 other ranks. Then two days later, Operation Pied Piper took place, to comb the area for German deserters and Dutch Nazis, as a result of which fifty-three arrests were made. The 1st Leicesters moved to Hilversum, where they also started to disarm the Wehrmacht. There was a certain grim satisfaction in doing so, and a carnival atmosphere in the town every evening. The 2nd Glosters were given the pleasant duty of disarming the 346th Infantry Division at Amersfoort, 12 miles from Utrecht. That division had opposed the 56th Sphinx Brigade in Normandy throughout their advance to Stampersgat and again at Arnhem. The regimental historian ended by saying: 'It was altogether a very satisfactory arrangement!' By 12 May all German divisional troops were disarmed and concentrated. HQ, signals and administrative companies of the German 88th Corps were disarmed by the Recce Regiment on the 13/14th.

The islands north of the Scheldt were captured by the British 4th Commando Brigade and 116th Royal Marine Infantry Brigade and E-boats, U-boats and many kriegsmarines were made prisoner. T-Force, the intrepid

Thieving Magpies had eight Category A and 140 Category B targets to investigate, so 30th Battalion of the Royal Berkshires and two companies of the Buckinghamshires advanced into Holland on 8 May to carry out their invaluable searches. In the Utrecht area T-Force found a torpedo-firing pistol unit for use in *midget* submarines and a number of botanical laboratories specialising in moulds and fungus for a penicillin equivalent. At Haaksbergen the Polar Bears gave T-Force permission to move ahead to identify targets. Capt. Lowe of the Buckinghamshires reached Rotterdam and met the NBS. National Archives WO/71/5161 shows that A Company entered Amsterdam, B Company Utrecht, C Company Rotterdam and D Company The Hague and islands near the Hook of Holland. The Thieving Magpies trawled through Groningen, Deventer, Wageningen, Leeuwarden, Harlingen, Norden, even Borkum island and Delft as well as the major cities for 'secrets' and 'secret men' of all kinds.

Many victory parades were held all over Holland on 21 May. The most important was held in The Hague with the salute taken by HRH Prince Bernhard in the presence of Queen Wilhelmina and General Crerar. Each Polar Bear battalion—twelve of them in all—was present with 200 men each, and sixteen pipe and five brass bands provided appropriate music. Overhead flew No 84 RAF group of fighters and fighter bombers.

There was spit and polish of course for the Polar Bears under their RSMs and they had a heavy infantry drill practice the day before. Lt Colonel D. A. D. Eykin's orders to his 11th Royal Scots Fusiliers included: 'Each company will provide ten men of not less than five feet ten inches in height. Decorated men will be given preference. Medals will be worn. Best battledress will be worn, boots will be highly polished. Brasses will be highly polished. Webbing, belts and gaiters will be blancoed. Caps (tam-o'-shanters) will be worn.'

On 25 May, 117,629 German troops (the Dutch renegade SS were left for local justice) moved from the Netherlands to concentration areas in the Wilhelmshaven/Emden peninsula. General Blaskowitz was responsible for co-ordination and control of evacuation and chose the route and the transit camps for the batches of 10,000 Wehrmacht who covered 15 miles per day into captivity.

During the war 205,900 Dutch men and women had died. The Netherlands had the highest death rate in Western Europe: 2.36 per cent of their population of about nine million. The Jewish suffered the worst with 104,000 deaths; forced labour in Germany another 27,000; in the

Resistance 23,000 died; 20,400 civilians died of starvation or bombing; and 7,850 armed forces were killed. The balance of 27,450 deaths was 'unclassified'.

In the final throes of retribution and justice over 200,000 cases of pro-Nazi activity were investigated. Of the many subsequently tried by democratic courts, forty received the death sentence, but many others were sentenced to between one and five years' imprisonment. Seyss-Inquart was hanged at Nuremberg on 16 October 1946; Anton Mussart was hanged at The Hague on 7 May 1946; General Johannes von Blaskowitz committed suicide in 1946. *Festung* Holland had been conquered and liberated.

On the 40th anniversary of the liberation of Arnhem on 15 April 1945, a Dutch postage stamp was issued that showed an Allied soldier in action. Initially it was supposed to be a Polish soldier, but the photographer, Mr Van-de-Weerd of Ede identified it as Pte Joseph Slatter, C Company, 2nd Essex Regiment (the Pompadours). The photo was taken on the Utrecht Weg, a hill near the Gemeente Museum in Arnhem. The Essex Regiment, part of 56th Brigade of the 49th Polar Bear Division, had fought in Operation Quick Anger west of Ijssel, on their way to Rijnbrug and Eusebuiskert. On 4 May, the Essex Regiment was in the front line at Wageningen when the German High Command surrendered. The postage stamp is reproduced below.

The 1985 Liberation stamp of Private Joseph Slatter, 2nd Essex.

„Poolse" soldaat blijkt Engelsman

(Van één onzer verslaggevers)

ARNHEM-EDE – De „Poolse Soldaat in Arnhem" die een van de bevrijdingspostzegels van de PTT siert, die op 5 mei, worden uitgegeven, blijkt een Engelsman te zijn. Het is Joseph Slatter die deel uitmaakte van de 2nd Battalion van The Essex Regiment, ook wel „The Pompadours" genaamd.

De Edese amateur historicus E. van de Weerd wist de gebruikte afbeelding direct thuis te brengen. Zij staat namelijk in een boekje over The Essex Regiment „'D' Day to 'Ve' Day". „De foto is gemaakt op de Utrechtseweg nabij de helling naar het Gemeentemuseum in Arnhem. Waarschijnlijk op 15 april", aldus Van de Weerd.

Joseph Slatter moet, als hij nog leeft, ongeveer 65 jaar zijn. Na de oorlog is hij teruggekeerd naar Londen waar hij waarschijnlijk in het zuidoostelijke deel heeft gewoond. Op dit moment is Van de Weerd bezig met naspeuringen om uit te vinden of Slatter nog in leven is.

Slatter was „Private" (soldaat) in de C-Compagnie. „The Pompadours" maakten deel uit van de 56ste brigade die bij Normandië landde en later met de Polar Bear Divisie optrok naar Nederland.

In de nacht van 12 op 13 april is The Essex Regiment nabij Westervoort de IJssel over gezet. In de loop van de 13e april heeft men zich een weg gevochten naar de Rijnbrug en de Eusebiuskerk. Een dag later werd de binnenstad gezuiverd en de dag daarna, de 15e april (de dag waarop de foto werd gemaakt) staat bij de kenners bekend als een dag van „consolidatie en reoganisatie". Later heeft de Essex Regiment nog in de frontlijn bij Wageningen gelegen. Vier mei was het ook voor hen voorbij.

* *De postzegels van de PTT waarop de Engelsman Slatter voor Pool wordt aangezien.*

TRANSLATION OF ATTACHED CUTTING FROM THE DUTCH NEWSPAPERS

1)
    Polish Soldier now proved to be an Englishman.

Arnhem-Ede.
        The Polish soldier in Arnhem, featured in the commemoration, liberation stamps issued by the Post Office, to mark the anniversary of the 5th May, has been found to be English.
        He is Joseph Slatter, of The 2nd, Battalion The Essex Regiment, also known as (The Pompadours). The amateur historian from Ede, Mr. E, Van-de-Weerd, recognised him from a photograph which he had at home. He is currently writing a book on The Essex Regiment, entitled "D" Day to "VE" Day. The photo, was taken on the Utrecht Way, on the hill near the Gemeente Museum, in Arnhem. Probably on the 15th April, said Mr. Van-de-Weerd.
        Joseph Slatter, if he is still alive, must be nearly 65 years old. (actually nearer 70 years old). After the war he returned to London, and was de-mobbed to an address in the South East. At this moment Van-de-Weerd, is researching his where-abouts, and if he is still alive.
        Slatter, was a Private, in "C" Comapny. The Pompadours, formed part of the 56th Brigade, during the Normandy landings, and later with the Polar bear, Divisions, march up through Holland.
2)
        During the night of the 12th/13th of April. The Essex Regiment, advanced to the West of Ijssel, and stayed. In the advance of the 13th of April, they fought their way to Rijnbrug, and Eusebiskerk. A day later they had taken the old town and the following day (the day the photograph was taken) their leaders agreed it should be a day of consolidation and re-organisation. Later The Essex Regiment, were in the front line at Wageningen. By the 4th of May they were victorious.

Polar Bears reach Amsterdam first.

2nd Essex move into Zetten, Private Slatter's comrades-in-arms. (*R. E. Gough*)

CHAPTER 17

Liberation of Denmark

All the Scandinavian countries emerged from the First World War with their faith in neutrality unshaken; it was a cardinal principle of their foreign policy. In 1939, Germany had a treaty of friendship with Norway and Denmark.

Denmark, a peaceful, democratic monarchy, with a population of over four million, had a special word to define the country—*Hyggelig*—which means cosy, comfortable and agreeable. This later earned the nickname 'Hitler's little canary'. King Christian X was very popular and his public image combined quiet heroism with regal dignity. Denmark's southern border with German Schleswig Holstein meant that many families intermarried and relations remained cordial between the two countries.

Adolf Hitler knew how to suborn the territories that in *Mein Kampf* he indicated he would subjugate. Looking at photographs of the Youth Group leaders from Norway, Denmark and Holland, his *Table Talk* biographer Martin Bormann recorded what he said:

Even in Denmark the opposition of the older generation will not prevent the youth from adopting in ever-increasing numbers the German way of thought for they feel they spring from the same racial origins. By methodically supporting the development of this movement I am cutting the ground from under the feet of the old King of Denmark and drawing his people away from him ... I have endowed the Hitler Jugend with the bold motto '*Die Jugend von Jugend gefürt werden soll*' (Youth must be led by Youth). I have set up in their very early years a process of selectivity amongst young people whereby the little group leaders soon select themselves. It is between the ages of ten and 17 that youth exhibits both the greatest enthusiasm and the greatest idealism

Copenhagen, Amalienborg Palace and harbour in 1945.

and it is for this period of their lives that we must provide them with the best possible instructors and leaders.

Having digested the capture of Poland, Hitler determined to attack and capture Norway and Denmark before, as he expected, Winston Churchill sent a joint Anglo-French expeditionary force to Norway to seize the vital ports. Lt General Nikolaus von Falkenhorst was appointed by Hitler to plan and execute Operation Weseruebung. The conquest of Denmark appeared to be easy—it was flat, open and ideal for tank warfare. Falkenhorst deployed two Wehrmacht divisions, a motorised rifle brigade with Mark I and II tanks, three motorised SP gun battalions, two batteries of heavy guns and three armoured trains. The Luftwaffe supplied a company of paratroops and some AA mobile guns. The Danish government had received specific information about an attack from friendly military attachés in Berlin, but Capt. Kjolsen, the Danish naval attaché's report was simply not believed. Nor did King Christian believe an attack was imminent.

In April 1940 the Danish army consisted of 15,000 poorly trained troops. In February of that year Winston Churchill had told journalists: 'I could not reproach Denmark if she surrendered to Nazi attack. The other two Scandinavian countries, Norway and Sweden, have at least a

Copenhagen Town Hall and centre, *c.* 1945.

ditch over which they can feed the tiger, but Denmark is so terribly near Germany that it would be impossible to bring help. Personally I would in any case not undertake to guarantee Denmark.'

At dawn on Tuesday 9 April the 170th Wehrmacht Division and 11th Motorised Rifle Brigade smashed across the border into Jutland. Panzer units were unopposed. On the island of Fyn assault troops captured Middelfart and Nyborg without a fight. In Copenhagen, General Kurt Himer, chief of staff of the German battlegroups involved, had personally in civilian clothes made a comprehensive survey of the city's defences. The troopship *Hansestadt Danzig* with a German assault battalion aboard, passed the coast forts without a challenge, tied up at Langelinie Pier, swept ashore and, before 0500hrs captured the city's Citadel. The king conferred with his ministers in the palace at Amalienborg Square. General W. W. Prior, the Danish C-in-C, wanted to fight but Luftwaffe bombers flying *en masse* low over Copenhagen persuaded the King to surrender at 0620hrs. Danish casualties in the three-hour war were thirteen killed in action and twenty-three wounded (in Jutland). The Germans had twenty casualties.

In his book *The Bitter Years* Richard Petrow wrote: 'Denmark led by its government and [seventy-year-old] king had embarked on a road that would earn for the country the reputation of Germany's model protectorate. Nevertheless fear and anger seethed below the outwardly calm exterior. The invasion sent a hard knife edge of terror through the country's eight thousand Jews and among thousands upon thousands of patriotic Danes the performance of the Danish Army and Navy was cause for shame and humiliation.' To this author it was clear that the very modest army, full of recruits, stood no chance at all against Hitler's stormtroopers and above all, his Luftwaffe, who had terrorised the huge Polish forces in 1939.

For three years Denmark retained a degree of independence, which diminished steadily. The German Foreign Minister in Denmark, Cecil von Renthe-Finke, was sympathetic to the Danes, who supplied huge agricultural exports of meat and butter to the Reich. But in July 1940, severe press censorship was imposed and the King appointed the pro-German Danish politician Erik Scavenius to head the Danish Foreign Ministry. His policy was: 'Denmark should not under any circumstances come into conflict with its great neighbour in the south. The great German victories which have struck the world with astonishment and admiration have begun a new era in Europe which will bring with it a New Order in political and economic spheres under Germany's leadership. It will be Denmark's task to find its place in mutual active co-operation with Greater Germany.' A Danish-German Association was designed to foster better relations between the two countries. Dr Fritz Clausen was the leader of the Danish National Socialist Workers Party (DNSAP), who were in effect Danish Nazis; and Lt Colonel P. C. Kryssing became the commanding officer of Frikorps Danmark, which became the SS Viking unit and fought for Germany on the eastern front against Russia. The 1,000-strong battalion suffered heavy casualties south of Leningrad. In the book, *Hitler's Table Talk*, it is recorded on 27 February 1942:

> As regards the monarchs the worst nuisances are those who've grown old in harness. They become in a sort of way, tabu [sic]. You scarcely touch them and everybody begins to howl ... If the Dane goes about it like the old Swede (who does nothing but gather his strength by playing tennis he'll reach the age of Methuselah) ... It's by dint of doing nothing that these puppets become impudently old. In Denmark, we already have the successor. That's Clausen. When we've reached that point, we'll have three men who'll have sinned so much that they'll be obliged to remain allied to us whatever happens. We can count on Clausen and likewise on Mussert [in Holland].

Hitler kept on stepping up pressure on the Danes as minor resistance, demonstrations, secret newspapers and evidence of SOE activities increased. Dr Werner Best, a leading Gestapo and SD agent was sent by Hitler as German Commissioner to Denmark and was ordered by the Führer to 'rule with an iron hand'. Lt General Hermann Hannekin, a tough Wehrmacht officer, took over the army command. Best produced figures that showed that eighty-five German civilians and an additional 130 employees 'governed' Denmark!

SOE sent Captain Rottboll and a wireless operator on 16 April 1942, and a group called 'Table' was started up; they made contact with the 'Dansk Samling' and 'The Princes', who were linked to the Danish General Staff. By the end of 1942 all the SOE operators were caught and either killed or captured by the Gestapo, except for 'Hammer'. In February 1943 SOE had two successful sorties and landed eight men and two radios. Flemming Bruuin Muus became SOE's chief organiser for the next eighteen months, with Duus Hansen, alias 'Napkin', plus Flemming Junker from Jutland as key agents. In the summer of 1943 no less than 28 sabotage attacks were made by fire and explosive on shipyards and factories working for the Germans, and there were also some attacks on German shipping. The Germans reacted predictably. President Scavenius resigned and on 29 August the Danish Army and Navy were disbanded. Many officers were arrested or fled to Sweden. However, Lt Svend Truelsen, a lawyer and reserve officer, soon worked up a first-class intelligence network. Rather surprisingly, the Swedish government co-operated and formed Danish police battalions. They eventually expanded to become Danforce, with 5,000 men and two British officers for liaison. Sabotage increased rapidly and in the first six months of 1944 there were fifty 'incidents'; from October 1944 to the end of April 1945 there were no fewer than 252 major incidents. On 22 June 1944 eighty saboteurs attacked the Dansk Industri Syndikat in Copenhagen, which was making guns for the Germans. Other attacks were made on the large Burmeister and Wain shipyard in Copenhagen. A general strike in June 1944 was followed by the Germans burning down the Tivoli Gardens.

The Danish Freedom Council was created in the autumn of 1943, and included Professor Mogens Fog with several other communists, and representatives of 'Ringen' and 'Dansk Samling' with Flemming Muus as the SOE representative. Ronald Turnbull was the SOE's London representative for Sweden and Denmark. Major Winkelhorn became

Planning Officer of the SOE Danish section, which from 1 May 1944, was integrated into SHAEF Mission for Denmark (September 1944) under Major General Dewing.

On 6 October 1943 the Danish physicist Niels Bohr, who had identified vanadium-235 as being a vital ingredient of what became the nuclear fission atomic bomb, was smuggled out of Denmark to Sweden in a fishing boat. On 6 October he was flown in the bomb bay of a BOAC Mosquito on the first stage of a journey to the United States.

By the end of the war, fifty-seven SOE-trained Danish agents had been sent in, of whom thirteen were captured and six killed. There were 414 aircraft sorties of which 285 were successful, but with the loss of seventeen aircraft. Some 6,670,000 Danish Krone were expended in cash and repaid later by the government of the day.

In August 1943 national strikes and several hundred acts of sabotage by the Resistance groups, often equipped by SOE agents, forced martial law by the German occupying forces. The Danish army had to surrender their arms and the Danish navy scuttled or sank twenty-nine vessels and many more were severely damaged; thirteen escaped to Sweden and only thirteen small ships were captured by the Germans. In September, Heinrich Himmler sent his Gestapo agent K. H. Hoffmann and the horrible Dr Rudolf Mildner, an expert of extermination camps in Katowice (Poland) and Auschwitz, to plan a 'Final Solution' to the 8,000 Danish Jews who had been relatively unscathed since the occupation in 1940. Major Rolf Günther, a deputy of Adolf Eichmann, was to carry out this operation on 1–2 October just after Rosh Hashanah, the Jewish New Year. Two German freighters arrived in Copenhagen harbour to take the intended Jewish captives back to the Reich's extermination camps. Richard Petrow charts their remarkable escape in his book *The Bitter Years*. The vast majority escaped to Sweden by fishing boat and 'only' 284 men, women and children were arrested. Adolf Eichmann, Rolf Günther and their Führer were all furious. However, the fishing boat captains earned fortunes.

The Communist-led underground group BOPA and the Freedom Council (Freihetradet) carried out many spectacular sabotage acts in 1944 and early 1945. So much so that the 9,000-strong Danish police were arrested, disbanded and several thousand deported to Germany. The British RAF sent daring Mosquito fighter-bomber attacks: three squadrons destroyed the Gestapo HQ in Aarhus on 31 October 1944 and on 21 March 1945 the Gestapo Copenhagen HQ in Shellhus building and Odense HQ in April. Despite civilian casualties these three daring and successful raids smashed up the Danish Gestapo teams and records.

Demobilised veterans of the Danish SS Frikorps founded the pro-German Danish Schalburg Corps, known as Hipos or Hilfepolizei and controlled by Nazi officers, began a retaliatory campaign of sabotage and terror against facilities and objects dear to most Danes. This reprisal was known as *Schalburtage* and they set fire to the Royal Danish porcelain factory, put incendiary bombs into the famous Tivoli Gardens, wrecked the Students' Union at Copenhagen University, bombed the main community centre in the city and set fire to the East Asiatic Company HQ. In June 1944 there was a huge national demonstration at the end of which 226 Danes were killed or wounded. The Hipos were extremely dangerous, well-armed fanatics who terrorised most Danish towns and villages.

Scandinavian prisoners, a mixed collection of policemen, teachers, journalists, diplomats, clergymen and underground Resistance workers, were imprisoned in camps in Poland and Germany. After complicated negotiations between Count Folks Bernadotte, Himmler, Ernst Kaltenbrunner—chief of Germany's secret police, and Ribbentropp, the vast majority of the Scandinavians were transferred to Neuengamme concentration camp near Hamburg. By 1 April 1945, 2,200 Danes and Norwegians from Sachsenhausen camp, 600 from Dachau, 1,600 from Buchenwald, and smaller groups from other camps including Natzweiler, were assembled in Neuengamme. The original prisoners there—Russians, Poles, Ukrainians, Dutch, French and others were sent off, mostly to Braunschweig and Belsen. These poor devils, called 'Mussulmen', walking skeletons, almost certainly died of starvation in the next few weeks.

Astonishingly, Himmler agreed that the Jutland Corps' 'White Bus' charitable group could transfer by 21 April 7,100 Scandinavians to Froslev in Denmark; but 2,100 died in captivity in Germany.

As the British Liberation Army swept into Hamburg and Schleswig Holstein, urgent negotiations started between Admiral Doenitz in his Flensburg HQ and the German gauleiters in Denmark, Norway and Holland. Should they continue the struggle against the Allies even after their Führer's death on 30 April in his Berlin bunker?

General Georg Lindemann was GOC of the German troops in Denmark. They numbered 136,000 Wehrmacht, 19,000 Kriegsmarines and 17,000 Luftwaffe—a total of 172,000. However, Admiral Skagerrak, who was Naval C-in-C Denmark, had 40,200 men under his command on 1 April 1945.

Mr Jens Andersen of the Copenhagen Museumscenter Hanstholm has kindly supplied the map of the German dispositions in Denmark at 4 May 1945. The 233rd Panzer Division, stationed on the frontier, only had twenty-five battle tanks including two Panther Mk IVs. All the units were for training recruits, and equipment was scarce. The Luftwaffe had 1,100 planes on Danish airfields but only 261 tons of petrol to fuel them! In Copenhagen harbour were the heavy cruiser *Prinz Eugen* and light cruiser *Nurnberg* in a combat-ready state but with insufficient fuel. About 10 per cent of Lindemann's troops were non-German: Hungarians, Russians and Poles. Many troops were elderly, portly or convalescing from wounds. No élite regiment served in Denmark—Hitler needed them to help defend the Reich.

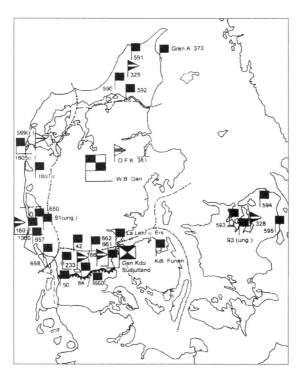

Concentration of German forces in Denmark.

In 1944 when the end of the war in Europe was approaching, the Russians and the Western Allies realised that, as their armies started to converge, clear rules of engagement would be needed to avoid accidental clashes. The plan for Operation Eclipse laid down the zones of occupation and lines of demarcation, later approved at the Yalta Conference in February 1945. These lines of demarcation, later named 'the Iron Curtain' by Winston Churchill, ran from Wismar in North Germany to Switzerland, with *Denmark and the Danish islands firmly in the Allied Sector.*

The BBC Danish radio at 2035hrs on 4 May broadcast the news that the German High Command had surrendered all their forces in north-west Germany, Denmark, Norway and Holland to Field Marshal Bernard Montgomery.

In Operation Eclipse the British High Command had made intricate and careful military preparations by air, sea and land to occupy *Norway* but, as will be seen, Denmark was another matter! It is a complicated story with many threads and strands. Winston Churchill cabled his deputy, Anthony Eden, who was in Washington, on 5 May: 'sending Monty to Lübeck to cut off any Soviet advance from the Baltic to Denmark: we are sending in a moderate holding force to Copenhagen by air and the rest of Denmark is being rapidly occupied from henceforward by our fast-moving armoured columns. I think therefore having regard to the joyous feeling of the Danes and the abject submission and would-be partisanship of the surrendered Huns, we shall head our Soviet friends off at this point too.'

The American General Bradley wrote of Field Marshal Montgomery about 21–22 April: 'Monty, denied the glory of taking Berlin, had lost all heart for the fight... I believe he viewed his primary mission of sealing off the Danish border as demeaning ... Monty no longer seemed to have a sense of urgency about his mission.' After visiting Churchill in London on 20 April, Eisenhower flew back to meet Montgomery in Diepholz, south-west of Bremen, on the next day. Monty grumbled about his lack of manpower so he was allocated General Ridgway's US 18th Airborne Corps to help him on his drive to the Baltic. Monty wanted time to complete the capture of Bremen, which eventually fell on 27 April. Ike warned Monty that Marshal Konstantin Rokossovsky was making rapid progress through Hecklenburg heading for the Elbe and the Baltic beyond. It was a race alright and at Wismar at 0900hrs on 2 May the

3rd Parachute Brigade mounted on Royal Scots Greys' tanks arrived *within half an hour* of the Russians.

In early April 1945 British and American leaders had learnt, from their most secret Intelligence source, Ultra, the Germans' own coded radio signals, that the Soviet army was preparing to take political advantage of its advance along the Baltic by occupying Denmark. This knowledge altered Allied strategy and was to bring the British troops to the Baltic as the occupying, and for some, the liberating power. A top secret diplomatic despatch from the Japanese Ambassador in Sweden to the Foreign Ministry in Tokyo, which had been intercepted on 7 April, showed that the Russian move and Britain's response had been noted. The despatch began:

> From the Russian declaration that Denmark will shortly be liberated it is plain that Russia intends to bring Denmark into her sphere of influence and thus secure an outlet from the Baltic into the North Sea. Moreover the Russians have recently been making covert inquiries about what the Danish people who have taken refuge in Sweden have been doing. These are probably intended to provide material for their designs on Denmark. It is a fact also that the free Danish minister here recently left for Moscow in company with Kollontay, the Russian Minister here.
>
> While not a word had been said in public in Britain about Soviet intentions the British have since changed the direction of the drive on the Western Front by Montgomery's armies and turned it towards Hamburg. Moreover the recent heavy bombing of Kiel seems not so much to have been directed against the Germans as intended to prevent the Russians from being able to use it.

Viewing Anglo-Soviet disputes in the most optimistic light, from a Japanese perspective, the Japanese Ambassador told his government: 'The problems of the future of Denmark, the Near and Middle East, the Aegean Sea and China are very likely to provide the *motives for a third world war.* (Source: 'British-Soviet relations', Top Secret Ultra, telegram sent at 12.30 p.m., 7 April 1945; circulated to the Prime Minister and others, London 11 April 1945. Reference HW1/3683, Public Record Office, Kew.)

Vice Admiral Tom Baillie-Grohman commanded a considerable fleet of Royal Navy warships. In effect his mission was a Grand Tour encompassing all the Norwegian ports, Copenhagen, and finally Kiel.

176

The cruisers Birmingham and Dido soon after their arrival at Copenhagen. Between them is the destroyer Zodiac. The destroyers Zest, Zephyr, and Zealous were moored farther along the quayside. Cheering crowds greeted the arrival of the British warships.

The Times article of the British arrival in Copenhagen, 5 May 1945.

He despatched a flotilla to clear the enemy minefields and then steam to Copenhagen. So the mine-sweeping flotilla under Captain Palmer DSC cleared the minefields in Kattegat and led cruisers *Birmingham* and *Dido* and four Z-class destroyers, *Zephyr, Zeus, Savage* and *Iroquis* into Copenhagen harbour on 4 May. Captain H. W. Williams, OC of the whole powerful squadron, took the surrender of the German Admiral Skaggerack's fleet: not only the *Prinz Eugen* and *Nürnberg*, but the *Leipzig*, three destroyers, two torpedo boats, ten minesweepers, thirteen Flak ships, nineteen armed trawlers and two armed merchant ships—fifty-one vessels altogether in Copenhagen, Aabenraa and other Danish ports. There were 600,000 tons of merchant shipping lying in the bay off Copenhagen harbour. Admiral Baillie-Grohman visited Kiel harbour on 8 May to take the surrender of the badly damaged *Hipper* and *Emden* cruisers and the battleship *Scheer*, sunk there by the RAF on 9 April.

The RAF was involved in Operation Eclipse. On 4 May a squadron of Typhoons landed at Kastrup airport outside Copenhagen, followed by another squadron two days later. Quite soon 8304th Air Disarmament

6th Airborne land in Copenhagen.

Wing landed in Denmark to inspect the 1,100 forlorn Luftwaffe planes and equipment. The RAF also provided thirty Curtis Commando planes for the VE celebration.

On 5 May Danforce, 5,000 soldiers residing in Sweden, crossed over the Kattegat with the SOE liaison officer Major Ray, who became the first British officer to enter liberated Denmark.

Alan Moorehead was nearly always the first of the team of authorised journalists to get to crucial episodes in North Africa and North-west Europe. In his book *Eclipse* he details his Scandinavian adventures. A dozen Dakotas with a considerable fighter escort took off from Luneburg airfield on the morning of 5 May:

> A company of airborne troops in their red berets and curious lizard-coloured camouflage jackets, a general [Dewing], an admiral and their staffs ... the general idea was destination Copenhagen and we should take over Denmark from the Germans. A pair of gleaming leather top-boots was passed on board. Young officers ran about ticking off names. The sun came down on the red caps and the red tabs and a Rolls Royce drove up debouching brigadiers ... so this was peace and peace this morning seemed wonderful. A full three months had passed since we had come into Germany; three months of army rations, and no

fraternisation; three months of refugees and ruined cities; of shuttered shops and no electric light and no hot baths; of lumpish German women and traffic blocks and artillery and mud and the endless dragging knowledge that the war dragged on. All this time we had been promising ourselves Scandinavia. Out through Germany into the light again. Past Lübeck and Kiel and out over the Baltic. German ships seeing us coming ran up the white flag and turned away apprehensively. Then, one after another the green Danish islands. Every house on that liberation morning flew the national flag on a pole, the white cross on the red background and from the air the effect was as if one was looking down on endless fields strewn with poppies. On arrival there was no fighting. The German General Lindemann surrendered to General Dewing, and all German troops were confined to barracks. The Danish Resistance troops took control.

We passed in a procession of 20 to 30 cars with Dewing at the head, wreathed in chrysanthemums, into the lovely city. We had never seen such pretty girls, such gay dresses, such glistening shops and gardens. Each time the procession stopped the crowd closed in on us touching our sleeves and tunics to make sure we were real.

[Dewing made his HQ in the Hotel Angleterre] The scene in the lobby bordered on hysteria … recollections of corks coming out of champagne bottles, of tables laden with smoked salmon and caviar, of grilled steaks and strawberries, of singing, of laughing faces, of bright flowers.

General Dewing inspecting MILORG resistance troops in Copenhagen.

179

Enthusiastic welcome for British 6th Airborne troops. (*Imperial War Museum*)

Moorehead and the others visited the Royal Palace and listened to the brass band playing in the pleasure gardens of the Tivoli.

Major A. A. McLoughlin, B Company, 13th Battalion 5th Parachute Brigade, was the first to arrive in Copenhagen from Wismar: 'accompanied by more war correspondents than I would have believed possible'. He was the bodyguard keeping Dewing and the VIPs safe.

8th Parachute Battalion of 8th Parachute Brigade landed in thirty Curtiss Commando planes at 1500hrs. on 6 May at Kastrup airport. Pte Raymond Hutchings, a twenty-one-year-old, wrote: 'We collected our gear and piled into a large lorry commandeered by the Danish Resistance. On one side was painted HOLGER DANSKE, the mythical personage who lives in the underworld and whenever Denmark was in trouble he goes into action and everything is all right again.' 8th Para chased the Gestapo General Gunther Pancke, who was later captured.

Lt General 'Bubbles' Barker commanded 8th Corps and sent battle groups into Denmark including 4th (Black Desert Rats) Armoured Brigade with the 2nd Dragoons (Royal Scots Greys) tanks, 1st Royal Dragoons armoured cars and 2nd KRRC motorised infantry. The Greys had 'carried' 6th Airborne troops to Wismar where they met the

Russians. Lt Edwin Bramall, who later became a field marshal, had spent 5 May with 2nd KRRC near Hamburg. On VE Day they moved north to Pinneburg. 'The whole area was in chaos. The SS and other potential war criminals were trying to avoid capture. To our relief two or three days later the battalion was given orders to move into Denmark. We crossed the frontier at Flensburg where Doenitz had set up Germany's final supreme HQ and entered a different world of cheering and welcoming crowds and with a countryside free from the ravages of war where food and female company were plentiful.'

Lt J. A. Dimmond was a troop commander with the 1st Royal Dragoons, whose CO was Lt Colonel Anthony Pepys. The regiment spent six months helping to garrison Denmark. He wrote: 'Like Caesar's Gaul, Denmark is in three parts. On the left the tall feature of Jutland extends 250 miles northwards from the German border. In the centre the small island of Fyn (pronounced Foon) included the second city, Odense. On the right the larger island of Sjaeland (pronounced Seeland) contains the capital. There are numerous smaller islands and away towards the Arctic Circle the huge colony of Greenland.' Initially A at Arhus and B Squadrons were stationed in Jutland, C in the citadel in Copenhagen, and D, HQ and RHQ in Odense and Juelsburg. After six months, ninety young Royal Dragoons were engaged to Danish girls.

T-Force was ordered to move into Denmark in the general capacity as troops on the ground in addition to 4th Armoured Brigade and the Paratroop battalions. They also, of course, had many targets to investigate. On 7 May, the 5th Kings detachments crossed the frontier, one group heading for Kolding and the other for Aarhus. Lt Tom Pitt-Pladdy's column had several jeeps, a captured Wehrmacht Opel, three armoured cars of 1st Royal Dragoons, four large Mack trucks with the Pioneer Corps troops, a ration truck and two 'liberated' amphibious DUKWs. In Kolding the Stald-Gaarden Gestapo HQ was a key target. On the island of Fano was a V-2 rocket experimental plant. A batch of German scientists at Horuphav was held for interrogation. At Sæby, one-man torpedos had to be identified and sent back to the UK. In Arhus, twelve midget submarines, torpedos for harbour defence and other items of naval interest were found.

When the 100 men of the 5th Kings arrived in Arhus they found the German garrison was 8,000 strong and was refusing to surrender to the Danes. They had already 'surrendered' to Field Marshal Montgomery!

5th Kings Regiment of T-Force in Denmark.

The Danish Resistance all over Denmark was hounding the Gestapo and this caused mini civil wars. The 5th Kings obtained a Danish army liaison officer, which helped calm down the warring tribes. Batches of 200 German prisoners were marched off to the frontier with Schleswig Holstein. One truck of Kings men carried food and blankets for the prisoners of war. Major Brian Urquhart's report on T-Force in Denmark is in the PRO at Kew (WO205/1049). One comment was: 'a tremendous and stupefying welcome was, and still is, being extended to those fortunate detachments.'

The island of Bornholm, 57 miles east of Copenhagen was Danish owned, garrisoned by a German force under Commander Kamptz with the chief Danish administrative officer, Peter Stemann. It was a strong garrison of 20,000 men. Kamptz would surrender to the British and the Royal Navy ships, which were only half a day's sail away. Russian aircraft bombed Nekso and Ronne, settlements on the island. Curiously neither the Danish government nor the British forces were interested in solving the problem. So the Russians sent a 50-bomber force, which dropped 1,500 200-pound bombs on the island. On 9 May, the Russians landed without opposition and by the 16th the German garrison had been shipped off into captivity. Rather surprisingly, eleven months later the Russians returned the island to the Danish government.

Field Marshal Montgomery in a victory parade in Copenhagen, 12 May 1945.

The 160,000 troops under General Lindemann were marched in large batches, armed, carrying some loot, to the Danish frontier where grateful dragoons and Kings men relieved them of everything before the undefeated Germans entered the nearest camp in Schleswig Holstein.

The main German villains, Werner Best, Major General Herman Hanneken, SS General Gunther Pancke and Otto Bovensiepen, Gestapo Chief, were all tried for war crimes. The death penalty for Pancke and Bovensiepen was later, on appeal, reduced to imprisonment. In the post-war period, 20,000 Danes were arrested; 12,877 men and 631 women received prison sentences. Life sentences were imposed on sixty-six men and foty-six were executed for war crimes.

Jørgen Nissen, a schoolboy aged ten when the Germans invaded in 1940, grew up during their occupation:

We had a great many troops in the area because Europe's biggest fortress was on our doorstep. The Hanstholm fortress was part of the Atlantic Wall and was—together with a fortress in Norway and extensive minefields in the Skagerrak—supposed to seal off the entrance to the Kattegat and the Baltic. It had artillery ranging from 17 cm guns up to four massive 38 cm guns, weighing

Field Marshal Montgomery inspects 6th Airborne in Copenhagen, 12 May 1945.

110 tonnes each. A bit like *Guns of Navarone*! Even Rommel paid us a visit I'm told. When they did the first trial shoot, windows were shattered all over town. Later fortifications were built all along the North Sea coast to prepare for an 'English' invasion (British was always called English), that never came of course.

By the beginning of 1945 it was clear that the end of the war was near, but we didn't know whether we would become a battlefield for a last stand effort by the Germans and whether the Russians would get to us before the British. But as the Germans started exchanging their good troops with inexperienced troops and a motley mix of troops from the East: Russians (deserters from the Russian army), Poles, etc their focus was clearly on the war in Germany itself.

During 1945 there was intense activity of our resistance movement sabotaging our railways and any facility relevant to the German war effort including supply facilities. An increasing number of soldier and civilian refugees came across the border and many ended up with us, and in February, Count Folke Bernadotte of Sweden brought back 7,000 Danes and Norwegians from German concentration camps and there were rumours that he was go-between in surrender negotiations.

Our link to the outside world was Danish broadcasts from the BBC World Service and we all remember how it was interrupted at 20.35 on 4 May with the news of the capitulation to Montgomery. We wondered about Norway, but they had to wait for the complete surrender to Eisenhower on the 8th, and Bornholm, our island in the Baltic, was occupied by the Russians who didn't leave until April 1946—so it was a close run thing!

The German troops started next morning walking back to Germany— not marching or singing as they usually did—throwing their weapons and ammunition by the wayside. We were a well-armed bunch of boys those days!

In Haderslev, the Freedom Council of Denmark noted: 'Montgomery's brave men, we know you have fought and won. We know you have fought and suffered and that you too have men that fell on the field of glory for their beloved country ... Together we have fought the Nazidom which has desecrated the word man, through bloody cruelty. Together you and we will make part of the Allied front in times to come and watch and guard around the peace and freedom we won. Blood and tears were the price of the fight, and happiness and right are to be made safe through the victory.' A bit convoluted but the right spirit!

The Danish resistance troops were immensely active during the liberation period. Much of their time was spent bringing the hundreds of dangerous Hipo terrorists to book. When Field Marshal Montgomery arrived in Copenhagen on 12 May he was given a hero's welcome by resistance and civilians alike. After all he was *the* commander to whom the gauleiters of Denmark, Norway and Holland surrendered.

CHAPTER 18

Liberation of *Festung* Norwegen

The first incident of the Second World War that involved Norway was unfortunate. Richard Petrow in *The Bitter Years* devotes a fascinating chapter to the 'Altmark Affair' of September 1939. The powerful pocket battleship *Admiral Graf Spee* had sunk many British merchant ships in the Atlantic and had transferred 300 British seamen to its supply ship, an 11,000-ton naval auxiliary tanker, the *Altmark*. He recounts the classic naval encounter when three lightly armed British cruisers, *Exeter*, *Ajax* and *Achilles* so chivvied and harassed the mighty German ship that it took refuge in Montevideo on the river Plate. It was sufficiently damaged by gunfire that Captain Langsdorff scuttled it rather than face ignominious capture by the three 'hounds' waiting for it at sea. The *Altmark* under its wily captain, Heinrich Dau, headed north towards Germany and entered Norwegian waters. Despite being stopped and interrogated three or four times by amateurish Norwegian naval officers the *Altmark* was eventually pounced upon by Captain Philip Vian, with HMS *Cossack*, who boarded and rescued the 300 British merchant seamen imprisoned below decks with the memorable cry 'The Navy's here!'. The Norwegian actions were shameful. The whole of Britain rejoiced and Hitler was absolutely furious.

Norway was the vital conduit for the supply of iron ore from the Kiruna-Gallivare district of northern Sweden, using mainly the Norwegian port of Narvik. Germany needed 750,000 tons of ore *per month*, or it would have risked major industrial breakdown. The renegade Norwegian Nazi, Vidkun Quisling and his Nasjonal Samling Party put up a plan to Hitler's adviser Alfred Rosenberg to mount a coup. At a meeting in Berlin on 14 December 1939 between Hitler and Quisling, the latter stated: 'A British landing is planned in the vicinity of Stavanger and Kristiansand as a possible British base. The present Norwegian government and parliament and the whole foreign policy are controlled by the well-known [Carl] Hambro—a Jew—and President of the Norwegian Parliament.' Hitler promised financial and moral support. He then ordered 'Studie Nord', a preliminary plan for the Scandinavian assault. In February, the plan became 'Weseruebung' under Captain Krancke, the skipper of the cruiser *Scheer*. By the middle of the month the Anglo-French Supreme War Council pursued their Scandinavian venture. Both the German and the Anglo-French war plans would violate the neutrality of Scandinavia.

General Alfred Jodl, chief of OKW (Armed Forces High Command) recommended Lt General Nikolaus von Falkenhorst to command Weseruebung. He wanted a full Wehrmacht division to attack and secure Oslo, Stavanger, Bergen, Trondheim and Narvik harbour. On 1 March, Hitler issued his official directive, with all forces assembled for the 10th and embarked on the 13th. But when Marshal Mannerheim surrendered Finland to Russia, a consequence was that the Allied Operation Wilfred and the German OperationWeseruebung were, by coincidence delayed until 9 April.

Admiral Raeder commanded the kriegsmarine armada of warships and transport ships, and Marshal Herman Goering the Luftwaffe air

The German top brass in Norway in March 1945 during a ceremony at the German cemetery near Oslo. In front General der Gebirgstruppen Frantz Böhme, C-in-C of the Wehrmacht in Norway (giving a Nazi salute) and Dr Herr Reichskommisar Joseph Terboven. Second from left, Chief of the German Air forces in Norway General Ernst Roth, Böhme's Chief of Staff Major General Hölter, Chief of the German Navy in Norway, Admiral Krancke, and extreme right Lt General Baesler, Commandant of Oslo.

fleet of 500 transports, 300 bombers and 200 Stuka dive-bombers. Both the Danish and the Norwegian governments received advice of the forthcoming onslaught from friendly embassies in Berlin. They chose to do nothing although the Norwegian High Command had assigned an army division to guard the six most important civilian and military centres.

Hitler's bold all-arms attack and conquest took only eight weeks in the period 7 April–10 June 1940. The Anglo-French army were defeated and King Haakon and his government sailed sadly from Narvik on the British cruiser *Devonshire*. The Royal Navy had performed superbly as one might expect and gave the Führer many anxious moments. The German casualties were 3,692 and the Allies 6,165 (British 4,400, Norwegian 1,335 and French and Poles 530). The Royal Navy lost the aircraft carrier *Glorious*, cruisers *Effingham* and *Curlew*, and nine destroyers and four submarines. The Germans came off worse. The cruisers *Blucher*, *Königsberg* and *Karlsruhe*, ten destroyers, six submarines and sixteen other naval craft were sunk. The pocket battleships—pride of the German Navy—*Scharnhorst* and *Gneisenau*, and battleships *Luetzow*, *Hipper* and *Emden* were also damaged. The only comfort Winston Churchill could take was that Germany only had one heavy cruiser and two light cruisers fit for action. This was: 'of major importance potentially affecting the whole future of the war'. Weseruebung was however a superb success for German arms as the Luftwaffe played a significant part in the campaign. Hitler was pleased: 'The Norwegian campaign was not only bold but one of the sauciest undertakings in the history of modern warfare.' He had secured his vital supply line for Swedish iron ore and secured excellent Norwegian harbours for his warships, when repaired, and U-boats to try to dominate the North Sea and Atlantic.

For Norway the campaign was a disaster. Soon a crushed and demoralised country of over three million inhabitants would be ruled initially by the renegade Vidkun Quisling, and then by Hitler's Reichskommissar Joseph Terboven, who was a tough loyal Nazi street fighter who ruled Norway until his noisy death in May 1945. Terboven introduced the usual terror actions which were set up in every conquered country. The concentration camp in Grini outside Oslo (later renamed Ilebu) initially harboured hundreds of Norwegian school teachers, then resistance loyalists, Jews (700 were deported) and dissidents. Terboven was 'a short, thin, humourless man with an icily cold manner' according to Richard Petrow's *Bitter Years*.

The Gestapo arrived at No. 19 Mollergaten and their HQ was on Victoria Terrasse, Oslo. The SS police general was Wilhelm Rediess who also came to a noisy, sticky end in May 1945, as did Jonas Lie, the Quisling police chief.

Total censorship soon followed and all political parties were forbidden except for the Nasjonal Samling Youth movement, which was modelled on the Hitler Youth movement in Germany. Quisling made membership compulsory for all Norwegian youngsters aged between ten and eighteen. By the end of 1940, membership stood at 26,000 and had doubled by the end of the war. The Norwegian SS Legion of 5,000 misguided young men was sent to fight on the Russian front, where 700 died.

There was one brave resistance movement in Norway, Milorg (military organisation) which soon developed links with the Special Operations Executive (SOE) in England. Often split by warring factions on the thorny problem of either very active resistance, which would bring heavy and brutal retaliation on the Norwegian public, or a steady 'go-slow' pinprick campaign of discreet sabotage. Often betrayed by informers or alert police or Gestapo, the first three years were not happy at all.

There are two interesting vignettes in the book *Hitler's Table Talk*:

On 2 August 1941: 'The exploitation of electricity generated by water power is in Germany only in its infancy ... if water flows it's enough to build a dam to obtain energy ... One day Norway will have to be the electrical centre of Northern Europe. In that way the Norwegians will at last find a European mission to fulfil.'

In May 1942 the Führer to Martin Bormann: 'In Terboven I am pleased to have found a man capable of assuming control of Norway, the most difficult commissarship of the Reich. As he told me this very day, if he relaxes his authority for a single instant, he feels as though he were standing on quicksands. He was compelled to arrest a number of Norwegian teachers who had seen fit to try to sabotage certain measures taken by the German High Command. He is now employing them in building fortifications.'

Early in 1943 a 28-year-old lawyer named Jens Christian Hauge took over command of Milorg. A meeting in Stockholm with representatives of the Norwegian High Command from London proved very helpful. Also an agreement was made with the civilian resistance at home. A policy was agreed to establish an underground army, ready to spring into action when Allied rescue was imminent—and a minimum of sabotage.

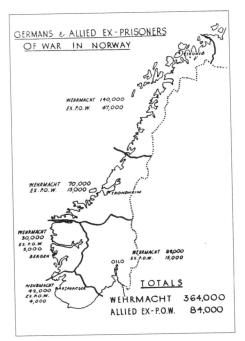

GERMANS & ALLIED EX-PRISONERS OF WAR IN NORWAY

WEHRMACHT 140,000
EX.P.O.W. 47,000

WEHRMACHT 70,000
EX.P.O.W. 15,000   TRONDHEIM

WEHRMACHT 30,000
EX.P.O.W. 5,000   BERGEN

WEHRMACHT 42,000
EX.P.O.W. 4,000   STAVANGER

WEHRMACHT 88,000
EX.P.O.W. 15,000   OSLO

TOTALS
WEHRMACHT   364,000
ALLIED EX-P.O.W.   84,000

Location of German armed forces and Allied POWs in Norway, May 1945.

Winston Churchill had always been interested in plans for further operations in Norway. The first was Wilfrid, to mine the Norwegian ports in 1940, before the ill-fated expedition. Operation Jupiter in the spring of 1942 was a plan to land a British Expeditionary Force (BEF) in northern Norway to wipe out the Luftwaffe airports preying on the Allied shipping convoys. Considerable U-boat fleets did immense damage in the North Atlantic, operating from Namsos, Narvik, Trondheim, Bergen and Stavanger. Hitler was convinced in mid-1942 that the British would once again invade Norway and in 1943 there were eighteen divisions and even early in 1945 no fewer than seventeen, with a total armed manpower of over 300,000 including kriegsmarines and Luftwaffe. In Operation Fortitude in May/June 1944, the 'fake' attack or attacks by the Allies against Hitler's Atlantic Wall, planned radio leakage convinced the Führer that a subsidiary attack would come against Norway.

In the 'Bitter Years' of 1940 to early 1945, the RAF bombed many targets including stranded pocket battleships and the heavy water plant in Vemork, the Norsk hydro-electric installation. The SOE sent dozens of missions. In March 1941, a large-scale raid by Combined Operations and SOE was made against the Danish-owned Lofoten Islands off Narvik. For the Allies it was a total success. Four fish oil factories and six ships were blown up and 314 Lofoteners volunteered to join the Norwegian forces in the UK. The Germans reacted brutally as feared and seventy men were sent to Grini concentration camp; many homes on the islands were burnt as reprisal. Operation Archery was a repeat performance in late December 1941 against the coastal towns of Måløy and Vagsöy and again on the Lofotens (Operation Anklet). Both raids were completely successful and so unfortunately were the inevitable German reprisals. Milorg was not involved in the raids and thought that their fairly peaceful existence was threatened.

The German conquerors and Norsk Hydro technicians had repaired the extensive damage to their plant buildings done by the SOE saboteurs, and the first heavy water was being shipped to Germany in August 1943. The American General Leslie Groves, head of the Manhattan Project (development of an atomic bomb) was so worried at the German development that on 16 November 155 Flying Fortress bombers dropped over 700 bombs on the Vemork plant. It was not successful. The Norwegian civilian casualties upset the Norwegian government in exile but the Germans decided to move all the heavy water equipment to Germany including 14 tons of heavy water. Lt Knut Haukelid, a very brave SOE agent, succeeded in blowing up and destroying the ferry boat carrying the potentially deadly cargo from Norway to Germany. He thoroughly deserved the award of the Distinguished Service Order (DSO).

In late 1944, the success of the Russian army in capturing Finnmark northern province with Finnish support had caused SHAEF to make plans in case the Red Army sought to conquer Norway by capturing Narvik and continuing south. Fortunately Stalin was concentrating his main efforts on the Eastern Front, with modest help from Dutch, Danish and Norwegian renegade SS battalions. Colonel Arne Dahl, the CO of a Norwegian Mountain Company sailed on the British cruiser *Berwick* to Murmansk in late October 1944 and, in early 1945, took part with the Russians in a renewed push from Finnmark using Kirkenes as his base. His force had been built up to 3,000 and it reached Lyngenfjord. To everyone's surprise all Russian troops left northern Norway by May 1945.

In the spring of 1945, Lt General Franz Böhme had taken over the command of the German forces in Norway after General Falkenhorst had returned to Germany. Böhme's HQ was at Lillehammer. Admiral Kranke, based in Oslo, commanded the bulk of Hitler's navy. General Lothar Rendulic commanded the 20th Mountain (Gebirg) Army, which had been defending Finnmark, the most northerly province at the North Cape, against Russian and Finnish attacks. Rendulic's troops had been forced back and had obeyed Hitler's order of scorched-earth policy, laying waste Hammerfest and a dozen large villages. His army, reduced to 140,000 men, guarded a 450-mile coastal strip from Namsos to Lyngenfjord. The German 33rd Korps commanded by General Titel in Oslo had five defence sectors: General von Nissen (Trondheim with 70,000 men); General Vogel (Hamar); General Weckman (Stavanger with 42,000 men); General de Boer (Bergen with 30,000 men); and General Bezeler (Oslo with 82,000 men). The Luftwaffe 14th Division under the two divisional generals Brabener and Remolt had many significant airfields including Gardermoen, Skoganvarre and a dozen or more radar stations along the coast. General Stumpf commanded Luftflotte 5 at Stavanger. For attacks on the convoys to Russia the Luftwaffe often deployed over 200 bombers.

SHAEF had drawn up various plans for the British Army, Navy and Airforce units to take over *Festung* Norwegen. Various operation code words were Amber, Apostle and Doomsday, all part of the overall Operation Eclipse, the final control of the Third Reich.

It was anticipated that General Böhme, the German C-in-C, would obey Admiral Doenitz's order from Flensberg to surrender the huge forces of almost 400,000, despite containing die-hard Nazis such as Joseph Terboven, Quisling, Jonas Lie, Henrik Rogstad and many fanatical members of Nasjonal Samling (56,000 strong in May 1945). On 1 May Böhme and Terboven were summoned to Doenitz in Flensberg, where he convinced or perhaps ordered them to surrender unconditionally. However, at 2215hrs on Monday 7 May, Böhme told his troops over Radio Oslo:

> The Foreign Minister Count von Krosigh has announced the unconditional surrender of all fighting forces. This capitulation hits us very hard, because we are unbeaten and in full possession of our strength in Norway, and no enemy has dared to attack us. In spite of all that in the interest of all that is German, we also have to obey the dictates of our enemy. Clench your teeth and keep discipline and order. Obey your superiors. Remain what you have been up to

now—decent German soldiers who love their people and homeland more than anything else in the world.

The *Daily Express* article of 8 May had the headline: 'No one dared attack us' after Böhme's speech.

The Milorg forces came out of the darkness into the open and began—as instructed under the leadership of Jens Christian Hauge—to occupy important plants and military installations. They were organised in twenty-two districts, each divided into two-four sub-districts: East Norway (strength 24,130); South and West (6,240); Central (1,100); and North (750). On VE Day another 10,000 joined, bringing their strength to 40,000. They were, of course, invaluable.

By 10 May 13,000 Norwegian troops trained in Scotland or Sweden had arrived to join the liberation forces. They comprised eight battalions of police reserves and eight state police companies. A further 3,000 Norwegian police returned from refuge in Sweden.

Scottish Command had been harbouring the Norwegians who had escaped by the Shetland Bus (fishing boats which carried cargoes of men or arms from one country to the other), or other means. As early as September 1941 Scottish Command harboured all the practical elements for an eventual rescue of Norway from the Nazi *Festung* Norwegen. Operation Rankin later became Operation Apostle. In August 1944 SHAEF decided that 'Force 134', a *theoretical* invasion force of a British infantry division, initially 52nd Lowland, a US Task Force (reinforced infantry regiment) plus the existing Norwegian brigade (in exile) would be required. Liaison with Milorg in Norway was of course vital. Eventually, as late as 5 May, SHAEF was able to allot 1st Airborne Division (the reinforced survivors of Market Garden) and the key commander, the highly experienced General Sir Andrew Thorne, as C-in-C of the liberation force. One airborne brigade was detached to reinforce the Danish liberation force and the airborne artillery units were co-opted into being their replacement. 38th Group RAF was ready to fly the division into Norway. Rear Admiral Ritchie would command the Royal Navy fleet and Air Vice Marshal Boret commanded the RAF air fleet. At the last moment a Special Air Service brigade (SAS) was also made available.

Since the Allied invasion force at full strength would not exceed 30,000, plus Milorg of course, it would be extremely difficult to control, disarm,

War games with the Scottish Command in the autumn of 1944. The Norwegian C-in-C, Crown Prince Olav, is seated centre with the British General Sir Andrew Thorne, set to become Allied Chief for the liberation of Norway, on his left. Behind Thorne (standing) is Brigadier General Percy Hansen of Scottish Command. To the left are seated Major General Johan Beichmann of the Norwegian Army Command and Major General A. T. Millar of Scottish Command. Major General Strugstad of Norway and Lt General Grasset from Eisenhower's staff at SHAEF to the extreme right.

intern, guard and administer an enemy twelve times as numerous, and heavily armed as well. SHAEF approved the only possible solution: that the Germans should be left as an army in administration and that Allied control should be effected through the German system of command. This would be highly unpopular with the Norwegian population who would expect to see every German safely behind barbed wire as quickly as possible. So control and disarmament parties called 'Heralds' were quickly organised and trained by the brigadier (Disarmament) R. Hilton. He led the SHAEF mission that reached Oslo on the afternoon of 8 May and the band of Heralds made their way to Lillehammer, 80 miles north of Oslo where General Böhme had his HQ.

However, several mildly impetuous sorties 'beat the whistle' and arrived earlier than they should have done. Alan Moorehead, that dashing journalist, had had a wonderful day when General Dewing's posse liberated Copenhagen on Monday 7 May. The following morning, he, Alexander Clifford, another journalist fluent in German, two

RAF air commodores in uniform, two stray Swedes in green, and two photographers flew in a RAF Dakota to find out what was happening in Norway. Flying over Anholt, Laso, Jutland and the Skaggerak: 'The most uplifting scenery passed below us. Mile after mile of inlets, and scattered waterways among the pines, a world of bright lakes, little beaches and gabled hamlets made of timber. Far ahead the eternal snow sat on the great backbone of the country. We swooped down towards Oslo. Considerable crowds were scuttling about the streets and open places like black ants. Two German Messerschmitt fighters, black and evil, shot by and vanished.' A German colonel festooned with medals followed by his officers made for 'our two commodores'. When Clifford explained who the British party were, the colonel replied: 'We had no warning of your coming. We were told to expect an Allied mission to discuss terms, flying in a Catalina and Sunderland painted white. In any event the German capitulation does not take place until midnight tonight.' The RAF commodore, the journalist, the photographers, plus three RAF officers who had broken out of their prison camp that morning, hurtled the five miles into Oslo in three battered brown Wehrmacht cars driven by Germans, to be greeted by ecstatic crowds: 'At first the people did not recognise the airforce blue uniforms but then seeing the khaki [which the three journalists wore] they became lost to all reason. They rushed headlong upon the cars ... This was different from Denmark. Different also from France and Belgium and Holland and the other places. There was a convulsive quality about their welcome, something almost religious, deriving from what could one say? ... The Norse temperament? ... Here in Oslo this afternoon we were seeing all gradations of the human power to feel happiness. The overall expression was clear enough: spontaneous, explosive, full of contagious colour and noise. The people poured themselves into the streets and once there they took fire from one another, from the flags, from one another's excitement ...'

Encrusted with flags, emblems, bunches of flowers, they reached the Grand Hotel and 'were pushed out on to a balcony overlooking the central square. The people flowed out beyond the square, up into the sidestreets, a great pink carpet of upturned faces and waving red flags.' Everyone made speeches. Everyone sang the National Anthem—several times, and *Hallelujah* for some reason. Champagne flowed. At the Bristol Hotel the group met the town governor, the chief of police, and the

British paratroops of 1st Airborne Division land near Oslo, 11 May 1945. (*Imperial War Museum* CL 2629)

former British Legation solicitor and were told: 'Quisling has resigned awaiting arrest by the Allies.' Then quickly back to the airport: 'Far down the fjord a Catalina and a Sunderland, both painted white, were heading past us towards Oslo. Norway was out of the war. Denmark was out of the war ... so many liberations. So much tragedy between them.'

On 6 May Wing Commander Len Ratcliffe with the Norwegian Captain Hysing-Dahl flew in a Hudson plane to Trondheim to take the surrender of the 50,000-strong garrison. On arrival they were greeted by 300 Resistance Milorg fighters.

In the *Daily Telegraph/Morning Post* of Tuesday 8 May, W. E. Mundy reported from Stockholm that Von Krosigk, the Reich Foreign Minister, had unconditionally surrendered all forces: 'An Allied naval force of 48 ships has been sighted at the entrance to Oslo Fjord said Swedish Radio tonight.'

General Sir Andrew Thorne, the Commander-in-Chief Allied Land Forces Norway, mentions the composition of the huge Royal Navy fleet that took part in Operation Eclipse:

Press article: 'Our Sky-Men of
Arnhem Take Over in Norway.'

1st Airborne arrive in Norway.

197

SHAEF mission in Norway: General Sir Andrew Thorne in the middle with Air Vice Marshal J. A. Boret to his right and Rear Admiral J. S. M. Ritchie to his left.

Cruisers *Devonshire, Norfolk, Bellona, Diadem, Dido, Berwick, Birmingham, Conrad* (Polish)

Destroyers *Campbell, Iroquois* (US Navy), *Savage, Onslow, Obdurate, Orwell, Offa, Opportune, Onslaught, Obedient, Arendal* (Norwegian), *Stord* (Norwegian), *Piorun* (Polish), *Zambesi, Zebra, Haida* (US Navy), *Huron* (US Navy), *Carysfort, Scourge, Hesperus, Havelock, Mackay, Viceroy, Zest, Zephyr* (25)

Minelayers *Apollo, Ariadne*

Anti-Aircraft *Broadway, Venomous*

Frigates *Conn, Stayner, Seymour, Flint Castle, Oakham Castle*

Minesweepers *Bangor, Blackpool* and many others

Motor Torpedoboats *54th* (Norwegian) *Flotilla*

On 13 and 18 May two destroyers were sent to Oslo, Kristiansand, Stavanger, Bergen, Trondheim and Tromso. Commander Bob Welland, commanding the destroyer *Haida* sailed into Trondheim to liberate the area occupied by 84,000 German troops. He sent his unarmed 'Liberty men' ashore to celebrate with the Norwegians but warned them to be on their best behaviour as his crew were outnumbered by 1,000 to one! Each pair of destroyers carried Herald parties to supervise disarmament

Preparations for a victory parade in Oslo, General Thorne is in the centre foreground.

and detachments for counter intelligence, civil affairs, and coffee, sugar etc as presents to the Norwegian population. In fact, the SHAEF mission had arranged that 43,000 tons of food be brought in between 8 May and 13 July and distributed to six distribution points: Oslo, Kristiansand, Stavanger, Bergen, Trondheim and Tromso. The supplies consisted of flour, biscuits, canned meat, canned milk, fats, sugar, coffee, salt, V-chocolate, peanut butter and wheat. And in the same period soap, clothing, footwear, battledress, overcoats, berets, steel helmets and Dodge trucks, destined for the 50,000 Milorg and police units.

From 9 May General Thorne's troops were flown or shipped in daily from 1st Airborne Division under Major General R. E. Urquhart, much under strength after the September 1944 Arnhem disaster. Commanders were Brigadier Bower, 1st Airlanding Brigade (Oslo north area); Brigadier Loder-Symonds, Artillery Brigade (Stavanger); Brigadier Calvert (SAS Brigade). Two new infantry brigades had been formed in the UK from units, mainly AA artillery, which were not needed in the final months of the war. These arrived in June with 303rd Brigade under Brigadier Smith (Trondheim) and 304th Brigade under Brigadier

Saunders (Tromso). SHAEF also sent an American task force with 474th US Infantry Regiment under Colonel Edwin Walker.

A considerable RAF presence included 88th Group with twenty-five wing commanders under Air Vice Marshal J. A. Boret. The units were 8,301 (Air Disarmament), 1,318 and 1,336 (RAF Regiment) and 128, 129, 130 and 132 operational wings. RAF units were located at Oslo, Fornebu, Stavanger, Kristiansand, Bergen, Trondheim and Tromso.

The Norwegian brigade arriving from Scotland was soon deployed and measures were taken to expand them into a small national defence force with arrivals from Sweden.

SHAEF were highly organised. General Böhme's staff of 1,200 was reduced to 400 and moved from Lillehammer to a camp at Bogstad; 150 senior generals and staff officers were flown out of Norway to captivity in the UK. And 2,700 members of the sinister SIPO, SD, Gestapo and Abwehr were identified and put under arrest for possible war crimes tribunals to investigate.

One very difficult problem was that 87,000 Allied prisoners of war in over 400 stalags were located all over Norway, even on isolated islands. The majority were Russian, and a mission under General Ratov arrived on 31 May; 72,000 were identified many of them very ill, even starving, and by early June 40,000 had been repatriated by rail to Sweden, thence by sea to Murmansk. There were 15,000 Poles, 14,600 Czechs and 6,500 French. The whole situation was complicated because many had served with the Wehrmacht; 9,000 were displaced persons, who were deemed unacceptable to return home—for instance Sudeten Germans. Altogether there were 37,000 non-German/Austrian personnel belonging to forty nationalities.

On 12 May three British cruisers arrived in Oslo carrying more troops and Norway's Crown Prince Olav who held the title of Chief of the Norwegian Forces. With him were three ministers from the Norwegian government in exile. Their welcome was less warm. Midshipman C. B. Koester served on HMS *Devonshire*. In Operation Kingdom the Crown Prince sailed on HMS *Apollo*, which flew the Norwegian Royal Standard:

We overtook the minesweeping flotilla, reduced speed to remain astern of *Apollo*. We had air cover all the way consisting of Sunderlands, Catalinas, Mosquitoes and Beaufighters. On Sunday 13 May we passed through the

Skaggerak into Oslofjord, met by people in small boats, decorated with fir boughs. There were motor boats, canoes, kayaks, fishing boats, row-boats, sail boats, every craft that could float packed full of people waving, cheering, singing, shouting, old men waved their hats, women, handkerchiefs, partisans stood up and presented arms and boy scouts saluted. Our baker had made extra bread that morning and our sailors threw the white loaves down to the people in the boats. The jetties and landing places along the fjord were lined with people. At every flagstaff a Norwegian flag was flying. We were saluted from shore so often that we stationed two signalmen aft to dip our ensign in return … As we approached Oslo, ferries towing up to 20 boats each joined the throng of small craft. Many of their passengers were shouting 'Kronsprins! Kronsprins!' We pointed aft to *Apollo* and *Ariadne* overtook us to lead the Task Force into harbour. We paraded a Royal Marine Guard and band on the quarter deck to salute as they passed. We heard for the first time that beautiful Norwegian anthem 'Ja Vi Elsker Dette Landet', which we were to know by heart and in Norwegian before we left.

[The crew went ashore]. It was a vast holiday crowd. Women and girls in national costume or summer frocks, blond, freckled boys in shorts, students of all ages wearing their black, tasselled student caps, and sailors from the British, Canadian, American and Norwegian ships of the Task Force all mingled in one happy crowd of holidaymakers. Yet there was a grimmer side as well. The British airborne troops, Norwegian police, some Swedish-trained Norwegian soldiers and partisans all armed with rifles or tommy-guns slung over their shoulders, and the Germans still to be seen on the streets wore pistols in their belts. They were largely ignored by liberators and liberated alike.

Young midshipman Koester and HMS *Devonshire* sailed back to Rosyth, and on 5 June was part of the RN task force to bring King Hakon VII safely back to his kingdom. *Norfolk* was the flagship for the king and *Devonshire* was followed by *Onslow, Obdurate, Orwell* and *Stord*. They passed a flotilla of six U-boats being escorted from Wilhelmshaven to a UK port, chaperoned by two RN frigates. Early on 7 June, the task force reached Oslo and the Crown Prince came out to meet his father the King, and similar rejoicing occurred. On 12 June the task force left for Copenhagen.

Justice and retribution soon followed. Reichskommissar Joseph Terboven and General Riedess of the SS blew themselves up in a bunker. The head of the Norwegian SS, Jonas Lie, shot himself dead. Other

Quisling officials took their own lives. By 1 July, 14,000 suspects of the NS Party were in prison. By the end of 1945, 90,000 had been arrested, investigated or interrogated. More than 46,000 were convicted of wartime offences, 18,000 received prison sentences and 28,000 fined or deprived of their civil rights. Thirty Norwegian collaborators and fifteen Germans were sentenced to death for wartime treason or atrocities. Vidkun Quisling's trial started on 20 August in Oslo's main Freemasons' Lodge. Found guilty, he appealed and on 13 October the court upheld the original verdict. In the courtyard of Akershuis castle on 24 October, Norway's most infamous man was shot to pieces by a ten-man military execution squad.

By the end of May, 272,000 Germans were corralled in their resettlement areas, with a further 32,900 due to arrive. Eventually, by the summer of 1946, the last batch of German prisoners of war were expatriated via Sweden to their home country. The vast majority— undefeated in battle—had behaved well. They had obeyed Admiral Doenitz's orders and those of General Böhme. They had clenched their teeth and kept discipline and order.

It was the end of Hitler's *Festung* Norwegen.

CHAPTER 19

Liberation of POW Camps

International rules governing the humane treatment of prisoners had been agreed at The Hague conventions of 1899 and 1907. Only Russia, out of the six major combatants in the European battlegrounds, was the exception. Civilised standards were set and prisoners of war (POW) were to be decently housed, properly fed and allowed privileges of religious worship, medical treatment and correspondence with their families. They were not to be beaten, interrogated, tortured or severely punished even for attempts to escape. The rank and file could be put to work and there were often many *arbeit* outstations located around POW camps in Germany. Officers were to be held in separate quarters. All were to be accessible for inspection by the International Red Cross.

130,000 Allied POWs were held in captivity, including 60,000 British in German oflags and stalags: veterans from Dunkirk, North Africa, and bailed out bomber crews. The 4.5 million German prisoners in Russia and 5.2 million Russian prisoners in Germany fared very badly indeed and comparatively few survived. Under Stalin's Order No. 270, which treated their own prisoners as deserters, those who were returned and repatriated were charged with treason. The officers were shot and the rank and file sent to gulags with little chance of survival.

There were officially twenty-three POW camps in Germany, known as stalags; five of them were Luft camps for captured RAF and USAAF personnel. Some of them like IV-C Colditz Castle were oflags, for officers only. In theory the Germans kept to the Geneva Conventions allowing Red Cross parcels and occasionally visits by the Swiss Red Cross inspectors. Under the Third Geneva Convention the use of POWs to produce explosives and gunpowder was prohibited.

The BLA liberated a number of these camps but the biggest prize was on 16 April when the armoured cars of the indomitable 11th Hussars, the Cherry Pickers, nosed their way into Fallingbostel camp, situated 20 miles north of Hannover. Major P. H. Huth's B Squadron found on their arrival at the great prison camp south-west of Fallingbostel, an extraordinary sight. RSM Lord, a Grenadier guardsman, had taken over. Sentries from the 1st Airborne Division captured at Arnhem, immaculate in scrubbed belts and gaiters and well-creased battledress were guarding the main gate. RSM Lord was in 'his' office giving orders to his Orderly Warrant officers. Soon Lt Colonel H. Moore, chief admin officer of 7th Armoured Division, had provided as requested rations, cigarettes and even newspapers. Chester Wilmot, the intrepid journalist, who always seemed to be in the right place at the right time reported:

16 April 1845. Twenty thousand Allied prisoners of war gained their freedom today when British tanks liberated two large prison camps, Stalag 11b and Stalag 357. More than 10,000 of them were British or American, and the British troops included 600 men of the 1st Airborne Division captured at Arnhem last year, and many more who were taken at Dunkirk.

This morning, when tanks of the 8th Hussars reached these two camps near Fallingbostel, 35 miles southeast of Bremen, they found that our troops (the prisoners) had already taken charge of the camp and interned their German guards. An airborne sergeant major, an ex-Guardsman, was in command, and the British guards were as spick and span as any parade ground troops. Their boots were polished, their trousers pressed, and their belts and gaiters blancoed. The British troops had taken over the German offices, and their liberators found clerks busy typing out nominal rolls on German typewriters.

The prisoners had been running the camp since last Friday, when three-quarters of the German guards departed, leaving a skeleton force of 60 to carry on. For the past four days German and British troops have been on guard together, but this morning the Germans were disarmed.

This afternoon, at Stalag 11b, I saw some of the 20,000 and learned from padres, doctors and NCOs how they'd been treated. They told me that in this camp there were 4,256 British troops and 2,428 Americans. Of these 6,700, more than 1,000 are in hospital suffering from wounds, injuries, or starvation, and I saw several thousand more suffering from starvation who should have been in hospital in any civilised country.

Above: British
section of the
prison camp at
Fallingbostel,
Stalag X1B/357.

Right: Over
12,000 released
prisoners of war
at Fallingbostel.

16 April 1945, British
POWs, veterans of
Dunkirk and Normandy
and others greet their
liberators at Stalag 11B,
Fallingbostel. (*Imperial
War Museum*)

Here in this camp I saw clear evidence of the German neglect and wanton disregard for the lives and health of their prisoners. Of the 4,250 British prisoners, some 2,500 have come into the camp in the last three weeks. The Germans have marched them from Poland, lest they should be set free by the Russian advance. Ten days ago in this camp there were 3,000 other British and American prisoners who had made this terrible trek from Poland; but when the 2nd Army crossed the Weser, the Germans put these 3,000 on the road again, and sent them marching back towards the Russians. They were determined to stop the 3,000 being liberated, because they were airmen and paratroops.

How far they'll be able to march I don't know, for I saw today the pitiable condition of those who have already made the nightmare journey from Poland. They certainly were exhausted at the end of that journey. I saw them in hospital—drawn, haggard, starved—starved beyond description—limbs like matchsticks, bodies shrunken till their bones stood out like knuckles.

The doctor in charge of them said to me, 'Nothing has kept these men alive except Red Cross parcels and their own spirit'. But on that journey from Poland they had very few Red cross parcels, and some got none.

One padre who was captured at Calais in 1940 told me that this party had marched 400 miles in 52 days, and their rations, in the depth of winter, had been nothing but a bowl of watery soup and a couple of slices of army bread per day. He had marched with 800 British and 6,500 American airmen, many thousands of whom had been sent marching back again almost as soon as they'd finished their journey.

I wish those people who think the Germans should be treated lightly had seen what I saw today. But I also saw something that was inspiring and encouraging. All this German oppression and brutality and starvation hadn't been able to kill the spirit and self-respect of these men of Arnhem, men of Crete, of Dunkirk and Calais, men of Bomber Command and the 8th Air Force. They'd managed to rise above their sordid environment and today those of them who were on guard or on duty were as soldierly in their bearing as they were the day they were captured. They were proud that they had their own camp running when our tanks got there. They felt they had almost liberated themselves. And this afternoon they had the supreme pleasure of watching their German guards being marched away to our prison cage; and as they watched, they cheered.

Robert Barr, another journalist, covered part of the American army advances and wrote:

Other Arnhem prisoners were liberated by the US 9th Army and celebrated their freedom by strolling to a nearby village, where they quickly established a typically British atmosphere.

17 April 1945. How can I explain what that village looked like—it had become an English village—there were hundreds of British paratroopers lining its pavements—happy, smiling, giving the 'thumbs-up' sign, some sunning themselves by the village duckpond, some playing around on bicycles. Two of them were trying to get a stubborn motor-cycle to work. Most of them were parading the pavements in twos and threes—they were parading the village streets, just as you saw them walk out of an evening in England; clean-shaven, smart, walking in step, and this village had suddenly become more than just an English village, its pavements held a living cavalcade of our story in this war, because amongst the Red Devils—outnumbered by them but not outshone— were other British soldiers, and New Zealanders and Australians whose stories briefly told were the story of our part in the war. It was an American officer, I think, who summed up that spirit; he said 'Prisoners? Gee, I thought they were troops going into the line.' That was no exaggeration—they looked just like it—if you'd seen them today you would have been proud. But what I don't understand is where some of them got the blanco.

Later in the campaign, near the river Elbe, 11th Armoured Division liberated 1,600 RAF officers on 2 May at Westerau. The Guards Armoured had to negotiate with Lt General Roth, GOC the 15th Panzergrenadier Division, for the relief of Westertimke on 26 April, which contained over 8,000 POW, half of them British Merchant Navy (and forty-two Guardsmen).

Close by was the even larger camp of Sandbostel on the way to Bremenvorde, with 22,000 prisoners, of whom half were civilians, mainly French and Russian but there were also 300 British POW. Lt Colonel T. W. Davidson, the Director of Medical Services of 30th Corps, with Brigadier Gwatkin and Lt Colonel Moore of Guards Armoured toured the camp on 28 April.

Lt General Horrocks wrote in his memoirs:

Sandbostel, one of those horror camps. When General Adair and I entered we came across the most ghastly picture I have ever seen. The floor of the first hut we visited was covered with emaciated figures, clad in the most horrible striped pyjamas. Many were too weak to walk, but on seeing us they heaved themselves up and gave a pathetic cheer. Most of them had some form of chronic dysentery and the stench was so bad that I disgraced myself by being sick in the corner. I was so angry that I ordered the Burgomeister of every one of the surrounding towns and villages to supply a quota of German women to clean up the camp and look after these unfortunate prisoners who were dying daily at an alarming rate. When the women arrived we expected some indication of horror or remorse when they saw what their fellow countrymen had been doing. Not a bit of it. I never saw a tear or heard one expression of pity from any of them.

Brigadier Prior-Palmer, commanding 8th (Red Fox's Mask) Armoured Brigade, also visited the Sandbostel camp and sent 168th Light Field Ambulance and six lorries of food supplies from each of his seven regiments to help feed the prisoners.

Sandbostel X-B and Westertimke were official prisoner of war camps but with the intense pressure on the German systems squeezed into a sandwich with the Russians in the east and the Allies in the west, tens of thousands of refugees were crammed into camps which simply could not cope with the extra numbers.

The rescue of Colditz Oflag was a far happier event. At Colditz, more than a thousand British, French, Polish, Czech, American and other

On 27 April 1945, Westertimke POW Camp was freed by the British. Russian ex-POWs were loaded on to lorries in Stittensen, to go to a camp run by the British Army.

About 80 per cent of five million Soviet POWs died in German captivity. Most of the survivors were killed by the NKVD on return to the USSR.

More than 7,000 former Allied prisoners of war, liberated by the Americans at VII-A
Moosburg on 29 April 1945.

Allied prisoners of war, all of them officers who had earlier escaped from
other camps and been caught before reaching freedom, were confined
within a formidable fortress. An eyewitness reported the scene:

> On 15 April a single GI arrived. An Allied officer standing near the gate
> advanced with outstretched hand and shook the hand extended by the
> American, who grinned at him and said cheerfully: 'Any doughboys here?' The
> spell was broken.
>
> Suddenly a mob was rushing towards him, shouting and cheering and struggling
> madly to reach him, to make sure that he was alive, to touch him, and from the
> touch to know again the miracle of living, to be men in their own right, freed
> from bondage, outcast no more, liberated by their Allies and their friends, their
> faith in God's mercy justified, their patience rewarded, the nobility of mankind
> vindicated, justice at last accomplished and tyranny once more overcome.
>
> Men wept, unable to restrain themselves. It was not enough that the body
> was free once more to roam the earth. Feelings, pent up and dammed behind

Westerau—2 May 1945. Liberated RAF officers and German POWs.

the mounting walls of five successive torturing, introverted years, had to erupt.

They welled up like gushing springs, they overflowed, they burst their banks, they tumbled unhindered and uncontrolled. Frenchmen with tears streaming down their faces kissed each other on both cheeks—the salute of brothers. They kissed the GI, they kissed everyone within range. The storm of emotion burst. The merciful rain descended. The grey clouds drifted from the horizon of the mind, borne on fresh salt and moisture-laden breezes across the unchained oceans of memory from the far-off shores of love. Home and country beckoned; loved ones were waiting. Wives and sweethearts, mothers, fathers, and children never seen, were calling across the gulf of the absent years.

POW Camps in Germany

Stalags

IX-C	Bad Sulza
XI-B	Fallingbostel
79	Brunswick
VII-B	Eichstatt
XIII-D	Nurnberg
VII-A	Moosburg
XIII-C	Hammelburg
IV-C	Colditz Castle
XI-A	Alten Grabow
III-A	Luckenwalde
IV-B	Mühlberg
VIII-A	Gorlitz
XX-B	Marienburg
XX-A	Thorn
344	Lamsdorf
VIII-B	Teschen
Luft-1	Barth
Luft-4	Gross Tychow
Luft-7	Bankau
Luft-6	Heydekrug
X-B	Sandbostel
Marlag und Milag Nord	Westertimke
Luft-3	Sagan

CHAPTER 20

Freedom for Hitler's Slaves

Primo Levi wrote in his book *The Re-Awakening*, when on 27 January 1945 he was liberated from Auschwitz extermination camp: 'There were men, but a good number of women and children. There were Catholics, Jews, Orthodox Christians and Muslims, people with white or yellow skins and Negroes in American uniforms … In Germany they had found bread, barbed wire, hard work, German order, servitude and shame. They were often herded into open cattle trucks, frightened, their closed bitter faces, their evasive eyes displayed a disturbing animal-like humiliation and resignation.' They became the displaced persons when they were freed.

Fritz Saukel, the Third Reich Director of Labour (1942–45) ordered five million people from occupied Europe to work as slaves in Germany. In March 1942 Hitler decreed the mobilisation of labour, both German and foreign to meet the demands of Albert Speer's armaments and munitions production. In 1942, the Third Reich dominated 400 million subjects so this seemed to be a reasonable task. Sauckel (1894–1946) was Hitler's Plenipotentiary for Employment and he extracted 5.8 million workers from the occupied territories.

Forced labour in the Reich was directed mainly at farming, mining, metallurgy, chemicals, building and transport. This is where Sauckel brought his slaves from:

USSR	2,406,895	Czechoslovakia	177,679
Poland	1,440,254	Belgium	177,451
France	954,966	Holland	174,358
Italy	486,326	TOTAL	5,817,929

213

German labour camp workers.

Of these 75 per cent were civilians, 4,375,882, and the rest were various prisoners of war.

On 20 April 1942 Sauckel stated his policy:

> The aim of the new gigantic labour mobilisation is to use all the rich and tremendous sources conquered and secured for us by our fighting armed forces under the leadership of Adolf Hitler for the armament of the armed forces and also for the nutrition of the Homeland. The raw materials as well as the fertility of the conquered territories and their human labour power are to be used completely and conscientiously to the profit of Germany and her Allies ... All prisoners of war from the territories of the West, as well as the East, actually in Germany must be completely incorporated into the German armament and nutrition industries ... consequently it is an immediate necessity to use the human reserves of the conquered Soviet territory to the fullest extent. Should we not succeed in obtaining the necessary amount of labour on a voluntary basis we must immediately institute conscription or forced labour. The complete employment of all prisoners of war as well as the use of a gigantic number of new foreign civilian workers, men and women, has become an indisputable necessity for the solution of the mobilisation of the labour programme in the war.

At the Nuremberg trial Sauckel admitted: 'Out of the five million workers who arrived in Germany not even 200,000 came voluntarily.' His instructions in April 1942 were: 'All men must be fed, sheltered and treated in such a way as *to exploit them to the highest possible extent, at the lowest conceivable degree of expenditure.*' Many prisoners of war, particularly Soviets, were compelled to work in munition factories and even be deployed as Ack-Ack gunners.

On 4 January 1944 Hitler directed Sauckel to obtain four million *new* workers from the occupied territories. It was called the Slave Labour Programme. Albert Speer, as chief of the Organisation Todt, desperately needed these slaves not only to build the Atlantic Wall, but also military highways and to man the vast range of industries under his control. Alan Moorehead noted:

> As soon as we crossed the Rhine *we were confronted by a problem almost as big as Germany herself* [author's emphasis], the millions upon millions of semi-slave workers. With every mile we went into Germany they grew more numerous on the roads: little groups of Frenchmen, then Dutch, then Belgians and Czechs and Poles and Italians and finally, in overwhelming majority, the Russians in their bright green uniforms with 'S.U.'—Soviet Union—painted in white on their backs. Half the nationalities of Europe were on the march, all moving blindly westward along the roads feeling their way by some common instinct towards the British and American lines in the hope of finding food and shelter and transportation there. These millions lived a vagabond life. At every bend of the road you came on another group, bundles on their shoulders, trudging along the ditches in order to avoid the passing military traffic. The Germans were terrified of the Russians.

About a million captured Soviet soldiers out of the 5.7 million in total who surrendered joined some form of service with Germany. The Russian general Andrei Andreivich Vlasson, who was captured in July 1942, was persuaded to accept command of the Russian Liberation Army but the enrolled men were either working in the Todt organisation (Fritz Todt was Speer's predecessor) or in separate auxiliary units until March 1945. Because Hitler was scraping the barrel for 'bodies', Vlasson found himself in command of two renegade Russian divisions on the Eastern Front. Eventually captured by the Russians, Vlasson was hanged and the survivors of the Russian Liberation Army almost certainly never

German refugees walk westward along one of Hitler's pre-war motor roads.

Ostflucht. Not waiting to be expelled, a flood of Germans from East Prussia and other eastern provinces took to the road.

got as far as the gulags. As a result, *all* the Russian prisoners of war in Germany were decreed by Stalin to be 'traitors'. So of the original 5,754,000 Russians captured, 3,700,000 died in captivity—many simply were starved to death and in May 1945 there were more than two million Russian soldiers and slaves at large.

After the German surrender Russian commissars were allowed—they were still Allies—to supervise repatriation of their unfortunate compatriots.

By 1953, 5,457,856 Soviet citizens had been returned to the Soviet Union. Russian historians estimate that at least 20 per cent were executed or given a life sentence—25 years imprisonment in the gulags. Some three million served shorter sentences.

An estimated nine and a half million people were on the roads of Europe in the week following VE Day, most—not all—longing to get home. Among those leaving the rubble-strewn cities of Germany in the immediate aftermath of the war were more than eight and a half million people: 2,400,000 Russians, 2,100,000 Frenchmen, 1,500,000 Poles, 600,000 Lithuanians, 570,000 Belgians, 560,000 Latvians, 420,000 Italians and 400,000 Dutchmen. Tens of thousands of Danes, Yugoslavs, Greeks, Estonians, Bulgarians, Roumanians, Hungarians and Czechs were also on their way home. Fleeing in a counter-direction were nine and a half million German civilians. Half a million of these were from Roumania, Hungary and Yugoslavia: Germans who had been living outside Germany for several centuries. Two million were German citizens expelled from East Prussia.

Nothing on earth would have kept the industrial slave workers in the factories, some underground, and the mines, once their German masters were gone. First the rescued slaves rushed out into the streets to loot. Some tried to take physical revenge on German families. Part of the loot was of course, drink. Moorehead reported that liquor at the moment of liberation caused as much uproar as anything else. The Poles and the Russians especially, in their first wild moments of freedom, would run roaring on to the hated factory machines and smash them with crowbars.

Most of the war's finest journalists were travelling with the Allied armies into the Third Reich and their reports to the BBC make sad but fascinating reading.

Matthew Halton, Canadian Broadcasting Company, sent this report to the BBC on 12 April:

Even some
Germans welcome
the British as
liberators.

Your hate rises against everything German when you see Dutchmen who have been tortured to death. And it rises again when you see the streams of freed slaves thronging down the roads. This astonishing sight is one we see every day. In the areas we've already overrun in Germany we've liberated over two million of these slaves, chiefly Russian and Polish but also French, Czechs, Yugoslavs and others. We've seen them in bands of several hundred at a time. They're not always emaciated, starving, ragged. Sometimes you wouldn't know they were slaves, except for their language, and the fact that they're laughing and chattering away, and waving and singing. But I've seen others, hungry, and even barefooted, mad with hate of the Germans, looting shops for food and clothes. What an extraordinary thing this is, in the 20th century! You see these things and wonder if you're not back in the pages of an historical novel, back in the Thirty Years War. Freed bondsmen—ten or twelve million men and women of Europe have been uprooted by the Germans and enslaved. It makes you hate all right when you question some of them, and women tell you how they were brought from Russia, put up on auction blocks, pawed and mauled by lecherous fat Germans, and sold into slavery. I've seen women on their knees, tears running down their cheeks as British tanks rolled past and they knew they were free. What a story that told, millions of Ruths sick for home, who stood in tears amid the alien corn, and even now many of them

Retribution on a German foreman by forced foreign workers.

will go back and find their homes destroyed and their families dead or gone. Is there any measure for the rivers and tides of sorrows and tears that the Nazis have set flowing in Europe?

Halton's countrymen, the gallant Canadian Army, had been struggling in the *verdronken* land of the Scheldt delta in the autumn of 1944. Now he was over the Rhine. And a few days later Wynford Vaughan-Thomas wrote this report for the BBC:

22 April 1945. The basis of German agricultural prosperity was slave labour, and as soon as the Allied armies swept by these prosperous farms, the slaves, very naturally, stopped working. We've opened the floodgates of a dam, and every single person who can get away is off. The roads of Germany today are one of the unforgettable sights of the war. You can walk a few hundred yards from the transmitter from which I'm speaking and you'll see for yourself the wealth of the German farmlands flowing away to the west. There go the farm tractors, towing the German farmers' carts, filled with jubilant Poles or Yugoslavs; there go his farm horses ridden by Russian prisoners of war, there go his bicycles and his lorries, and his eggs and his chickens and his pigs. This great flood goes steadily on day after day, and now in the semi-deserted fields the German farmer has got to work himself; you see him with his wife and

his daughter and the young children, for his sons have long since left for the army, maybe they'll never be coming back to this farm. You see him working to salvage something out of the wreck. It's impossible he can salvage enough to feed the townsfolk of Germany, for the labour with which he cultivated these rich fields is gone or is living on his farm as self-invited guests. Yes, the Germans are in for a grim winter. But then, they might have thought of that before they based their agriculture on slave labour.

George Blake, who was 'embedded' with 52nd Lowland Division, encountered dreadful conditions as the battle for Bremen ended:

The civilian population of Bremen was beyond resisting. It was, in the physical sense, bomb happy after the terrible pounding it had received from the Lancasters a few nights before; it was psychologically in the desperate state of crazy abandonment that so often comes on people who cannot bring themselves to stare the bleak face of defeat in the face. They had gone wild, looting, drinking, fighting among each other for what are called consumer goods; their frenzy was complicated by the presence among them of large numbers of utterly demoralised displaced persons from internment camps in the countryside round about. For two or three days towards the end of April 1945 Bremen was probably among the most debauched places on the face of God's earth: all sanctions broken down among those Germans who rioted in their shocking inability to accept the consequences of their own political stupidity.

The control of this bear-garden was a heavy responsibility on the cool and terribly tired Scottish soldiers who had taken the city after such a long and gruelling battle. It was immensely complicated by the litter of smashed and fallen masonry left by the bombers. A central area of the city, some four miles by one, had ceased to exist. All who have seen something of Germany since the war ended have their own pet notions as to degrees of degradation among the smashed German towns—Essen, Munster, Halle, Cologne, Berlin or what you will. The present writer thought that the ruins of Hamburg, seen from a draughty jeep through the drizzle of a darkling January evening, was as much as he ever wished to see of destruction; but Bremen on a bright February afternoon seemed even more calamitous, its undoubtedly handsome, metropolitan air all sullied and humbled by the bombs.

Policing and patrolling the great, smashed seaport and its bewildered population was continuous work for at least a brigade. Some units left the area to mount guard over groups of DP camps.

Mass graves of slave workers were found in the woods near Soltau. Desert Rats made local civilians disinter the bodies and give them proper burial.

What the DPs urgently needed were registration cards (new identity cards), soup kitchens, medical aid, and DDT dustings to combat the filth and squalor of their initial interim abodes. They wanted some kind of security, law and order, without threats of violence and death.

Every German woman feared rape as the Red Army plundered, pillaged, looted and raped its way through the German regions they overran in late April 1945. As the British armour moved up to and over the river Elbe the vast, moving, sad human frieze kept pouring down the roads increasing in numbers with every new town or village that was captured and liberated. Moorehead again: 'One began to get a new picture of Nazi Germany. What we were seeing was something from the Dark Ages, the breaking up of a medieval slave state. All the Nazi flags and parades and conquests in the end were based on this one thing—slave labour. There was something monstrous about the wired-in workers' compounds and sentry boxes round each factory, something that was in defiance of all accepted ideas of civilisation ... we had only begun to glimpse the extent and depth of the Nazi terror system, but already one sensed the utter disregard of the value of human life in Germany. And now the Reich was collapsing at its roots because the slaves were melting away.'

221

By mid-May ten million German soldiers had become prisoners in the hands of the Allies. The Russian NKVD reported they were holding 1,464,803 Germans including 93 generals in camps in their conquered sector of East Germany. As a result nearly all the German men were either prisoners, wounded or dead.

The military achievement of conquest was backed by an equally remarkable ordering of the chaos that followed the Reich's implosion Hard on the heels of troops fighting through cities, Allied military government officers moved in to take control. Their task was to set up administrations to restore law and order, to secure water, food and fuel supplies, and shelter. Riots in cities such as Hannover and Osnabruck—total anarchy—needed force to restore some order.

Public order was the essential prerequisite of any revival of a proper social existence. In many towns, order was admirably enforced, and tensions defused by imperturbable public safety officers—mostly bobbies drawn from British police forces.

The Allied military administrators directed Germans to dig, build and clear wreckage, insisting that only by work could they feed and shelter themselves. They had expected some hostility, but often found people willing to co-operate; for most civilians the arrival of a military government signalled the welcome ending of the war. The new military governments sought out local leaders, preferably of anti-Nazi sentiment and installed them as mayors to help get basic services going. The military authorities provided tent camps for thousands of displaced persons and, wherever possible, made Germans feed them.

Overall, Germany was in a worse mess than planners had envisaged millions were homeless. The breakdown of transport, local government and communications was almost total.

Food was an urgent problem. The Allies were determined that the Germans, who had eaten well by ransacking conquered territories should not have more than newly liberated peoples.

However, a balance had to be struck. Famine would bring catastrophic disorder and disease. The Allies drew calorie scales and rations: not so high as to enrage the liberated countries, not so low as to make the black market worse. Ordinary people were rationed to 1,550 calories a day men doing heavy work to 2,800 calories. The Allies set a daily ration of 12.7 oz of bread and 10.5 oz of potatoes. In reality many people had much less.

German refugees, trudging westward, pass a Soviet poster, July 1945.

Even before the surrender of German forces it was seen that there would be disaster if the harvest were not gathered. The military government launched Operation Barleycorn and half a million German servicemen were ordered to bring in the corn.

The British had a particular difficulty in the industrial powerhouse of the Ruhr, which was under their control. Ruhr miners needed more food if they were to hew coal to power the factories. Feeding them was a matter of economic necessity, so the Allies sent them food.

In November 1943 a conference took place in Atlantic City, New Jersey USA for the founding of the United Nations Relief and Rehabilitation Administration (UNRRA). This was dedicated to the welfare of refugees and the distressed population of liberated countries in the warfare of the future. In the wake of Operation Torch in North Africa the first UNRRA help was deployed. In the next four years, 1943–47, it was to dispense US$44 billion of radical, practical help to refugees in 17 countries. UNRRA was mainly funded by the USA, Canada and Britain and was a gigantic global relief effort.

In December 1944 President Roosevelt's key advisers, Harry Hopkins and Dean Acheson, realised: 'The war can be lost in the liberated countries. It cannot be won with success in the liberated countries.

Liberated people are the most combustible material in the world. They are fighting people. They are violent and restless. They have suffered unbearably ... to win the war requires that we win the battle of the liberated countries.'

More than 100 UNRRA teams were soon in the field after VE Day, assisted by 697 Allied Liaison Officers. Field Marshal Montgomery had organised very thoroughly the division of the British Army of the Rhine into 'fiefs' with his soldiers responsible for law and order until the German police had been disbanded from their duties fighting alongside the Wehrmacht. The UNRRA teams would always find the military very helpful. Accommodation had to be found for the multitude of displaced persons in former military barracks, summer camps for children, hotels, castles, hospitals, private homes, even partly demolished houses. A Central Tracking Bureau was started in conjunction with the International Red Cross to identify individuals and trace their families. Soon one million names were on the register. Soon ethnic and religious groups tended to concentrate in certain camps. German universities were compelled to take a quota of DP students.

By the end of 1945 AMGOT, UNRRA, the Red Cross and other aid agencies had repatriated six million DPs, but it was evident that a hard core of well over one million could not, or would not be repatriated. Few DPs *wanted* to return to Stalin and the Communist dictator of Yugoslavia, Tito. Most of the free world grieved for these dispossessed souls. By 1950 Israel had taken 650,000 Jews; USA eventually accepted 600,000; Australia 182,159; Canada 157,000; Belgium 20,000, mainly coal miners; France 30,000. The Latin American countries accepted 80,000. The UK instituted Operation Westward Ho and accepted 86,000 DPs plus 115,000 Polish Army veterans and 12,000 of the Ukranian Halychyna Division.

CHAPTER 21

Retribution:
War Crimes Tribunals

A United Nations War Crimes Commission was set up in London in 1943. In November the British, Americans and Russians declared that Germans responsible for abominable deeds would be sent back to where they had committed them to be tried by the liberated countries. The massacres of many American soldiers at Malmédy during the German Ardennes offensive in December 1944 convinced America of the need to punish the guilty. It was agreed by May 1945 that an international tribunal should sit with American, British, French and Russian judges and prosecutors. In August it was decided that Nuremberg should be the location for the trials because it had been the site of the great Nazi party rallies. There would be four possible counts: crimes against peace (planning and making war); war crimes (responsibility for crimes during warfare); crimes against humanity (to cover racial persecution); and conspiracy (to commit crimes alleged in other courts). The teams of prosecutors would come from the Allies, and the defence lawyers would be German. The tribunal also put Third Reich organisations on trial. If an organisation was declared criminal, any member of it could be tried on that count alone. The SS and the Waffen SS, the Gestapo, the SD (Sicherheitsdienst, the Nazi Party's own intelligence and security body) were all declared guilty organisations, as were the senior ranks of the Nazi Party from the rank of kreisleiter upwards.

The whole world followed the great trial, which sat from November 1945 to September 1946. Twenty-one defendants were tried. The sentences were: death for Frank, Frick, Goering, Jodl, Keitel, Kaltenbrunner, Ribbentropp, Rosenberg, Saukel, Seyss-Inquart and Streicher; life imprisonment for Funk, Hess and Raeder; 20 years for

Twenty-four Nazi leaders on trial.

von Schirach and Speer; 15 years for von Neurath; 10 years for Doenitz. Those condemned to death were hanged in October 1946.

Smaller war crimes tribunals were set up in various places where major crimes had been committed. In 1939 the British government published a White Paper on the German concentration camps and a widely read Penguin book on international affairs (1939) listed Dachau, Buchenwald, Oranienburg and Papenburg. There were two categories of camps. Between 1933 and 1945 a total of 1,600,000 people were sent to concentration *work* camps, and over one million died. In the even more infamous *extermination* camps, such as Auschwitz, Sobibor, Treblinka and Chelmno, where upwards of 18 million people were sent, up to 11 million were killed. There were camps outside Germany, many in Poland, and also into Austria and Czechoslovakia. Most camps were commanded by an SS officer of the rank of colonel or major and were divided into military style companies. Each camp block was under the charge of a senior prisoner or *kapo*. The SS charged industrial companies four to eight Deutschmarks per day for the use of prisoners working a full 12-hour day. The average survival of a prisoner in a work camp was nine months. The SS could count on a net gain of 1,431 marks per labourer for their short life.

In the war crimes tribunals set up in the post-war period in Poland, where there were seven camps, 631 war criminals were executed; in the US zone of Germany 278; in the British zone 240; in Hungary 149; and in the French zone of Germany 104; a total of 1,402. In Auschwitz camp under Commandant Höss, between two and four million inmates were murdered. The majority of the dead were Jewish.

Nearly two million German soldiers and civilians had to be screened in the British zone at the end of the war. German bureaucratic records were fortunately excellent. There were five categories to be identified from their Nazi records:

Above: Court room at Nuremberg.

Right: Ruins of Nuremberg in 1945: more than half of the city had been destroyed by Allied bombing, but the survival of its courthouse and prison determined the trial's value. (*Getty Images*)

227

1) *Hauptschuldige* (offender)
2) *Belastete* (an active military record involved in war crimes)
3) *Minderbelastete* (a minor offender, a Party member, not known to have committed any crime)
4) *Mitlaufer* (person who joined the Nazi Party to keep a job)
5) *Entlastete* (innocent, proved anti-Nazi)

Since the liberation of the Bergen-Belsen concentration camp on 15 April by the author's battlegroup of 11th Armoured Division, the British press were justifiably baying for blood. *The Illustrated London News* described Joseph Kramer, the camp commandant, as: 'a typical German brute—a sadistical, heavy-featured Nazi. He was quite unashamed.' Raymond Phillips, a barrister who edited the official published transcript of the Belsen trial, wrote afterwards: 'To many it seemed superfluous that there should be a trial at all, and the popular cry was for a summary identification and execution of the offenders.' In some of the camps liberated by American forces, SS guards were simply lined up and shot. Some guards were lynched by the prisoners immediately after they were freed. On 27 April, twelve days after the liberation, a team of war crimes investigators consisting of two majors, a captain and some NCO translators, plus another team of fifteen who joined in May, were allotted to a camp of nearly 60,000 witnesses, two-thirds of them Polish, Hungarian and Roumanian Jews.

The Belsen trial opened on 17 September 1945. The defendants were sixteen male members of the SS, including Joseph Kramer, commandant, Dr Fritz Klein, camp doctor, and Franz Hössler, commandant of Camp 2. Also accused were sixteen female SS guards, including Irma Grese, who commanded a compound, and Elizabeth Volkenrath, the camp overseer of the women's camp. Grese, twenty-one, with long blond hair, high leather boots and a short whip for her guard dogs, was what the tabloid press wanted. Also on trial were a dozen *kapos* accused of mistreating their fellow prisoners.

The British authorities were determined to follow the practices being laid out by the UN War Crimes Tribunal. 'Arch' criminals would be tried at Nuremberg: 'ordinary war criminals in the custody of Allied military authorities could be dealt with by military courts'. Kramer and his fellow guards fell into the 'ordinary' category and faced a court made up of five British military officers. Colonel T. M. Backhouse led the prosecution team as senior Judge Advocate General of the legal staff of the new British Army of the Rhine (BAOR). The forty-four accused were represented by eleven British regimental officers, including Captain Lionel Cranfield, who was the author's solicitor post war, and one Polish officer.

The trial took place in a specially built dock in a gymnasium on the outskirts of Luneburg, a town 40 miles north-east of Belsen. The army painstakingly gathered evidence, produced witnesses, provided the accused with defence counsel, allowed the defence to answer the charges against them and treated the prisoners with a degree of respect.

The Belsen defendants were not on trial for crimes against Jews, not for genocide, but for mistreating and abusing *Allied nationals*. This included Jews and others from Allied nations such as Poland and Russia. The insistence on correct and traditional British justice was immediately criticised by the Russian and French press as being 'unnecessarily attentive to the rights of the defendants'.

Twelve of the accused had appalling track records and had worked in Auschwitz previously; these included Kramer, Klein, Hössler, Grese and Volkenrath. Kramer had spent his *entire* career in camps. He had joined the SS in 1932 aged twenty-six, and then worked in Dachau, Sachsenhausen, Malthausen, Auschwitz, was commandant at Natzweiler, back to Auschwitz, commandant of Birkenau in Poland, the extermination camp for Russian officers, then in December 1944 to Belsen. Grese had started at Ravensbruck, then Auschwitz, then back to Ravensbruck and finally Belsen.

Two of the star witnesses were Brigadier Llewelyn Glyn Hughes, who gave precise medical details of the camp upon its liberation, as did Captain Derek Sington. The court watched a film made of the camp in April by the British and the court toured the camp grounds, which were burned by Crocodile-tank flame-throwers after the trial. The defence counsel did their best. Colonel H. A. Smith argued that concentration camps had been legal in Germany since 1933, therefore what went on there was legal by German law. Most of the evidence was witness statements. Another theme was that Kramer and the others were simply taking orders from their superiors in Berlin, Richard Glücks and Oswald Pohl, who was Heydrich's No. 2, but was remarkably similar to Oskar Schindler, as in *Schindler's Ark* by Thomas Keneally.

Colonel Backhouse, in his closing summary, went over the details of the transport, beatings, shaving, tattooing, forced labour, starvation, selections and crematoria. The only difference between Auschwitz and Belsen was that the latter had no gas chambers. He also stated that: 'the martyrdom of the Jews … was a war crime which has never been equalled.'

On 16 November 1945 the court adjourned and six hours later delivered the verdicts. Thirty out of forty-four defendants were declared guilty on one or both counts of mistreating Allied nationals at Auschwitz and Belsen. Eleven defendants: Kramer, Klein, Hössler, Grese, Bormann, Volkenrath and five others were sentenced to death and hanged on 12 December. Nineteen others received sentences from life in prison to a mere one year in jail.

Belsen was, in effect, the first war crimes trial in the British zone. There were several others and the author was involved in two of them: in Hamburg and also in Oldenburg. In each case a British Judge Advocate General supervised and made sure that the same high legal standards applied. There was an interpreter for the Crown and another for the defence who had to agree on the accuracy of the witnesses' testimony. The judges and jury were a lt colonel, a major and the author, a lieutenant who always had to give his verdict first for obvious reasons.

Oldenburg War Crimes Tribunal: September 1946. The author was a junior member of the three man court (judge and jury) seen back to the camera with two gleaming RHA stars (Lieutenant). Trial of Willi Erold and eleven others charged with the murder of 300 persons (POWs and DPs) at a 'people's camp' in April 1945. The verdict was death by hanging for Erold and six others. The remaining persons on trial received lesser sentences.

The Oldenburg trial in September 1946 was of Willi Erold and eleven others charged with the murder of 300 at a 'People's Camp' in April 1945. Erold and six others were found guilty and sentenced to death by hanging. The other five faced other lesser charges.

The author was Intelligence Officer of 3rd Regiment Royal Horse Artillery at the time of both trials. On 13 December 1945 he was one of fifty officers of BAOR who witnessed Mr Albert Pierrepoint, the official British hangman, execute thirteen convicted war criminals in Hameln.

It is true to say that thousands of war crimes went untried and unpunished. For instance when the SS units left Belgium in a hurry in early September 1944, they or the Hitler Jugend, and some Wehrmacht, committed undeniable war crimes in Ghlin, Jemappes, Quaregnon, Quevaucamps, Sovet, Anhée, Godinne, Bouillon, Hun, Warnant, Rivière, Faillon and Bonsin.

This author and separately Alan Moorehead, the journalist, witnessed the SS camp at Breendonck, just south of Antwerp, an absolute charnel house of butchery of civilians who might, or might not, have been members of the Belgian Resistance.

Alfred Pierrepoint (1905–1992) first flew to Germany on 11 December 1945 and the next day executed eleven Belsen guards, plus two more Germans convicted of murdering a RAF pilot on 11 March. Altogether Pierrepoint made twenty-five visits to the British zones in Germany and Austria and hanged over 200 war criminals in a four-year period.

CHAPTER 22

The Holocaust and the
Death Camps

As soon as Hitler took power in the Third Reich in January 1933 his SA (Sturm Abteilung), tough brownshirts, unemployed ex-soldiers, began rounding up all possible enemies and putting them under guard, initially in Dachau, Oranienburg, Buchenwald, Gross-Rosen, Mautausen and Sachsenhausen. In 1939 and 1940 came Flossenburg, Ravensbruck, Neuengamme, Theresienstadt (Czechoslovakia), and Auschwitz 1, 2 and then 3 in Poland. In 1941 Stutthof, Natzweiler (Alsace) and a batch of five more in Poland: Birkenau, Chelmno, Belzec, Sobibor, Treblinka and Lublin-Majdanek. Bergen-Belsen opened as late as 1943. All the camps were run by the SS Death's Head Formation, camp colonels, under the overall chief inspector Theodor Eicke (1892–1943). He was succeeded by Richard Glucks (1889–1945). The whole system was supervised by the infamous Reichsführer SS Heinrich Himmler (1900–1945).

The two main types of camp, excluding POW and work camps, were concentration and extermination or death camps. The former included Dachau, Belsen and Sachsenhausen, which were defined as penal camps under a very harsh regime. There was no release and the average life expectancy was six months before death from overwork, starvation, diseases such as typhus, and of course intense brutality. If a concentration camp held 60,000 inmates, then the deaths would be about 100 a day. The SS defined them as 'camps of protective custody'.

A typical concentration camp like Dachau had five departments: 1 for the commandant and his staff; 2 was the political office run by the Gestapo; 3 was for the SS officers responsible for work schedules and discipline; 4 was the camp administration—initially there were *totenbuch* or death registers identifying the victims and cause and date

The main concentration, extermination camps and prisoner of war camps.

of death; 5 was the medical section who often caused severe medical problems, theoretically for research, besides a minimum of aid for sick prisoners.

Towards the end of the war, usually in 1944, camps were being overwhelmed as Himmler's SS rounded up victims for *schutzhaft* (protective custody): trade unionists, communists, homosexuals, petty criminals, dissenters of all kinds. Coloured patches were worn: green for criminal, black for anti-social, pink for homosexuals, red for politicals, blue for stateless or potential escapees from the Third Reich, and violet for religious fundamentalists. Bergen-Belsen, according to Joseph Kramer, was overwhelmed, but starvation, typhus and SS brutality caused the scenes that were photographed and shown round the world. Most of the concentration camps were in the centre of a circle of cheap labour industries. At the end of 1944, 13 parent camps in Germany had 500 sub-camps.

The second category of extermination or death camps were limited to reception areas, often railways, temporary accommodation, gas chambers and crematoria, used exclusively for the Holocaust and genocide. Killing people by gas was perfected in December 1941 after the

Above left: A concentration camp victim is buried in a mass grave.
Right: The scene at one concentration camp.

use of zyklon B gas at Chelmno (Kulmhof) near Lodz west of Warsaw. It is estimated that 320,000 Jews were killed there 1941–45. The three purpose-built death camps in Poland were constructed in 1942. Sobibor killed over 300,000 Jews, Belzec 600,000 and Treblinka over 700,000.

Rudolf Höss, Commandant of Auschwitz, told the Nuremberg Tribunal that in the period 1 May 1940 to 1 December 1943 he estimated that 2,500,000 were exterminated and a further 500,000 died from disease and starvation. In that last month the Red Army were getting close, so the SS dynamited the main installation and drove 60,000 prisoners on a march of death. The Judgement of Nuremberg 1946, details Höss's testimony of the screening and the actual killing. Adolf Eichmann, who was put in charge of 'The Final Solution' by his Führer, estimated that his policies killed six million Jews, four million of them in the extermination camps. Poles accounted for three million, Russians for two million, and Germans one million.

From January 1945 when 750,000 concentration camp prisoners were driven from the eastern camps into western Germany, at least 250,000 of them died on the way.

CHAPTER 23

The Nazi Nuclear Option

The Nazis had been the leaders in the race for technology that could produce V weapons: V for Victory or Vengeance. They produced the world's first operational jet fighters (ME 262s), ballistic missiles, electro high-speed submarines, flying bombs, infra-red gun sights, rocket planes and dangerous new chemical weapons such as Sarin and Tabun. Hitler was devoted to the development of new battlefield weapons.

In 1920 Hitler had a great respect for Professor Philipp Lenard of Heidelberg University, a Nobel Prize laureate in physics. Lenard joined the Nazi Party in its early days and told Hitler that: 'science, like every other human product, is racial and conditioned by blood'. Lenard attacked Einstein and the theory of relativity and persuaded Hitler that: 'the Jew conspicuously lacks understanding for the truth ... being in this respect in contrast to the Aryan research scientist with his careful and serious will to truth ... Jewish physics is thus a phantom and a phenomenon of degeneration of fundamental German physics.' Professor Wilhelm Müller of Aachen Technical College and Professor Ludwig Bierback of Berlin University were unanimous in their agreement: modern physics and this included nuclear physics, was in reality a bid for 'Jewish world rule'. So to Hitler nuclear physics were Jewish physics. Thus Alfred Rosenberg, later Minister of Education, took his cue from his master and failed to support nuclear research. Nevertheless work and research did continue and Dr Hans Süss began searching in 1940 for a nuclear 'moderator' to control an atomic reactor, and the physical characteristics of heavy water, which has the chemical formula of D_2O rather than the usual H_2O. German War Office planners estimated that they needed five *tons* of heavy water to control chain reaction in a uranium pile. None was available in

Copenhagen Physics Conference, June 1936. First row (left to right): Pauli, Jordan, Heisenberg, Born, Meitner, Stern, Franck; second row: Weizsäcker and Hund behind Hiesenberg, Otto Frisch (second from right); third row: Kopfermann, Euler, Fano; fourth and fifth rows, second from left: Peierls and Weisskopf; standing along wall: Bohr and Rosenfeld.

Germany but Norsk Hydro plant at Vemork in Norway was producing ten kilograms of heavy water per month. In January 1940 a representative of the great I. G. Farben, which held shares in Norsk Hydro, visited the plant and offered to buy their stock of 185 kilograms of heavy water and would start purchasing 100 kilograms per month. The sensible Norwegians, however, sold this stock to a French group which included the renowned physicist, Frédéric Joliot-Curie. They were experimenting with an atomic pile and took delivery in February. After that blow a batch of German scientists descended on the plant during 1940, urging that output should be increased to an annual output of 1,364 kilograms. Then Lt Commander Eric Welsh, head of the Norwegian section of British Intelligence, the SOE and RAF sprang into action for Operations Swallow, Grouse, Freshman and Gunnerside to destroy Norsk Hydro. Many brave Norwegians, such as Knut Haugland, Helberg, Kjelstrup, Ronneberg and finally, Knut Haukelid, eventually completely sabotaged the heavy water project.

Goebbels' diary of 21 March 1942 noted: 'Research into the realm of atomic destruction has now proceeded to the point where results may possibly be used in the present war. It is essential that we should keep ahead of everybody.'

General Friedrich Fromm, Chief of Army Armaments, suggested to Albert Speer in April that the only chance of Germany winning the war lay in developing a weapon with totally *new* effects. So Speer chaired a meeting at Harnack House, the Berlin centre of the Kaiser Wilhelm Gesellschaft, with General Fromm, Admiral Witzell, Field Marshal Milch and various scientists including Nobel Prize-winners Otto Hahn and Werner Heisenberg. The latter was bitter about the lack of support for nuclear research in Germany. He also tabled a report on 'atom smashing', and the development of the cyclotron, a particle accelerator or atom-smashing machine. Heisenberg stated that Germany had found the scientific solution to nuclear fission and that theoretically building an atom bomb was possible given time, money and more scientific staff.

In the same way that secret personal armies were developed in the Third Reich, such as Goering's huge land-based parachute army, unbeknownst to others, so it was with scientific research. All three branches of the armed forces, also the SS, even the postal service, had separate research facilities. Thus progress on the development of nuclear fission was negligible. Speer in 1942 had immense power as Armaments Minister. He could have, perhaps, centralised all the key research facilities and asked Hitler for funds to continue and develop a nuclear missile.

T-Force, the 'thieving magpies', had a rather important role in tracking down and politely capturing scientists involved in nuclear research. They included Professor Wilhelm Groth, Dr Paul Harteck, an associate who had used an ultra-centrifuge at Celle on the separation of uranium 235 and 238 (FO 1032/205) and Professor Otto Hahn, head of physics at the Hannover Technische Hochschule, who was perhaps the most famous, with his discovery of fission or uranium and thorium in medium-heavy nuclei.

Operation Alsos was the American secret group searching for evidence of the Nazis' atomic research programme. In October 1945, the movements of ten nuclear scientists (three in particular) were vital in case they fell into the hands of the Soviets: Heisenberg, Gerlach, Diebner, Hahn, von Laue, von Weizsäcker, Wirtz, Bagge, Korshing and Harteck were 'persuaded' to live on parole in East Anglia, although British authorities initially wanted them to go to Bonn University *en masse*.

T-Force discovered the Mega Research Association, anti-military, anti-industrial, pure researchers; an alliance of physicists devoted to pure atomic and nuclear research who knew 'everybody' in Germany connected with nuclear research.

Above left: Farm Hall, where ten German physicists were detained in 1945.
Above right: Max von Laue resisted the Nazis while remaining in Germany during the war.
Below left: Carl Friedrich von Weizsäcker, Heisenberg's younger colleague in the Nazi bomb project.
Below right: Paul Harteck solicited funding for atomic-bomb research from Army ordnance in 1939.

Alsos picked up several leads: Professor Fleischmann, a leading physicist working at Strasbourg University, and in November 1944 a group of scientists hidden in a wing of Strasbourg Hospital masquerading as medical officers. Professor Samuel Goudsmit, the scientific head of Alsos, later concluded that: 'their pile work was still in a very early state, and had been unable to produce a chain reaction'. In February 1945 the Auer factory at Oranienburg, north of Berlin, was manufacturing uranium metals and thorium ore for atomic energy.

When Carl Friedrich von Weizsäcker's obituary was published in the *Daily Telegraph* it mentioned that he and fellow scientists were briefly interned near Cambridge where their conversations were *secretly* recorded. In one Weisensäcker, on hearing that the USA had dropped atom bombs on Hiroshima and Nagasaki, remarked: 'If they were able to finish it by summer '45 then with a bit of luck we could have been ready in winter '44–45.' At the end of the war the scientists had been interned at Farm Hall, Godmanchester after Cambridge. The taped transcripts revealed that Weizsäcker had taken the lead in arguing for an agreement among the group that they would claim they had *never* wanted to develop a German bomb. This story, which they knew to be untrue, was known within their circle as *die lesart* (the version).

After Dresden was battered and burned between 13 and 15 February 1945 by the RAF and USAAF, Hitler was beside himself with fury and spoke to Dr Giesing in the Berlin Chancellery: 'I'm going to start using my Victory weapon [*siegwaffe*] and then the war will come to a glorious end. Some time ago we solved the problem of nuclear fission and we have developed it so far that we can exploit the energy for armaments purposes [*rüstungszwecke*]. They won't even know what hit them! It's the weapon of the future. With it Germany's future is assured.'

Albert Speer had visited the Krupp armaments works and was shown parts of Germany's first cyclotron. And at Heidelberg in the summer of 1944 he was shown 'our first cyclotron splitting an atomic nucleus' by Professor Walter Bothe. Professor Walther Gerlach was the Reich chief of nuclear research; Professors Werner Heisenberg and Carl Friedrich von Weizsäcker were developing an experimental atomic pile at Haigerloch. Hitler's boast was valid. In his memoirs Speer wrote that he was convinced that Hitler would have used the atomic bomb on London and Moscow.

The seminal book on this subject is John Cornwell's *Hitler's Scientists*. He recounts the agonised conversation in the Farm Hall 'camp' where

Werner Heisenberg, Otto Hahn, Paul Hartech, Max von Laue, Erich Bagge, Kurt Diebner, Walter Gerlach, Karl Wirtz and, of course, von Weizsäcker were benevolently imprisoned. He describes their secret (so they thought) conversations and their agreement to *lesart*. The conspirators drew up a detailed memorandum but carefully omitted: (1) Paul Harteck's approach to their key minister, Bernhard Rust for funding to push forward uranium research with the aim of creating weapons of mass destruction; (2) Weizsäcker's 1940 report on the neptunium path to a bomb; (3) Fritz Houterman's speculations about plutonium; and (4) no mention was made of the theoretical research on graphite as a moderator.

Perhaps the Allies were fortunate after all.

CHAPTER 24

Operation Unthinkable

Winston Churchill was deeply angry and also extremely gloomy about the fate of Poland and evidence of Soviet barbarism in the territories which they had 'liberated'. On 13 May 1943, he cabled President Truman in Washington:

Our armed power on the continent is in rapid decline. Meanwhile what is to happen about Russia[?] I have always worked for friendship with Russia but, like you, I feel deep anxiety because of their misinterpretation of the Yalta decisions, their attitude towards Poland, their overwhelming influence in the Balkans excepting Greece, the difficulties they make about Vienna ... and above all their power to maintain very large armies in the field for a long time. What will be the position in a year or two, when the British and American armies have melted ... and when Russia may choose to keep two or three hundred [divisions] on active service? An iron curtain is drawn down upon their front ... Surely it is vital now to come to an understanding with Russia, or see where we are with her before we weaken our armies mortally, or retire to the zones of occupation. I should be most grateful for your opinion or advice ... To sum up, this issue of a settlement with Russia before our strength has gone seems to me to dwarf all others.

Truman answered: 'From the present point of view, it is impossible to make a conjecture as to what the Soviets may do when Germany is under the small forces of occupation and the great part of such armies as we can maintain are fighting in the Orient against Japan.' The President agreed with Churchill that a tripartite meeting with Stalin had become urgently necessary.

On 24 May Churchill instructed the chiefs of staff to consider the military possibilities of pushing the mighty Red Army back eastwards *before* the Anglo-American armies were demobilised: 'impose upon Russia the will of the United States and British Empire to secure a square deal for Poland'. The target date for Operation Unthinkable— the launching of an assault would be—1 July 1945. It was a marvellous pipe-dream story—but true—and recounted with Max Hastings' usual brio in his book *Finest Years*.

Joseph Stalin, the Russian dictator.

CHAPTER 25

The U-Boat Warfare

Grand Admiral Doenitz's staff produced these figures:

1. September 1939 U-boat strength 57.
2. During the course of the war a further 1,113 U-boats were commissioned (ready for action). Of these 1,099 were built in German yards, 4 in foreign yards and 10 seized from the enemy
3. Of the grand total of 1,170 U-boats 836 became operational
4. Losses were 630 at sea, 123 in port, total 758
5. At the end of the war 215 U-boats were either sunk or blown up by their crews. Flensburg 53, Lübeck 33, Kiel 26, Bremen 50, Hamburg 62
6. At the end of the war 153 U-boats were handed over to the Allies, mainly the British
7. 148 Allied warships were sunk and 45 more damaged during the war by the German U-boat fleet, and 2,759 merchant ships with 14,119,413 tonnage sunk
8. The Todt organisation built huge bomb-proof shelters for U-boats in the French ports of Lorient, La Pallice, Brest, St Nazaire and Bordeaux. In August 1944 after the successful Allied landings all boats were sent to safer harbours along the Norwegian coast
9. During the last months of the war some 50,000 naval ratings were deployed in Marine divisions around Hamburg and on the Eastern Front. Their use of large sea mines destroyed a number of Allied AFVs, and the marines caused 53rd Welsh and 15th Scottish Divisions a great deal of trouble
0. In early 1945 Doenitz deployed all available merchant ships under Rear Admiral Engelhardt to rescue more than 2 million German refugees from West and East Prussia and Pomerania

Alpenfestung: Goebbels' Hoax

In the autumn of 1944 stories began to circulate in Switzerland that the Nazis had set up a vast military complex in the mountains of southern Germany and Austria. They probably derived from Dr Joseph Goebbels, that master of spin. Agents of the SD (SS Intelligence Department) forwarded this 'information' to Gauleiter Hofer of the Tyrol. In November, Hofer sent a report to Martin Bormann, the deputy Führer, to the effect that US experts had forecast unacceptably high casualty rates for the campaign by the Americans to overcome this final bastion. Moreover Hofer noted that 'East-West tension will become visible if the war drags on too long'. This situation could be exploited by the Nazis who should open negotiations with the West at the expense of the Soviet Union. Hofer urged that a defence redoubt *festung* be set up in mountainous areas, such as his own Gau (shire) in the Tyrol. In fact, Hofer had strengthened areas already, which he modestly called 'The Hofer Line'. He recommended that Allied POW camps be moved there to deter Allied air interdiction. The garrison would need élite military units backed by 30,000 men of the Standschutzen (local defence unit's equivalent to the Volkssturm). General Ritter von Hengl was ordered by Berlin to command the redoubt garrison, but his mountain troops' corps, between 1–5 April 1945, consisted of only 30,000 men. He produced a thoroughly damning report and dismissed the Hofer plan as a slogan: 'The Alpine Redoubt existed merely on paper.'

Goebbels wrote about Hofer's recommendations as though they were operational: food stocks were already stockpiled; underground factories were in full production; the élite units garrisoning the *Alpenfestung* were in action; and German scientists were working hard to produce another super vengeance weapon, which would ensure a German victory!

244

On 11 March 1945 SHAEF produced this intelligence summary: 'Accumulated information and photographic evidence made possible a more definite estimate of the progress of plans for the "Last Ditch Stand". German defence policy is to safeguard the Alpine Zone. Defences continue to be constructed in depth in the south through the Black Forest to Lake Constance and from the Hungarian frontier to the west of Graz ... In Italy defence lines are built up in the foothills of the Italian Alps. The results of air reconnaissance show at least 20 sites of recent underground activity as well as numerous natural caves mainly in the region Golling, Feldkirch, Kufstein and Berchtesgaden [Hitler's personal chalet-retreat atop a mountain] ... accommodation for stores and personnel. The existence of several underground factories has also been confirmed ... As regards actual numbers of troops, stores and weapons ... evidence indicates considerable numbers of SS and specially chosen units are engaged on some type of defence activity at the most vital strategic points ... The most important ministries are established within the Redoubt area ... while Hitler, Goering, Himmler and other notables are said to be in the process of withdrawing to the mountain stronghold.'

At SHAEF a large map was on display headed 'Unconfirmed Installations in Reported Redoubt Area' covering 20,000 square miles, the Alpine meeting point of southern Germany, northern Italy and western Austria with Hitler's Berghof near Berchtesgaden in their midst. Moreover symbols were printed on the base of the map indicating ammunition and fuel dumps, HQs and barracks, food depots, radio installations, factories, troop locations and a chemical warfare site.

Adolf Hitler received Hofer's November 1944 memorandum during April 1945 and ordered that the gauleiter's plans be put into immediate effect. At that late stage it was an impossible pipedream.

Nevertheless Eisenhower, Bradley and Lt General Walter Bedell Smith, in particular, felt strongly that: 'After the Ruhr was taken we were convinced there would be no surrender at all so long as Hitler lived. Our feeling then was that we should be forced to destroy the remnants of the German Army piece by piece, with the final possibility of a prolonged campaign in the rugged Alpine area of Western Austria and Southern Bavaria known as the National Redoubt.'

The SHAEF summary continued: 'This area is by the nature of the terrain practically impenetrable. The evidence suggests that considerable numbers of SS ... are being systematically withdrawn to Austria ... Here defended

American paratroops reached the Berghof, Hitler's retreat in the Bavarian Alps, in May 1945. This is Hitler's own residence, with an RAF bomb crater in the foreground.

The Berghof, April 1945. An American GI looks at Hitler's home. The Nazis' 'last stand' in a non-existent Alpine redoubt.

both by nature and by the most efficient secret weapons yet invented the powers that have hitherto guided Germany will survive to reorganise her resurrection. Here armaments will be manufactured in bomb-proof factories, food and equipment will be stored in vast underground caverns and a specially selected corps of young men will be trained in guerilla warfare [Werewolves] so that a whole underground army can be fitted and directed to liberate Germany from the occupying forces.'

General Eisenhower's report 'D-Day to VE Day' published in 1946 devotes several pages to the Redoubt. There is no doubt that Eisenhower concluded that the National Redoubt was now of greater significance than Berlin: 'Military factors when the enemy was on the brink of final defeat were more important in my eyes than the political considerations involved in an Allied capture of the capital since this no longer represented a military objective of major importance.' By taking a unilateral decision (but backed by General Marshal in Washington) his new plans involved his right wing of armies driving south-east to meet the Russians in the Danube valley, west of Vienna, and *seizing the Redoubt before the Nazis could organise it for defence.*

Churchill was furious. Montgomery was furious. They had always wanted the Allies to get to Berlin come what may. On 28 March Eisenhower sent his plan direct to Marshal Stalin, who was undoubtedly delighted. Ike wrote: 'The Prime Minister was greatly disappointed and disturbed because my plan did not first throw Montgomery forward with all the strength I could give him *from American forces* in a desperate attempt to capture Berlin before the Russians.'

Alpenfestung was of course a brilliant Goebbels hoax! What actually happened was that by mid-April most of the key ministries from Berlin had been moved to the Berchtesgaden area, and had taken their documents and administrators with them. Most of the OKW staff (Supreme Command) had also been transferred to the Redoubt area. However, on 20 April, Hitler decided to stay in Berlin—and die there—defending the city to the last. SHAEF had probably noted the movement of staff to the area—and assumed that the Wagnerian Götterdammerung would follow. A new German Army, the 11th, under General Walter Wenck, had five modest divisions which, in theory, guarded the Redoubt as part of their command area. On 18 April Wenck's 10,000 men were trapped by the US 1st Army around Dessau near the Harz Mountains. That was the end of *Alpenfestung.*

Rogues' Gallery

These mini-biographies are short sketches of the main characters who marched on and off the stage of the Third Reich and who are also mentioned in this book. In particular, focus is given on how they met their end. Where a character is prominently illustrated in the text, no head-shot is provided. Appropriate illustrations are not available for every person mentioned.

Amann: Max Amann (1891-1957)

Amann was an official with the honorary rank of SS-Obergruppenführer. He was Hitler's sergeant during the First World War and became his literary agent, publisher—he published Mein Kampf—financial adviser and almost, but not quite, a friend. Arrested after the War, Amann was deemed a Hauptschuldiger ('main guilty one') and sentenced, in 1948, to ten years in a labour camp, but was released in 1953. Stripped of his property, pension rights and practically all of his fortune, he died in poverty on 30 March 1957.

Axmann: Artur Axmann (1913-1996)

Axmann succeeded Baldur von Schirach as Reich Youth Leader (Reichsjugendführer) of the Nazi Party in 1940. In 1941, he was severely wounded on the Eastern Front, losing an arm. During the last weeks of the War his units consisted mostly of children and adolescents. In May 1949, a Nuremberg de-Nazification court classified him as a 'major offender', sentencing him to prison for three years and three months. Axmann became a prosperous businessman after the War.

Bechstein: Helene Bechstein (1876-1951)

Helene, with her husband Edwin (d. 1934), of the famous piano manufacturing firm, was a close friend of Hitler's. She bestowed many gifts on him including his first luxury car, a red Mercedes costing 26,000 marks, and frequently invited him to Berchtesgaden, her family's villa. It was always Helene expectation that Hitler would marry her daughter, Lotte.

Beck: Ludwig August Theodor Beck (1880-1944)

A German general and Chief of Staff between 1935-38, Beck became increasingly disillusioned with the Nazi Party, standing in opposition to the increasing authoritarianism of the regime and Hitler's aggressive foreign policy; he resigned from his post in August 1938. In 1943, he planned two abortive attempts to kill Hitler by means of a bomb. In 1944, he was one of the driving forces behind the 20 July assassination plot. It was proposed that Beck would become the head of the provisional government that would assume power in Germany after Hitler had been eliminated. The plot failed, and by the next morning Beck was in the custody of General Friedrich Fromm. He offered to commit suicide and shot himself, but in severe distress, he succeeded only in severely wounding himself; a sergeant was brought in to administer the coup de grâce.

Blomberg: Werner Eduard Fritz von Blomberg (1878-1946)

Blomberg was a German Field Marshal, Minister of War and Commander-in-Chief of the Armed Forces until January 1938. He advised Hitler to allow Germany more time to re-arm before pursuing a high-risk strategy of localized wars likely to trigger a much larger conflict. Goering and Himmler tried to discredit Blomberg by accusing him of being a homosexual; he and his wife were subsequently exiled for a year to the isle of Capri. Having spent the War in obscurity, Blomberg was captured by the Allies in 1945 and gave evidence at the Nuremberg Trials. In March 1946, while at Nuremberg, he died of cancer.

Bormann: Martin Ludwig Bormann (1900-1945)

In May 1941, Hess's flight to Britain cleared the way for Bormann to become head of the Party Chancellery. Bormann was a master of intricate political infighting; as Hitler's private secretary, his proximity to the Führer made him the enemy of Goebbels, Goering, Himmler, Rosenberg, Ley, Speer and a plethora of other high-ranking officers and officials, both public and private. Bormann took charge of all of Hitler's paperwork, appointments and personal finances. Hitler came to have complete trust in Bormann, giving the latter tremendous influence. He died attempting to escape from Berlin in May 1945.

Brandmayer: Balthaser Brandmayer (1892-1960)

Balthaser was a war comrade of Hitler's in the Bavarian Reserve Infantry Regiment 16. After the War he worked as a bricklayer in Bruckmühl. In 1932, together with the publisher Heinz Bayer, Brandmayer wrote Two Messengers, a book on the experiences shared with Hitler during the War. In the same year he joined the party and in 1934, as Hitler's former comrade, he was employed by the Deutsche Reichsbahn. In 1937 Hitler gave him 5,000 Reichsmarks 'to clarify his economic circumstances'. After the War he returned to bricklaying.

Brandt: Karl Brandt (1904-1948)

Brandt was SS-Gruppenführer in the Allgemeine-SS and SS-Brigadeführer in the Waffen-SS. Among other positions, he headed the administration of the euthanasia programme from 1939 and was selected as Hitler's personal physician in August 1934. Along with his deputy Werner Heyde and others, Brandt was involved in criminal human experimentation. He was convicted of crimes against humanity and hanged on 2 June 1948.

Brauchitsch: Heinrich Alfred Walther von Brauchitsch (1881-1948)

Brauchitsch was promoted to Field Marshal in 1940 and was a prominent architect of Hitler's 'blitzkrieg' war, making modifications to the original plan to overrun France. In 1941, the army's failure to take Moscow earned him Hitler's enmity, and after suffering a serious heart attack, he was relieved of his command on 10 December 1941. At the end of the War, Brauchitsch was arrested and charged with war crimes, but he died in Hamburg in 1948 before he could be prosecuted.

Braun: Eva Braun (1912-1945)

Eva Braun first met Hitler in 1929 while she was assistant to the beer-loving Heinrich Hoffmann, the Third Reich's official photographer. Eva attended the Nuremberg Rally in 1936, and Hitler's Berghof villa became her gilded cage. The staff referred to her as 'EB', addressed her as 'Madame' and kissed her hand. She referred to Hitler as 'Chief' and he called her 'Patscherl'. Over the years they exchanged hundreds of letters and Hitler paid her monthly wages to the Hoffmann studios until the end of their lives. She committed suicide with Hitler on 30 April 1945 in his underground bunker in the Reich Chancellery gardens in Berlin.

Braun: Wernher Magnus Maximilian, Freiherr von Braun (1912-1977)

Braun was one of the leading figures in the development of rocket technology. In his twenties and early thirties he was the central figure in Germany's rocket development programme, responsible for the V-2 combat rocket. After the War, he and some of his rocket team were taken to the United States as part of the secret Operation Paperclip. Braun was the chief architect of the Saturn V launch vehicle, the superbooster that propelled the Apollo spacecraft to the moon.

Brueckner: Wilhelm Brueckner (1884-1954)

On 9 November 1923, Brueckner took part in the Beer Hall Putsch in Munich and was sentenced to a year and a half in prison. In 1930 he became Adolf Hitler's adjutant and bodyguard, later rising to Chief Adjutant, one of Hitler's closest confidants next to Goebbels and Dietrich. On 18 October 1940, he was suddenly relieved of his position for having an argument with Hitler's house manager, Arthur Kannenberg; an event probably manipulated by Bormann. Julius Schaub succeeded Brueckner, who joined the Wehrmacht, becoming a colonel by the end of the War.

Bruckmann: Elsa Bruckmann (1865-1946)

Born as Princess Cantacuzene of Romania, Elsa was the wife of publisher Hugo Bruckmann. She managed the 'Salon Bruckmann' and made it her mission to introduce Adolf Hitler to leading industrialists.

Buch: Walter Buch (1883-1949)

Buch was an early member of the NSDAP. Following the abortive Beer Hall Putsch, Buch maintained contact between Hitler, imprisoned in Landsberg, and the illegal party leadership in Austria. He was instrumental in Roehm's downfall, and as a jurist he was also responsible for the 'legalisation' of the anti-Semitic vandalism carried out by party members during the so-called Kristallnacht (9 November 1938). After the War, Buch was seized and sentenced to five years in a labour camp. In July 1949, in the course of yet another wave of de-Nazification, he was classified as a 'Hauptschuldiger' ('main guilty one'), meaning that he was considered to be an especially culpable war criminal. On 12 November, he ended his own life by slitting his wrists and throwing himself into the Ammersee.

Buechner: Bruno Buechner (1871-1943)

Buechner was a famous bicycle road racer and pioneer pilot in German Africa. With his wife Elisabeth he bought the Moritz Pension in Obersalzburg which he renamed Platterdorf Hotel. The Buechners were friends of Hitler, and Elisabeth, a towering Brünhilde type, gave the Hitler a rhinoceros-hide dog whip.

Buehler: Joseph Buehler (1904-1948)

Buehler joined the NSDAP in 1922 and was one of the members of the attempted putsch in Munich on 9 November 1923. He was appointed Minister of Justice for Bavaria in 1933 and was secretary and deputy governor to the Nazi-controlled General Government in Kraków. Buehler attended the Wannsee Conference on 20 January 1942 as the representative from the Governor General's office. After the War he was tried before the Supreme National Tribunal of Poland for crimes against humanity; he was condemned to death, and executed in Kraków.

Burgdorf: Wilhelm Burgdorf (1895-1945)

Burgdorf was a Wehrmacht general. He was promoted to Chief of the Army Personnel Office and Chief Adjutant to Hitler in October 1944. At that time, he was further promoted in rank to Lieutenant General. On 14 October 1944, Burgdorf arrived at the Rommel home. He had been instructed to offer Rommel a choice—take poison, receive a state funeral, and obtain immunity for his family and staff, or face a trial for treason. Rommel drove away with Burgdorf and Maisel; Rommel's family received a telephone call 10 minutes later saying that he had died. On 29 April 1945, Burgdorf, Krebs, Joseph Goebbels, and Martin Bormann witnessed and signed Hitler's last will and testament. On 2 May, following the earlier suicides of Hitler and Goebbels, Burgdorf and his colleague, Chief of Staff Hans Krebs, also committed suicide by gunshot to the head.

Canaris: Wilhelm Franz Canaris (1887-1945)

Canaris joined the German Imperial Navy in 1905 and served during the First World War. In 1935, Canaris was made head of the Abwehr, Germany's official military intelligence agency. Later that year, he was promoted to Rear Admiral. In 1938, with the support of MI6, Canaris devised a plan to assassinate Hitler, precipitating the dissolution of the entire Nazi Party before the invasion of Czechoslovakia, but nothing came of this. The assassination of Heydrich in Prague, organised by MI6, was done in part to preserve Canaris in his important position. Evidence mounted that he was playing a double game, and at the insistence of Himmler, who had suspected him for a long time, Hitler dismissed Canaris in February 1944, replacing him with Schellenberg. Canaris was put under house arrest, preventing him from taking any direct part in the 20 July plot. Himmler kept Canaris alive for some time because he planned to use him secretly as a future contact with the British. When Himmler's plan failed to materialise, he received Hitler's approval to send Canaris to his death. He was humiliated before witnesses and then led to the gallows barefoot and naked on 9 April 1945.

Christian: Gerda Christian (1913-1997)

Gerda Christian was one of Hitler's secretaries. She had been engaged to Hitler's driver Erich Kempka, but this fell apart and she later married Luftwaffe officer Eckhard Christian in 1943. In April 1945, after his promotion to the Luftwaffe Command Staff, Eckhard Christian was stationed in Berlin at the Führerbunker HQ. He left the bunker complex on 22 April 1945 to become Chief of the Liaison Staff of the Luftwaffe to OKW Command Staff North. Gerda and Traudl Junge both volunteered to remain with Hitler in the Führerbunker. After Hitler's death, Gerda tried to escape Berlin, but she was captured by the Russians the following day. She was a committed Hitler loyalist, and divorced Eckhard Christian in 1946 because he did not remain with her in the Führerbunker until after Hitler's death. Gerda moved to Düsseldorf, where she worked at a hotel and died at the age of 83 in 1997.

Ciano: Galeazzo Ciano (1903-1944)

Count Ciano held diplomatic posts in South America before marrying Edda Mussolini in 1930. In 1936, he was appointed by Mussolini as Minister of Foreign Affairs. Ciano was a supporter of the German alliance, but objected to the way that Hitler ordered the invasion of Poland without consulting Italy. Mussolini followed Ciano's advice to keep out of the Second World War until the fall of France in May 1940. In 1942 Ciano became increasingly dissatisfied with Mussolini and in February 1943, after a series of heated arguments, he resigned as Foreign Minister. Ciano left Rome after Mussolini was overthrown, but he was captured by the Germans. On 11 January 1944, on Mussolini's order, Ciano was given a mock trial and executed by a shot to the head while tied to a chair.

Darré: Richard Walther Oscar Darré (1895-1953)

In 1933, Darré became Reich Minister of Food and Agriculture, serving from June 1933 to May 1942. He developed a plan for Rasse und Raum (Race and Space) which provided the ideological background for the Nazi expansionist policy, called Drang nach Osten and Lebensraum (Drive to the East and Living space). Darré strongly influenced Himmler in his goal to create a German racial aristocracy based on selective breeding. He was forced to resign in 1942. At Nuremberg he was sentenced to seven years, but was released in 1950 and died of cancer in 1953.

Dietrich: Joseph 'Sepp' Dietrich (1892-1966)

Prior to 1929, Dietrich was Adolf Hitler's chauffeur and bodyguard but received rapid promotion after his participation in the murder of Hitler's political opponents during the 'Night of the Long Knives'. Hitler promoted him within the Wehrmacht and he fought in France, Greece and Yugoslavia before taking command of the I.SS-Panzerkorps, attached to Army Group Centre on the Eastern Front. In 1943, Dietrich was sent to Italy to recover Benito Mussolini's mistress Clara Petacci. He commanded the 6.SS-Panzer-Armee in the Battle of the Bulge in 1944 and received numerous German military medals, but also became notorious for his mistreatment of prisoners of war. He was sentenced to life imprisonment, but this was later reduced to twenty-five years. He was eventually released in 1958. Dietrich died of a heart attack in 1966.

Dodd: Martha Eccles Dodd (1908-1990)

Martha was the vivacious young daughter of US Ambassador Professor William E. Dodd. She was very attracted to Hitler and was invited to have tea with him at the Kaiserhof Hotel on a number of occasions. She once declared that she was in love with him and wanted to organise him a tour of the United States. This did not meet with the approval of Goering, who spread the rumour that Martha was a Soviet agent; Hitler refused to see her again and banned her from all future diplomatic receptions. Soon after, reports circulated that she had attempted suicide by slashing her wrists. In 1938 she married American millionaire investment broker, Alfred Kaufman Stern, and became active in left-wing politics.

Doenitz: Karl Doenitz (1891-1980)

At the start of the Second World War, Doenitz was the senior submarine officer in the German Navy. In January 1943, he replaced Grand Admiral Erich Raeder as Commander-in-Chief of the German Navy. On 30 April 1945, after the death of Adolf Hitler and in accordance with Hitler's last will and testament, Doenitz was named Hitler's successor as Staatsoberhaupt (Head of State), with the title of Reichspräsident (President) and Supreme Commander of the Armed Forces. On 7 May 1945, he ordered Alfred Jodl to sign an official German surrender in Rheims, France. Doenitz remained as head of the temporary Flensburg Government until it was dissolved by the Allied powers on 23 May 1945. Doenitz was imprisoned for ten years in Spandau and released October 1956.

Drexler: Anton Drexler (1884-1942)

Drexler was instrumental in the formation of the anti-communist German Workers' Party. The German Workers' Party was the precedent for the Nazi Party; Drexler served as mentor to Hitler during his early days in politics. Drexler changed the name of the party to the National Socialist German Workers' Party early in 1920. By 1921, Hitler was rapidly becoming the undisputed leader of the party and Drexler was thereafter reduced to the purely symbolic position of honorary president; he left the party in 1923. He had no part in the NSDAP's re-founding in 1925, and he rejoined the party only after Hitler had come to power in 1933. He received the party's Blood Order in 1934 and was still occasionally used as a propaganda tool until about 1937, but was largely forgotten by the time of his death.

Eckhart: Dietrich Eckhart (1868-1923)

Dietrich Eckhart, a nationalist poet, founded the Deutsche Arbeiterpartei with Gottfried Feder and Anton Drexler, which later became the NSDAP. Eckhart met Adolf Hitler when Hitler gave a speech before party members in 1919. He introduced Hitler to Erich Ludendorff, who was later imprisoned with Hitler in Landsberg, and Alfred Rosenberg. On 9 November 1923, Eckhart participated in the failed Beer Hall Putsch; he was arrested and placed in Landsberg Prison along with Hitler and other party officials, but was released and died of a heart attack in Berchtesgaden on 26 December 1923.

Eichmann: Adolf Eichmann (1900-1962)

Eichmann was an SS-Obersturmbannführer and one of the major organisers of the extermination camps in German-occupied Eastern Europe. After the War, he fled to Argentina and lived under a false identity. He was captured there by Mossad operatives and taken to Israel to face trial, where he was found guilty and executed by hanging in 1962.

Elser: (1903-1945)

Elser was an opponent of Nazism. He planned and carried out an assassination attempt on Hitler on 8 November 1939 in Munich at Hitler's annual speech on the anniversary of the failed Beer Hall Putsch. Hitler left the beer hall at about 13 minutes before Elser's bomb exploded as planned at 21:20. Elser was arrested by chance at 20:45, about 35 minutes before the bomb exploded, by the customs border police in Konstanz when he tried to cross the border into Switzerland. After his confession to the crime in Munich, Elser was taken to the Berlin headquarters of the Gestapo where he was severely tortured. He was imprisoned in Sachsenhausen and Dachau concentration camps, and just three weeks before Hitler's own suicide, the Führer ordered Elser to be executed.

Epp: Franz Ritter von Epp (1868-1946)

Epp served during the First World War and subsequently formed the Freikorps Epp, a right-wing paramilitary formation mostly made up of war veterans, of which future leader of the SA, Ernst Roehm, was a member. Epp became a member of the party and then of the Reichstag in 1928, holding this position until 1945. He served as the NSDAP's head of its Military-Political Office from 1928 to 1945, and later as leader of the German Colonial Society, an organisation devoted to regaining Germany's lost colonies. At the end of the War, he was imprisoned by the Americans and died in a prison camp in 1946.

Esser: Hermann Esser (1900-1981)

Esser entered the Nazi Party with Hitler in 1920 and became the editor of the Nazi paper Völkischer Beobachter and a Nazi member of the Reichstag. In the early days of the party, he was Hitler's de facto deputy. Esser was a renowned pervert; after a scandal whereby he sexually assaulted the underage daughter of a businessman, he was suspended from the party. Even Hitler said of him: 'I know Esser is a scoundrel, but I shall hold on to him as long as he is useful to me.' From 1939 to the end of the War he served as the Under-Secretary for Tourism in the Reich Propaganda Ministry. He was imprisoned twice and died in 1981.

Feder: Gottfried Feder (1883-1941)

Feder was an economist, an important early member of the Nazi Party, and the party's economic theoretician. Initially, it was his lecture in 1919 that drew Hitler into the party. Hitler eventually decided to move away from Feder's economic views; when he became Chancellor in 1933, he appointed Feder as Under-Secretary at the Ministry of Economics. After the 'Night of the Long Knives', Feder began to withdraw from the government, finally becoming a professor at the Technische Hochschule in Berlin in 1936, where he stayed until his death in 1941.

Freiser: Roland Freiser (1893-1945)

Freiser joined the Nazi Party in 1925. He rose to become Reich Minister of Justice 1934-42 and was at Wannsee Conference. In 1942 he became President of the People's Court; the number of death sentences rose sharply under his stewardship and he was known for humiliating defendants and shouting at them. He was killed during an American bombing raid in February 1945.

Fritsch: Werner Thomas Ludwig Freiherr von Fritsch (1880-1939)

Fritsch was a prominent Wehrmacht officer and a member of the German High Command. Himmler and Goering accused him of being homosexual, but Fritsch had never been a womaniser and had preferred to concentrate on his army career. He was forced to resign on 4 February 1938. It soon became known that the charges were false, and Fritsch was acquitted on 18 March, but the damage to his name had been done. He was the second German general to be killed during the Second World War—by a Polish bullet on 10 September 1939.

Fromm: Friedrich Fromm (1888-1945)

Fromm was Commander-in-Chief of the Reserve Army, responsible for training recruits and replacing personnel in the Wehrmacht. Though he was aware that Stauffenberg was planning an assassination attempt against Hitler, he remained quiet. When the plot failed, Fromm immediately had the conspirators executed to cover up potential allegations that he himself was involved. These actions did not save him, and he was eventually executed by firing squad on 12 March 1945.

Gansser: Emil Gansser (1874-1941)

Gansser was a pharmacy and chemical engineer. He joined the party in 1921 and mediated between the NSDAP and Siemens. Through his party and Siemens connections, he acquired wealth which he salted away in Swiss Banks.

Goebbels: Joseph Goebbels (1897-1945)

Goebbels came into contact with the Nazi Party in 1923 during the French occupation of the Ruhr, and became a member in 1924. He rose to power in 1933 along with Hitler and was appointed Propaganda Minister. One of his first acts was the burning of books. He exerted totalitarian control over the media, arts and information in Germany. Goebbels remained with Hitler in Berlin to the end; after Hitler's suicide, Goebbels succeeded him as Chancellor, but along with his wife Magda, he killed their six young children and then committed suicide.

Goering: Hermann Goering (1893-1946)

Goering fought in the First World War, initially in the infantry and then as a fighter pilot, finally commanding the famous Richthofen Squadron. A member of the party from its early days, he was wounded in 1923 during the failed Beer Hall Putsch. He suffered from a lifelong addiction to morphine after being treated with the drug for his injuries. He founded the Gestapo in 1933 and was appointed Commander-in-Chief of the Luftwaffe in 1935. At Nuremberg he was sentenced to death by hanging, but committed suicide by taking cyanide the night before his execution.

Graf: Ulrich Graf (1878-1950)

Graf became Hitler's personal bodyguard from 1920 to 1923. He was present at the Beer Hall Putsch, where, with Rudolf Hess, he cleared Hitler's way to the platform. In a mêlée at a subsequent march, Graf shielded Hitler with his body, receiving several bullets and probably saving Hitler's life. He was elected to the Reichstag in 1936, became an Oberführer in the SS in 1937 and on 20 April 1943, Hitler's birthday, he became an SS Brigadeführer. Graf survived the War and died in 1950.

Grynszpan: Herschel Grynszpan (1921-1944?)

Herschel was a German-born Jewish refugee of Polish parents. In Paris on 7 November 1938 he shot and killed Ernst vom Rath, a junior German Embassy official, saying he was acting in the name of 12,000 persecuted Jews. Grynszpan made no attempt to resist or escape, and identified himself correctly to the French police. Grynszpan was seized by the Gestapo after the German invasion of France and brought to Germany where he was last heard of in prison in 1944. His eventual fate is not known, but may be guessed at. He was eventually declared dead in 1960.

Guderian: Heinz Guderian (1885-1954)

General Guderian was a pioneer in the development of armoured warfare, and was the leading proponent of tanks and mechanisation in the Wehrmacht. He became Inspector-General of Armoured Troops, rose to the rank of Colonel General (Generaloberst), and was Chief of the General Staff of the Heer in the last year of the War. Guderian surrendered to American troops on 10 May 1945 and remained in US custody as a prisoner of war until his release on 17 June 1948. Despite Russian and Polish government protests, he was not charged with any war crimes.

Guensche: Otto Guensche (1917-2003)

Guensche first met Hitler in 1936 and was his SS orderly officer from 1940 to 1941. He then had front-line combat service until January 1943 when he became a personal adjutant for Hitler. In 1944, Guensche fought on the Eastern Front and then in France until March, when he again was appointed as a personal adjutant for Hitler. He was present at the 20 July 1944 assassination attempt on Hitler at the Wolf's Lair in Rastenburg. Guensche was entrusted by Hitler to ensure that his body was cremated after his death on 30 April 1945. He stood guard outside the room as Hitler and Eva Braun committed suicide. He was captured by Russian troops and after various prisons and labour camps he was released from Bautzen Penitentiary in 1956.

Gutmann: Hugo Gutmann (1880-1971)

Gutmann was a German-Jewish officer and Hitler's superior officer during the First World War. In 1938, Guttman was arrested by the Gestapo but released due to sympathetic SS personnel, who knew his history. In 1939, he and his family escaped to Belgium and in 1940, he emigrated to the USA just prior to the invasion. Guttman eventually settled in the city of St Louis, Missouri, where he changed his name to Henry G. Grant. He died in 1971.

Haase: Werner Haase (1900-1945)

In 1935 Haase began serving as Hitler's deputy personal physician. In the last days of the fighting in Berlin in late April 1945, Haase, with Ernst Guenther Schenck, was working to save the lives of wounded Nazis in an emergency casualty station located in the large cellar of the Reich Chancellery. On 29 April, Hitler expressed doubts about the cyanide capsules he had received through Himmler's SS. To verify the capsules' potency, Haase was summoned to the Führerbunker to test one on Hitler's dog Blondi. A cyanide capsule was crushed in the mouth of the dog, which died as a result. Haase was made a Russian prisoner, but died in captivity in 1945.

Halder: Franz Halder (1884-1972)

General Halder was Chief of the Army General Staff from 1938 until September 1942, when he was dismissed after frequent disagreements with Adolf Hitler. During the summer of 1942, Halder had told Hitler that he was underestimating the number of Russian military units, while Hitler argued that the Russians were nearly broken. Hitler concluded that the General no longer possessed an aggressive war mentality. Following a speech in which Hitler announced his plan to find a replacement for Halder, Halder walked out stating 'I am leaving' and was retired into the 'Führer Reserve' on 24 September 1942. Hitler had him imprisoned in early 1945 and he was turned over to US troops on 4 May 1945, spending the next two years in an Allied prisoner of war camp.

Hanfstaengl: Ernst 'Putzi' Hanfstaengl (1887-1976)

Hanfstaengl had an American mother and was brought up and educated in the USA where, in 1920, he married Helene Elise Adelheid Niemeyer. He returned to Germany in 1922 and soon became one of Hitler's most intimate followers. For much of the 1920s, Hanfstaengl introduced Hitler to Munich's high society and helped polish his image. He also helped to finance the publication of Mein Kampf, and the party's official newspaper, the Völkischer Beobachter. Hanfstaengl wrote both Brownshirt and Hitler Youth marches, based on his memories of Harvard football songs; he later claimed that he devised the chant 'Sieg Heil'. Several disputes arose between Hanfstaengl and Goebbels which led to him being removed from Hitler's staff in 1933. He and Helene divorced in 1936. Hanfstaengl fell completely out of Hitler's favour after he was denounced by Unity Mitford, a close friend of both the Hanfstaengls and Hitler. He moved to England where he was imprisoned as an enemy alien after the outbreak of the Second World War. In 1942 he was turned over to the US and worked for President Roosevelt's 'S-Project', revealing information on approximately 400 Nazi leaders.

Hanisch: Reinhold Hanisch (1884-1937?)

In 1909 Hanisch came to Vienna, where he met Hitler. In 1910 he lived with Hitler in the Meldemannstrasse men's dormitory. They created an informal partnership: while Hitler painted postcards and pictures, mostly watercolours, Hanisch would sell them. The men shared equally the sums received, but they later fell out. Hanisch served in the First World War and in 1918 he married. He was imprisoned for theft in 1923 and divorced in 1928. After 1930, to earn a basic living, he produced watercolours, which he sold as alleged works of Hitler from their years in Vienna. His fraud was discovered and in 1932 he was sentenced to three days in jail. He continued to forge Hitler pictures until a major prison sentence in 1936. After Hitler's rise to power, Hanisch made money from numerous interviews with national and international newspapers. His memoir of Hitler posthumously appeared in 1939 in The New Republic. He appears to have died in prison in 1937, but it is unknown how he died.

Hanke: Karl Hanke (1903-1945)

Hanke joined the party in 1928 and the SA in 1929. In 1932 he was made Chief Gau Organisational Director and personal adjutant to Goebbels. Hanke was the first party official to establish contact with the young architect Albert Speer and they became close friends. Hanke rose within the party but came unstuck in 1938 due to a liaison with Magda Goebbels who intended to leave her husband for him. He then joined the army and SS, rising to Reichsführer-SS. In May 1945, he escaped to Prague, but was captured and executed by Czech partisans.

Hanussen: Erik Jan Hanussen (1889-1933)

Hanussen was an Austrian Jewish publicist and clairvoyant performer acclaimed in his lifetime as a hypnotist, mentalist, occultist, and astrologer; he taught Hitler a great deal about the importance of dramatic effect. Predicting the Reichstag fire was his most famous feat of clairvoyance. After a miscalculated use of inside information, he was assassinated on 25 March 1933, most likely by a group of SA men.

Haushofer: Karl Haushofer (1869-1946)

Following the First World War, Haushofer forged a friendship with Hess who became his scientific assistant. In 1919 he became Privatdozent for political geography at Munich University and professor in 1933. After the establishment of the Nazi regime, Haushofer remained friendly with Hess, who protected him and his wife from the racial laws. After the plot of 20 July 1944, Haushofer's son Albrecht was arrested and later shot. From 24 September 1945 onwards, Haushofer was informally interrogated to determine whether he should stand trial at Nuremberg. On 10 March 1946 he and his wife committed suicide.

Heiden: Erhard Heiden (1901-1933)

Heiden was an early member of the party and in 1925 he joined a small stormtrooper bodyguard unit known as the Schutzstaffel (the SS). Heiden was an early advocate of separating the SS from its master organisation, the Sturmabteilung (SA). Heiden hired Himmler to serve as his deputy, regarding him as a 'keen young clerk'; he was soon dismissed by Hitler and succeeded by Himmler as Reichsführer-SS. In April 1933 he was arrested on Himmler's orders and killed shortly after.

Heines: Edmund Heines (1897-1934)

Heines joined the party and the SA. From 1931 to 1934, he served as an SA leader in Silesia and as Ernst Roehm's deputy. He was arrested during the 'Night of the Long Knives' and was caught in bed with an 18-year-old youth. He refused to cooperate and get dressed. When this was reported to Hitler, he went to the room and ordered him to get dressed within five minutes or risk being shot. Heines still refused to cooperate and Hitler became so furious that he ordered some SS men to take him and the boy outside to be executed.

Hess: Rudolf Hess (1894-1987)

After hearing Hitler speak for the first time in May 1920, Hess became completely devoted to him. He joined the fledgling Nazi Party in 1920 as one of its first members and commanded an SA battalion during the Beer Hall Putch. Hess served seven and a half months in Landsberg Prison and acted as Hitler's private secretary there, transcribing and partially editing Mein Kampf. He rose in Hitler's estimation and on the eve of the invasion of Poland, Hitler announced that should anything happen to both him and Goering, Hess would be next in the line of succession. On 10 May 1941 he flew solo to Scotland in an attempt to negotiate peace with the United Kingdom, where he was arrested and became a prisoner of war. Hess was tried at Nuremberg and sentenced to life imprisonment, which he served at Spandau Prison, Berlin.

Hettlage: Karl Maria Hettlage (1902-1995)

Hettlage was an SS captain and one the founding members of the National Socialist German Law Academy. From 1934 to 1938 he was city treasurer of Berlin and from 1938 to 1951 he served as a board member of Commerz and Private Bank. Until 1945, Hettlage was one of Speer's representatives and remained very close to him. Surprisingly, he was able to resume his career after the War without much difficulty, although the stain of his former position in the SS could not be completely erased. He served in Konrad Adenauer's post-war government.

Hewel: Walther Hewel (1904-1945)

Hewel was one of the earliest members of the party, joining as a teenager. After Hitler's imprisonment following the Beer Hall Putsch, Hewel stayed in Landsberg Prison with him and acted as his valet for several months. He served as a diplomat in the Foreign Ministry, and on 15 March 1939, he transcribed the conference between Hitler and Czech president, Emil Hácha. However, he spent most of the War without an official portfolio. Hewel usually ended up dealing with situations and events that Hitler could not handle; he remained in his inner circle right up to Hitler's suicide on 30 April 1945. Hewel was the last individual to engage in a long, personal conversation with Hitler, and was said to have tried to cheer him up. He killed himself on 2 May 1945, biting down on a cyanide capsule while shooting himself in the head.

Heydrich: Reinhard Tristan Heydrich (1904-1942)

Heydrich was one of the main architects of the Holocaust. He was an SS-Obergruppenführer, General der Polizei, Chief of the Reich Main Security Office and Stellvertretender Reichsprotektor of Bohemia and Moravia. Heydrich chaired the January 1942 Wannsee Conference, which laid out plans for the 'Final Solution' to the 'Jewish Question'. He helped organise Kristallnacht, a series of co-ordinated attacks against Jews throughout Germany and Austria. In Operation Anthropoid on 27 May 1942, Heydrich was attacked in Prague by a British-trained team who had been sent by the Czechoslovak government-in-exile to kill him. He died from his injuries a week later.

Himmler: Heinrich Luitpold Himmler (1900-1945)

Himmler joined the party in 1923 and the SS in 1925. In 1929 he was appointed Reichsführer-SS by Hitler. Himmler developed the SS into a powerful group with its own military. Following Hitler's orders, he set up and controlled the Nazi concentration camps. From 1943 onwards, he was both Chief of German Police and Minister of the Interior, overseeing all internal and external police and security forces, including the Gestapo. On Hitler's behalf, Himmler formed the Einsatzgruppen and built extermination camps. Late in the War, Hitler gave Himmler command of the Army Group Upper Rhine and the Army Group Vistula; he failed to achieve his assigned objectives and Hitler replaced him in these posts. Shortly before the end of the War, without Hitler's knowledge, Himmler attempted to open peace talks with the Western Allies. Hearing of this, Hitler dismissed him from all his posts in April 1945. Himmler was arrested by British forces and he committed suicide on 23 May 1945.

Hindenberg: Paul Ludwig Hans Anton von Beneckendorff und von Hindenburg (1847-1934)

After a long career in the Prussian Army, Hindenburg retired in 1911 but was recalled in 1914, becoming Chief of the General Staff from 1916. He was recalled to public life in 1925 to be elected as the second President of Germany. Hindenburg despised Hitler and condescendingly referred to him as that 'Bohemian corporal'. He dissolved the parliament twice in 1932 and eventually was forced by circumstances to appoint Hitler as Chancellor in January 1933. He died the following year.

Hitler: Paula Hitler (1896-1960)

Paula was seven years younger than her brother. At one time she worked as a secretary for a group of doctors in a military hospital, but she kept her identity a secret. Whenever she saw a small chapel when travelling in the mountains, she would go in and say a silent prayer for her brother. In March 1941, Hitler was staying at the Imperial Hotel in Vienna and it was here that Paula met him for the last time. Hitler never mentioned her in his writings because of his embarrassment at her weak mental state. After the War, she lived unmarried in a two-bedroom flat near Berchtesgaden. Her main interest was the Catholic Church. She died on 1 June 1960.

Hoesch: Leopold von Hoesch (1881-1936)

Hoesch was a career diplomat who began his political career in France in 1923. In 1932, Hoesch was transferred to London, where he remained until his death. He was well liked by most British statesmen, including Sir Anthony Eden. By 1934, Hoesch was beginning to challenge Hitler indirectly, sending communiqués to Konstantin von Neurath, Foreign Minister, detailing Hoesch's mistrust of Ribbentrop whom Hitler had appointed to serve as commissioner of Disarmament Questions. The relationship between Hoesch and Hitler continued to sour as Ribbentrop gained more power within the German government. By 1936, Hoesch was quickly becoming a thorn in Hitler's side. Before Hitler could take action against him, he died of a heart attack on 11 April 1936.

Hoffmann: Heinrich Hoffmann (1885-1957)

Hoffmann worked in his father's photographic shop and as a photographer in Munich from 1908. He joined the party in 1920 and was chosen by its new leader, Hitler, as his official photographer. Hitler and Hoffman became close friends. Hoffmann's photographs were published as postage stamps, postcards, posters and picture books. Following Hoffmann's suggestion, both he and Hitler received royalties from all uses of Hitler's image, making Hoffman a wealthy man. In 1933 he was elected to the Reichstag and in 1938 Hitler appointed him a 'Professor'. He was arrested on 10 May 1945 and sentenced to four years imprisonment for Nazi profiteering.

Hohenlohe: Stephanie Julianne von Hohenlohe (1891-1972)

Stephanie married Friedrich Franz von Hohenlohe-Waldenburg-Schillingsfürst in 1914, but the couple divorced in 1920. Despite being Jewish, she became friendly with Hitler who called her his 'dear princess'. She developed a very close friendship with Goering, and Himmler even declared her an 'honorary Aryan'. In a 1938 MI6 report, British intelligence said that 'she is frequently summoned by the Führer who appreciates her intelligence and good advice. She is perhaps the only woman who can exercise any influence on him.' She also befriended Lord Rothermere and was able to get him to pay her a £5,000 annual retainer, which ceased in 1939 leading to a court case. On the outbreak of war she returned to England, and then moved to the USA. After the War she rebuilt influential connections in Germany. She died in Geneva in 1972.

Hossbach: Friedrich Wilhelm Ludwig Hossbach (1894-1980)

Hossbach served on the Eastern Front in the First World War, rising to the rank of Senior Lieutenant (Oberleutnant). He remained in the army and is best known for the 'Hossbach Memorandum', a report of a meeting held on 5 November 1937 between Hitler, Blomberg, Fritsch, Raeder, Goering, Neurath and Hossbach. In May 1945, Hossbach (who was largely opposed to the Nazi regime) was warned by friends to expect a visit from the Gestapo. They arrived at his house an hour before the Americans; Hossbach, armed with a pistol, engaged his visitors in a firefight until they fled. He was taken into American custody.

Jodl: Alfred Joseph Ferdinand Jodl (1890-1946)

Jodl served during the First World War and remained in the army. He was nominally assigned as an artillery commander from 1938 to August 1939 during the Anschluss, but from then until the end of the War he was Chief of Operation Staff OKW. Jodl acted as a Chief of Staff during the swift occupation of Denmark and Norway. He was injured during the 20 July 1944 plot to assassinate Hitler and was awarded the special wounded badge alongside several other leading Nazi figures. He was found guilty at Nuremberg and hanged on 16 October 1946.

unge: Gertraud Junge (1920-2002)

Gertraud (Traudl) was the youngest of Hitler's three secretaries.
At the age of 22 she worked at Hitler's HQ at Rastenburg in
East Prussia and later in the Berlin Bunker. In June 1943, she
married Hans Junge, Aide-de-Camp to the Führer, who was
killed a year later when a Spitfire strafed his company on the
Normandy Front. Gertraud Junge survived the last chaotic days
in Berlin, typing Hitler's last will and testament. She was arrested
by the Russians and then the Americans and interrogated for
hours. She died childless in 2002.

Kahr: Gustav Ritter von Kahr (1862-1934)

Kahr became Prime Minister of Bavaria in 1920 and was
instrumental in the failure of Hitler's Beer Hall Putsch. Hitler and
Ludendorff sought Kahr's support, but he had his own plan with
Seisser and Lossow to install a nationalist dictatorship without
Hitler. On 30 June 1934—the 'Night of the Long Knives'—Kahr
was punished for his 'treason' during the Beer Hall Putsch. He was
abducted in Munich and hacked to death with axes by SS members
and then thrown into a swamp near Dachau.

Keitel: Wilhelm Bodewin Johann Gustav Keitel (1882-1946)

Keitel served on the Western Front during the First World War.
He remained within the army after the War and by 1938 he
was promoted to the Supreme Command of the Armed Forces,
effectively making him War Minister. Soon after his appointment
to OKW, he convinced Hitler to appoint his close friend, Walter
von Brauchitsch, as Commander-in-Chief of the Army. During
the Second World War, Keitel was one of the primary planners
of the Wehrmacht campaigns and operations on the western and
the eastern fronts. In 1940, after the French campaign, he was
promoted to Field Marshal along with several other generals. After
the failed plot of 20 July 1944, Keitel sat on the army court that
handed over many officers to Freisler's notorious People's Court.
Following the Nuremberg trials he was executed by hanging.

Kempka: Erich Kempka (1910-1975)

Kempka joined the Nazi Party in 1930 and two years later was
one of eight founding members of the SS-Begleit-Kommando. He
was present at the arrest of Ernst Roehm in 1934, and in 1936 he
replaced Julius Schreck as Hitler's primary chauffeur and chief of
his car fleet. Unless in the company of an important personality,
Hitler would sit in the front, next to Kempka, with his valet
behind him. In April 1945, Kempka accompanied Hitler to the
Führerbunker. He was one of those responsible for the burning
of Hitler and Eva Braun's corpses after they committed suicide
together on the afternoon of 30 April 1945. On 20 June 1945,
he was captured by US troops at Berchtesgaden and eventually
released in 1947. He died in 1975.

Kesselring: Albert Kesselring (1885-1960)

Kesselring served on both the western and eastern fronts during the
First World War and remained in the army until 1933, when he was
discharged to become head of the Department of Administration
at the Reich Commissariat for Aviation. During the Second World
War, Kesselring commanded air forces in the invasions of Poland
and France, the Battle of Britain and Operation Barbarossa. As
Commander-in-Chief South, he was overall commander in the
Mediterranean theatre including North Africa. In the final campaign
of the War, he commanded German forces in Western Europe.
Kesselring was sentenced to death at Nuremberg, but the sentence was
subsequently commuted. He was released in 1952 and died in 1960.

Klausener: Erich Klausener (1885-1934)

Klausener served as an ordnance officer on the western and eastern
fronts during the First World War; he was later imprisoned for a
short time for participating in boycotts during the French occupation
of the Ruhr in 1923 and 1924. Beginning in 1928, Klausener became
head of the Catholic Action group and prior to 1933 he energetically
supported the police battle against unlawful Nazi activities. After
the 'Night of the Long Knives', a squad of SS men, apparently acting
on the orders of Goering and Heydrich, entered his office at the
Transportation Ministry and shot him dead at his desk.

Kluge: Guenther Adolf Ferdinand 'Hans' von Kluge (1882-1944)

Kluge was a staff officer during the First World War, and in 1916 he fought at the Battle of
Verdun. By 1936 he was a lieutenant general, and in 1937 he took command of the Sixth Army
Group. He led the Sixth into battle in Poland in 1939. In October 1943 he was badly injured in
a car accident and was unable to return to duty until July 1944, when he became Rundstedt's
replacement as commander of the German forces in the West. When Stauffenberg attempted to
assassinate Hitler on 20 July 1944, Kluge was with him in his headquarters in La Roche-Guyon.
On 17 August 1944 he was replaced by Model and recalled to Berlin for a meeting with Hitler.
Thinking that Hitler would punish him as a conspirator, he committed suicide by taking cyanide
near Metz that same day.

Kordt: Erich Kordt (1903-1969)

Kordt spoke perfect English and joined the German Foreign Office
in 1928, later serving in the London Embassy under Ribbentrop,
for whom he developed a personal dislike. Despite this, he became
a member of the Nazi Party in November 1937, and in February
1938, when Ribbentrop became Foreign Minister, he was appointed
head of the Foreign Office's 'Ministerial Bureau'. In June 1939,
Kordt went to London to warn Robert Vansittart, the diplomatic
advisor to the British government, of the secret negotiations
between Germany and the Soviet Union. He was dismayed that all approaches made by the
German Resistance Movement within the German Foreign Office were ignored by the British.
In April 1941, Kordt was posted to Tokyo as the German Embassy's First Secretary, and later to
Nanking as German Consul, where he worked as an agent for the Russians until 1944. From
1951, Kordt was a professor of international law at the University of Cologne.

Krebs: Hans Krebs (1898-1945)

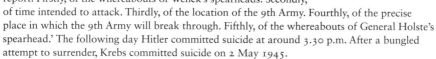

Krebs remained in the army after the First World War, rising to
become a general of infantry. As Chief of the Army General Staff
(OKH), Krebs was in the Führerbunker below the Reich Chancellery
garden during the Battle of Berlin. On 28 April 1945, Krebs made
his last telephone call to Field Marshal Wilhelm Keitel at the new
Supreme Command HQ in Fürstenberg. He told Keitel that, if
relief did not arrive within 48 hours, all was lost. The following
day Krebs, Burgdorf, Goebbels, and Bormann witnessed Hitler
signing his will. Late that evening, a somewhat delusional Krebs
radioed Jodl with the following demands: 'Request immediate
report. Firstly, of the whereabouts of Wenck's spearheads. Secondly,
of time intended to attack. Thirdly, of the location of the 9th Army. Fourthly, of the precise
place in which the 9th Army will break through. Fifthly, of the whereabouts of General Holste's
spearhead.' The following day Hitler committed suicide at around 3.30 p.m. After a bungled
attempt to surrender, Krebs committed suicide on 2 May 1945.

Kriebel: Hermann Kriebel (1876-1941)

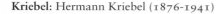

Kriebel was a retired lieutenant colonel; he fought with the Freikorps during the White counter-
revolution and in 1923 became the military leader of the Kampfbund. Kriebel was a key figure
in the Beer Hall Putsch of 8-9 November 1923, and was convicted with Hitler in 1924, serving
his sentence in Landsberg Prison just outside Munich. Kriebel maintained his ties with the party,
but he did not benefit from Hitler's rise to power. He later became Consul General in Shanghai.

Kubizek: August 'Gustl' Kubizek (1888-1956)

Kubizek and Hitler first met while competing for standing room
in the Landestheater in Linz, Austria. They quickly became close
friends; the two shared a small room from February to July 1908.
Kubizek was accepted into the Vienna Conservatory where he quickly
made a name for himself. In 1908 Hitler abruptly broke off the
friendship and drifted into homelessness. Kubizek did not attempt
to contact Hitler until 1933, when he wrote to congratulate him
on having become Chancellor of Germany; they eventually met in 1938, the last meeting being
in 1940. Kubizek was arrested and his home was searched by US forces in 1945, but the Hitler
correspondence and drawings were not found. He was released from prison on 8 April 1947.

Lammers: Hans Heinrich Lammers (1879-1962)

Having served in the First World War, Lammers resumed his career
as a lawyer, becoming an Under-Secretary at the Ministry of the
Interior by 1922. In 1932 he joined the party and by 1937 he
was Reich Minister without portfolio. On 30 November 1939 he
became a member of the Council of Ministers for the Defence of
the Reich. Following the battle of Stalingrad, Lammers, Bormann
and Keitel attempted to create a three-man junta representing the
Nazi Party. Goebbels, Speer, Goering and Himmler all saw this
proposal as a power grab and Lammers eventually lost influence as the continuation of the War
rendered his post irrelevant. In April 1945, Hitler ordered SS troops to shoot Lammers, but
he was rescued when he was captured by US forces. His wife, however, committed suicide. At
Nuremberg he was sentenced to ten years' imprisonment, but he was released in 1952.

Lange: Martin Franz Erwin Rudolf Lange (1910-1945?)

Lange went to the University of Jena and received a doctorate in law in 1933. He joined the SA in November of that year, and the SS in 1936. He worked for the Gestapo in Berlin, Vienna, Riga and Stuttgart. In November 1941 he was deeply involved in planning and executing the murder of 24,000 Latvian Jews from the Riga ghetto. He was called to the Wannsee Conference by Heydrich where, as an SS-Major along with Eichmann, the recording secretary of the conference, Lange was the lowest ranking of the SS officers present. Heydrich, however, viewed his first-hand experience in conducting the mass murder of Jews as valuable for the conference. He was said to be killed in action in February 1945; he may have committed suicide, but the records are unclear.

Lenard: Philipp Eduard Anton von Lenard (1862-1947)

Lenard was a distinguished scientist and won the Nobel Prize in 1905. He was a strong German nationalist who despised English physics, which he considered as having stolen its ideas from Germany. He joined the Nazi Party and was an outspoken proponent of the idea that Germany should rely on 'Deutsche Physik' and ignore what he considered the fallacious and deliberately misleading ideas of 'Jewish physics', by which he meant chiefly the theories of Albert Einstein. As an advisor to Hitler, Lenard became Chief of Aryan Physics under the Nazis. He was expelled from his Heidelberg post by Allied occupation forces in 1945, and he died in 1947.

Ley: Inge Ley (d. 1942)

Gossip circulated throughout Germany about the beautiful Inge's (Inga) relationship with Hitler and the cause of her suicide. She and her husband, Robert Ley, had three children, but she was troubled by her husband's acute alcoholism. She was well known to have had a passion for Hitler. She was an exceptionally beautiful woman and Ley commissioned a life size portrait of her in the nude which he displayed prominently in his house. According to Robert Ley's private secretary, Inge shot herself on 29 December 1942, suffering depression following complications during childbirth which had left her drug-dependent.

Ley: Robert Ley (1890-1945)

Ley served as an aviator during the First World War. After the War he gained a doctorate at university and joined the party having read Hitler's speech at his trial following the Beer Hall Putsch. When Hitler became Chancellor in January 1933, Ley accompanied him to Berlin. In April, when the trade union movement was taken over by the State, Hitler appointed him as head of the German Labour Front (DAF), where he freely embezzled funds. In 1942, his second wife Inge shot herself after a drunken brawl. Ley's subordinates took their lead from him, and the DAF became a notorious centre of corruption. Despite his failings, Ley retained Hitler's favour; until the last months of the War he was part of Hitler's inner circle along with Bormann and Goebbels. He was captured on 16 May 1945 and indicted at Nuremberg. Three days later he strangled himself using a noose made by fastening strips of his towel to the toilet pipe in his cell.

Linge: Heinz Linge (1913-1980)

Linge was an SS officer and worked as Hitler's valet from 1935 until Hitler shot himself on 30 April 1945. Linge was one of the last people to leave the bunker and was subsequently arrested by the Russians who interrogated him about the circumstances of Hitler's death. He was eventually released from Russian captivity in 1955 and then gave numerous television interviews. He died in Bremen in March 1980.

Lossow: Otto von Lossow (1868-1938)

Lossow was a lieutenant colonel during the First World War and remained in the army, becoming a commander in Bavaria. By 1923 he was politically aligned with Kahr and Seisser and the three had their own plans for a nationalist government without Hitler. At the Beer Hall Putsch they ostensibly supported Hitler, but seeing the way matters were heading they went over to General von Seeckt and helped put down the coup.

Lubbe: Marinus van der Lubbe (1909-1934)

Lubbe joined the Dutch Communist Party in 1925. After an injury at a building site where he worked, he moved to Leiden in 1927 where he learned to speak some German and founded the Lenin House, where he organised political meetings. According to the Berlin police, Lubbe claimed to have set the Reichstag building on fire as a cry to rally the German workers against fascist rule. Under torture, he confessed again and was brought to trial along with the leaders of the opposition Communist Party. He was guillotined on 10 January 1934.

Ludendorff: Erich Friedrich Wilhelm Ludendorff (1865-1937)

Ludendorff was a general during the First World War. Convinced that the German Army had been betrayed by Marxists and Republicans in the Versailles Treaty, he joined Hitler in the unsuccessful Beer Hall Putsch. In 1925 he ran for president against his former colleague, Paul von Hindenburg. After 1928, Ludendorff went into retirement, having fallen out with the Nazi Party. He no longer approved of Hitler and began to regard him as just another manipulative politician. In an attempt to regain Ludendorff's favour, Hitler paid him an unannounced visit on his birthday in 1935 and offered to make him a Field Marshal if he came back into politics. Ludendorff did not welcome Hitler or his offer.

Maurice: Emil Maurice (1897-1972)

Maurice was an early member of the party and became the SA commander of the newly established Stabswache, a special SA company responsible for guarding Hitler at political rallies. He was imprisoned with Hitler after the Beer Hall Putsch. In 1925, Hitler refounded the Stabswache as the SS and Maurice became SS member No. 2, after Hitler himself. He reportedly had a brief relationship with Geli Raubal, Hitler's niece, and therefore lost his job as Hitler's chauffeur. Himmler later recommended that Maurice be expelled from the SS, along with other members of his family due to their Jewish ancestry, but to Himmler's annoyance, Hitler stood by his old friend. In 1948 Maurice was sentenced to four years in a labour camp.

Milch: Erhard Milch (1892-1972)

Milch commanded a fighter wing, Jagdgruppe 6, at the end of the First World War. In 1933, following an early career at Junkers, he took up a position as State Secretary of the Reich Aviation Ministry, answering directly to Goering. In this capacity he was instrumental in establishing the Luftwaffe. In 1944 Milch sided with Goebbels and Himmler in attempting to convince Hitler to remove Goering from command of the Luftwaffe. When Hitler refused, Goering retaliated by forcing Milch out of his position. For the remainder of the War, he worked under Speer. He was sentenced to life imprisonment at Landsberg Prison by the Allies, but his sentence was commuted to fifteen years in 1951. He was released in 1954.

Mitford: Diana Mitford (1910-2003); Unity Valkyrie Mitford (1914-1948)

Diana was the third daughter of Lord Redesdale. She was married first to Bryan Walter Guinness, heir to the barony of Moyne, and secondly to Sir Oswald Mosley, 6th Baronet of Ancoats, leader of the British Union of Fascists. Her second marriage, in 1936, took place at the home of Goebbels, with Hitler as guest of honour. She was interned for three years during the Second World War and later moved to Paris. Unity was the fourth daughter of Lord Redesdale. Along with her sister Diana she was a prominent public supporter of Nazism, and from 1936, a part of Hitler's inner circle of friends for five years. Following the declaration of war, she attempted suicide and Hitler arranged for her to be sent home to England. She never fully recovered and died in 1948.

Model: Otto Moritz Walter Model (1891-1945)

Model served during the First World War and remained in the army. He was a supporter of the Nazi regime and served throughout the War. At various times in 1944 he commanded each of the three major army groups on the Eastern Front. By August 1944 Model was transferred to defence in the west where he successfully held the Arnhem bridge. Three months later, following a joint plan developed with Runstedt, led the push for Antwerp, culminating in the Battle of the Bulge. The failure of this attack marked the end of Model's special relationship with Hitler. He shot himself in the head on 21 April 1945.

Moltke: Helmuth James Graf von Moltke (1907-1945)

Moltke studied legal and political sciences. In 1935, he declined the chance to become a judge because he would have been obliged to join the Nazi Party. He helped victims of Hitler's regime emigrate, and between 1935 and 1938, he regularly visited Britain. He was drafted into the High Command of the Armed Forces (OKW), Counter-Intelligence Service, Foreign Division under Admiral Canaris. Moltke led the 'Kreisau Circle' but opposed the assassination of Hitler. He was not involved in the 29 July 1944 plot, but he was arrested, and in January 1945 he stood along with several of his fellow regime opponents before the People's Court of Roland Freisler. Because no evidence could be found, Freisler had to invent a charge de novo. Moltke was sentenced to death on 11 January 1945 and executed twelve days later.

Morell: Theodor Gilbert Morell (1886-1948)

Morell served as a medical officer during the First World War. He joined the Nazi Party in 1933 and later met Hitler at an event at the Berghof. He was constantly recommended to other members of the Nazi leadership, but most of them, including Goering and Himmler, dismissed him as a quack. By April 1945, Hitler was taking twenty-eight different pills a day, along with numerous injections every few hours and intravenous injections of methamphetamine almost every day. On 22 April 1945, about a week before committing suicide, Hitler dismissed Morell from the Führerbunker in Berlin, saying that he did not need any more medical help. Morell was captured, but was never charged with any crimes. He died in 1948 after a stroke.

Mueller: Renate Mueller (1906-1937)

Mueller was a popular actress in Berlin in the late 1920s. A blue-eyed blonde, she was considered to be one of the great beauties of her day. She starred in more than twenty German films, including Viktor und Viktoria (1933). With the rise of the Nazi Party, Mueller came to be regarded as an ideal Aryan woman and was courted and promoted as Germany's leading film actress. A meeting with Adolf Hitler in the mid-1930s resulted in Mueller being offered parts in films that promoted Nazi ideals. She died after a fall from her hotel window—presumably suicide, but this is not clear.

Mueller: Heinrich Mueller (1900-1945?)

At the end of the First World War, Mueller served as a pilot for an artillery spotting unit. He was later employed in the political department of the police headquarters and rose quickly through the ranks of the SS. During the Second World War, he was heavily involved in espionage and counter-espionage. After the assassination attempt against Hitler on 20 July 1944, Mueller was placed in charge of the arrest and interrogation of all those suspected of involvement in the resistance. Over 5,000 people were arrested and about 200 were executed, including Canaris. In the last months of the War, Mueller remained at his post, apparently still confident of a German victory. He remains the most senior figure of the Nazi regime who was never captured or confirmed to have died.

Mussolini: Benito Amilcare Andrea Mussolini (1883-1945)

Mussolini created the Fasci di Combattimento in 1919 and following the 'March on Rome' in October 1922, he became Prime Minister of Italy. He began using the title 'Il Duce' in 1925. He inaugurated public works programmes which included the 'taming of the Pontine Marshes'. He was also dedicated to the improvement of job opportunities and public transports. On 10 June 1940, Mussolini led Italy into the Second World War, but after the 1943 Allied invasion of Italy, King Victor Emmanuel had him arrested. On 12 September 1943, Mussolini was rescued from prison in the daring Gran Sasso raid by German special forces. On 28 April 1945 he was captured and summarily executed near Lake Como by Italian partisans. His body was then taken to Milan where it was hung upside down at a petrol station. Two days later Hitler shot himself. The war in Europe came to an end just ten days after his death.

Neurath: Konstantin von Neurath (1873-1956)

Neurath served as an officer during the First World War. By 1932 he was Minister of Foreign Affairs and he continued to hold that position under Chancellor von Schleicher and then under Hitler. In 1937, Neurath became a member of the Nazi Party, but Hitler sacked him in February 1938. In March 1939, Neurath was appointed Reichsprotektor of Bohemia and Moravia and Hitler chose him in part to pacify the international outrage over the German occupation of Czechoslovakia. In 1941 he was relieved of his day-to-day powers and replaced by Heydrich and Daluege. At Nuremberg he was sentenced to fifteen years' imprisonment, but was released in 1954.

Papen: Franz Joseph Hermann Michael Maria von Papen (1879-1969)

Papen was expelled from the USA during the First World War and later served as an officer, first on the Western Front and later in Palestine. He entered politics and was a member of the Parliament of Prussia in 1921-32. Hindenburg appointed him Chancellor, but the cabinet he formed with the assistance of General Kurt von Schleicher was weak; by 1933 he was replaced by Hitler, himself becoming Vice-Chancellor. Hitler and his allies quickly marginalised Papen and the rest of the cabinet. During the 'Night of the Long Knives', General von Schleicher was gunned down along with his wife, but Papen managed to survive. He was later sidelined by being made Ambassador to Austria. Hitler dismissed him from his mission in Austria in 1938, and he later served as Ambassador to Turkey in 1939-44. At Nuremberg he was acquitted, but a later de-Nazification court sentenced him to eight years' hard labour. Papen was released on appeal in 194

Paulus: Friedrich Wilhelm Ernst Paulus (1890-1957)

Paulus served during the First World War and after the Armistice he fought with the Freikorps in the east as a brigade adjutant. Paulus was promoted to Lieutenant General in August 1940 and named Deputy Chief of the German General Staff, in which role he helped draft the plans for Operation Barbarossa. In January 1942 he was promoted to General and became Commander of the German Sixth Army, leading the drive on Stalingrad during that summer. He fought the Soviet defenders for three months, but following a massive counter-offensive, Paulus found himself surrounded. He surrendered on 31 January 1943, a day after he was promoted t the rank of Field Marshal. In Russian captivity, Paulus became a vocal critic of the Nazi regime He was released by the Russians in 1953.

Poetsch: Leopold Poetsch (1853-1942)

Poetsch was Hitler's teacher in geography and history from 1901 to 1904. He was a fervent believer in pan-Germanic rule and Hitler was captivated by his teachings; at this time Hitler began regularly reading a local anti-Semitic newspaper. In his later years, Hitler spoke of Poetsch as a 'great man' and he was clearly influential in Hitler's self-imposed mission to exterminate all Jews. In 1936 some teachers in Linz sent their now-famous pupil photographs to remind him of them, and they asked Poetsch to join them, but he refused, arguing that he d not agree with Hitler in his defamation of Austria as he had sworn an official oath to Austria.

Quisling: Vidkun Abraham Lauritz Jonssøn Quisling (1887-1945)

On 14 December 1939, Hitler met Quisling, a Norwegian right-wing politician, and promised to respond to any British invasion of Norway, perhaps pre-emptively, with a German counter-invasion. In the early hours of 9 April 1940, Germany invaded Norway by air and sea, intending to capture King Haakon VII and the government. In the afternoon, Quisling was told by German liaison Hans Wilhelm Scheidt that should he set up a government, it would have Hitler's personal approval. From 1942 to 1945 Quisling served as Minister-President, working with the occupying forces. His government was dominated by ministers from Nasjonal Samling, the party he founded in 1933. Quisling was put on trial during the legal purge in Norway after the War and found guilty of charges including embezzlement, murder and high treason. He was executed by firing squad on 24 October 1945.

Raeder: Erich Raeder (1876-1960)

Raeder joined the Imperial Navy in 1894 and was promoted to Admiral in 1928. As head of the German Navy, he focused all of his efforts on rebuilding the High Seas Fleet. He was a believer in battleships and was hostile towards submarines and aircraft carriers. Raeder was interested in using Norway as a base to allow the Kriegsmarine to attack the North Atlantic sea-lanes to Britain; he was instrumental in Hitler's decision to invade Norway. Raeder was opposed to Operation Sea Lion and also had doubts about Germany's ability to gain air superiority over the English Channel. In the autumn of 1942, in an attempt to limit Doenitz's power, Raeder retracted Doenitz's responsibility for training U-boat crews, only to see Doenitz ignore his orders. Raeder resigned from Kriegsmarine in May 1943 and was succeeded by Doenitz. After the War, Raeder was sentenced to life imprisonment at the Nuremberg Trials for waging a war of aggression. The sentence was later reduced and he was released in 1955.

Raubal: Angela Franziska Johanna Raubal, née Hitler (1883-1949); Angela Maria 'Geli' Raubal (1908-1931)

Angela Hitler was the second child of Alois Hitler and his second wife, Franziska Matzelsberger. Her mother died the following year. She and her brother Alois Hitler Jr were raised by their father and his third wife Klara Pölzl. Her half-brother Adolf was born six years after her, and they grew very close. She married Leo Raubal (1879-1910) and had two children, Leo and Geli. Angela lost contact with her half-brother for ten years, and then in 1928 she and Geli moved to the Berghof where she became Hitler's housekeeper. After Geli's suicide, Angela left Berchtesgaden and moved to Dresden. Hitler broke off relations with Angela and did not attend her second wedding to the architect Professor Martin Hammitzsch. Angela died of a stroke in 1949. Geli (junior) was close to her uncle Adolf from 1925 until her suicide in 1931. She moved into Hitler's Munich apartment in 1929 when she enrolled in medicine at university. Hitler was infatuated with her and refused her any freedom or permission to go to Vienna. While Hitler was absent at a meeting, Geli shot herself in the Munich apartment with Hitler's pistol. Hitler treated Geli's room at the Berghof as a shrine and it was kept as she had left it; he hung portraits of her in his room there, and at the Chancellery in Berlin.

Reinhardt: Fritz Reinhardt (1895-1969)

Reinhardt joined the party and with his talent for speaking and his knowledge of economic and taxation systems, he quickly built up a career. From 1928 to 1930 he was the Governor of Upper Bavaria. In 1930 he became a member of the Reichstag and took the leading role in the party's financial issues. In 1933, he became an SA Gruppen-führer and a member of Hess's staff. He was the chief architect of the Tax Reconciliation Act of October 1934. He was publisher of the tax newspaper Deutsche Steuerzeitung, which along with all his other publications was made required reading for all finance officials. After the War, Reinhardt was placed in Allied custody, and in 1949 he was classified as a 'main culprit' and sentenced to four years in a labour prison. He is pictured here between Otto Skorzeny and Kurt Zschirnt.

Reitsch: Hanna Reitsch (1912-1979)

Reitsch became Germany's leading female stunt pilot and later chief test pilot for the Luftwaffe. She worshipped Hitler and the Nazi ideology and became the only woman to win the Iron Cross. Hanna Reitsch spent three days in the Führerbunker shortly before Hitler's suicide; she then flew out with the newly appointed Chief of the Luftwaffe, General Robert Ritter von Greim, whose orders were to mount a bombing attack on the Russian forces that were now approaching the Chancellery and Führerbunker. Hanna Reitsch survived the War and died in 1979.

Ribbentrop: Ulrich Friedrich Wilhelm Joachim von Ribbentrop (1893-1946)

Ribbentrop was first introduced to Hitler in 1928 and became a secret emissary between him and Papen. From the start, Ribbentrop was Hitler's favourite foreign-policy adviser. In August 1936, Hitler appointed him Ambassador to Britain with orders to negotiate the Anglo-German alliance, but this came to nothing. In 1938 he succeeded Neurath as Foreign Minister and his most successful moment came with the signing of the Non-Aggression Pact with Russia in August 1939. He was against the attack on the USSR in 1941 and passed a word to a Soviet diplomat: 'Please tell Stalin I was against this war, and that I know it will bring great misfortune to Germany.' As the War progressed, Hitler found Ribbentrop increasingly tiresome and sought to avoid him; his position weakened further when many old Foreign Office diplomats participated in the 20 July 1944 assassination attempt on Hitler. In April 1945, Ribbentrop attended Hitler's 56th birthday party in Berlin. Three days later, he attempted to meet with Hitler, only to be told to go away. This was their last meeting. He was arrested after the War, tried at Nuremberg, and executed in 1946.

Roehm: Ernst Julius Guenther Roehm (1887-1934)

Roehm joined the German Workers' Party, which soon became the Nazi Party. He also met Hitler and they became political allies and close friends. Following the Beer Hall Putsch, Roehm was found guilty, but was granted a conditional discharge. At Landsberg Prison in April 1924, Roehm was given full powers by Hitler to rebuild the SA in any way he saw fit. By August 1933, Roehm and Hitler were so close that he was the only Nazi who dared address Hitler as 'Adolf,' rather than 'mein Führer'. Despite this friendship, Roehm represented a challenge to Hitler, who by now desired the support of the army. In the 'Night of the Long Knives' on 30 June 1934, Roehm and the entire leadership of the SA was purged; Roehm was shot in the chest at point-blank range.

Rosenberg: Alfred Ernst Rosenberg (1893-1946)

Rosenberg became one of the earliest members of the German Workers Party, later to become the Nazi Party, joining in January 1919, ten months before Hitler. After the Beer Hall Putsch, Hitler appointed Rosenberg as a temporary leader of the party. He was named leader of the party's foreign political office in 1933, but he played little practical part in the role. Rosenberg reshaped Nazi racial policy over the years, but it always consisted of Aryan supremacy, extreme German nationalism and anti-Semitism. Following the invasion of Russia, he was appointed head of the Reich Ministry for the Occupied Eastern Territories. At the Nuremberg Trials he claimed to be ignorant of the Holocaust; he was sentenced to death and executed on 16 October 1946.

Rundstedt: Karl Rudolf Gerd von Rundstedt (1875-1953)

Runstedt served during the First World War and remained in the army. He commanded Army Group A during the invasion of France, and was promoted to Field Marshal on 19 July 1940. In the Russian campaign he commanded Army Group South, responsible for the encirclement and the Battle of Kiev. He was dismissed by Hitler in December 1941, but was recalled in 1942 and appointed Commander-in-Chief in the West. He was dismissed again after the defeat in Normandy in July 1944, but was again recalled as Commander-in-Chief in the West in September, and dismissed for a final time March 1945. Rundstedt was aware of the various plots to depose Hitler, but he did not support them. He was charged with war crimes but did not face trial and was released in 1949.

Saxe-Coburg: Charles Edward, Duke of Saxe-Coburg and Gotha (1884-1954)

Saxe-Coburg was a grandson of Queen Victoria and Prince Albert, and also, until 1919, the Duke of Albany and a Prince of the United Kingdom. The duke supported Germany during the First World War, but never held a major command. He joined the Nazi Party in 1935 and became a member of the SA. He also served as a member of the Reichstag representing the Nazi Party from 1937 to 1945, and as President of the German Red Cross from 1933 to 1945. The duke attended the funeral of his first cousin King George V in his SA uniform and approached the new King-Emperor, Edward VIII, about the possibility of a pact. Nothing came of these talks. Nonetheless, he continued to send Hitler encouraging reports about the strength of pro-German sentiment among the British aristocracy. After the War he lost most of his assets and died in seclusion.

Schacht: Hjalmar Horace Greeley Schacht (1877-1970)

Schacht was an economist, banker, liberal politician, and co-founder of the German Democratic Party. He served as the Currency Commissioner and President of the Reichsbank under the Weimar Republic. He was a fierce critic of Germany's reparation obligations following the Treaty of Versailles. In 1934 Hitler appointed Schacht as his Minister of Economics. Schacht supported his public works programmes, most notably the construction of autobahns to alleviate unemployment. He disagreed with what he called 'unlawful activities' against Germany's Jewish minority and in 1935 made a speech denouncing Julius Streicher. He objected to high military spending, and thereby came into conflict with Hitler and Goering. In November 1937 he resigned as Minister of Economics, but remained President of the Reichsbank until Hitler dismissed him in January 1939. He had no role during the War and was imprisoned after the 20 July 1944 plot. He was tried at Nuremberg and acquitted.

Schaub: Julius Schaub (1898-1967)

Schaub was born in Munich, and in 1925 he was hired privately by Hitler as a personal assistant. Schaub was one of Hitler's personal adjutants until 1945, and was in constant close contact. Near the end of the War, on 23 April 1945, Hitler ordered Schaub to burn all of his personal belongings and papers from the Reich Chancellery and the Führerbunker. Schaub then flew to Munich and did the same in Hitler's private apartment at Prinzregentenplatz and at the Berghof in Obersalzberg. He was arrested on 8 May 1945 and remained in custody until February 1949.

Schellenberg: Walther Friedrich Schellenberg (1910-1952)

Schellenberg joined the SS in May 1933 after graduating in Law at the University of Marburg. He met Heydrich and went to work in the counter-intelligence department of the SD. From 1939 to 1942 he was Himmler's personal aide and a deputy chief in the Reich Main Security Office under Heydrich, who answered only to Himmler. In 1940 he was charged with compiling the Informationsheft G.B., a blueprint for the occupation of Britain. A supplement to this work was the list of 2,300 prominent Britons to be arrested after a successful invasion of Britain. At the end of the War, Schellenberg persuaded Himmler to try negotiating with the Western Allies through Count Folke Bernadotte and personally went to Stockholm in April 1945 to arrange their meeting. He was taken into custody by the British in June 1945. During the Nuremberg Trials, he testified against other Nazis. In the 1949 Ministries Trial he was sentenced to six years' imprisonment, during which time he wrote his memoirs, The Labyrinth. He was released in 1951 and died the following year.

Scheubner-Richter: Max Scheubner-Richter (1884-1923)

Scheubner-Richter was an early member of the Nazi Party and it was he, along with Rosenberg, who devised the plan to drive the German government to revolution through the Beer Hall Putsch. He was a Baltic German born in Riga and lived a large part of his life in Imperial Russia. After the First World War he was involved in the Russian counter-revolution and moved to Germany with Rosenberg in 1918. At the end of September 1923, Scheubner-Richter provided Hitler with a lengthy plan for revolution. During the Beer Hall Putsch, walking arm-in-arm with Hitler, he was shot in the lungs and died instantly. Hitler claimed Scheubner-Richter to be the only 'irreplaceable loss'.

Schirach: Baldur Benedikt von Schirach (1907-1974)

Schirach had an American mother and English was his first language. He married Henriette Hoffmann in 1932, daughter of Heinrich Hoffmann, Hitler's personal photographer and close friend. Through this relationship, Schirach became part of Hitler's inner circle. In 1931 he was a Youth Leader and in 1933 he was made head of the Hitler Youth. He fell into disfavour with Hitler in 1943, but remained at his post. He surrendered in 1945 and was one of the officials put on trial at Nuremberg. He was one of only two men to denounce Hitler. On 1 October 1946, he was found guilty of crimes against humanity for his deportation of the Viennese Jews. He was sentenced to twenty years' imprisonment at Spandau, and was released in 1966.

Schleicher: Kurt von Schleicher (1882-1934)

Schleicher entered the German Army in 1900 as a lieutenant and in his early years made two friendships that played an important role in his life; one was to Franz von Papen, and the other, to Oskar von Hindenburg. In the early 1920s, Schleicher had emerged as a leading protégé of General von Seeckt, who often gave Schleicher sensitive assignments. Between September 1923 and February 1924, the army took over much of the administration, a task in which he played a prominent role. The appointment of Groener as Defence Minister in January 1928 did much to advance his career. After a complex career with myriad political manoeuvres, Schleicher became Chancellor in 1933, but stepped down shortly afterwards when he was unable to control a government. Initially he supported Hitler, but this turned out to be a fatal mistake; seventeen months later he was shot down during the 'Night of Long Knives'.

Schoengarth: Karl Georg Eberhard Schoengarth (1903-1946)

In 1933, Schoengarth became a member of the SD Intelligence Service of the SS. During the German attack on Poland he was Senior Inspector of SiPo Security Police in Dresden. In January 1941 he was sent to Krakow, Poland, as the Senior Commander of SiPo and SS intelligence, where he formed several Special Action Groups with the intention of perpetrating massacres. He was responsible for the murder of up to 10,000 Jewish citizens between July and September 1941. From early July 1944 until the end of the War, he worked as Commander of the Gestapo in the Netherlands. He was captured by the Allies and charged with the crime of murdering a downed Allied pilot. He was tried by a British Military Court in Burgsteinfurt and was found guilty on 11 February 1946. He was sentenced to death by hanging.

Schreck: Julius Schreck (1898-1936)

Schreck served during the First World War and joined the Nazi Party in 1920 at about the same time as Hitler; the two developed a deep friendship. In 1921 Schreck was one of the founders of the SA and also helped form the Stabswache, which was an early company of SA troops assigned as bodyguards to Hitler. In 1923 he participated in the Beer Hall Putsch. In 1925, he was asked by Emil Maurice to help establish a new bodyguard for Hitler which would be known as the Stosstrupp Adolf Hitler. Later that year, the group of eight men was renamed as the Schutzstaffel and Schreck became SS Member No. 5. He also worked as Hitler's chauffeur. In 1930 he was appointed as an SS-Standartenführer, but had little power. In 1936 he developed meningitis and died in May.

Schroeder: Christa Schroeder (1908-1984)

Schroeder was employed as a stenotypist in the Oberste SA-Führung, the SA high command. Hitler met her there in early 1933 when he had been appointed Chancellor; he took a liking to her and hired her the same year. She lived at the Wolf's Lair near Rastenburg, Hitler's initial Eastern Front headquarters. On 20 April 1945, during the Battle of Berlin, Schroeder, Bormann and several others were ordered by Hitler to leave Berlin by aircraft for the Obersalzberg. She was arrested on 28 May 1945 in Hintersee near Berchtesgaden and interrogated by the French liaison officer Albert Zoller serving in the 7th US Army. She was released on 12 May 1948.

Schwarz: Franz Xaver Schwarz (1875-1947)

Schwarz served during the First World War as a second lieutenant in the infantry. He joined the Nazi Party in 1922 and his membership number was six. He participated in the failed Beer Hall Putsch of November 1923, and with the re-establishment of party in 1925 he became full-time Treasurer. Hitler gave Schwarz full authority for the financial affairs of the party and attended his 60th birthday celebration on 27 November 1935. Schwarz's able administration of party funds insured a cash balance of one billion reichmarks by the end of the War. He was arrested by US troops and died in an Allied internment camp near Regensburg on 2 December 1947. He was posthumously classified by the Munich de-Nazification court as a 'major offender'.

Speer: Albert Speer (1905-1981)

Speer joined the Nazi Party in 1931 and reported to the party's leader for the West End of Berlin, Karl Hanke, who hired Speer to redecorate a villa he had just rented. Hanke was enthusiastic about Speer's work and launched his career within the party. He became a member of Hitler's inner circle and was commanded by him to design and construct a number of structures, including the Reich Chancellery and the Zeppelinfeld stadium in Nuremberg where party rallies were held. As Minister of Armaments, Speer was so successful that Germany's war production continued to increase despite massive and devastating bombing. He was tried at Nuremberg and sentenced to twenty years' imprisonment for his role in the Nazi regime, principally for the use of forced labour. He served his full sentence, most of it at Spandau Prison in West Berlin, and was released in 1966.

Stauffenberg: Claus Schenk Graf von Stauffenberg (1907-1944)

Stauffenberg was commissioned as second lieutenant in 1930. Following the outbreak of war in 1939, he and his regiment took part in the attack on Poland, the invasion of France and Operation Barbarossa. He was later transferred to the Tunisian campaign as part of the Afrika Korps, and was severely wounded in April 1943. While recuperating he became involved in the resistance movement. Early plans came to nothing, but in July 1944 he had an opportunity, code-named 'Operation Valkyrie'. On 20 July 1944, Stauffenberg entered the briefing room at the Wolf's Lair carrying a briefcase that contained two small bombs. Some minutes later, he excused himself and left the room. Stauffenberg had been heroic, but suffered two unfortunate set-backs which caused the plan to fail. First he only had time to arm one of the two bombs; secondly, after he had left the room, another officer moved his briefcase behind a strong oak base of the table. Hitler survived and the conspirators were tracked with appalling reprisals.

Strasser: Gregor Strasser (1892-1934)

Strasser served during the First World War, rising to the rank of First Lieutenant. In 1919 he and his brother Otto joined the right-wing Freikorps with the young Heinrich Himmler as his adjutant. In 1921, Strasser's group joined forces with Hitler's Nazi Party. His leadership qualities were quickly recognised and he took an active part in the Beer Hall Putsch. After 1925, Strasser's organisational skill helped the NSDAP to take a big step from a marginal South German splinter party to a nationwide mass party with wide appeal. In 1932 he toyed with the idea of joining Sleicher's government. On 30 June 1934, the 'Night of the Long Knives', Strasser was arrested and killed on Hitler's personal order by the Berlin Gestapo.

Streicher: Julius Streicher (1885-1946)

Streicher served during the First World War, rising to the rank of Lieutenant. In 1919 Streicher became politically active and was a supporter of Hitler after hearing him speak in 1922. He took part in the Beer Hall Putsch. Streicher was the publisher of Der Stürmer, a newspaper which promulgated anti-Semitic propaganda and orchestrated anti-Jewish campaigns. He had numerous enemies, especially Goering, and in spite of his special relationship with Hitler, he was stripped of his party offices and withdrew from the public, although he was permitted vto continue publishing Der Stürmer. At Nuremberg, he was found guilty of crimes against humanity and hanged on 16 October 1946.

Stuckart: Wilhelm Stuckart (1902-1953)

In 1922 Stuckart studied law and political economics at Munich and Frankfurt, where he also joined the Nazi Party. From 1932 to 1933 he worked as a lawyer and legal secretary for the SA in Stettin, and upon Himmler's recommendation, he joined the SS in 1933. In 1935 he was given the task, alongside Loesener and Medicus, of co-writing the anti-Semitic Law for the Protection of German Blood and German Honour and The Reich Citizenship Law, together better known as the Nuremberg Laws. Stuckart later represented Wilhelm Frick, the Interior Minister, at the Wannsee Conference on 20 January 1942. In 1945 he was tried and imprisoned for his role in formulating and carrying out anti-Jewish laws. He was eventually released in 1949. He died in a car accident in 1953, but there was suspicion of Mossad involvement.

Weber: Christian Weber (1883-1945)

Weber was an early friend of Hitler's and was among his earliest political associates. Well-known as a thug, he had the habit of carrying a riding crop with him—a habit shared by Hitler in the early years. His name became a by-word for corruption in Munich and it was regularly questioned how this former hotel bellboy had come to own a number of hotels, businesses and smart residences. Numerous Jewish businesses and assets fell into his open lap. On the 'Night of the Long Knives', Weber was among those SS men who travelled to Bad Wiessee to purge the Sturmabteilung leadership. At the end of the War he was killed by Bavarian insurrectionists.

Wessel: Horst Ludwig Wessel (1907-1930)

Wessel joined the Nazi Party in 1926 and soon impressed Goebbels, the Party Governor. In October 1929 he dropped out of university to devote himself full-time to the Nazi movement. Wessel played the schalmei, a type of oboe popular in Germany, and he founded an SA Schalmeien-kapelle, which provided music during SA events. In early 1929, Wessel wrote the lyrics for a new Nazi fight song which was first published in Goebbels's newspaper Der Angriff; this song later became known as 'Horst Wessel Song', with a tune stolen from an old Imperial Navy folk song. On the evening of 14 January 1930, Wessel answered a knock on his door and was shot in the face and fatally wounded. Albrecht Hoehler, an active member of the local Communist Party branch was sentenced to six years' imprisonment for the shooting, and was executed by the Gestapo after the Nazi accession to power in 1933. Wessel's death was a propaganda coup for Goebbels who whipped up anti-communist hysteria.

Wiedemann: Fritz Wiedemann (1891-1970)

Wiedemann served alongside Hitler during the First World War when, as regimental adjutant, he was Corporal Hitler's superior. After the War, Wiedemann left the army and became a farmer, initially refusing an offer from Hitler at the regimental reunion in 1922 to help organise the SA. However, when Hitler came to power, Wiedemann accepted a new offer to link up with his former corporal, initially in the offices of Rudolf Hess before taking up his post at Hitler's side. He became a member of the Nazi Party on 2 February 1934, and from then on Wiedemann remained constantly at Hitler's side as an adjutant. In 1939 he fell out of favour with Hitler and his rival, Julius Schaub, rose as the more important adjutant. To side-line him, he was appointed Consul General to the USA in San Francisco. Wiedemann gave evidence at Nuremberg after the War. Charges against him were dropped in 1948.

Zeitzler: Kurt Zeitzler (1895-1963)

Zeitzler served during the First World War and received an officer's commission as a reward for outstanding bravery. He was placed in command of an infantry battalion. Between 1919 and 1937 he served as a staff officer in the army, and then as a staff officer for the Oberkommando des Heeres (OKH). He served under General Siegmund List during the invasion of Poland, and under General von Kleist in the invasion of France. He was part of the German force that successfully resisted the Dieppe raid on 19 August 1942. He was promoted to General of the Infantry and simultaneously appointed Chief of Staff of the Army General Staff on 24 September 1942, replacing Franz Halder. Following the débâcle at Stalingrad, Zeitzler's relations with Hitler became strained. After a series of violent rows with Hitler, he abruptly left the Berghof on 1 July 1944. Hitler had him dismissed from the army in January 1945 and refused him the right to wear a uniform. After the War, Zeitzler was held in British captivity until February 1947. He died in 1963. In the photograph Zeitler is on Hitler's left.

Bibliography

BBC War Report, Despatches: D-Day to VE Day (OUP, 1946)

Blake, George, *Mountain & Flood* (Jackson & Co, 1950)

Churchill, Winston, *Triumph & Tragedy* (Cassell, 1951)

Cornwell, John, *Hitler's Scientists* (Penguin, 2004)

Davies, Norman, *Europe at War* (Pan, 2007)

De Guingand, Francis, *Operation Victory* (Hodder & Stoughton, 1941)

Delaforce, Patrick, *Churchill's Secret Weapons* (Pen & Sword, 2006)

Delaforce, Patrick, *The Rhine Endeavour* (Amberley, 2010)

Delaforce, Patrick, *Monty's Rhine Adventure* (Fonthill 2014)

Delaforce, Patrick, *Invasion of Hitler's Third Reich* (Fonthill 2014)

Ford, Ken, *Rhineland 1945* (Osprey, 2000)

Gilbert, Martin, *The Day the War Ended* (Harper Collins, 2001)

Gilbert, Martin, *Second World War* (Phoenix, 2009)

Hastings, Max, *Finest Years (Churchill)* (Harper Press, 2009)

Hastings, Max, *Armageddon* (Pan, 2004)

Hauge, Jens Chr, *Liberation of Norway* (Norsk Forlag, 1950)

Hitchcock, William, *Liberation, Bitter Road to Freedom* (Faber, 2009)

HMSO, *By Air to Battle (Airborne Divisions)* (1945)

HMSO, *World War 2 Collection* (2001)

Horrocks, Brian, *A Full Life* (Collins, 1960)

Longden, Shaun, *T-Force, Race for Nazi Secrets* (Constable, 2009)

Lucas, James, *Last Days of the Reich* (Arms & Armour, 1986)

Moorehead, Alan, *Eclipse* (Hamish Hamilton, 1945)

Petrow, Richard, *The Bitter Years* (Purnell Book Services, 1975)

Rosse & Hill, *Guards Armoured* (Geoffrey Bles, 1956)

Saunders, Hilary, *Red Beret* (Michael Joseph, 1950)

Shulman, Milton, *Defeat in the West* (Secker & Warburg, 1947)
Speer, Albert, *Inside the Third Reich* (Sphere, 1971)
Stacey, C. P., *History of the Canadian Army* (Queens/Ottawa, 1960)
Taylor & Shaw, *Dictionary of the Third Reich* (Penguin, 1997)
Trevor-Roper, Hugh, *Hitler's Table Talk* (Enigma Books, NY 2000)
Whiting, Charles, *Monty's Greatest Gamble* (1985)
Wilmot, Chester, *Struggle for Europe* (Collins, 1957)

Also Divisional Histories: *Red Crown and Dragon, Polar Bears,
Fighting Wessex Wyverns, The Black Bull, Churchill's Desert Rats,
Monty's Ironsides, Monty's Northern Legions, Monty's Highlanders* by
Patrick Delaforce.

Glossary

German and Dutch Terms

Abteilungen	Combat Units
Abwehr	Military intelligence department of the OKW
Festung	German Garrison designated only by Hitler
Flak Units	German anti-aircraft units
Hitler Jugend	Young and highly indoctrinated Nazis, fanatically loyal to Hitler
Kampfgruppe	Impromptu German battle group
Kranken	Wounded convalescent formation
Kriegsmarine	Members of the German Navy
Landsturm Nederland	Dutch Nazi volunteers
Luftwaffe	German Air Force
Minnenwerfer	German mortars known by the Allies as 'Moaning minnies'
Nebelwerfer	Mortar that fired chemical or HE shells
OKW	Oberkommando der Wehrmacht
Panzerfaust	Cheap German one-shot anti-tank weapon
Panzergrenadier	German motorised or mechanised infantry
Panzerjaeger	Armoured units designed to fight tanks, usually SP guns
Schmeisser	German submachine-gun, also known as the MP-40
Schu mine	Wooden cased anti-infantry mine
Schwerpunkt	Concentrated method of advance upon a focal point with co-ordinated

	armour and infantry and appropriate flank protection
Spandau	German machine-gun
Stonk	German word for a sudden artillery bombardment, also used by the British
Teller	Cylindrical, powerful anti-tank mine
Verdronken land	Flooded region in Holland
Volksgrenadier Divisions	Emergency divisions created in 1944 to combat the German manpower crisis
Wehrmacht	The unified armed forces of Germany

Military Abbreviations

AA	Anti-Aircraft
ADC	Aide-de-camp
AFV	Armoured fighting vehicle
AVRE	Armoured Vehicle Royal Engineers; special Churchill tank
BAOR	British Army of the Rhine
BEF	British Expeditionary Force
BLA	British Liberation Army
CAS	Close Air Support, usually by RAF planes
CIGS	Chief of the Imperial General Staff
CO	Commanding Officer
CRA	Commander Royal Artillery
CRE	Commander Royal Engineers
Crocodile	Churchill tank with flame-thrower
CSM	Company Sergeant-Major
DCLI	Duke of Cornwall's Light Infantry
DCM	Distinguished Conduct Medal
DD Tanks	Duplex Drive Tanks
DLI	Durham Light Infantry
DP	Displaced Person
DSO	Distinguished Service Order
DUKW	Wheeled amphibious landing craft
DZ	Drop zone for paratroops
FOO	Artillery Forward Observation Officer
GOC	General Officer Commanding
HAA	Heavy anti-aircraft gun

HLI	Highland Light Infantry
Kangaroo	Armoured infantry carrier on selfpropelled tank-type chassis
KOSB	King's Own Scottish Borderers
KOYLI	King's Own Yorkshire Light Infantry
KRRC	King's Royal Rifle Corps
KSLI	King's Shropshire Light Infantry
LAA	Light Anti-Aircraft artillery
LCA	Landing Craft Assault
LZ	Landing zone for glider troops
MC	Military Cross
MM	Military Medal
MMG	Medium Machine Guns
NAAFI	Navy, Army and Air Force Institutes
NCO	Non-Commissioned Officer
OBE	Order of the British Empire
OC	Officer commanding
PBI	Poor Bloody Infantry
PIAT	Projector Infantry Anti-Tank
PIR	Parachute Infantry Regiments
RA	Royal Artillery
RAC	Royal Armoured Corps
RAMC	Royal Army Medical Corps
RB	Rifle Brigade
RE	Royal Engineers
REME	Royal Electrical and Mechanical Engineers
RHA	Royal Horse Artillery
RSF	Royal Scots Fusiliers
RTR	Royal Tank Regiment
RWF	Royal Welch Fusiliers
SHAEF	Supreme Headquarters Allied Expeditionary Force
SOE	Special Operations Executive
TCV	Troop Carrying Vehicle
VE Day	Victory in Europe Day
UNRRA	United Nations Relief & Rehabilitation Administration